Oxford English Grammar Course
Intermediate

A grammar practice book for
intermediate and upper-intermediate
students of English

OXFORD
UNIVERSITY PRESS

Great Clarendon Street, Oxford OX2 6DP

Oxford University Press is a department of the University of Oxford.
It furthers the University's objective of excellence in research, scholarship,
and education by publishing worldwide in

Oxford New York

Auckland Cape Town Dar es Salaam Hong Kong Karachi
Kuala Lumpur Madrid Melbourne Mexico City Nairobi
New Delhi Shanghai Taipei Toronto

With offices in

Argentina Austria Brazil Chile Czech Republic France Greece
Guatemala Hungary Italy Japan Poland Portugal Singapore
South Korea Switzerland Thailand Turkey Ukraine Vietnam

OXFORD and OXFORD ENGLISH are registered trade marks of
Oxford University Press in the UK and in certain other countries

ISBN: 978 0 19 442080 8   Student's book with answers
ISBN: 978 0 19 442082 2   Student's book and CD-Rom pack with answers

Printed in China

This book is printed on paper from certified and well-managed sources.

Michael Swan & Catherine Walter

Oxford English Grammar Course

Intermediate

A grammar practice book for
intermediate and upper-intermediate
students of English

With answers

OXFORD
UNIVERSITY PRESS

publisher's acknowledgements

The authors and publisher are grateful to those who have given permission to reproduce the following extracts and adaptations of copyright material:

p45 Adapted extract from *Playback* (1958) by Raymond Chandler © Copyright Raymond Chandler Limited, a Chorion company. All rights reserved. Reproduced by permission.

p139 'Stopping by Woods on a Snowy Evening' from *The Poetry of Robert Frost* edited by Edward Connery Lathem, published by Jonathan Cape. Reprinted by permission of The Random House Group Ltd.

p181 'First Fig' by Edna St. Vincent Millay. Copyright © 1922, 1950 by Edna St. Vincent Millay. Reprinted with permission of Elizabeth Barnett, The Millay Society.

p237 The featured records have been supplied courtesy of Guinness World Records Ltd.

p281 From 'Rondeau Redoublé' taken from *Making Cocoa for Kingsley Amis* © Wendy Cope. Reproduced by permission of Faber and Faber Ltd.

p322 'Three Rusty Nails' by Roger McGough from *In the Glassroom* (© Roger McGough, 1976) is printed by permission of United Agents (www.unitedagents.co.uk) on behalf of Roger McGough.

Illustrations by:

Stefan Chabluk: p.168; **Mark Duffin**: pp: 28, 53, 170, 182, 296; **Neil Gower**: p. 18; **Maureen and Gordon Gray**: p.66, 102; **Sophie Joyce**: pp: 19, 36, 157(instructions); **Pete Lawrence**: pp: 9(cartoons). 26, 30, 32, 36(cartoons), 44, 46, 54, 65, 86, 142, 157(cartoons), 175, 180, 243; **Gavin Reece**: pp: 194, 232, 249, 322; **Phillip Scramm/Meiklejohn agency**: pp 9(objects), 14, 88, 90, 112, 117, 125, 136, 158, 201, 210, 230, 265, 273

The publisher would like to thank the following for permission to reproduce photographs:

Alamy Images pp120 (Brushing hair/mediablitzimages (uk) Limited), 120 (Hand on steering wheel/FourT4), 120 (Riding a bike/Oleksiy Maksymenko 2), 120 (Phoning/MatthiolaC), 205 (Red deer/Brian Hewitt), 205 (Red snappers/Martin Strmiska), 312 (Motorbike/Motoring Picture Library); Getty Images p120 (Kim Clijsters); **OUP** pp120 (Sipping coffee/Digital Vision), 151 (Bin filled with paper/Photodisc), 312 (Apple/Photodisc), 312 (Bicycle/Photodisc), 312 (Butterfly/Ingram), 312 (Car/Luminis), 312 (Cat/Photodisc), 312 (Dog/Photodisc), 312 (Goldfish/Photodisc), 312 (Frog/Photodisc), 312 (Orange/Ingram), 312 (Parrot/Photodisc); **Photolibrary** pp120 (Woman reading/beyond fotomedia), 312 (Pram/Photolibrary); **PunchStock** p120 (Washing hands/BlueMoon Stock); **Elizabeth Whiting and Associates**: p11; **5W Infographics**: p.39 (human migration map)

The publisher would like to thank the following for their permission to reproduce cartoons:

Mel Calman: p.168 ('equality for women'); **Sidney Harris**: pp 71 ('should we walk upright?'), 149 ('vowels'), 307; **Anthony Hutchings**: p23/Anthony; **MirrorPix**: p.167 /Sax('yes of course'); **Punch Cartoon Library**: pp 25/Handelsman/Schwadron, 31/Nick, 67/Handelsman/Sally Artz, 71/Barsotti, 73/Dickinson, 79/Haefeli, 93/Chase, 122/Handelsman, 129, 139/Sally Artz, 149/W. Scully, 156/H. Martin, 165('one night'), 165/H. Martin, 167/Haefeli ('straighten your tie'), 182/Nick/Ken Pyne, 187/Schwadron('it's your birthday'), 189/Haefeli, 193/W Scully, 199/Handelsman, 203/Nick, 212/Holte, 212('Right, Mr Wilson'), 217/Holte, 231/Graham, 253/Heath, 267/Schwadron, 288, 289, 291/Donegan, 309/Noel Ford, 326; **Private Eye**: p.215/Ken Pyne; **Ken Pyne**: p.221; **The Cartoon Bank/Conde Nast Publications Inc/ww. cartoonbank.com**: pp 20/Peter Steiner, 64/Cotham. 103/Mick Stevens, 119/Christopher Weyant, 189/Mick Stevens, 259/John Donohue, 286/Joseph Farris, 293.Peter C. Vey, 293/CAJ; **The Spectator**: pp 5/Tony Husband, 7/Pugh, 23/AJSingleton, 27/Robert Thompson, 139/W Scully, 187('He's right here beside me');**The Telegraph Media Group**: p.207/Matt; **Tessa Sayle Literary agency**: pp: 143, 187/Ronald Searle

contents

authors' acknowledgements

We owe a continuing debt to the many people whose advice and comments helped us with earlier versions of this material. The present book has benefited enormously from the hard work and professionalism of our editorial and design team at Oxford University Press. In particular, we would like to acknowledge the contributions of our remarkable editor, Sarah Parsons, and our equally remarkable designer, Phil Hargraves, who have made it possible for us to write the book that we wanted to, and whose input is evident on every page.

introduction

Who is this book for?

The *Oxford English Grammar Course* (Intermediate Level) is for all intermediate and upper-intermediate learners who want to improve their knowledge of English grammar.

What kind of English does the book teach?

This book teaches the grammar of spoken and written British English. But it can also be used by students of American, Australian or other kinds of English – the grammatical differences are very small and unimportant.

How is the book organised?

There are 22 sections. A section covers one part of English grammar (for example: making questions and negatives; present tense verbs; problems with nouns). Each section contains:

- a presentation page which introduces the point of grammar
- several short units with explanations and exercises
- two 'More Practice' pages: these include 'Grammar in a text' exercises and internet exercises
- a short revision test.

---

3 Grammar in a text. Put in expressions from the box. Use the present progressive.

| become less common | continue | continue | get ✓ | get | get | go down | increase |

People [1] *...are getting...* happier. According to a recent report from the Western Statistics Office, 73% of people say that they are happy 'most of the time', compared with only 47% at the beginning of the century. Perhaps this is partly because the world is less crowded: the Western population [2] .... by about 1.3% per year. And life expectancy [3] ....: in 1970, men lived for an average of 69 years and women 75; both sexes now can expect to live for 113 years. We [4] .... richer, too. The average income in 2096 was 146,000 Western Credits – twice as much as in the year 2018.

Not everything [5] .... better, though. The climate [6] .... to change for the worse, and sea levels [7] .... to rise. If average temperatures go on increasing, scientists are afraid that more of the world's capitals will go the same way as London, Paris and New York. Perhaps one day we will all have to move to the mountains.

Religious belief [8] .... In 2018, 65% of Western Federation citizens said that they believed in God; in 2096 the figure was only 24%, and only half of these went to church regularly.

(From *The Times*, 18 July 2098.)

---

7 Internet exercise. Use a search engine (e.g. Google) to find five or more simple sentences beginning *"I have never been given"*. Write them out.

....
....
....
....
....

Two levels

Some units are marked 'Revise the Basics': these revise elementary points of grammar which may still cause problems. More advanced units are marked 'Level 2'.

Using the book to study particular points

If you want to know more about a particular point (for example present tenses, the difference between *should* and *must*, or the position of adverbs), look in the index (pages 377–386) to find the right unit(s). Read the explanations and do the exercises. Check your answers in the answer key (pages 329–376).

Using the book for systematic study

If you are working without a teacher, we suggest:

1   DON'T go right through the book from beginning to end – some parts will be unnecessary for you.
2   Decide which sections you most need to study. Section 1, 'be and have', for example? Section 8, 'questions and negatives'? Section 19, 'relatives'? Or other sections?
3   Go to the pages that you need. Read the grammar explanations, do the exercises, and check your answers in the answer key (pages 329–376).
4   In some units there are 'Grammar and vocabulary' exercises for students who would like to learn more words. Try these as well if you want to.
5   There are also some 'Do it yourself' exercises, which will give you a chance to discover rules for yourself.
6   Do some or all of the exercises in the 'More Practice' pages.
7   Go to the revision test at the end of the section, and try some or all of the questions.
8   Check your answers. If you still have problems, look at the explanations again.

Website

On the website there are tests which will help you to decide what you need to study, or to find out how well you have learnt the different points of grammar. There are also extra exercises and games to give you more practice on some of the points.

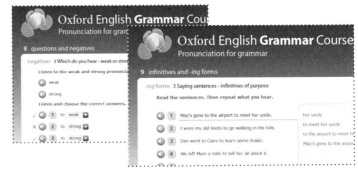

Pronunciation

The 'Pronunciation for grammar' CD-ROM will help you to pronounce structures fluently, with good rhythm and stress.

Examinations

This book teaches all of the grammar (and more!) that is needed for Common European Framework Levels B1 and B2 and is suitable for learners studying for Cambridge FCE.

If you know everything in the book, will you speak perfect English?

No, sorry!

1   Not many people learn foreign languages perfectly. (And not many people need to.) But this book will help you to speak and write much more correctly.

2   Books like this give short practical explanations. They cannot tell you the whole truth about English grammar, and they cannot give you enough practice to get all the difficult points right. If you follow the rules in this book, you will not make many mistakes. But you will probably need to practise using the structures in different situations. (The website material will help with this.) You will find more complete information about difficult points in the Advanced Level of the Oxford English Grammar Course, or in Michael Swan's Practical English Usage (Oxford University Press).

3   Grammar is not the only important thing in a language. You also need a wide vocabulary, and – very important – you need a lot of practice in listening and speaking, reading and writing. Remember: this is a grammar practice book, not a complete English course.

We hope that you will enjoy using our book.

With our best wishes for your progress in English.

Michael Swan.   Catherine Walter

words for talking about grammar

active and **passive:** *I see, she heard* are **active** verbs; *I am seen, she was heard* are **passive** verbs.

adjectives: for example *big, old, yellow, unhappy*.

adverbs: for example *quickly, completely, now, there*.

affirmative sentences or **statements** are not questions or negatives – for example *I arrived*.

articles: *a/an* ('indefinite article'); *the* ('definite article').

auxiliary verbs are used before other verbs to make questions, tenses etc – for example *do you think; I have finished; she is working*. See also **modal auxiliary verbs**.

clause: see **sentence**.

comparatives: for example *older, better, more beautiful, more slowly*.

conditional: a structure using the conjunction *if*.

conjunctions: for example *and, but, because, while*.

consonants: see **vowels**.

contractions: short forms like *I'm, you're, he'll, don't*.

conversational: see **formal**.

countable nouns: the names of things we can count – for example *one chair, three cars*; **uncountable** (or 'mass') **nouns:** the names of things we can't count, like *oil, rice*.

determiners: words like *the, some, many, my*, which go before (adjective +) noun.

double letters: *pp, tt, ee* etc.

formal, informal, conversational: We use **formal** language with strangers, in business letters etc: for example 'Good afternoon, Mr Parker. May I help you?' We use **informal** or **conversational** language with family and friends: for example 'Hi, John. Want some help?'

future verbs: for example *I will go; Ann is going to write to us*.

imperatives: forms like *Go home, Come and sit down, Don't worry*, which we use when we tell or ask people (not) to do things.

indirect speech: the grammar that we use to say what people say or think: for example *John said that he was tired*.

infinitives: *(to) go, (to) sleep* etc.

informal: see **formal**.

-ing forms: *going, sleeping* etc.

irregular: see **regular**.

leave out: If we say *Seen John?*, we are **leaving out** *Have you*.

modal verbs or **modal auxiliary verbs:** *must, can, could, may, might, shall, should, ought to, will* and *would*.

negative sentences are made with *not*: for example *I have not seen her*.

nouns: for example *chair, oil, idea, sentence*.

object: see **subject**.

opposite: *hot* is the **opposite** of *cold; up* is the **opposite** of *down*.

passive: see **active**.

past perfect tense: see **perfect tenses**.

past progressive tense: see **past tenses**.

past tenses: for example *went, saw, stopped* (**simple past**); *was going, were eating* (**past progressive**).

past participles: for example *gone, seen, stopped*.

perfect tenses: forms with *have/has/had* + past participle: for example *I have forgotten* (**present perfect**); *It has been raining* (**present perfect progressive**); *They had stopped* (**past perfect**).

personal pronouns: for example *I, you, us, them*.

plural: see **singular**.

possessives: for example *my, your; mine, yours; John's, my brothers'*.

prepositions: for example *at, in, on, between*.

present participles: for example *going, sleeping* etc (also called **-ing forms**).

present perfect tenses: see **perfect tenses**.

present tenses: for example *He goes* (**simple present**); *She is walking* (**present progressive**).

progressive (or '**continuous**'): for example *I am thinking* (**present progressive**); *They were talking* (**past progressive**).

pronouns: for example *I, you, anybody, themselves*.

question tags: for example *isn't it?, doesn't she?*

reflexive pronouns: *myself, yourself* etc.

regular: plurals like *cats, buses*; past tenses like *started, stopped*; **irregular:** plurals like *teeth, men, children*; past tenses like *broke, went, saw*.

relative clauses: clauses that begin with relative pronouns: for example *the man who bought my car*.

relative pronouns: *who, which* and *that* when they join clauses to nouns: for example *the man **who** bought my car*.

sentence, clause: A sentence begins with a capital letter (A, B etc) and ends with a full stop (.), like this one. A sentence may have more than one clause, often joined by a conjunction. For example *I'll come and see you when I'm in London*.

simple past tense: see **past tenses**.

simple present tense: see **present tenses**.

singular: for example *chair, cat, man*; **plural:** for example *chairs, cats, men*.

spelling: writing words correctly: for example, we spell *necessary* with one *c* and double *s*.

subject and **object:** In *She took the money – everybody saw her*, the **subjects** are *she* and *everybody*; the **objects** are *the money* and *her*.

superlatives: for example *oldest, best, most beautiful, most easily*.

tense: *She goes, she is going, she went, she was going, she has gone* are different **tenses**.

third person: words for other people, not *I* or *you*: for example *she, them, himself, John, has, goes*.

uncountable nouns: see **countable nouns**.

verbs: for example *sit, give, hold, think, write*.

vowels: *a, e, i, o, u* and their usual sounds; **consonants:** *b, c, d, f, g* etc and their usual sounds.

other useful words

Here are some other words that are used in this book. Find them in your dictionary and write the translations here.

action ....

choose ....

common ....

complete (*verb*) ....

correct ....

description ....

difference ....

event ....

exclamation ....

explain ....

expression ....

form (*noun*) ....

go on, happen ....

in general ....

introduction ....

join ....

mean (*verb*) ....

meaning ....

necessary ....

news ....

normal ....

normally ....

particular ....

plan ....

polite ....

politely ....

possibility ....

possible ....

practise ....

predict ....

prefer ....

probable ....

pronounce ....

pronunciation ....

repeat ....

report ....

revision ....

rule ....

section ....

similar ....

situation ....

stressed (pronunciation) ....

structure ....

unnecessary ....

unusual ....

use (*noun*) ....

use (*verb*) ....

(word) order ....

list of units

SECTION 1 *be* and *have*

GRAMMAR SUMMARY

be (*am*/*are*/*is*/*was*/*were*)

- We can use **adjectives**, **nouns** or expressions of **place** after *be*.
  *She **is early**.   I'm **tired**.   **Are** you a **student**?   **Is** anybody **at home**?*

- We can use *be* to talk about **age**, **size**, **height**, **weight** and **colour**.
  *My sister's 22.   What size **are** your shoes?   I'**m** 1 metre 85 and 80 kilos.
  What colour **are** the baby's eyes?*

- We use **there** + **be** to introduce things: to tell people that they exist.
  ***There's** a good film on TV tonight.   **There are** some people at the door.*

- *Be* can be an **auxiliary verb** in progressive tenses (see pages 14, 41) and passives (see page 94–95).
  *It **is** raining.   This **was made** in 1850.*

have (*have*/*has*/*had*)

- We can use *have* to talk about **possession**, **relationships** and some other ideas.
  ***Do** you **have** a pair of walking boots?   I **don't have** any children.*

- *Have* is often used with **got**.
  *I'**ve got** a headache.*

- And we can use *have* to talk about some kinds of **actions**.
  *I'm going to **have breakfast**.   Let's **have a party**.*

- *Have* can also be an **auxiliary verb** in perfect tenses (see Section 5).
  *I **haven't heard** from Alan.   I thought that I **had seen** her before.*

'People can have it in any colour –
as long as it's black.'
(*Henry Ford, talking about the Model T Ford car*)

'Don't throw away your old shoes until
you have got new ones.'
(*Proverb*)

'The future is black.'
(*James Baldwin*)

'All the world's a stage
and all the men and women merely players.
They have their exits and their entrances.'
(*Shakespeare: As You like It*)

'The so-called white races are really pinko-grey.'
(*E M Forster*)

'Be contented when you have got all
you want.'
(*Holbrook Jackson*)

'I am black, but O! my soul is white.'
(*William Blake*)

'I've got plenty of nothing
and nothing's plenty for me.'
(*Gershwin: Porgy and Bess*)

'Eyes too expressive to be blue,
too lovely to be grey.'
(*Matthew Arnold*)

'The East is red.'
(*Chinese communist slogan*)

'In the beginning there was nothing,
and it exploded.'
(*Terry Pratchett*)

revise the basics: *be* and *have*

1 Put in *am, are, is, was, were* or *will be*.

▶ I ...*am*........ ready.

1 We .... in Dublin yesterday.

2 My brother .... a dentist. He works in London.

3 'You .... late.' 'Sorry. The train .... late.'

4 It .... cold tomorrow.

5 I .... ill last week.

6 'We .... surprised to see you yesterday.' 'And I .... surprised to see you.'

7 We .... in France all of next year.

8 I .... really happy today.

9 There .... a big storm last night.

10 My great-grandmother .... a writer, and her two sisters .... writers too.

11 Sue and Peter .... in America all this year.

12 We .... on the wrong bus. Let's get off now.

2 Make questions (?) or negatives (-).

▶ Liam in the office yesterday was ? ...*Was Liam in the office yesterday?*...................

▶ book this interesting is - ...*This book is not interesting.*...........................

1 will here be tomorrow you ? ....

2 Anne's teacher father a was ? ....

3 are ready we - ....

4 when birthday was your ? ....

5 chocolates those good very were - ....

6 Mary at home will next be week - ....

7 train this late morning the was ? ....

8 am for exam I ready the - ....

9 gloves in my the are car ? ....

10 were my brother happy and at I school - ....

11 there in kitchen telephone is the a ? ....

12 lesson will there tomorrow a be - ....

3 Make questions (?) or negatives (-) with *have*. Use *do/does*.

▶ you / a dog ? ...*Do you have a dog?*...........................

▶ Wendy / much money - ...*Wendy doesn't have much money.*...................

1 we / a car / We don't - ....

2 they / any children ? ....

3 James / a cold ? ....

4 my mother / a cat - ....

5 Cindy / any brothers or sisters ? ....

6 I / enough work - ....

7 John / a girlfriend ? ....

8 Why / you / two bicycles ? ....

9 This house / a garden - ....

10 you and Alan / an evening free next week ? ? ....

4 Make statements (+), questions (?) or negatives (–) about Sharon. Use *have got*.

▶ a TV + *She's got a TV.*
▶ any boyfriends ? *Has she got any boyfriends?*
▶ a horse – *She hasn't got a horse.*
1 a brother ? ....
2 a car – ....
3 three dogs + ...
4 a lot of money – ....
5 long hair ? ....
6 any sisters – ....
7 a nice flat ? ....
8 a good job + ...
9 problems with her family + ...
10 much free time – ....

5 Write these sentences with contractions. (There are sometimes two possible answers.)

▶ It is cold. *It's cold.*
1 We are all here. ....
2 They are tired. ....
3 I am ready. ....
4 My name is Mike. ....
5 You are very kind. ....
6 Nina has got a headache. ....
7 I do not have a car. ....
8 They are not ready. ....
9 I am not well. ....
10 You are not very polite. ....
11 What is your name? ....
12 What has the dog got in its mouth? ....
13 Where is the station? ....
14 I did not have a good time at school. ....
15 The house does not have central heating. ....
16 There is not much cheese in the fridge. ....

6 Correct (✓) or not (✗)?

▶ Are you ready? ✓
▶ I got a headache. ✗
1 This coffee is'nt hot. ......
2 We don't got much time. ......
3 The hotel does not have a bar. ......
4 Steve doesn't got a girlfriend. ......
5 There has a man at the door. ......
6 Who's that woman? ......
7 I amn't ready yet. ......
8 I gotn't your address. ......
9 Do you have got a car? ......
10 I won't be at home tonight. ......

7 *Be* or *have*? Circle the correct form.

▶ *Is* / *Has* your brother at home?
1 *Are* / *Have* you thirsty?
2 Alice *is* / *has* three brothers.
3 My sister *is* / *has* 25 today.
4 'I *am* / *have* cold.' 'Put on a sweater.'
5 I *am* / *have* too much work.
6 Emma *is* / *has* very happy today.
7 *Are* / *Have* you interested in history?
8 What size *are* / *have* your shoes?
9 'It's 10.00.' 'You *are* / *have* wrong. It's 9.00.'
10 Everybody *is* / *has* problems sometimes.

In some answers, both contracted forms (for example *I'm*, *don't*) and full forms (for example *I am*, *do not*) are possible. Normally both are correct.

BE AND *HAVE*   **3**

revise the basics: *there is/was* etc

THE MOST COMMON STRUCTURES WITH *THERE + BE*		
there is/are	*there was/were*	*there will be*
there is/are going to be	*there has/have been*	*there had been*
Questions: *is there, are there* etc		
Contraction: *there's* (pronounced /ðəz/, like the beginning of *the zoo*)		

We use **there is** to say that **something exists** (or doesn't exist) somewhere or at some time.

There is *a hole in my sock.* **There's** *snow on the mountains.*
There are *two men at the door.* *Once upon a time* **there were** *three little pigs.*
There will be *rain tonight.* **There has** *never* **been** *anybody like you.*

In an informal style we often use *there's* before a plural noun.

There's some grapes *in the fridge.*

1 **Put in the correct form of *there is(n't)*.**

1 .... no water in the Atacama desert.
2 .... no railways in the 18th century.
3 Once upon a time .... a beautiful princess.
4 Tomorrow .... snow.
5 .... some soup, if you're hungry.
6 .... any potatoes?
7 .... wars all through history.
8 .... many tigers left in the wild.
9 .... an accident – can I use your phone?
10 I'm afraid .... time to see Granny.
11 Do you know if .... any tickets left?
12 .... a letter for me yesterday?
13 .... going .... a test tomorrow.
14 I'm sorry, but .... any rooms free.
15 How many US Presidents .... since 1900?
16 I don't think .... any reason to worry.
17 .... a meeting tomorrow: everybody's away.
18 .... never .... land animals in Antarctica.
19 .... going .... a general election soon, do you think?
20 Why .... so much rain in the last two months?

There is introduces **indefinite** subjects. Compare:

There's a window *open.*
The window's *open.* (**NOT** *There's the window open.*)

2 **Complete the sentences with your own ideas.**

1 In 1800 there weren't any ....
2 500 years ago there ....
3 5000 years ago there ....
4 Next year there ....
5 In 100 years there ....
6 In 1000 years there ....

more about *there is* *There seems to be a delay.*

THERE IS: MORE COMPLICATED STRUCTURES	
with *seem/appear*	There seems to be a delay.
with modal verbs	There may be a problem. There must be a car park somewhere.
with *certain/sure/likely*	Is there likely to be a test?
with *need/sense/point/use*	There's no point in asking questions.
with *something/anything/nothing + wrong*	Is there anything wrong?
infinitive	I don't want there to be any trouble. I'd like there to be more hours in the day.
in question tags	There will be enough, won't there?
with auxiliary *be*	There were some children playing in the garden. (= Some children were playing …)

1 **Put the beginnings and ends together.**

0	According to the forecast,	A	'He says there's nothing wrong with me.' ......
1	I can't see how to open the door.	B	'There seems to be something lying in the road.' ......
2	I'm looking forward to the party.	C	any noise while I'm on the phone. ......
3	OK, children, now I don't want there to be	D	We've got plenty of time. ......
4	That must be Jeff.	E	but there may be some tomorrow. ......
5	There are too many people	F	if you've got a headache – you won't enjoy it. ......
6	There aren't any tickets now,	G	there's likely to be more snow tonight. ..*0*..
7	There's no need to hurry.	H	looking for too few jobs in this country, aren't there? ......
8	There's no point in going to the cinema	I	There are sure to be some nice people there. ......
9	'Why have we stopped?'	J	There can't be two people who look like that. ......
10	'What did the doctor say?'	K	There must be a keyhole somewhere. ......

We **don't** use *it is* like *there is*. We usually use *it is* for something that we have **already talked about**, or that people **already know about**.

There's a car outside. It's a Ford. (**NOT** ~~It's a car outside.~~)

2 **Put in *there's* or *it's*.**

1 .... a cat in your bedroom.
2 .... ice on the roads.
3 I've got a new job. .... interesting.
4 'Whose is that dog?' '.............. mine.'
5 .... a letter on the table.
    .... for Alex.
6 .... a car park just round the corner.
7 'What's that noise?' '.............. the wind.'
8 .... a problem with the TV.
9 Do you like my new coat?
    .... very warm.
10 .... a funny smell in the kitchen.

'Right, children, there are going to be a few changes this term.'

In some answers, both contracted forms (for example *I'm, don't*) and full forms (for example *I am, do not*) are possible. Normally both are correct.

BE AND *HAVE*   **5**

have with *got* and *do*   *We haven't got / don't have time.*

Have can be used to talk about **possession**, **relationships**, **characteristics** and similar ideas.
The short forms *I have, have I?, I have not* etc are **unusual** in an informal style.
Instead, we generally use forms with **have got** or **do ... have**.
Have got is **not present perfect** in this use. It means exactly the same as *have*.

INSTEAD OF	WE USE
I/you etc have	*I've got, you've got* etc
have I/you? etc	*have I got?* etc **OR** *do I have?* etc
I/you etc haven't	*I haven't got* etc **OR** *I don't have* etc
had I/you? etc	*did I have?* etc
I/you etc hadn't	*I didn't have* etc

I've got a headache. (More natural than *I have a headache.*)
Have you got a credit card with you? (More natural than *Have you a credit card ...?*)
We haven't got much time. (More natural than *We haven't much time.*)
Do you have today's paper? (More natural than *Have you today's paper?*)
Did Lily have your keys? (More natural than *Had Lily your keys?*)

Got-forms are most common in the **present**. The past forms *I/you* etc *had* are more common **without** *got*.
*I **had** a bad cold last week.*

Do and *got* are not used together. (**NOT** ~~Do you have got any children?~~)

1 Complete the sentences.

1 I've .... a new boyfriend.
2 .... your sister got a car?
3 I haven't .... your keys.
4 The school does not .... adequate sports facilities.
5 .... you .... good teachers when you were at school?
6 We .... got any bread in the house.
7 .... you .... Anne's address? OR .... you .... Anne's address?
8 'Can I borrow your bike?' 'Sorry, I .... one.' OR 'Sorry, I .... one.'
9 .... you .... a headache? OR .... you .... a headache?
10 Ruth and Joe .... any children. OR Ruth and Joe .... any children.

2 If you're homeless, you haven't got a home. Write sentences using *If you're ...* , *you haven't got a/any ...* to explain these words:

1 bald ....
2 penniless ....
3 childless ....
4 unemployed ....
5 toothless ....
6 lonely ....
7 starving ....
8 an orphan ....
9 unmarried ....

3 Complete the conversations, using *have got*, *has got* etc.

1 '............................ an aspirin?' '............................ a terrible headache.' 'I'll just look. I think .... some in my bag. Oh, no, sorry, ... any.'

2 'How many brothers and sisters .... ?' 'Just one brother.'

3 'We .... a new car.' 'Really?' 'Yes. .... four-wheel drive, power steering and anti-lock braking.' 'Fascinating.'

4 'I'm afraid .... some bad news for you.' 'Oh, no. What is it this time?'

5 'Why .... dark glasses on?' '............................ something wrong with my eyes.'

6 '............................ dirt on my nose?' 'No, but .... something funny in your hair.'

7 'Sally .... a new boyfriend.' 'What's he like?' 'Very good-looking. He's quite tall, and .... big dark brown eyes and a lovely smile. But she says .... a terrible temper.'

8 '............................ any idea why Rob wants to see us?' 'Not really. Maybe .... a problem with Sarah again.'

9 'You .... a new flat, haven't you?' 'Yes, and it .... a view of the river.'

10 '............................ anything to drink?' 'Only water. Is that OK?'

4 Change the sentences as in the examples.

▶ Have you got my keys? *Do you have my keys?* ....

▶ Does Sue have your address? *Has Sue got your address?* ....

1 We haven't got a TV. ....

2 Do you have a dog? ....

3 Bill doesn't have a job any more. ....

4 My mother hasn't got time for a holiday. ....
....

5 Luke doesn't have any friends. ....

6 I haven't got a very good temper. ....

7 Why have you got that funny hat on? ....
....

8 Do we have a meeting this evening? ....
....

9 Has anybody got a map of the town? ....
....

10 Have you got time to look at something? ....
....

5 Complete some of these sentences about yourself.

1 I've got plenty of ....

2 I haven't got a ....

3 I haven't got much ....

4 I haven't got many ....

5 I haven't got any ....

6 I've got too much ....

7 I've got too many ....

8 I've got enough ....

9 I haven't got enough ....

'I think we've got a leadership problem.'

In some answers, both contracted forms (for example *I'm*, *don't*) and full forms (for example *I am*, *do not*) are possible. Normally both are correct.

BE AND *HAVE*   7

habitual and repeated actions *Do you often have colds?*

Got-forms are **not** generally used to talk about **habits** and **repeated actions**.

We **have** meetings on Mondays. (**NOT** ~~We've got meetings on Mondays.~~)
Do you often **have** colds? (**NOT** ~~Have you often got colds?~~)

1 Here is a child's school timetable. Write five or more sentences beginning
She has … / She doesn't have …

	M	T	W	Th	F
9.00–10.00	maths	French	English	maths	physics
10.15–11.15	history	maths	chemistry	French	chemistry
11.30–12.30	biology	physics	Russian	geography	English
2.00–3.00	English	geography	sociology	Russian	maths
3.15–4.15	games	economics	games	English	games

▶ .....She has maths at nine o'clock on Mondays.......................................
▶ .....She has economics once a week...
▶ .....She doesn't have French on Wednesdays...
....
....
....
....
....

2 Write some sentences about what happens in your week.
▶ .....I usually have a lie-in on Sunday mornings.....................................
▶ .....I have English lessons three times a week..
....
....
....
....
....
....

3 Use *have* with words from the box to complete the sentences.

a medical check-up   a service   bad dreams   difficulty   exams   fish ✓
long holidays   meetings   terrible headaches

▶ We always ...have fish........................ on Fridays.

1 Students here .... at the end of every term.

2 My car .... every 10,000 miles.

3 I'm not usually ill, but I .... sometimes.

4 Do you ever .... those .... when you can't wake up?

5 We .... with the manager every Monday morning.

6 I .... at the hospital twice a year.

7 Children in Britain .... in the summer.

8 I often .... remembering names and faces.

have for actions *I'm going to have a swim.*

We use *have* in a lot of fixed expressions to talk about actions, especially in an informal style.

COMMON EXPRESSIONS

have breakfast, lunch, coffee etc   *have a wash, bath* etc   *have a rest, sleep, lie-down, dream* etc
have a good time, bad day, nice evening, day off, holiday etc   *have a good flight, trip, journey* etc
have a talk, word, conversation, disagreement, quarrel, fight etc   *have a swim, walk, dance, ride, game* etc
have a try, a go, a look   *have difficulty in, trouble in … ing*
have a baby   *have an accident, an operation, a nervous breakdown*

In this structure, *have* is an ordinary verb with progressive forms, and with *do* in questions and negatives.

'Where's Jane?' 'She's having a bath.'   *What time do you have lunch?*

1 **What can you do with these things / in these places? Use *have* with the words in the box.**

dinner   a drink   a game of cards   a game of tennis   a rest   a shave   a shower   a swim   coffee

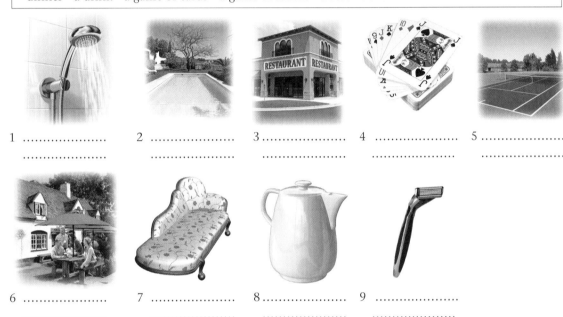

1 ....   2 ....   3....................   4 ....   5 ....
....

6 ....   7 ....   8....................   9 ....
....

2 **What are they going to do? Use *have* with the words in the box.**

an accident   a baby   a fight   a nervous breakdown   an operation

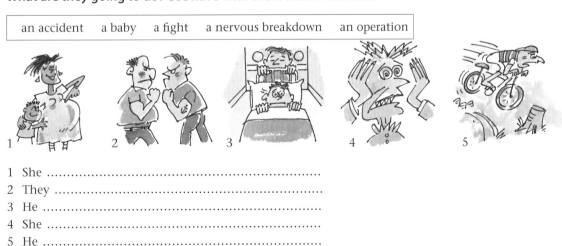

1   2   3   4   5

1 She ....
2 They ....
3 He ....
4 She ....
5 He ....

In some answers, both contracted forms (for example *I'm, don't*) and full
forms (for example *I am, do not*) are possible. Normally both are correct.

be and have: more practice

1 *There is.* **Use words from the three boxes (or your own words) to make 10 sentences.**

There must be There might be There can't be There is/are (not) likely to be I would like there to be	green elephants a horse three small dogs pizza life teachers *your idea*	on the moon on Mars somewhere in the universe in Scotland upstairs in this street *your idea*

▶ ...There are not likely to be green elephants on the moon.

....

....

....

....

....

....

....

....

....

....

2 *Be*, **not** *have.* **Write five or more sentences with** *I am (not)* **to say how you feel now. Use some of the words in the box.**

cold hot hungry ill sleepy thirsty warm well wide awake

....

....

....

....

....

3 **Internet exercise. Use a search engine (e.g. Google). How many examples are there of the following?**

"They are hungry" ..*585,000*.... "They have got hunger" ..*0*.............

"She was cold and" .... "She had cold and" ....

"We are a new car" .... "We've got a new car" ....

"What size are your shoes?" .... "What size have your shoes?" ....

"What colour are her eyes?" .... "What colour have her eyes?" ....

"I am happy now" .... "I have happy now" ....

"They were afraid" .... "They had afraid " ....

"They were a long journey" .... "They had a long journey" ....

4 **DO IT YOURSELF** **Which of the three rules is correct? Use a dictionary if necessary.**

In English, we often use *be*, not *have*, to talk about:

A possessions, travel and illness.   B feelings, colour and size.   C feelings, possessions and clothing.

Answer: Rule ...... is correct.

5 Grammar in texts. Here are some 'contact' advertisements from a magazine. Write sentences about some of the things that the people *are* and *have got* (according to them).

1 handsome, intelligent male, 6ft, 31, athletic build, Porsche, seeks attractive girlfriend, under 30, for fun and friendship. Box 329.

2 natural woman, 37, intelligent, fun-loving, tall, brown hair, blue eyes, good sense of humour, enjoys cinema, theatre and travel, seeks sincere, well-educated man, 35-55, for honest, caring relationship. Ring 093 22815.

3 attractive, professional black lady, slim, 5ft 6in, nice smile, own apartment, likes long hair, brains in a man. Ring 038 9734.

4 successful businessman, 35, attractive, tanned, nice home, yacht, requires exciting, slim female. Photograph. Ring 045 37943.

▶ *The man in advertisement 1 is handsome. He has got an athletic build.* ....

....

....

....

....

6 Grammar in a text. Here is a rather unnatural conversation. Can you make it more natural?

A: Good morning, Helen. Have you a moment? *Have you got a moment?* ....

H: For you, Amanda, I always have a moment. ....

   Have you a problem? ....

A: Yes, Helen. I have a small problem. ....

   But first, I have a question. ....

   Have you a dog? ....

H: Yes, Amanda. I have three. ....

A: I see. Now I have a garden. ....

   And yesterday I had flowers. But today I have no flowers. ....

   ....

H: I have no idea what you are talking about. ....

A: Really? Well, Helen. I have a gun. ....

   And now I must go. I have work to do. ....

7 GRAMMAR AND VOCABULARY. Houses. Read the advertisement with a dictionary and complete the sentences.

▶ *There are two* .... floors.
▶ *There is a modern* .... kitchen.
1 .... living room.
2 .... study.
3 .... cloakroom.
4 .... two ....
5 .... four ....
6 .... gas...........................
7 .... garage.
8 .... large ....

Price: £ 650,000　　　　　**ref.no.671749**

Large new house situated in the village of Wickfield.

Modern kitchen, large living room, small study, downstairs cloakroom and shower room, 4 bedrooms, 2 bathrooms, gas central heating, double garage, large garden.

be and *have*: revision test

① Put in *there's* or *it's*.

1 .... a new teacher in the school.
2 .... some fresh milk in the fridge.
3 '............... no sugar in your coffee.'
4 'Whose is that coat?' '............... Ann's.'
5 .... a problem with the car.
6 .... a present in my bag. .... for you.
7 .... a mistake on this page.
8 'What's that noise?' '............... the children playing.'
9 We've got a new flat. .... quite small.
10 'Have you seen my purse?' '............... on the floor.'

② Put the words in the right order.

1 problem seems to there be a ....
2 much soup is there in salt the too ....
3 snow is to tomorrow there likely be ....
4 any I there don't to want be trouble ....
5 any for letters me there were ? ....
6 with wrong something there is car the ....
7 singing the bus was a woman there on ....
8 shout to there no need is ....
9 must somebody be there home at ....
10 there an exam next will week be ? ....

③ Are these normal English expressions or not?

▶ have a bath ...Yes........
▶ have a write ...No........
1 have a good journey ....
2 have a conversation ....
3 have an eat ....
4 have a look ....
5 have a play ....
6 have trouble ....
7 have a work ....

8 have a try ....
9 have a baby ....
10 have a good time ....
11 have an operation ....
12 have a find ....
13 have happiness ....
14 have an accident ....
15 have a dream ....

④ Correct (✓) or not (✗)?

1 I have often got headaches. ......
2 There might be snow tomorrow. ......
3 I would like that there is good weather for my holiday. ......
4 It's a big dog in the garden. ......
5 Are you having a good time? ......
6 We've got too much work. ......
7 Are you having any brothers or sisters? ......
8 How much money do you have got? ......
9 Did you have a good journey? ......
10 I'm going to have a talk with John. ......

In some answers, both contracted forms (for example *I'm, don't*) and full forms (for example *I am, do not*) are possible. Normally both are correct.

SECTION 2 present tenses

GRAMMAR SUMMARY

> SIMPLE PRESENT: *I work, she works, he doesn't work* etc
> PRESENT PROGRESSIVE: *I am working, she is working, he isn't working* etc

English has **two 'present' tenses**.

- We use the **simple present** mostly to talk about **things that are always true**, and **things that happen repeatedly**.
  *Dogs **eat** meat.*   *My aunt **lives** in Leeds.*   *I **don't work** on Saturdays.*

- We can use the **simple present** in **commentaries**, **instructions**, **stories** and **jokes**, to describe events that happen **one after another**.
  *Smith **passes** to Peters, Peters **passes** to Ollis, Ollis **shoots** – and it's a goal!*
  *First you **break** three eggs into a bowl. You **add** butter, salt and pepper. Then you **take** a fork …*
  *This man **goes** into a pub, and he **says** to the barman …*

- We use the **present progressive** (or 'present continuous') to talk about things that are happening just **around the time when we speak**.
  *Look! The dog's **eating** your shoe.*   *I'm **working** hard these days.*

- We use the **present progressive** to talk about **changes** that are happening.
  *Prices **are going** up.*   *Transport **is getting** worse.*

- We can also use the **present progressive** to talk about the **future** (see pages 27, 30).
  *I'm **seeing** Lucy tomorrow.*

JUST WORDS

I hate you
I love you
you get on my nerves
you're destroying me
darling
don't leave me
it's your fault
you always
you never
darling
you never listen to me
don't listen to me
it's just words.

Why computers are like women:

Nobody understands the language that they use when they talk to other computers.

They never tell you what is wrong; and if you don't know, you're in trouble.

They remember your smallest mistakes for ever.

Why computers are like men:

They know a lot of things but they are very stupid.

After you get one for yourself, you soon see a better one.

They like to go fast but they always crash.

revise the basics: which present tense?

	SIMPLE PRESENT	PRESENT PROGRESSIVE
+	I/you/we/they **work** he/she/it **works**	I **am**, you **are** etc work**ing**
?	**do** I/you/we/they work? **does** he/she/it work?	**am** I, **are** you etc work**ing**?
−	I/you/we/they **do not** work he/she/it **does not** work	I **am not**, you are not etc work**ing**

- things that are **always true**
- things that happen **all the time, repeatedly, often, sometimes, never** etc.

- things that are happening **now**
- things that are happening **around now**

You live in North London, don't you?
No thanks. I don't smoke.
Chetford Castle stands on a high hill.
Alice works for an insurance company.
What do frogs eat?
I play tennis every Wednesday.
The sun rises in the east.

My sister's living with me just now.
Look – Ann's smoking a cigar.
Why is that girl standing on the table?
Phil's not working at the moment.
Hurry up! We're waiting for you.
'What are you doing?' 'I'm writing letters.'
Why are you crying? What's wrong?

1 **DO IT YOURSELF** Study the above examples. Which of these words and expressions go best with the simple present (SP), and which go best with the present progressive (PP)?

▶ *permanent* ...SP....
1 *temporary* ....
2 *habit* ....
3 *just around now* ....

4 *always* ....
5 *usually* ....
6 *just at this moment* ....
7 *these days but not for very long* ....

2 **GRAMMAR AND VOCABULARY: things to read**
Look at the pictures and numbers, and write sentences with *often* and *now*.
Use a dictionary if necessary.

▶ (2, 1) She *often reads newspapers, but now she's reading a short story.*
▶ (3,4) She *often reads magazines, but now she's reading a biography.*
1 (5,9) He ....
2 (8,10) She ....
3 (1,7) He ....
4 (4,2) I ....
5 (2,6) They ....
6 (3,5) He ....

1 short stories

2 newspaper

3 magazine

4 biography

5 poems

6 notice

7 cookery book   8 comic

9 autobiography

10 grammar

3 Here are some exchanges from an interview between an American journalist and a French film star. Can you complete them with the correct tenses?

1 'How do you start work on a film?' 'I .... the script and .... notes.' (*read; make*)

2 'I .... notes of our interview. I hope you don't mind.' 'No, that's OK.' (*make*)

3 'What languages ....?' 'English, French and Spanish.' (*you speak*)

4 'I'm glad we .... this interview in English. My French isn't very good.' (*do*)

5 'Who .... that guitar?' 'My son, when he has time.' (*play*)

6 'Who .... the piano upstairs?' 'My sister. She's got a concert tomorrow.' (*play*)

7 'What ....?' 'I think it's a piece by Mozart.' (*she play*)

8 '........................... anything else?' 'The violin. She's very musical.' (*she play*)

9 'Your daughter's very keen on sport, isn't she?' 'She .... tennis.' (*play*)

10 'Where is she now?' 'She .... tennis, as usual.' (*play*)

11 'What's that delicious smell?' 'My husband ....' (*cook*)

12 'Is that usual?' 'Yes, normally I .... and my husband ....' (*shop; cook*)

13 'What a lovely clock!' 'It .... , I'm afraid – it's been broken for years.' (*not work*)

14 'Could I use your phone?' 'I'm afraid it .... at the moment.' (*not work*)

Remember that some verbs are most often used in **simple** tenses, not progressive, even if we mean 'just now'.

I **like** this weather. (NOT ~~I'm liking this weather.~~)   What **does** he **want**? (NOT ~~What is he wanting?~~)

4 Circle the correct verb forms.

1 I *think / am thinking* you're right.

2 What *do you look / are you looking* at?

3 *Do you know / Are you knowing* that woman's name?

4 I *don't understand / am not understanding* this letter.

5 Why *do you drive / are you driving* so fast?

6 What *do you mean / are you meaning*?

7 I *hate / am hating* this music.

8 *Do you talk / Are you talking* to me?

9 I *don't remember / am not remembering* Andrea's phone number.

10 It *rains / is raining* again.

5 DO IT YOURSELF Write a rule in your own language to explain the difference between the two English present tenses. If you can work with other students who speak your language, compare your rule with theirs.

6 Choose the correct form of the cartoon caption.

'I *stand / am standing* under your foot.'

NOTE: We **don't** use a **present** tense to say **how long** something has been going on (see page 56).

I**'ve known** her for years. (NOT ~~I know her for years.~~)

In some answers, both contracted forms (for example *I'm, don't*) and full forms (for example *I am, do not*) are possible. Normally both are correct.

PRESENT TENSES 15

revise the basics: spelling

1 **DO IT YOURSELF** Look at the examples of third person singular (*he/she/it* ...) forms. Then circle 'A', 'B' or 'C' to complete the rules.

catches	cooks	does	eats	enjoys	fixes	flies	goes	lives	makes
misses	passes	plays	pushes	reads	replies	says	shops	smokes	
speaks	stands	teaches	thinks	tries	waits	washes	works		

1 **Most verbs: add**   **A** *-s*   **B** *-es*   **C** *-ies*
2 **Verbs ending in a vowel (for example *a* or *o*) + *y*: add**   **A** *-s*   **B** *-es*   **C** *-ies*
3 **Verbs ending in a consonant + *-y*: drop *-y* and add**   **A** *-s*   **B** *-es*   **C** *-ies*
4 **Verbs ending in *-s, -x, ch, sh*: add**   **A** *-s*   **B** *-es*   **C** *-ies*
5 ***Go* and *do*: add**   **A** *-s*   **B** *-es*   **C** *-ies*

2 Write the third person singular of these verbs.

box .... brush .... buy .... complete .... cry ....
defend .... excite .... expect .... fry .... guess ....
look .... pray .... reach .... rush .... spend ....
want .... watch ....

3 **DO IT YOURSELF** Look at the examples of *-ing* forms and complete the table.

helping	hoping	lying	making	running	sleeping	stopping	trying
waiting	wanting	working					

	Just add *-ing*	Double the last letter and add *-ing*	Change the end to *y* and add *-ing*	Drop the end and add *-ing*
most verbs	✓			
verbs ending in *-e*				
verbs ending in *-ie*				
short verbs ending in one vowel and one consonant				

4 Write the *-ing* forms of these verbs.

break .... clean .... come .... die .... dream ....
enjoy .... feel .... get .... go .... hit ....
jump .... live .... make .... play .... put ....
rob .... shop .... shout .... sit .... slim ....
stand .... turn .... wash .... write ....

NOTE: We only double letters in STRESSED syllables.

beGIN → beginning   forGET → forgetting   **BUT**   HAPpen → happening   OFFer → OFFering

5 Write the *-ing* forms of these verbs.

ANSwer .... preFER .... OPen .... GALLop ....
upSET .... VISit ....

present progressive for changes *Prices are going up.*

We use the **present progressive** for **changing** and **developing** situations.

The climate **is getting** warmer. (**NOT** ~~The climate gets warmer.~~)
That child**'s growing** bigger every day.
The universe **is expanding**, and has been since its beginning.
The price of petrol **is going up**. Everything **is getting** more expensive.
The economy **is getting** worse.

1 Look at the graph and say what is happening.

1 Milk...
2 Newspapers ....
3 Haircuts...

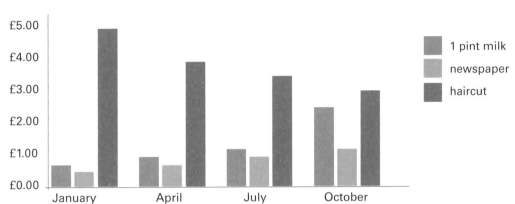

2 Say what is happening to some of the following.

the world's population	you (age)	your English	prices	days (length)	pollution
roads trains cars air travel the world's forests the political situation children					
cities medical care teenagers unemployment sprinters people's holidays the seas					

▶ *My English is getting better and better.* ....

....
....
....
....
....
....
....
....
....
....
....
....

In some answers, both contracted forms (for example *I'm, don't*) and full
forms (for example *I am, do not*) are possible. Normally both are correct.

PRESENT TENSES **17**

simple present: instructions etc *You take the first left*

We use the **simple present** to describe events that happen **one after another** in **commentaries** and **demonstrations**. We also use the **simple present** to ask for and give **instructions**.

Calvin **passes** to Peters, Peters to O'Malley, Lucas **intercepts**, Lucas to Higgins, Higgins **shoots** – and it's a goal!
First I **put** a lump of butter into the frying pan and **light** the gas; then while the butter's melting I **break** three eggs into a bowl …
'How do I get to the station?' 'You **go** straight on for half a mile, then you **come** to a garage, you **turn** left and then you **take** the first right.'

1 **Look at the map and follow the directions.**

When you come out of the station you turn right. Then you take the first left and keep straight on till you come to a T-Junction. You turn right and keep straight on till you get to a crossroads, and then turn right again.

Where are you? At ....

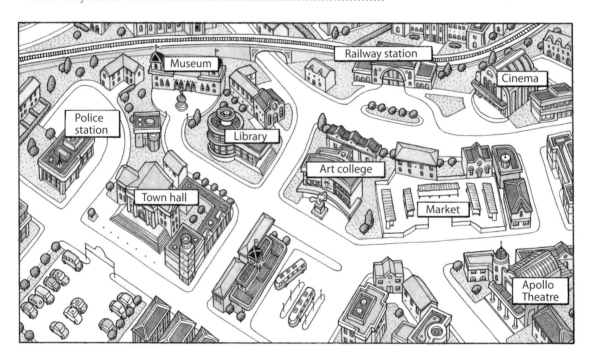

2 **Write similar directions: tell somebody how to get from the station to the Apollo Theatre.**

....
....
....

3 **Now tell somebody how to get from the Apollo Theatre to the car park.**

....
....
....

4 Look at the pictures and write the instructions for boiling an egg.

1   2   3   4

5   6   7

You put water in a saucepan. Then you

....

....

....

5 Write the instructions for cooking something else.

....

....

....

We often tell **stories** and **jokes** with **present tenses** in an informal style.
We use the **simple present** for **events** – things that happen one after another.
We use the **present progressive** for **background** – things that are already happening when the story starts,
or that continue through part of the story.

*There's this Scotsman, you see, and he's **walking** through the jungle when he **meets** a gorilla. And the gorilla's
eating a snake sandwich. So the Scotsman **goes** up to the gorilla and **says** …*

6 Number the parts of the story in order and put in the correct forms of the verbs.

ask   close   go   hold   keep   notice ✓   open   say   sit ✓   throw   work

...... 'But there are no elephants in these mountains,' .... the woman.

...... Suddenly the man .... the window, ... out the orange and ....
the window again.

...... 'Because we .... through the mountains. Oranges .... the elephants away.'

..1.. A woman ..*is sitting*.. in a railway carriage when she ..*notices*.. that the man opposite her
.... an orange in his hand and looking out of the window.

...... 'You see?' says the man. 'It ....'

...... 'Excuse me,' the woman .... , 'but why did you do that?'

7 You probably know a better story than this. Write it.

....

....

....

....

....

....

In some answers, both contracted forms (for example *I'm, don't*) and full
forms (for example *I am, do not*) are possible. Normally both are correct.

PRESENT TENSES   **19**

non-progressive verbs *I remember his face.*

Some verbs are most often used in **simple** tenses, not progressive, even if we mean 'just now'.

I **know** what you mean. (**NOT** ~~I'm knowing what you're meaning.~~)
You **seem** worried. (**NOT** ~~You're seeming~~…)

SOME COMMON NON-PROGRESSIVE VERBS

believe, forget, hate, know, like, love, mean, need, prefer, remember, seem, understand, want

Do you **believe** *what he's saying?*   *I* **remember** *her face, but I* **forget** *her name.*
What **does** *this word* **mean**?   *I* **like** *this weather.*
What **does** *she* **want**?

1 Use non-progressive verbs to complete the sentences. More than one answer may be possible.

  1 I .... you're right.
  2 .... you .... this music?
  3 She says she .... to see Fred.
  4 I .... a drink of water.
  5 I .... you don't .... me.
  6 I .... how old she is.
  7 She .... me and I .... her.
  8 'Beer?' 'I .... orange juice.'
  9 I .... his face, but not his name.
 10 What .... 'explicate' .... ?
 11 You .... unhappy today.
 12 I don't .... why she .... to go home.
 13 .... you .... who that woman is?
 14 I don't .... where I parked the car.
 15 We .... more bread.

'On the Internet, nobody knows you're
a dog.'

OTHER COMMON NON-PROGRESSIVE VERBS

agree, belong, contain, depend, matter, mind, own, realise, recognise, suppose

'This is a terrible film.' 'I **don't agree**.*'   'Sorry I'm late.' 'It* **doesn't matter**.'*
I **recognise** *her, but I don't remember her name.*
'Can I borrow the car?' 'It **depends**. *Until when?'*
'There's no more orange juice.' 'I **don't mind**. *I'll have water.'*

2 Choose the best verb to complete each sentence.

  ▶ His wife always ....*agrees*........ with everything he says. (*agree, realise, recognise*)
  1 This book .... to me. (*own, belong, contain*)
  2 I .... you're right. (*suppose, depend, mind*)
  3 His father .... a chain of hotels. (*contain, belong, own*)
  4 Money doesn't .... to me. (*depend, mind, matter*)
  5 That bottle .... petrol. (*contain, own, belong*)
  6 'Can you lend me some money?' 'It .... ' (*matter, depend, mind*)
  7 I .... that I've made a mistake. (*matter, realise, depend*)
  8 Do you .... if I open a window? (*matter, suppose, mind*)
  9 I .... it's time to go home. (*suppose, own, mind*)
 10 'He's a great president.' 'I don't .... ' (*matter, recognise, agree*)

3 Complete the sentences with your own ideas.

1 I like ....
2 I hate ....
3 I remember ....
4 I forget ....
5 I don't know what .... means.
6 I don't agree with ....
7 I don't mind if ....
8 My bag contains ....
9 I own ....
10 It doesn't matter if ....

Think, see, look, feel and *have* can be **non-progressive** with one meaning but **progressive** with another.

NON-PROGRESSIVE (*I think etc*)	CAN BE PROGRESSIVE (*I'm thinking etc*)
think (that ...) = 'have an opinion' *I think you're wrong.*	***think (about ...)*** = 'plan, look at ideas' *I'm thinking about the holidays.*
see = 'understand' *I see what you mean.*	***see*** = 'meet' *I'm seeing the doctor today.*
look like = 'seem like' *That looks like our train.*	***look*** = 'turn eyes towards' *What are you looking at?*
feel = 'have an opinion' *I feel you're making a mistake.*	***feel ill/tired*** etc (can be progressive or simple) *I'm feeling ill.* or *I feel ill.*
have (possession etc) *I have (got) a headache*	***have*** (actions) *We are having a great time.*

4 Put in the correct verb forms.

1 We .... the bank manager this afternoon. (*see*)
2 'I .... you're crazy.' (*think*)
3 Why .... that woman .... at me? (*look*)
4 I .... not .... much money just now. (*have*)
5 That girl .... like your sister. (*look*)
6 'I'm not going to help you.' 'I .... ' (*see*)
7 'What .... you .... about?' 'Life.' (*think*)
8 I .... very tired today. (*feel*)
9 'How's Jane doing?' 'She .... a wonderful holiday in Greece.' (*have*)
10 I .... you're wrong to get married. (*feel*)

'I know that you believe that you understood what you think I said, but I am not sure you realize that what you heard is not what I meant.'

(*Attributed to a US State Department spokesman*)

In some answers, both contracted forms (for example *I'm, don't*) and full forms (for example *I am, do not*) are possible. Normally both are correct.

PRESENT TENSES **21**

present tenses: more practice

1 **Mixed structures. Correct the sentences, or write 'Correct'.**

▶ Look! It rains. ....It's raining.........

▶ I'm getting tired. ....Correct...............

1 I'm watching TV every evening. ....

2 'What are you doing?' 'I'm reading.' ....

3 I'm not knowing Alicia's address. ....

4 Food gets very expensive these days. ....

5 A man's going into a shop, and he's asking for a newspaper. And the shopkeeper is saying …
   ....

6 'The sun goes round the earth.' 'No, it doesn't.' ....

7 I'm not feeling very well. ....

8 We're seeing the bank manager at two o'clock. ....

9 I'm not understanding what she wants. ....

10 It's getting late. ....

2 **Spelling. There are sixteen mistakes in the text. Can you find and correct the other fifteen?**

speaks

Annie ~~speakes~~ and writs three languages, and workes in an import-export office. She replys to letters

and emails, and she spends a lot of time answerring the phone. It's not very interesting work, and she's

not very good at it: she trys hard, but she keeps forgetting things and makeing mistakes. She

wishs she could change her job, so she's begining a computer course. She goes for lessons every

evening, and she's lookking forward to completeing the course and geting her certificate. At the

weekends she teachs karate. She really enjoyes that, and is hopping to open her own school one day.

3 **Grammar in a text. Put in expressions from the box. Use the present progressive.**

become less common   continue   continue   get ✓   get   get   go down   increase

People [1] ....are getting......... happier.
According to a recent report from the Western
Statistics Office, 73% of people say that they are
happy 'most of the time', compared with only
47% at the beginning of the century. Perhaps
this is partly because the world is less crowded:
the Western population [2] ....
by about 1.3% per year. And life expectancy
[3] ....: in 1970, men lived for
an average of 69 years and women 75; both
sexes now can expect to live for 113 years. We
[4] .... richer, too. The average
income in 2096 was 146,000 Western Credits –
twice as much as in the year 2018.

Not everything [5] .... better,
though. The climate [6] ....
to change for the worse, and sea levels
[7] .... to rise. If average
temperatures go on increasing, scientists are afraid
that more of the world's capitals will go the same
way as London, Paris and New York. Perhaps one
day we will all have to move to the mountains.

Religious belief [8] .... In 2018,
65% of Western Federation citizens said that they
believed in God; in 2096 the figure was only 24%,
and only half of these went to church regularly.

(From *The Times*, 18 July 2098.) ●

4 Non-progressive verbs. Write negative continuations, using verbs from the box.

agree ✓	agree	believe	matter	mind	recognise	remember

▶ 'He's a great singer.' I ...*don't agree.*...........

1 'I'm sorry. I've broken a glass.' 'It ....'

2 'What's Bill's phone number?' 'I ....'

3 Perhaps I've seen her before, but I .... her.

4 Peter says he's a student, but I .... him.

5 'Supper will be very late.' 'I .... I'm not hungry now.'

6 Lucy thinks everybody should study music, but I ....

5 Non-progressive verbs. Choose the best way to complete the sentences.

1 'Joich vallahava enstiuz sanschlowu.' ' .... ' (*I hope not, I know, I don't understand*)

2 'Is your English getting better?' ' .... ' (*I hope so, I know, I see*)

3 'I'm sorry, we're late.' ' .... ' (*I don't know, It depends, It doesn't matter*)

4 'Do you like dancing?' ' .... ' (*I don't remember, I don't know, It depends*)

5 'Where does your boss live?' ' .... ' (*I don't remember, I see, I don't think so*)

6 'Do you understand?' ' .... ' (*I see, I think so, I don't remember*)

7 'Meat is bad for you.' ' .... ' (*It doesn't matter, I don't agree, I don't understand*)

8 'The car's broken down, so we'll have to walk.' ' .... ' (*I don't mind, I don't know, It depends*)

6 Internet exercise. Use a search engine (e.g. Google) to find simple sentences containing some of the expressions in the box. Write the sentences.

"is increasing" "is getting better" "is getting worse" "are going up" "is changing"
"are changing" "is getting cheaper" "is getting more expensive" "is becoming impossible"

....

....

....

....

....

....

....

7 Changes. Complete the cartoon captions.

'Seems all right. How .... your English
.... ?' (*get on*)

'That funny noise ....
louder.' (*get*)

present tenses: revision test

1 Write the third person singular forms and the *-ing* forms.

accept *accepts, accepting*.   answer ....   begin ....

break ....   buy ....   catch ....

complete ....   cook ....   eat ....

enjoy ....   fetch ....   fix ....

forget ....   fry ....   gallop ....

happen ....   hope ....   make ....

miss ....   offer ....   open ....

park ....   pay ....   push ....

say ....   shop ....   sit ....

sleep ....   start ....   teach ....

try ....   wait ....   wash ....

2 Circle the correct form.

1 Vegetarians are people who *don't eat / are not eating* meat.

2 Look out! My husband *comes / is coming*.

3 Some people still think the sun *goes / is going* round the earth.

4 I *play / 'm playing* tennis every weekend.

5 Who *sits / 's sitting* in my chair?

6 What *happens / is happening* in golf if you lose the ball?

7 An alcoholic is a person who *drinks / is drinking* too much and can't stop.

8 Look! *She wears / She's wearing* the same shoes as me.

9 'What *are you looking / do you look* at?' 'A strange bird.'

10 I *stay / 'm staying* with John for a few weeks until my flat's ready.

11 We *usually stay / 're usually staying* with Peggy when we go to Chicago.

12 Can you explain why water always *runs / is running* downhill?

13 What *do you do / are you doing* with my coat?

14 Nobody *gets / is getting* up early for fun.

15 Not many passenger planes *fly / are flying* faster than sound.

3 Put in the correct tense (simple present or present progressive).

1 I .... he's away. (*think*)

2 You .... what I .... (*know; mean*)

3 Your sister .... you. (*look like*)

4 I .... we .... a mistake. (*feel; make*)

5 While the butter ...., you .... three
eggs and .... them into a bowl. (*melt; take; break*)

6 I .... about the weekend. (*think*)

7 Scientists .... the weather ....(*believe; change*)

8 I .... what the problem is. (*not see*)

9 Why .... at me like that? (*you look*)

10 Now I .... what she wants. (*understand*)

11 Let's go home. It .... late. (*get*)

12 Food prices .... again. (*go up*)

13 'Sorry. I can't play tennis tomorrow.' 'It ....' (*not matter*)

14 'Can you lend me some money?' 'It ....' (*depend*)

15 We .... Joe and Patsy on Saturday. (*see*)

In some answers, both contracted forms (for example *I'm, don't*) and full
forms (for example *I am, do not*) are possible. Normally both are correct.

SECTION 3 talking about the future

GRAMMAR SUMMARY

the most common ways to talk about the future

There are **three** common ways to talk about the **future** in English:

- with the *going to* structure.
  *I'm really **going to tell** her what I think of her.*
- with the **present progressive**.
  We're meeting Malcolm tomorrow.
- with *will*.
  *The treasurer **will be** in the office from 9.00 till 2.00.*

We use *going to* or the **present progressive** especially when the future has some **present** reality: for example to talk about plans that we have already made.

Will can also be used when we **decide**, **agree**, **promise** or **refuse**, and in **requests**.
'There's the doorbell.' 'I'll go.'   'Please write every week.' 'Of course I will.'
*She **won't** come out of the bathroom.   **Will** you get some milk while you're out?*

We can sometimes use the **simple present** to talk about the future.
*Her plane **arrives** at 15.30.   I'll phone you when I **know** something.*
*I'll see you tomorrow if I **have** a chance.*

other ways to talk about the future

- **future progressive**
  *This time tomorrow I'**ll be lying** on the beach.*
- *be* + infinitive
  *The President **is to visit** Scotland in September.*
- **future in the past**
  *I didn't realise what **would happen**.*
- **future perfect**
  *I'**ll have finished** the job by supper time.*
- **future perfect progressive**
  *Next summer I'**ll have been studying** English for six years.*

The future progressive, future perfect and future perfect progressive are not very common. They are included here for the sake of completeness.

'Separate futures, please.'

revise the basics: *going to*

We often use **present** verb-forms to talk about the **future**. For example, we say that something *is going to* happen. This happens when we can **see the future in the present** – when a future situation is **starting**, or clearly **on the way**.

 *Look – it's **going to** rain.*

 *They're **going to** crash!*

1 **Look at the pictures. What is going to happen?**

| ▶ | 1 | 2 | 3 |
| 4 | 5 | 6 | 7 |

▶ *He is going to dive.* ....

1 .... 4 ....

2 .... 5 ....

3 .... 6 ....

                                                    7 ....

We often use *going to* for plans and intentions, especially in conversation.

*We're **going to** get a new car soon.*   *When **are** you **going to** get your hair cut?*
*I'm **going to** keep asking her out until she says 'Yes'.*

2 **Put the verbs in the right places to complete the sentences. Use *going to*.**
Note: there are too many verbs.

1 Jane is ..*going to study*............ music in Vienna. She's .... to become a professional pianist. This summer, she's .... three months studying German. (*spend; try; work; study*)

2 Max is .... maths and science for his school-leaving exams. Then he's .... the summer learning to fly. In the autumn, he's .... a two-year training course for airline pilots. (*start; spend; go; do*)

3 Jennifer's eight, and she doesn't know what she's .... One day she says she's .... a dancer, and the next she says she's .... with animals. This summer, she's .... with her aunt in America. (*take; work; do; stay; be*)

4 Annie is .... the house this summer. Then she's .... two weeks walking in Scotland. In the autumn, she's .... a new job as a translator. (*start; decorate; spend; play*)

3 **Write some things that you are going to do in the future.**

....

....

....

revise the basics: present progressive for future

We often use the **present progressive** to talk about **future personal arrangements** and **plans that are already fixed now**, especially when we give the **time**, **date**, and/or **place**.

'What *are* you *doing* this evening?' 'I*'m washing* my hair.'
My car*'s having* a service next week.   We*'re going* to Spain in June.
Did you know I*'m getting* a new job?   What *are* we *having* for dinner?

1 **Look at the diary and correct the sentences.**

1 She's playing tennis on Sunday afternoon.
....

2 Matthew is coming to see her on Sunday morning.
....

3 She's having lunch with James at 12.30 on Tuesday.
....

4 She's flying to Rotterdam on Thursday.
....

5 She's meeting Mrs Parsons in the London office.
....

6 She's going to the meeting with Mrs Parsons by car.
....

7 She's going to a funeral on Wednesday afternoon.
....

8 She's meeting the accountants at 12.00 on Monday.
....

9 She's going to the theatre on Saturday evening.
....

10 She's spending Friday at the races.
....

AUGUST	Week 34

22 Sunday
Tennis with Barbara 10am
Matthew afternoon

23 Monday
10.15 Mrs Parsons
Oxford Office (9.00 train)
Accountants 4.00 pm

24 Tuesday

25 Wednesday
George's funeral 9.00
Lunch James 12.30

26 Thursday
To Amsterdam KLM 147, 8.00
Back 18.50 KLM 156

27 Friday

Theatre Royal with Polly

28 Saturday
RACES

2 **Write some sentences about your plans for the coming week.**

....
....
....
....
....
....
....
....

'Hi, it's me. Listen. It's David's birthday, so a few million of us are going out for a meal. Are you interested?'

revise the basics: *will*-future

We use **will** to **give or ask for information** about the future, when there is no reason to use a present verb-form (see pages 26–27, 30–31).

*We **will** need the money on the 15th.*   ***Will** all the family be at the wedding?*
*It **will** be spring soon.*   *She'll be here in a few minutes.*

We often use **will** to **predict** the future – to say what we **think**, **guess** or **calculate** will happen.

*Tomorrow **will** be warm, with some cloud in the afternoon.*
*Who do you think **will** win?*   *You'll never finish that book.*

1 GRAMMAR AND VOCABULARY: weather. Look at the map and complete the weather forecast. Use some of the words in the box, once or more than once.

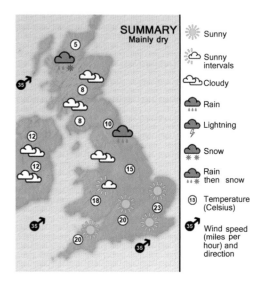

be	cold	dry	earthquakes	east	
hurricanes	ice	lightning	north	rain	
snow	south	thunder	warm	west	
wet	will	will be	winds		

Tomorrow will .... mainly ....,
but there .... some .... in the
north. There .... be strong ....
from the south-west later in the day. It will be quite
.... in the south, but Scotland ....
cold, and in the .... of Scotland the rain
.... turn to .... during the
afternoon.

2 Write your own weather forecast for the place where you are.

....
....
....
....

We usually say *I don't think … will*, NOT ~~I think … won't~~.

I don't think she'll be late. (NOT USUALLY ~~I think she won't be late.~~)

3 What do you think will happen? Make your own predictions, with *I think* or *I don't think*.
  ▶ ..*I think it will rain*.. tomorrow. (*rain*)
  ▶ ..*I don't think I'll get*.. money in the post tomorrow. (*get*)
  1 .... it .... tomorrow. (*snow*)
  2 .... I .... a letter from America tomorrow. (*get*)
  3 .... I .... rich in ten years. (*be*)
  4 .... I .... famous in ten years. (*be*)
  5 .... people .... English everywhere in the year 2100.
  (*speak*)

NOTE: We can say *I shall* and *we shall* instead of *I will* and *we will*. There is no difference of meaning in modern English. *Will* is more common.

→ For another use of *shall*, see page 82. For *will* in requests, promises etc, see page 29.

will in decisions, promises etc *OK, I'll go.*

We can use *will* when we **decide**, **agree** or **promise** to do things. We **don't** use the **simple present** in these cases.

We'll buy the tickets; you can buy supper afterwards. (**NOT** ~~We buy~~ …)
You'll get your money tomorrow. (**NOT** ~~You get~~ …)
I promise I'll stop smoking. (**NOT** ~~I promise I stop smoking.~~)
I'll hit you if you do that again. (**NOT** ~~I hit you if~~ …)

We often use *will* to announce a decision at the moment when we make it.

'There's the doorbell.' 'OK, I'll go.' (**NOT** … ~~I go.~~)

Won't can be used to talk about refusals.
He won't talk to anybody.   *The car won't start.*

1 **Complete the sentences with verbs from the box. Use *'ll* or *won't*.**

| answer   call   come   drive ✓   eat   go   send   tell   tell   wash   write |

▶ I ….*'ll drive*……… . Will you map-read?
myself.
1 I ……………… the cups. You can dry them.
2 I'm tired. I think I ……………… to bed now.
3 She ……………… us what's wrong.
4 The cat ……………… I think it's ill.
5 'The phone's ringing.' 'I ……………… it.'

6 I ……………… you the date when I know
7 I promise I ……………… to you every week.
8 That child ……………… out of the bathroom.
9 If you don't get out of here, I ………………
   the police.
10 I ……………… you all the papers on Friday.

Will you … ? can introduce instructions, orders and requests.
Would you … ? is softer, and can be used to make requests more polite.

Will you get me a paper while you're out?
Will you be quiet, please?
Would you watch the children for a few minutes?

2 **Use *Will you …?* to tell somebody to:**
▶ clean the bathroom. *Will you clean the bathroom?* ……………………………………………………
1 deliver the furniture on Friday. ……………………………………………………………………………………
2 send the bill to the office. ……………………………………………………………………………………
3 stop shouting. ……………………………………………………………………………………………………
4 lock all the doors. ……………………………………………………………………………………………
5 put the meat in the oven. ……………………………………………………………………………………

3 **Use *Would you …?* to ask somebody to:**
▶ get you a drink. *Would you get me a drink?* …………………………………………………………
1 switch the lights on. ……………………………………………………………………………………………
2 open a window. ……………………………………………………………………………………………………
3 buy some bread. ……………………………………………………………………………………………………
4 phone for a taxi. …………………………………………………………………………………………………
5 wake you up at 8.00. ……………………………………………………………………………………………

NOTE: *I'll have …* is often used when people order in cafés, restaurants etc.

I'll have a black coffee, please.

which future? *will, going to* or present progressive?

There are some differences between these three ways of talking about the future. The differences are not always important; often we can use two or three different forms to talk about the same thing.

PLANS
Going to and the **present progressive** are often both possible when we talk about plans.
We use the **present progressive** mostly for **fixed plans** with a definite **time** and/or **place**.

I'm going to see Ann some time soon.   *I'm meeting Pat at the theatre at 8.00.*
I think John's going to study biology.   *Sarah's starting university on September 17th.*

1 **In three of these sentences, the present progressive is possible. Which three?**
Rewrite them with the present progressive.

> Jack is going to arrive at 4.00.   I'm going to learn Spanish one of these days.
> I'm going to fly to Glasgow tomorrow.   Al's going to tell me about his problems.
> We're going to spend next week in Ireland.   Are you going to answer those letters?

1 ....
2 ....
3 ....

PREDICTIONS
Going to: we can **see** the future in the present: we see things coming or starting.
Will: we **think** or **believe** things about the future.

Look out! You're going to break that glass!
(I can see it now.)

Don't give him a watch – he'll break it.
(I think so, because I know him.)

2 **Circle the best form.**

▶ Mary *(is going to)* / *will* have a baby.
1 Perhaps we *are going to* / *will* meet again one day.
2 Be careful, or you *are going to* / *will* fall.
3 Look – Andy *is going to* / *will* fall off his bike!
4 I think you *are going to* / *will* love Scotland.
5 Look at those clouds: it*'s going to* / *will* rain.

DECISIONS
Will: we **are making** decisions.   *Going to*: decisions exist **now**: they **are already made**.

'We've got a letter from Jan.' 'OK, I'll answer it.'
'There are a lot of letters to answer.' 'I know. I'm going to do them all on Tuesday.'

3 **Put in *I'll* or *I'm going to*.**

▶ I've decided. ...*I'm going to*........ stop smoking.
1 'I don't want to cook tonight.' 'All right, then. .... cook.'
2 'I haven't got any money.' 'No? OK. .... pay.'
3 'Do you want to go out tonight?' 'No, ... wash my hair.'
4 'Those trousers are dirty.' 'Really? Oh, yes, they are. .... wash them.'
5 'Is Roberta eating with us?' 'Wait a minute. .... ask her.'

simple present *My credit card expires at midnight.*

We sometimes use the **simple present** to talk about the future. This happens mostly when we talk about **timetables**, routines and schedules.

*Next term **starts** on 6th April.   My train **leaves** at 3.17.*
*What time **does** the bus **arrive** in York?   **Do** you **have** classes next Saturday?*

1 **Choose the best tense.**

▶ The plane (*arrives*)/ *will arrive* at 10.00.
▶ I *write* / (*will write*) soon.
1 When *does* / *will* school start?
2 We *go* / *are going* to Spain some time soon.
3 I *stop* / *will stop* smoking after Christmas.
4 The exams *are* / *will be* in June.
5 I *have* / *will have* a lecture at 9.00 tomorrow.
6 The train *won't* / *doesn't* stop at Oxford.
7 I *come* / *will come* round after 7.00.
8 I *play* / *am playing* football tomorrow.
9 What time *does* / *will* the concert end?
10 I *post* / *will post* your letters.

'... And please hurry.
My credit card expires at midnight.'

The **simple present** can also be used to give and ask for **instructions**.

*When you get to the office you **go** up to the first floor, you **knock** on the first door on the right and you **ask** for Mrs Alstone. OK?*
*What **do** we **do** now?   Where **do** I pay?*

2 **Write sentences asking for instructions.**

You don't know:
▶ when to pay. *When do I pay?* ....
1 how to start the car. ....
2 where to put your coat. ....
3 who to write to. ....
4 where to go for the interview. ....
5 when to apply. ....
6 how to make spaghetti bolognese. ....
7 when to start. ....
8 who to ask. ....
9 how much to give the driver. ....
10 where to sign. ....

In other cases we **don't** use the **simple present** in simple sentences to talk about the **future**.

*Lucy's **coming** for a drink this evening.* (**NOT** ~~Lucy comes~~ ...)
*I'll **phone** you – I promise.* (**NOT** ~~I phone you~~ ...)
*There's the doorbell. I'll **go**.* (**NOT** ... ~~I go.~~)

→ For the simple present with a future meaning after *if, when, before, after, until* and other conjunctions, see pages 241 and 254.

In some answers, both contracted forms (for example I'm, don't) and full forms (for example I am, do not) are possible. Normally both are correct.

TALKING ABOUT THE FUTURE   **31**

future progressive *This time tomorrow I'll be skiing.*

| + *I will be working* etc | ? *will you be working?* etc | − *she will not be working* etc |

We can use the **future progressive** to say that something will be **going on at a certain time in the future**.

This time tomorrow I'll be skiing.   *We'll be thinking of you on Saturday.*

1 Mr Collins is a teacher. Look at the pictures and say what he will be doing at different times tomorrow. Use expressions from the box.

| cook supper | correct papers | drive to work | have a shower | have breakfast ✓ |
| have coffee | teach French | teach maths | train the football team | watch TV |

▶ ... *At 8.00 he will be having breakfast.* ....
1 ....
2 ....
3 ....
4 ....
5 ....
6 ....
7 ....
8 ....
9 ....

We can use the **future progressive** to **ask politely** 'What have you already decided?' Compare:

Will you stay in this evening? (request or order)
Are you going to stay in this evening? (perhaps pressing for a decision)
Will you be staying in this evening? (just asking about plans)

2 Make future progressive questions to ask somebody politely:
▶ whether they are planning to go out this evening. ...*Will you be going out this evening?*...
1 what time they are planning to get up. ....
2 what they plan to wear. ....
3 how they intend to travel to work. ....
4 how soon they intend to leave. ....
5 whether they expect to take the car. ....
6 whether they plan to have lunch out. ....
7 what time they intend to come back. ....
8 where they are planning to sleep. ....
9 how they intend to pay. ....
10 when they plan to go back home. ....

be + infinitive *You're to do your homework.*

We can talk about the future by saying that something **is to happen**. We often use this structure to talk about **official plans** and fixed **personal arrangements**.

*The President **is to visit** Scotland in September.*   *We **are to get** a pay rise.*
*I felt nervous because **I was** soon **to leave** home for the first time.*

1 Write five or more sentences about President Morton's schedule, using *is to . . .*

	08.00	Arrive Star City Airport. Inspect guard of honour.
	09.00	Working breakfast with President Jensen.
Schedule for	11.00–13.00	Tour of Star City; meet mayor and civic leaders.
Presidential Visit	13.00–14.00	Lunch with Foreign Minister Svendsen and guests.
to Northland	14.00–16.00	Visit inner city schools; open new eye hospital.
	16.00–20.00	Meet business leaders; rest.
MONDAY 27.6	20.00–23.00	Attend State Dinner as guest of President and Mrs Jensen.

▶ .....The President is to arrive at Star City at 8.00. ....
....
....
....
....
....
....

You are (not) to can be used (for example by parents) to **give orders**.

*You**'re to do** your homework before you watch TV.*
*She can go out, but she**'s not to be** back late.*

2 Put together sentences that a parent might say to a child, using expressions from the two boxes and *You're (not) to . . .*

clean up ✓	do	give chocolate	go to bed	leave dirty	leave empty	make
make your own	open door	polish				

by ten o'clock	bed	crisp-packets lying around	hour-long phone calls	
piano practice	room ✓	shoes	socks on floor	to cat to strangers

▶ .....You're to clean up your room. ....
1 ....
2 ....
3 ....
4 ....
5 ....
6 ....
7 ....
8 ....
9 ....

In some answers, both contracted forms (for example *I'm, don't*) and full forms (for example *I am, do not*) are possible. Normally both are correct.

TALKING ABOUT THE FUTURE **33**

future in the past *I was going to ring you yesterday.*

When we are talking about the past, we often want to say that something was still **in the future at that time.** To express this idea, we can use the **past progressive** (*was …ing*), *was going to …*, *would …* or *was to*.

*She was a little nervous, because she **was flying** to America the next day.*
*Sorry – I **was going to tell** you about Alice and Fred, but I forgot.*
*I knew that woman **would be** trouble.*
*They showed me the room where I **was to sleep**. My heart sank.*

1 Complete the sentences with expressions from the box.

> was going to happen   was going to ring   was going to say   was catching   was leaving
> was to change   was to regret   would be terrible   would be married   would spend

1 Carola and I hardly noticed each other that first evening. Two weeks later we
....
2 He .... that conversation for many years to come.
3 I .... you yesterday, but I forgot.
4 She .... in two hours, and she still hadn't started packing.
5 So this was the school where I .... the next five years.
6 The letter that .... my life arrived one Friday morning.
7 I couldn't decide what I .... to Mary.
8 I knew that the party ...., and it was.
9 I got up early because I .... the 7.50 train.
10 John was the only person who realised what ....

2 Complete the text with expressions from the box. Use a dictionary if necessary.

> was going   was going to be   was going to do something   was going to stay   was joining
> was starting   was to   was to get   was to report   were going to do
> would become well known   would come back   would sometimes envy   would marry

It was the last night at university; the last party. The mood kept changing from happy to serious to sad and back again. We talked about the past, remembering good and bad times; and we talked about the future and what we [1]..................................... David [2].....................................
into the theatre; we were all sure he [3]..................................... a star. I saw him years later in a James Bond film: one of those anonymous bad guys who get killed in the first ten minutes. Alistair [4]..................................... the army; he [5]..................................... to his regiment the following Monday. And he [6]..................................... killed for real, a few years later, in a stupid and unnecessary war. Chris Homer [7]..................................... in finance, he said, though it was not entirely clear what. He [8]..................................... into my life in a couple of years, walking into my office in torn jeans, smelling of drink and asking for money. The other Chris – the one we called 'egghead' – [9]..................................... post-graduate work the following year. He [10]..................................... become an eminent research scientist with an international reputation. Two others [11]..................................... in years to come: Keith as a prize-winning film director, and Robbie as a politician involved in a series of juicy sex scandals. My closest friend, Nigel, [12]..................................... his university girlfriend, have three children, and enjoy a quiet and happy life. Later I [13]..................................... him. I [14]..................................... at university and become an academic – I thought. (Do you know how to make God laugh? Tell him your plans.)
    I emptied my glass, said an emotional good-bye to everyone, and walked out into the future.

future perfect *He'll have finished the roof by Saturday.*

	SIMPLE	PROGRESSIVE
+	*I will have worked* etc	*I will have been working* etc
?	*will* you *have worked?* etc	*will* you *have been working?* etc
−	*she will not have worked* etc	*he will not have been working* etc

We can use the **future perfect** to say that something will have been **completed by a certain time in the future.**

*The builder says he'**ll have finished** the roof by Saturday.*
*The car **will soon have done** 100,000 miles.*

1 Complete the sentences with the verbs from the box. Use the future perfect.

drive   finish   not finish ✓   leave home   save   win

▶ I ....*won't have finished*.... the report by Monday, and it's needed for Monday morning.
1 In a couple of years the children ...., and we'll be able to move to
   a smaller house.
2 I .... painting the kitchen by bedtime.
3 I hope I .... enough money for a mountain bike by Christmas.
4 When I get home I .... 400 miles.
5 If we beat United, we................................... all our matches this season.

We can use the **future perfect progressive** to say **how long** something will have continued by a certain time.
*Next Christmas I'**ll have been teaching** for twenty years.*

2 Write three sentences about yourself with the future perfect progressive. For example, say how long you will have been learning English / working / living in your house.
1 By next summer, ...
2 By next summer, ...
3 By next summer, ...

3 A romantic novelist writes 300-page books. She writes ten pages a day, and takes no holidays. Use the future perfect to answer the questions.
1 How many pages will she have written after ten days?
   ....
2 – after a month? ....
3 – after a year? ....
4 – after ten years? ....
5 If she starts today, how soon will she have finished her first book?
   ....
6 How many books will she have written a year from now?
   ....
7 How long will she have been writing when she has written 120 books?
   ....
8 She earns $100,000 per book. How much money
   will she have made altogether after her 120th book?
   ....

In some answers, both contracted forms (for example *I'm, don't*) and full forms (for example *I am, do not*) are possible. Normally both are correct.

TALKING ABOUT THE FUTURE **35**

talking about the future: more practice

1 Promises. A boy left home for the first time to go to university. Look at the pictures, and write the promises he made to his parents. Begin: *I promise I'll ...* or *I promise I won't ...*

1 ....
2 ....
3 ....
4 ....
5 ....
6 ....
7 ....
8 ....
9 ....
10 ....
11 ....
12 ....

2 GRAMMAR AND VOCABULARY: two-word verbs. Make sure you know the verbs in the box. Use a dictionary if necessary. Then look at the pictures and complete the sentences with *is going to*.

| plug in   unplug   switch on/off   turn on/off   turn up/down |

▶ She *is going to* .... switch on the radio.
1 She .... off the radio.
2 .... turn up ....
3 .... down ....
4 .... on ....
5 .... off ....
6 .... turn on the tap.
7 .... the tap.
8 .... plug in the iron.
9 .... unplug the
   ....
10 .... the hair-dryer.
11 ....

3 DO IT YOURSELF **Are these rules correct (✓) or not (✗)? (Four of rules 1–7 are correct.)**

▶ We often use present forms for the future. ..✓..

▶ We often use past forms for the future. ..✗..

1 We often use *be going to* for the future. ......

2 We often use the present progressive for the future. ......

3 We often use the simple present for promises. ......

4 We often use the simple present when we decide things. ......

5 We often use the simple present when we talk about timetables. ......

6 We use present forms mostly when we can see the future in the present. ......

7 We never use *will* for predictions. ......

4 **Present or future verbs? Circle the best form.**

▶ Here's the builder's estimate. It *will cost /* (*is going to cost*) £7,000 to repair the roof.

▶ I think it (*will cost*)*/ is going to cost* about £3,000 to rebuild the garage.

1 *It will rain / It's going to rain* – look at those clouds.

2 If it gets any colder, *it will snow / it's going to snow*.

3 Alice *will have / is going to have* a baby.

4 With a bit of luck, the baby *will have / is going to have* Alice's eyes.

5 *I will play / I'm playing* tennis with Stan on Sunday.

6 *He'll win / He's winning* tomorrow. He always does.

7 Don't tell her. *She'll tell / She's going to tell* everybody else.

8 'What's wrong?' 'The car *won't start / isn't going to start*.'

9 One day everybody *will have / is going to have* proper housing.

10 *She'll get married / She's getting married* on Friday at the local church.

5 **Mixed structures. Complete the sentences with the structures in the box.**

> will be ...ing   will have ...ed   will have been ...ing   am/are/is to ...
> was/were going to ...   would ...

1 This time tomorrow I .... in the mountains. (*walk*)

2 I .... the painting by tomorrow night. (*finish*)

3 Children, you .... to bed NOW! (*go*)

4 Next summer I .... medicine for six years. (*study*)

5 I was surprised when Ann told us she and Bill .... married on Sunday. (*get*)

6 The President and his wife .... Ireland next month. (*visit*)

7 We could see that it .... (*rain*)

8 I didn't lend him money, because I knew that he .... it back. (*not pay*)

9 .... this evening? (*you go out*)

10 We'll start at 6 o'clock; I think everybody .... by then. (*arrive*)

6 **Internet exercise. Use a search engine (e.g. Google) to find simple sentences beginning as follows. Complete the sentences.**

1 "We promise we will"

....

2 "Soon we will have finished"

....

3 "The Prime Minister is to"

....

talking about the future: revision test

1 **Correct the mistakes, or write 'Correct'.**

▶ I'll ~~seeing~~ you tomorrow. ..see................

▶ We're having drinks with Phil this evening. ..Correct..........

1 Mary will have a baby. ....

2 Tomorrow will be warm and sunny. ....

3 I promise I pay you tomorrow. ....

4 The President arrives in London on Monday. ....

5 I going to get up early tomorrow. ....

6 'I've lost my keys.' 'I find them for you.' ....

7 I think it's raining this evening. ....

8 Look out! You fall! ....

9 Are you going to write to Patrick? ....

10 Who's cooking this evening? ....

2 **Here are some sentences taken from real recorded conversations. Can you put the beginnings and ends together?**

0	Buy the cat food here.	A	about you.	
1	Don't give her your keys.	B	and then your kids will laugh at you.	
2	Get John to have a look at the TV.	C	He'll fix it.	
3	'He'll grow up one day.'	D	It'll be cheaper. ..O..	
4	He'll need somebody	E	on May 12th.	
5	'How's June?'	F	'She'll be OK.'	
6	I must get back to work,	G	'I hope you're right.'	
7	No good sending her a bill, is it?	H	She'll just refuse to pay.	
8	One day you'll be old,	I	She'll only lose them.	
9	She'll be fourteen	J	otherwise I'll get the sack.	
10	Believe me, she'll forget	K	to help him.	

3 **Choose the correct forms to complete the sentences.**

1 I hope your exam goes well. I .... of you. (*will be thinking, will have been thinking, am to think*)

2 When I finish this job I .... on it for two years. (*am to work, will have been working, will be working*)

3 Tell the children they .... their room. (*will be tidying, would tidy, are to tidy*)

4 I hope by next summer I .... enough money for a holiday. (*will save, will be saving, will have saved*)

5 So this was the man that I .... work for. I didn't like the look of him. (*would be to, am going to, was going to*)

6 The Prime Minister .... the new hospital next month. (*is to open, will have opened, has opened*)

7 I didn't go to Pete's party, because I knew that I .... it. (*didn't enjoy, wouldn't enjoy, wasn't to enjoy*)

8 I saw Carola last year. She thought she .... to America, but I don't know if she went. (*would go, would have gone, had gone*)

9 What time .... up tomorrow? (*will you have got, will you be getting, are you to get*)

10 'Is my car ready?' 'No, but we .... by this evening.' (*have finished, would finish, will have finished*)

In some answers, both contracted forms (for example I'm, don't) and full forms (for example I am, do not) are possible. Normally both are correct.

SECTION 4 past tenses

GRAMMAR SUMMARY

SIMPLE PAST: *I worked, she worked, he didn't work* etc

PAST PROGRESSIVE (OR 'PAST CONTINUOUS'): *I was working, she was working, he wasn't working* etc

English has two 'past' tenses.

- We use the **simple past** for **complete finished actions**. We often use it in **stories**.
  *I **sent** ten emails yesterday.*   *A man **walked** into the library and **asked** …*
- We use the **past progressive** to talk about actions which were **unfinished** at a past time.
  *'What **were** you **doing** at 10.00 last night?'*   *'I **was writing** letters.'*

Past tenses can make **requests**, **questions** and **suggestions** less direct, and so **more polite**.
*I **wondered** if you **were** free this evening.*
*How much **did** you **want** to spend, sir?*
*I **was wondering** if I **could** use your phone.*

Where did we come from?

Most scientists now believe that our ancestors – the earliest Homo Sapiens – originated in Africa around 200,000 years ago. Perhaps between 80,000 and 60,000 years ago – dates are uncertain – these people gradually started migrating into the rest of the world. Some groups crossed the Red Sea (sea levels were much lower then because water was locked up in large ice caps at the North and South Poles). As these populations grew, they settled further and further along the sea coasts into South Asia and South-East Asia, reaching Australia perhaps 45,000 years ago. Other groups colonised Central Asia, Europe and East Asia, with some populations finding their way across the Bering Strait, perhaps around 15,000 years ago, into North and South America. ◆

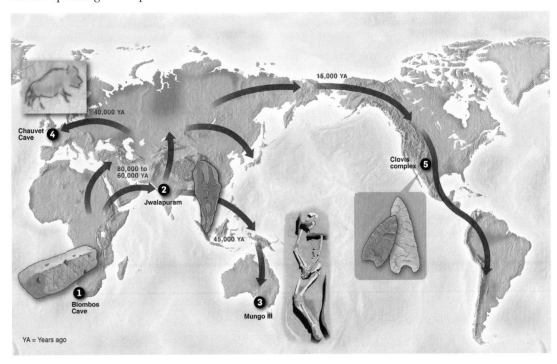

15,000 YA

40,000 YA

Chauvet Cave **4**

80,000 to 60,000 YA

2

Jwalapuram

Clovis complex **5**

45,000 YA

1

Blombos Cave

3

Mungo III

YA = Years ago

revise the basics: simple past forms

1 **DO IT YOURSELF** **Look at the examples and complete the table.**

enjoyed	helped	hoped	liked	planned	played	rained	replied	seemed
stopped	tried	waited	wanted	worked				

TO MAKE REGULAR SIMPLE PAST FORMS	Add -ed	Just add -d	Double the last letter and add -ed	Change the -y to -i and add-ed
most verbs	✓			
verbs ending in -e				
verbs ending in vowel + -y (-ay, -oy)				
verbs ending in consonant + -y				
short verbs ending in one vowel and one consonant				

2 **Write the simple past.**

annoy .... arrive .... carry .... change .... cook ....

cry .... fit .... hate .... hurry .... jump .... live ....

pass .... pray .... rain .... rob .... shave ....

shop .... shout .... slim .... slip .... start ....

stay .... study .... turn .... walk .... watch ....

NOTE: We only double letters in STRESSED syllables.

preFER → *preferred* **BUT** *WONder* → *wondered*

3 **Write the simple past.**

VIsit .... reGRET .... deVElop .... GALlop .... OPen ....

ANswer .... reFER ....

With **irregular** verbs, you have to learn the simple past forms one by one (see page 317).

go → **went**   *see* → **saw**   *buy* → **bought**   *pay* → **paid**

4 **Write as many of the simple past forms as you can. Check them on page 317, and learn the ones that you don't know.**

become .... begin .... break .... bring .... catch ....

come .... drink .... eat .... fall .... feel ....

forget .... get .... give .... hear .... hold ....

keep .... know .... learn .... leave .... let ....

make .... pay .... put .... read .... say ....

shut .... sit .... speak .... stand .... take ....

tell .... think .... write ....

→ For the spelling of *-ing* forms, see page 16.

revise the basics: which past tense?

	SIMPLE PAST	PAST PROGRESSIVE
+	I/you etc **worked**	I **was**, you **were** etc work**ing**
?	**did** I/you etc work?	**was** I, **were** you etc work**ing**?
−	I/you etc **did not** work	I **was not**, you **were not** etc work**ing**

We use the **simple past** to talk about a **complete** action (long or short).
We use the **past progressive** for actions which were **not complete** at a past time.

Joe got up at 7.00 and worked from 9.00 to 4.00.

| PAST | 7.00 | 9.00 | | 4.00 | NOW |

At 5.00, when Joe came home, I was reading.

| PAST | | 5.00 | NOW |

Note the difference when we use the **past progressive** and the **simple past** together.
Past progressive: longer action or situation.
Simple past: complete shorter action that **happened** while the longer action **was happening**.

While I was cooking supper,

| PAST | | NOW |

Ellie phoned.

As I was walking down the road,

| PAST | | NOW |

I saw Bill.

1 **Put in the correct tenses.**

▶ At 6.00 this morning I ...*was having*......... a wonderful dream, but then the alarm ...*went*......... off. (*have; go*)

▶ This time yesterday I ...*was lying*........... on the beach. (*lie*)

1 When I walked in they .... about babies. (*all talk*)

2 I .... in Paris for a long time. (*live*)

3 I saw Sid when I .... to work. He .... (*come; shop*)

4 She .... Jim while she .... (*meet; travel*)

5 While I .... to Mrs Singleton, somebody .... into my office and .... the computer. (*talk; walk; steal*)

6 When Jake .... in everybody .... talking. (*come; stop*)

7 I .... out of the window and .... that we .... over the mountains. (*look; see; fly*)

8 I .... up to find that water .... through the bedroom ceiling. (*wake; pour*)

9 He .... his leg while he .... football. (*break; play*)

2 **What were they all doing at midday yesterday? Put sentences together from the boxes.**
Can you make another sentence yourself?

▶ Edward ...*was eating eggs in Exeter.*...........

▶ Louise ...*was learning Latin in a launderette.*.......

1 Fred ....

2 Harry ....

3 Barbara ....

4 Steve ....

5 Ruth ....

6 Pete ....

7 ....

have	buy	fry	eat ✓	steal
ride	play	learn ✓		

Latin ✓	books	eggs ✓	a haircut
fish	poker	socks	racehorses

Rome	Folkestone	a supermarket
Exeter ✓	Paris	Hamburg
Birmingham	a launderette ✓	

In some answers, both contracted forms (for example *I'm*, *don't*) and full forms (for example *I am*, *do not*) are possible. Normally both are correct.

more about past tenses

We can use **when** in different ways with past tenses.

When Amy came home, John **was cooking** supper. (Amy came home **during** the cooking.)
When Amy came home, John **cooked** supper. (**First** Amy came home; **then** John cooked supper.)

1 **Put in the correct tense (simple past or past progressive).**

▶ When I went out, it ...*was raining.*............... (*rain*)

▶ When Mary got home, she ...*made*.......................... tea. (*make*)

1 When I saw Lucas, he .... (*shop*)

2 When Ben saw me, he .... (*stop*)

3 When we asked them, they .... 'No'. (*say*)

4 When I walked in, they .... (*talk*)

5 When I dropped the glass, it .... (*break*)

6 When I phoned William, he .... (*work*)

7 When the music stopped, everybody .... (*sit down*)

8 When I arrived at the station, I .... a taxi. (*take*)

9 When the police stopped her, she .... a gun. (*carry*)

Progressive forms are used mostly for temporary actions and situations. For longer, more permanent situations we prefer the **simple past**. **Compare:**

When I walked in I found that water was running down the walls.
Explorers believed that the river ran into the Atlantic.

We do **not** normally use the **past progressive** to talk about **past habits**, or to say **how often** something happened.

I played a lot of tennis when I was younger. (**NOT** ~~I was playing~~ ...)
She rang the bell three times. (**NOT** ~~She was ringing~~ ...)

2 **Circle the correct form.**

▶ When I was at university I (*went*)/ *was going* to a lot of parties.

▶ The Marlborough family (*lived*)/ *was living* in the same house for 400 years.

1 I looked out of the window. A strange man *stood* / *was standing* in the garden.

2 We took the road that *went* / *was going* along the river.

3 My sister *took* / *was taking* the driving test twelve times before she passed.

4 When I got there everybody *danced* / *was dancing* in the garden.

5 At my school we *played* / *were playing* rugby in winter and cricket in summer.

6 We started to hurry because it *got* / *was getting* late.

7 Where I grew up, most people *worked* / *were working* for the local farmer.

8 She *got* / *was getting* married four times – twice to the same man.

9 People used to believe that the sun *went* / *was going* round the earth.

10 When I saw Annie she *went* / *was going* round the corner to the church.

Remember that some verbs are not used in progressive forms (see page 20).

*I tried the cake to see how it **tasted**.* (**NOT** ... ~~how it was tasting~~.)

Past tenses can make requests, questions and suggestions **more polite**. (They sound less direct than present tenses.) **Simple past** forms are common.

*I **wondered** if you **were** free this evening.*   *How much **did** you **want** to spend, sir?*

The past modal forms ***would**, **could*** and ***might*** are often used in this way.

*I **thought** it **would** be nice to have a picnic.*   ***Could** I ask you to translate this for me?*
*You **might** see if the consulate can help you.*

1 **Make these sentences less direct.**

▶ We wonder if you feel like coming out with us.
   We wondered if you felt like coming out with us.
....

▶ I think you will like to see my holiday photos.
   I thought you would like to see my holiday photos.
....

1 How many days do you intend to stay?
....

2 Can you give me a hand?
....

3 We can ask Peter to help us.
....

4 I think it will be a good idea to invite Simon.
....

5 I wonder if you need any help.
....

6 We hope you will stay for dinner.
....

7 Are you planning to be here next week?
....

8 Do you want to pay now?
....

9 Will you tell Annie to come to my office?
....

10 It may be a good idea to apologise.
....

Past progressives can be used in the same way.

*I **was wondering** if I could use your phone.*

2 **Change the verbs *in italics* to make these sentences less direct.**

▶ I *hope* ...*was hoping*.... you *can* ...*could*............. lend me £10.
1 We *wonder* .... if you *have* .... two single rooms.
2 *Are* .... you looking for anything special?
3 I *wonder* .... if I *can* .... ask you a small favour.
4 We *think* .... it's .... time for you to look for a job.
5 I *hope* .... you *don't* .... need the car this afternoon.

In some answers, both contracted forms (for example *I'm, don't*) and full
forms (for example *I am, do not*) are possible. Normally both are correct.

PAST TENSES   **43**

past tenses: more practice

1 **GRAMMAR AND VOCABULARY: crimes. At 8.30 yesterday evening a crime was committed. The police asked eight known criminals what they were doing at that time. They all told lies. Study the pictures and complete the sentences, using the past progressive with expressions from the box.**

burgle house	feed pigeons	fish	forge banknotes	hold up security van
mug old lady	paint	play chess	poison husband	pray read poetry
rob bank	sell stolen property	shoplift	sing	study French

▶ *Fred told the police that he was reading poetry, but actually he was mugging an old lady.*

1 ....

2 ....

3 ....

4 ....

5 ....

6 ....

7 ....

TOLD THE POLICE:

ACTUALLY*:

Fred *Mrs Allen* *Bill* *Pete*

TOLD THE POLICE:

ACTUALLY:

Mrs Oliver *Miss Fry* *Jim* *Mr Lucas*

*Note: actually means 'really'.

2 Past tenses: mixed uses. Complete the sentences with the correct tenses.

▶ That summer, the river that ..*ran*.................... through the town dried up. (*run*)

1 When I .... home, Bill .... the washing machine. (*get; repair*)

2 We had a lovely room that .... out over the sea. (*look*)

3 On holiday I .... tennis every day. (*play*)

4 When I phoned Laurence he .... round straight away. (*come*)

5 I .... until I was thirty. (*smoke*)

6 Nobody .... why she married him. (*understand*)

7 I went upstairs and found that a bird .... round the bedroom. (*fly*)

8 The castle .... the road that .... from Carlisle to Edinburgh. (*protect, go*)

9 When I .... Jane she .... alone in the darkness. (*find; sit*)

10 When Carl was in China he .... to Maggie every week. (*write*)

11 When I walked in I .... the music that they ...., so I .... out again. (*not like; play; walk*)

3 Polite past tenses. (Circle) the most polite forms.

1 We *hoped / were hoping* you *can / could* come to dinner tomorrow.

2 I *wonder / wondered* if you *feel / felt* like playing something for us.

3 We *think / thought* you *will / would* like to hear all about our holiday.

4 How much *were / are* you thinking of paying?

5 *Would / Will* you give my best wishes to Sarah if you see her?

6 You're tired. It *might / may* be best if I *drove / drive*.

7 We *wondered / were wondering* if you were free on Saturday.

8 *Were / Are* you planning to use the car?

4 Grammar in a text. Complete the text with the verbs in the box (there is one verb too many). You will need five past progressives and three simple pasts. Use a dictionary if necessary.

ask come dance grin hold not dance order play throw

On the dance floor half a dozen couples [1].......................... themselves around. Most of them [2].......................... cheek to cheek, if dancing is the word. The men wore white tuxedos and the girls wore bright eyes, ruby lips, and tennis or golf muscles. One couple [3].......................... cheek to cheek. Mitchell's mouth was open, he [4].........................., his face was red and shiny, and his eyes had that glazed look. Betty [5].......................... her head as far as she could get away from him without breaking her neck. It was very obvious that she had had about all of Mr Larry Mitchell that she could take. A Mexican waiter in a short green jacket and white pants with a green stripe down the side [6].......................... up and I [7].......................... a double Gibson and [8].......................... if I could have a club sandwich.

Raymond Chandler: Playback (adapted)

5 Internet exercise. Use a search engine (e.g. Google) to find simple sentences on the internet containing the expressions *"he robbed"*, *"he burgled"*, *"they mugged"*, *"he poisoned"*, *"was shoplifting"*. Write the sentences.

1 ....

2 ....

3 ....

4 ....

5 ....

past tenses: revision test

1 **Write the simple past forms.**

accept ...*accepted*... agree .... answer .... arrive ....

become .... begin .... believe .... carry ....

develop .... drop .... enjoy .... fit ....

gallop .... hope .... leave .... open ....

plan .... prefer .... regret .... reply ....

rob .... seem .... sleep .... slim ....

slip .... start .... stay .... stop ....

study .... visit .... write ....

2 **Look at the picture, and choose the correct caption.**

A Somebody was stealing his wallet
while he was having lunch.

B Somebody was stealing his wallet
while he had lunch.

C Somebody stole his wallet while
he had lunch.

D Somebody stole his wallet while
he was having lunch.

3 **Correct or not? Correct the sentences, or write 'Correct'.**

▶ When you woke me I ~~had~~ a wonderful dream. ...*was having*........

▶ This time yesterday I was playing tennis. ...*Correct*..............

1 When I got to the party everybody had a great time. ....

2 When Columbus left Europe, he thought he sailed to India. ....

3 Everybody was knowing that she was unhappy. ....

4 We lived in New York when I was small. ....

5 Did you want to pay now? ....

6 I was learning the violin at school. ....

7 Where I grew up, nobody was having a car. ....

8 We were on the wrong road. It went to Birmingham, not Manchester. ....

9 When I was seeing Joe, he was talking to Angela. ....

10 I broke my leg while I was skiing. ....

11 When the music started, everybody stood up. ....

12 I wondered if you were free this evening. ....

13 I was smoking when I was younger. ....

14 The Moreton family was living in that house for 300 years. ....

15 When the police were stopping him, he carried two guns. ....

4 **Change the verbs *in italics* to make these sentences less direct.**

▶ I ~~hope~~ ...*was hoping*........ you ~~can~~ ...*could*.............. help me.

1 I *think* .... it *is* .... best to say nothing to her.

2 I *wonder* .... if I *can* .... speak to you for a moment.

3 *Are* .... you looking for somebody?

4 *Do* .... you want to speak to Professor Austin?

5 I *wonder* .... if you *have* .... a special price for students.

In some answers, both contracted forms (for example *I'm*, *don't*) and full
forms (for example *I am*, *do not*) are possible. Normally both are correct.

SECTION 5 perfect tenses

GRAMMAR SUMMARY

(SIMPLE) PRESENT PERFECT: *I have worked, she has worked, he hasn't worked* etc
PRESENT PERFECT PROGRESSIVE: *I have been working, he has been working* etc
PAST PERFECT: *I had worked, she had worked* etc
PAST PERFECT PROGRESSIVE: *I had been working, he had been working* etc

- We use the **present perfect** to talk about **past** actions with some **importance now**.
  I've written to John, so he *knows what's happening*.

- We use the **present perfect progressive** mostly to say **how long** things have been going on **up to now**.
  I have been baking since breakfast time.

- When we are already talking about the past, we use the **past perfect** or past perfect progressive to talk about an **earlier time**.
  *Yesterday I found some old postcards that Kate **had sent** to me from Italy.*
  *When Ann arrived I **had been waiting** for 25 minutes.*

NOTE: The rules in this section apply to British English. There are some small differences in American English.

why are we getting
so much faster?

The Greek athlete Spiridon Louis won the Olympic marathon in 1896 in 2 hours 58 minutes 50 seconds. A little over a century later, the great Ethiopian runner Haile Gebrselassie ran the same distance in less than 2 hours 4 minutes: 30% faster than Spiridon. Women runners have also got faster. In 1926 the woman's marathon record stood at around 2 hours 55 minutes; in 1979 the Norwegian Grete Waitz broke two and a half hours. And less than a quarter of a century later, the Englishwoman Paula Radcliffe ran a marathon in 2 hours 15 minutes 25 seconds: faster than any man had run up to 1954! There has been similar progress over the last century at all other distances, from the half marathon down to the sprints. Usain Bolt's 100 metre record of 9.58 seconds, set in 2009, was an improvement of over 9% on the 1912 record. In contrast, horse race results have scarcely changed at all. In spite of all their trainers' efforts, horses run little faster now than they did a century ago. What is happening? Why are we the only animals that are speeding up? ◆

revise the basics: present perfect forms and use

| + | *I have worked/seen* etc | ? | *have I worked/seen?* etc | − | *I have not worked/seen* etc |

To make the **present perfect**, put *have/has* with the **past participle** (*worked*, *seen* etc).
Regular past participles end in *-ed*, like simple past forms (for spelling rules, see page 40).

work → **work**ed   hope → **hop**ed   stop → **stopp**ed   try → **tried**

With **irregular** verbs, the past participle is often different from the simple past form (see page 317).

see → **seen**   speak → **spoken**   go → **gone**   buy → **bought**

1 Write as many of the irregular past participles as you can. Check them on page 317, and learn the ones that you don't know.

become ..*become*.. begin .... break .... bring .... buy ....
come .... drink .... eat .... fall .... forget ....
give .... hear .... hold .... keep .... know ....
learn .... leave .... let .... make .... pay ....
put .... read .... say .... shut .... sit ....
stand .... take .... tell .... think .... write ....

The present perfect **connects the past and the present**.
We use it especially for **finished actions that are important now.**
They have **results now**, or they are **news**.

x------------------------x
past   **present**

I can't walk – I've hurt my leg.   **Have** *you* **heard**? *He's arrived!*
Look – he hasn't drunk his tea.   *You've passed your exam!*

Compare: *Brutus killed Caesar.* (**NOT** *… has killed …* – no present importance.)
We can often change a **present perfect** sentence into a **present** sentence with more or less the same meaning.

I've hurt my leg. = *I have a bad leg.*   *Sue's come back.* = *Sue is home.*
He's lost his keys. = *He can't find them.*   *He's gone.* = *He isn't here.*

2 Change these present perfect sentences into present sentences with similar meanings.
  ▶ I've cleaned the windows. ..*The windows are clean.*.................................
  1 The Foreign Minister has died. ....
  2 Lucy's had a baby. ....
  3 You've torn your coat. ....
  4 I've broken my leg. ....
  5 He's lost his address book. ....
  6 Have you made tea? ....
  7 I've done the washing up. ....
  8 She's gone to work for the BBC. ....
  9 We haven't found out where he is. ....
  10 The noise has stopped. ....
  11 I've forgotten your name. ....
  12 She's learnt French. ....

revise the basics: present perfect or simple past?

PRESENT PERFECT: WE THINK ABOUT THE PAST AND THE PRESENT TOGETHER
When we think about the **past and present together,** we normally use
the **present perfect**.

*I've phoned Ann, so she **knows** what's going on.*
I've made coffee. Would you like a cup?
Come and look – I've painted the kitchen.

SIMPLE PAST: WE THINK ONLY ABOUT THE PAST, NOT THE PRESENT
When we think **only about the past**, we most often use the **simple past**.

*My grandfather **worked** for a phone company.*
    (He's dead now; I'm not thinking about the present.)
I made a cake when Liz and Sandra came.
    (I'm not talking about the present.)
I painted the living room last week.
    (I'm thinking only about last week.)

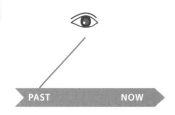

1 **Read the sentences and the questions, and circle the correct answers.**

▶ Claudia has bought a new car. *Has she got the car now?* (YES) / PERHAPS

▶ Susie went to stay with her grandmother. *Is she there now?* YES / (PROBABLY NOT)

1 I made coffee. *Is there coffee now?* YES / PROBABLY NOT

2 Jack has made tea. *Is there tea now?* YES / PROBABLY NOT

3 Amanda has come to stay with us. *Is she here now?* YES / DON'T KNOW

4 Mark has gone to work in Ireland. *Is he there now?* YES / DON'T KNOW

5 Simon and Roger opened a shop. *Is the shop still in business?* YES / DON'T KNOW

6 Oliver has started French lessons. *Is he taking lessons now?* YES / DON'T KNOW

7 The dog has run away. *Is the dog at home now?* NO / DON'T KNOW

8 We sent Pam to the doctor. *Is she with the doctor now?* YES / NO / PROBABLY NOT

9 Carl lost his glasses. *Has he got his glasses now?* NO / DON'T KNOW

10 Kate has cut all her hair off. *Has she got any hair now?* NO / DON'T KNOW

2 **Circle the correct verb forms.**

1 'Does Jeff know you're back home?' 'Yes, I *told* / *'ve told* him.

2 'What's Rosie's address?' 'Sorry, I *forgot* / *'ve forgotten*.'

3 I *made* / *'ve made* coffee. Would you like some?

4 Look – I *bought* / *'ve bought* a new jacket.

5 My mother *left* / *has left* school at 16.

6 Peter *lost* / *has lost* his job, and he's looking for a new one.

7 Julius Caesar *never reached* / *has never reached* Scotland.

8 We *got* / *have got* to know some very interesting people in America last year.

9 When we were at school we *studied* / *have studied* Latin.

10 Who *built* / *has built* the Tower of London?

In some answers, both contracted forms (for example *I'm, don't*) and full
forms (for example *I am, do not*) are possible. Normally both are correct.

PERFECT TENSES **49**

revise the basics: tenses with time words

We **don't** normally use the **present perfect** with **words for a finished time.**

I've met a really nice man. (**BUT NOT** ~~I've met a really nice man yesterday.~~)
A plane has disappeared over the Atlantic. (**BUT NOT** ~~A plane has disappeared at 3.15 this afternoon.~~)

1 (Circle) the words for a finished time.

two days ago   always   this year   last month   never   now   then   today   yesterday
when?   in 2007   before I was born   in my life   just after I got up   lately   when I was nine

2 Correct (✓) or not (✗)?

▶ Andy has changed his job. ..✓..
▶ Sarah has gone to France last week. ..✗..
1 John has left home in 2006. ......
2 I think everybody has gone now. ......
3 Lindsay has phoned at 10 o'clock. ......
4 I've forgotten Phil's birthday last Monday. ......

5 I've seen a good film the other day. ......
6 Look what Peter has given me yesterday! ......
7 Claire has written to me three weeks ago. ......
8 Sorry – I've forgotten your name. ......
9 The house is empty! What has happened? ......
10 When have you heard from Peter? ......

We can use the **present perfect** to ask if things **have happened up to now**, or to say that they **haven't happened up to now.**
This often happens with **words for an unfinished time:**
for example *today, ever, never, yet.*

Has *the boss* **phoned** *today?*   **Have** *you ever* **broken** *your leg?*
We **haven't been** *to Scotland this year.*
Mary **hasn't written** *to me yet.*
Recently, lately and **before** can be used like this.
Have *you* **heard** *from Phil recently?*
'Who's that?' *'I've never* **seen** *him before.'*

Have you ever **been** *to Paris?*

PAST ▷ ?EVER | EVER | EVER | EVER? ▷ NOW

I've never **been** *there.*

PAST ▷ NEVER ✗ NEVER ✗ NEVER ✗ NEVER? ▷ NOW

3 Make present perfect sentences.

▶ Eric / pay / for his ticket ?   *Has Eric paid for his ticket?* ....
1 you / see Carol / today ? ....
2 Simon / come back / from Spain / yet ? ....
3 the baby / have / anything to eat ? ....
4 I / not / play / tennis / this year ....
5 Alex / speak / to you / lately ? ....
6 Rob / never / write to me ....
7 you / ever / lose / your passport ? ....
8 my mother / never / travel by air ....
9 you / ever / write / a love letter ? ....
10 I / never / see / an iceberg ....

4 Circle the correct tense.

1 I *haven't seen / didn't see* much of Al lately.
2 'Who is she?' 'I *'ve never seen / never saw* her before.'
3 I *'ve done / did* a lot of stupid things in my life.
4 She *has left / left* school last year.
5 When *have you got / did you get* married?
6 I'm sorry. I *haven't finished / didn't finish* yet.

7 I *'ve often wondered / often wondered* what he does for a living.
8 He *has caught / caught* the plane at eight this morning.
9 I *'ve read / read* a lot of her books when I was at school.
10 *Have you seen / Did you see* any good films recently?

revise the basics: *already*, *yet* and *just*

We often use the present perfect with *already* (= 'earlier than somebody expected').
Note the word order: *already* comes **after** *have*.

'Coffee?' 'No, thanks. I**'ve** already **had** some.'
'Can I speak to Colette?' 'I'm afraid she**'s** already gone home.'

1 **Complete the sentences with *already* and verbs from the box (present perfect).**

| buy | find | leave ✓ | read | sell | tell |

▶ 'What time's the bus?' 'It *'s already left* '
1 'Shall I tell Sally?' 'I .... her.'
2 'Do you want the newspaper?' ' .... it.'
3 'I'll buy milk, shall I?' 'I .... some.'
4 Amelia lost her job last week, but she .... a new one.
5 'How much do you want for your car?' ' .... it.'

We also often use the present perfect with *yet* (= 'up to now') in questions and negatives.
Note the word order: *yet* usually comes at the end of a sentence.

'**Have** you **paid** the electrician yet?' 'No, he **hasn't sent** his bill yet.'

2 **Make questions and negatives with *yet*.**

1 you / have breakfast **?** ....
2 Cheryl / find a flat **-** ....
3 you / finish the painting **?** ....
4 John / phone **?** ....
5 Carole / come back from holiday **-** ....
6 the newspaper / come **-** ....

And we often use the present perfect with *just* (= 'a short time ago'). *Just* comes **after** *have*.

I**'ve** just **heard** from the tax office.   The snow **has** just **stopped**.

3 **Write five things that have just happened (in your family, in the world, …)**

▶ My sister has just got married.   A famous pop star has just died.
....
....
....
....

4 **You probably want to do a lot of things in life. Write five things that you haven't done yet.**

▶ I haven't seen a volcano yet.
....
....
....
....

NOTE: In American English, the simple past is often used with *already*, *yet* and *just*.

'Where's Serena?' 'She **went** home **already**.'   '**Did** you **eat yet**?'   I **just had** a great idea.

In some answers, both contracted forms (for example *I'm*, *don't*) and full
forms (for example *I am, do not*) are possible. Normally both are correct.

finished time or time up to now? *this morning; at school*

Some expressions can refer either to an **unfinished** or to a **finished time**. The tense depends on the meaning. Compare:

I haven't seen Carl this morning. (said in the morning)
I didn't see Carl this morning. (said in the afternoon)
I've made lots of friends at university. (said by a student)
I made lots of friends at university. (said by an ex-student)

1 **Read the sentences and circle the correct answers.**

▶ 'A lot of people came to see me in hospital.' *Was the speaker in hospital when he/she said this?*
A Yes. (B) No.

1 'I didn't enjoy school.' *Was the speaker at school when he/she said this?*   A Yes.   B No.

2 'I've been to sleep three times during the lesson.' *When did the speaker say this?*
A During the lesson.   B After the lesson.

3 'I didn't travel much in December.' *When did the speaker say this?*   A In December.   B Later.

4 'My computer has crashed three times this morning.' *When did the speaker say this?*
A In the morning.   B Later.

5 'Joseph Adams made many friends during his life.' *Was Joseph Adams alive when the speaker said this?*
A Yes.   B No.

6 'We've had a lot of problems at the club.' *Is the speaker a member of the club now?*   A Yes.   B No.

7 'The police called again this afternoon.' *When did the speaker say this?*
A In the afternoon.   B Later.

8 'I spent too much money during the holiday.' *Is the speaker still on holiday?*   A Yes.   B No.

9 'Peter has done some very stupid things in his first job.' *Is he still in his first job?*   A Yes.   B No.

10 'During her time as President she has done a great deal of good for her country.' *Is she still President?*
A Yes.   B No.

We can **think of a finished or unfinished time** without putting the time in words. Compare:

Did you see 'Hamlet'? (It was on TV **last night**.)
Have you seen 'Hamlet'? (= Have you **ever** seen 'Hamlet'?)

2 **Put in the simple past or present perfect.**

1 You .... a beautiful baby. (*be*)

2 I .... her latest book. (*not read*)

3 .... India? (*you visit*)

4 My great-grandmother .... in Glasgow. (*live*)

5 Columbus .... America: the native Americans already
.... where it was. (*not discover; know*)

6 The company is in trouble; it .... a lot of money. (*lose*)

7 Who .... Shakespeare his first job? (*give*)

8 How many times .... in love? (*you be*)

9 I .... a holiday as much as this one. (*never enjoy*)

10 ' .... the thunder?' 'No, nothing wakes me up.' (*you hear*)

Note the difference between *gone to* and *been to*.

*Alex has **gone to** Rome.* (He's there now.)   *Sorry I'm late. I've **been to** the shops.* (And come back.)
We often use the **present perfect** to say **how much** we have done **up to now**.

I've done six different jobs since Christmas.
I've done no work at all so far (='up to now') today.
Joe is saving €20 a week. He started 8 weeks ago. Up to now he's saved €160.
Benjamin's been to Africa several times this year.
I've climbed a lot of mountains, but I've never been up Mont Blanc.

3 Look at the pictures and complete the sentences.

▶ I ..*have washed up thirty*........... glasses this morning. (*wash up*)

1 I .... cups of coffee today. (*drink*)

2 I .... letters since breakfast. (*write*)

3 I .... books this week. (*read*)

4 Joe .... kilometres so far this year. (*drive*)

5 I .... in .... different
houses in my life. (*live*)

6 That child .... already ....
chocolates today. (*eat*)

30

6

5   **20**   **40,000 km**   **8**

8

4 Complete the sentences with the present perfect or simple past.

1 I .... a lot of tennis this year. (*play*)

2 She .... six different jobs since she left school. (*have*)

3 He .... away from school three times when he was fourteen. (*run*)

4 How many cups of tea .... today? (*you make*)

5 In those days, Andrew .... to stay with us most weekends. (*come*)

6 Shakespeare .... poems as well as plays. (*write*)

7 Since my brother lost his job, he .... two books. (*write*)

8 I'm not cooking today – I .... all the meals yesterday. In fact,
I .... most of the meals this week. (*cook; cook*)

9 Would you believe I .... twenty-three phone calls today? (*make*)

10 Our team are rubbish. They .... eight games this year. (*lose*)

5 GRAMMAR AND VOCABULARY: entertainments. Make sure you know all the words in the box.
Use a dictionary if necessary. Then write sentences to say how often you have been
to the different kinds of entertainment.

| the cinema   the circus   the opera   the theatre |
| a rock / jazz / classical music concert   a rock / jazz festival |

I've been to the circus once in my life. I've been to a rock concert twice this year.
I've never been to the opera.

....

....

....

....

In some answers, both contracted forms (for example *I'm*, *don't*) and full
forms (for example *I am*, *do not*) are possible. Normally both are correct.

PERFECT TENSES   **53**

news *We've found oil in the garden!*

We often use the **present perfect** to give **news**: to tell people about **new things** that have happened.

*The Prime Minister **has arrived** in Washington for talks with the President.   Jessica **has bought** a new car.*
*A plane **has crashed** at Heathrow Airport.   Some new people **have moved** into the house next door.*

1 When John Wells arrived home from work, his family gave him a lot of news.
Complete the sentences.

> come   die   eat   find ✓   go   steal   win

▸ Hello, dear. We ....*'ve found*..... oil in the garden!

1 Dad! The cat .... your supper!

2 Hi, John. Mary .... to Australia with a soldier!

3 Dad! You .... a lot of money in the lottery!

4 Hi! Somebody .... the car!

5 Surprise! Grandma .... to stay for a month!

6 Daddy! The goldfish .... !

2 Here are some sentences from radio news broadcasts. Put in the correct verbs.

> arrest   arrive ✓   close   delay   die   disappear   discover   give   leave   marry   set fire

▸ England footballers ....*have arrived*........ back in Britain after their match in Rome.
1 Singer Alex Haverty .... his long-time girlfriend Katy Bowen.
2 Charles Blackstock, Member of Parliament for East Chilbury, ... at the age of 57.
3 Once again, bad weather .... the tennis final.
4 The Foreign Minister .... London for a two-day visit to Berlin.
5 Heavy snow .... hundreds of roads in Scotland.
6 Demonstrators .... to cars in a suburb of Paris.
7 A plane with 150 passengers .... over the Indian Ocean.
8 A Birmingham businessman .... £10m to cancer research.
9 A Northamptonshire farmer .... hundreds of Roman coins in a field.
10 Customs officers .... three suspected drug smugglers at Luton airport.

REMEMBER: we don't normally use the **present perfect** with words for a finished time.

We've found oil in the garden. **BUT NOT** ~~We've found oil in the garden yesterday.~~
A plane has crashed at Heathrow Airport. **BUT NOT** ~~A plane has crashed at 3.15 this afternoon.~~

NOTE: In American English it is quite common to give news with the simple past.

'Somebody stole my car!'

news and details   *A plane has crashed. It came down . . .*

1 When we **first** give **news**,
we often use the **present perfect**.

2 When we give or ask for **more** past
details, we change to the **simple past**.

finished action   *news now*

PAST	NOW

past details

PAST	NOW

A plane **has crashed** in Yorkshire.   →   It **came** down in a field outside York.
The Prime Minister **has met** business leaders.   →   They **talked** for four hours.
Stephanie **has gone** to Australia.   →   She **left** last night.
'I**'ve found** your keys.'   →   'Thanks. Where **were** they?'

REMEMBER: we don't normally use the **present perfect** when we **give** or **ask about** a finished time.

Joe **has left** *home.*   **OR**   *Joe* **left** *home last week.* (**BUT NOT** ~~Joe has left home last week.~~)
Have they **arrived?**   **OR**   *When* **did** *they arrive?* (**BUT NOT** ~~When have they arrived?~~)

1 Put in present perfect and simple past verbs.

▶ The cat ....*has eaten*.... your supper. She ....*took*.......... it off the table when I was out. (*eat; take*)

1 Anna .... her job at the bank. She .... her boss. (*leave; not like*)

2 I .... a beautiful dress. I .... it at Parker's yesterday. (*buy; find*)

3 Cathy and Sam .... their house. They .... a very good price. (*sell; get*)

4 'Dad .... his glasses.' 'Where .... he .... them?'
'Under his pillow.' (*find; find*)

5 Mrs Collins .... into hospital. She .... to the doctor this morning, and he
.... her straight in. (*go; go; send*)

6 Bill .... an accident. He .... off his bike last night. (*have; fall*)

7 I .... from Jenny. She .... us a postcard from Peru. (*hear; send*)

8 'I .... your mother about us.' 'What .... she .... ?' 'She was very
nice about it.' (*tell; say*)

9 Two climbers .... in the Alps. They .... their way in bad weather. (*die; lose*)

10 John and Sue .... yet. They .... the wrong train. (*not arrive; take*)

2 Make questions to ask for more details.

▶ 'I've bought a new jacket.' 'Oh, yes? ....*Where did you buy it?*................... ' (*where / you / buy it*)

1 'Ian's passed his exam.' ' .... ?' (*he / get / good marks*)

2 'Louise's moved to London.' ' .... ?' (*when / she / go*)

3 'Andy's lost his job.' 'I know.' ' .... ?' (*when / he / tell you*)

4 'My brother's been to San Francisco.' ' .... ?' (*where / he / stay*)

5 'Mark's sold his car.' ' .... ?' (*why / he / sell it*)

6 'Phil's bought a bike.' ' .... ?' (*how much / it / cost*)

7 'Paul's found a new girlfriend.' ' .... ?' (*where / he / meet her*)

8 'I've given up smoking.' ' .... ?' (*why / you / stop*)

In some answers, both contracted forms (for example *I'm, don't*) and full
forms (for example *I am, do not*) are possible. Normally both are correct.

PERFECT TENSES   **55**

revise the basics: present perfect progressive; *since, for*

| + *I have been working* etc | ? *have you been working?* etc | - *he has not been working* etc |

We make the **present perfect progressive** with *have/has been* + *...ing*.

*We **have been living** here since April.*   *John**'s been working** in the bank for three months.*

We use the **present perfect progressive** (with most verbs) to say **how long** things have been continuing **up to now**. We do **not** use a present tense with this meaning.

*I**'ve been learning** English **for four years**.* (NOT ~~I'm learning English for four years.~~)
*It**'s been snowing since Tuesday**.*   *Have you **been waiting long**?*

I've been walking all day.

PAST 👣👣👣👣👣👣👣 NOW 👣👣

1 **Complete the sentences with verbs from the box. Use the present perfect progressive.**

| cry   learn   live   play (*twice*)   rain   wait (*twice*)   walk   work |

1 It .... all day.
2 I .... English since I was six.
3 She .... tennis professionally for ten years.
4 We .... n't .... in this house for very long.
5 That man .... up and down the street for ages.
6 I .... very hard this week.
7 She .... non-stop since she got his letter.
8 He .... that music for hours. I wish he'd stop.
9 .... you .... long, sir?
10 They call him the waiter, but we .... for our coffee for half an hour.

We can say how long with *since* or *for*.
We use *since* when we give the **beginning** of the time (for example *since Tuesday*).
We use *for* when we give the **length** of the time (for example *for three days*).

It's been snowing since Tuesday.   *It's been snowing for three days.* (NOT ... ~~since three days.~~)
I've been working here since last week.   *I've only been working here for a short time.*
He's been waiting for a visa since April.   *He's been waiting for six months.*

2 **Put in *since* or *for*.**

1 .... two weeks   5 .... yesterday   9 .... August
2 .... Monday   6 .... lunchtime   10 .... last week
3 2006   7 .... a long time   11 .... a day
4 .... eight years   8 .... two minutes   12 .... this afternoon

3 Make present perfect progressive sentences. Use *for* or *since*.

▶ Oliver started learning the piano in January. Now it's May. (*for*)
  Oliver has been learning the piano for four months.

▶ It started snowing on Wednesday. It's still snowing. (*since*)
  It's been snowing since Wednesday.

1 My father started repairing his car on Sunday. Now it's Friday. (*for*)
  ....

2 We started travelling at six o'clock. Now it's eleven o'clock. (*for*)
  ....

3 We started waiting for the train at 7.30. (*since*)
  ....

4 Mr Andrews started making violins when he was 20. Now he's 50. (*for*)
  ....

5 Prices started going up fast last year. (*since*)
  ....

6 I started writing my great novel in January. (*since*)
  ....

7 The water started rising at midnight. Now it's 8.00 a.m. (*for*)
  ....

8 The people next door started playing loud music at 9.00 p.m. Now it's 2.00 a.m. (*for*)
  ....

9 I started trying to explain things to her an hour ago. (*for*)
  ....

10 The dog started barking at six o'clock. (*since*)
  ....

We can use the present perfect progressive just to say how we have been **filling our time** (up to now), especially when we talk about **present results**.

*'You look tired.' 'Yes, I***'ve been working** *in the garden.'*
*I'm sorry dinner isn't ready – I***'ve been helping** *Diana with her homework.*
*We***'ve been playing** *a lot of tennis in the last few weeks.*

4 Put together the beginnings and ends of the conversations.

0	'Aren't you hungry?'	A	'Helen's been looking at them.' ......
1	'Is it true that Philip's been arrested?'	B	'I've been moving furniture all afternoon.' ......
		C	'I've been swimming.' ......
2	'Janet seems very cheerful.'	D	'I've been talking to Henry, and he just goes on and on.'
3	'She's very dirty.'		......
4	'Why are my books all over the floor?'	E	'No, I've been eating all day.' ..*0*..
		F	'She's been cleaning the cellar.' ......
5	'Why's your hair wet?'		
6	'You all look very miserable.'	G	'She's been skiing with Roger for the last week.' ......
7	'You look tired.'	H	'Yes, he's been stealing things from shops.' ......
8	'You're very late.'	I	'Yes. I've been painting the ceiling.' ......
9	'Your hair's all white.'	J	'Yes, we've been telling each other our life stories.' ......

In some answers, both contracted forms (for example *I'm, don't*) and full forms (for example *I am, do not*) are possible. Normally both are correct.

present perfect or present perfect progressive?

We use the **present perfect** mostly for **finished** actions.
We use the **present perfect progressive** mostly for **unfinished** actions continuing up to now (often when we say **how long**).

PRESENT PERFECT: *I have written* etc

finished actions

Mike has learnt how to cook spaghetti.
I've read your book. (= I've finished it.)
I've written to John, so he knows everything.

PRESENT PERFECT PROGRESSIVE: *I have been writing* etc

unfinished actions ⟶ now

Jane has been learning Greek since August.
I've been reading your book: I'm enjoying it.
The children have been writing letters all day.

We use the **present perfect** to say **how much** or **how often**. Compare:

We've travelled to nine countries this year.
I've played tennis three times this week.

We've been travelling all this year.
I've been playing a lot of tennis recently.

1 Circle the correct form.

▶ How long have you *learnt* / been learning the piano?
▶ Look! I have *bought* / been buying a coat.
1 It has *rained / been raining* since Tuesday.
2 John has *broken / been breaking* his leg.
3 He hasn't *told / been telling* me his address.
4 How long have we *driven / been driving* now?

5 Have you ever *read / been reading* this book?
6 Hello! I've *waited / been waiting* for you for hours!
7 How long have you *sat / been sitting* here?
8 How many letters have you *written? / been writing?*
9 She has *learnt / been learning* German for six years.
10 She has *learnt / been learning* most of the irregular verbs.

The **present perfect progressive** can also be used for longer, more permanent situations. However, we often prefer a **simple present perfect**, especially when we are talking about unchanging states rather than actions. Compare:

He's been standing there for hours.   *The castle has stood on this hill for 900 years.*

2 Circle the best answer. (Both are correct, but one is more probable.)

1 We've *lived / been living* in London since January.
2 They've *lived / been living* in London all their lives.
3 My father has *worked / been working* here for 47 years.
4 I've *worked / been working* here for two weeks.
5 Her family has *farmed / been farming* this land since the tenth century.
6 She has only *farmed / been farming* for two years, but she's doing very well.
7 John has *run / been running* the village shop since his father died last year.
8 Alex has *run / been running* the company since it was founded in 1980.
9 Harris has *spent / been spending* the last ten years in prison.
10 I've *spent / been spending* a lot of time with the children recently.

We don't often use the **progressive** with *be, have* (meaning 'possess'), *know* and other non-progressive verbs (see page 20).

I've been here since Tuesday. (**NOT** ~~I've been being~~ …)
How long **have you had** your car? (**NOT** ~~How long have you been having~~ …)
We've only **known** each other for two weeks. (**NOT** ~~We've only been knowing~~ …)

3 **Make present perfect questions with *How long …?***

▶ you / be / in this country *How long have you been in this country?* ....

1 you / know / Mike ....

2 you / be / a student ....

3 your brother / be / a doctor ....

4 Andrew / have / that dog ....

5 David and Elizabeth / be / together ....

6 Mary / have / her job ....

7 your parents / be / married ....

8 you / know / about Carl's problem ....

4 **Put in the present perfect or present perfect progressive.**

▶ I *have had* .... these shoes for a year. (*have*)

▶ How long *have* .... you *been waiting* .... ? (*wait*)

1 It .... all day. (*snow*)

2 We .... this dog since Christmas. (*have*)

3 Emma .... all day. (*work*)

4 Matt .... ill this week. (*be*)

5 How long .... Ben? (*you know*)

6 My hands are dirty, because I .... the car. (*repair*)

7 I .... my job recently. (*not enjoy*)

8 George .... me in the office since Tuesday. (*help*)

9 I .... a headache since this morning. (*have*)

10 Anthony .... away for the last few days. (*be*)

5 **How long have you known people? Write sentences.**

▶ *I've known my English teacher since September.* ....

1 I've known .... for ....

2 I've...

3 ....

4 ....

5 ....

6 **How long have you had things? Write sentences.**

▶ *I've had these shoes for six months.* ....

1 I've had my .... since ....

2 ....

3 ....

4 ....

5 ....

Don't confuse: *How long* **have you been** here *(for)?* (= 'Since when … ?') and
How long **are you** here for? (= 'Until when … ?')

simple past and present perfect: summary

SIMPLE PAST: *I worked/wrote/drove* etc

finished actions

- **finished actions, no connection with present**
  My grandfather worked for a newspaper.   *I hated school.*

- **with words for a finished time, like *yesterday, in 2002, ago, then, when***
  I saw Ann yesterday. (NOT ~~I have seen Ann yesterday.~~)   *Bill phoned three days ago.*
  When did you stop smoking? (NOT ~~When have you stopped smoking?~~)

- **stories**
  A man walked into a café and sat down at a table. The waiter asked …

- **details (time, place etc) of news**
  The cat has eaten your supper. She took it off the table.
  Tim has had an accident. He fell off his bicycle when he was going to work.

(SIMPLE) PRESENT PERFECT: *I have worked/written/driven* etc

A finished actions

- **thinking about past and present together**
  I've written to John, so he knows what's happening now.   *Jane has found my glasses, so I can see again.*

- **news**
  A plane has crashed at Heathrow airport.   *The Prime Minister has left for Paris.*

- **up to now: how much/many; how often**
  I've drunk six cups of coffee today.   *My father has often tried to stop smoking.*

- **up to now: things that haven't happened; questions; *ever* and *never***
  Mark hasn't phoned.   *Has Peter said anything to you?*   *Have you ever seen a ghost? I've never seen one.*

- ***already, yet* and *just***
  'Where's Oscar?' 'He's already gone home.'   *Has the postman come yet?*   *'Coffee?' 'I've just had some.'*

- **NOT with words for a finished time**
  I saw Penny yesterday. She's getting married. (NOT ~~I have seen Penny yesterday.~~)

B unfinished actions continuing up to now
   (especially with *be, have, know* and other non-progressive verbs)

- **to say how long (often with *since* and *for*)**
  How long have you been in this country?   *We've had our car for seven years.*
  I've known Jake since 1996. (NOT ~~I know Jake since 1996.~~)

PRESENT PERFECT PROGRESSIVE: *I have been working/writing/driving* etc

unfinished actions continuing up to now (most verbs)

- **to say how long (often with *since* and *for*)**
  Have you been waiting long?   *I've been learning English since last summer.*
  We've been driving for three hours – it's time for a rest.

  DON'T use a present tense to say how long.
  I've been living here since January. (NOT ~~I'm living here since January.~~)

- **to say how we have been filling our time up to now**
  Sorry I haven't written. I've been travelling.   *'You look tired.' 'Yes, I've been working in the garden.'*

- **NOT USUALLY to talk about long, unchanging situations**
  The castle has stood on this hill for 900 years.

revise the basics: past perfect

➕ **I had been working** etc	❓ **had** you **been working**? etc	➖ he **had not been working** etc

To make the **past perfect**, put **had** with the **past participle** (*worked, seen, lost* etc).

*She didn't write to Steve because she'**d lost** his address.*   *It was a song that I **hadn't heard** before.*

We use the **past perfect** when we are already talking about the **past**, and want to talk about an **earlier past** time.

I bought a ticket and went up to the platform. But the train had already left.

EARLIER PAST   PAST   NOW

*We couldn't understand why Simon **hadn't paid** for the car.*
*I went into the office. It was empty. Natalie **had gone** home.*
*I was glad that I **had taken** an early flight.*   *Susie wondered if anyone **had told** Oliver.*

① Circle the correct answers.

▶ I (*didn't have*) / *hadn't had* much money after I *paid* / (*had paid*) for the plane ticket.

1 Carl *never saw* / *had never seen* a castle before he *went* / *had gone* to Europe.

2 No one *understood* / *had understood* how the dog *got* / *had got* out.

3 I *arrived* / *had arrived* at the cinema at 5.30, but the film *already started* / *had already started*.

4 Sarah *didn't play* / *hadn't played* golf on Saturday because she *hurt* / *had hurt* her leg.

5 After I *looked* / *had looked* in all the drawers for my keys, I *found* / *had found* them in my pocket.

6 I *didn't recognise* / *hadn't recognised* Lucy, because she *grew* / *had grown* her hair very long.

7 The man *told* / *had told* me that he *was* / *had been* in Russia a few years before.

8 Everything *was* / *had been* white and beautiful, because it *snowed* / *had snowed* in the night.

9 Because I *didn't make* / *hadn't made* an appointment, the manager *refused* / *had refused* to see me.

10 When I *did* / *had done* the washing up I *sat down* / *had sat down* and *read* / *had read* the paper.

② Put in the simple past or the past perfect.

▶ Joe ...*didn't tell*........... anybody where he ....*had got*.............. all that money. (*not tell; get*)

▶ Helen ...*went*............... to Mexico last week. Before that, she ...*had*................ never ...*been*............... outside the US. (*go; be*)

1 When their mother .... home, the children .... the cat. (*get; wash*)

2 Yesterday I .... a man who .... with my grandmother. (*meet; work*)

3 I .... her somewhere – I .... sure. (*see; be*)

4 Because he .... the oil for so long, the car .... (*not check; break down*)

5 She couldn't find the book that I .... her. (*lend*)

6 They .... where he .... the money. (*not know; hide*)

7 200 years ago, most people .... very much. (*not travel*)

8 I .... a letter on my desk that I .... to post. (*find; forget*)

9 When she .... in, we all knew where she .... (*come; be*)

10 The lesson .... when I .... (*already start; arrive*)

In some answers, both contracted forms (for example *I'm, don't*) and full forms (for example *I am, do not*) are possible. Normally both are correct.

more about the past perfect *after I had finished*

We often use the **past perfect** with *when* and *after* to show that something was **completely finished** before something else happened.

When he **had painted** the kitchen and bathroom, he decided to have a rest.
After I **had finished** the report, I realised that it was too late to email it.

1 **Make sentences using the past perfect.**

▶ 1. Jack finished his lunch.   2. He sat down to watch a film. (*when*)
.......*When Jack had finished his lunch, he sat down to watch a film.*....................

▶ 2. I went on a trip round America.   1. I finished my exams. (*after*)
.......*I went on a trip round America after I had finished my exams.*....................

1   1. He tried on six pairs of shoes.   2. He decided he liked the first ones best. (*after*)
....

2   1. Mary did all the shopping.   2. She took a short walk round the park. (*when*)
....

3   1. I washed and dried the last plate.   2. Paul came in and offered to help. (*after*)
....

4   2. He went to the café in the square for a cup of coffee.   1. He said goodbye to the visitors. (*after*)
....

5   2. I started on the dark chocolate.   1. I ate all the milk chocolate. (*when*)
....

6   1. Peter did his karate training.   2. He phoned his mother. (*when*)
....

7   2. Mike had a long hot shower.   1. He went for a run. (*after*)
....

8   2. Sandra went to bed.   1. She phoned the office to say she was ill. (*after*)
....

2 **Grammar in a text. Choose the correct tense (simple past or past perfect).**

I (▶ *go*) ...*went*......... to Paris last spring for a job interview; I (1 *not be*) .... there for five years. I (2 *arrive*) .... the evening before the interview, and (3 *decide*) .... to go for a walk. I (4 *spend*) .... a happy hour strolling round, thinking about the good times I (5 *have*) .... there as a student. As I was walking by the Seine, I suddenly (6 *see*) .... a familiar face – it was Nedjma, the woman I (7 *share*) .... a flat with when I was a student, and whose address I (8 *lose*) .... after leaving Paris. I could tell she (9 *not see*) .... me, so I (10 *call*) .... her name and she (11 *look*) .... up. As she (12 *turn*) .... towards me, I (13 *realise*) .... that she (14 *have*) .... an ugly scar on the side of her face. She (15 *see*) .... the shock in my eyes, and her hand (16 *go*) .... up to touch the scar; she (17 *explain*) .... that she (18 *get*) .... it when she was a journalist reporting on a war in Africa.

She (19 *not be*) .... uncomfortable telling me this; we (20 *feel*) .... as if the years (21 *not pass*) ...., as if we (22 *say*) .... goodbye the week before. She (23 *arrive*) .... in Paris that morning, and she (24 *have*) .... a hospital appointment the next day. The doctors (25 *think*) .... that they could remove the scar, but she would have to stay in Paris for several months. Both of us (26 *have*) .... the idea at the same time: if I (27 *get*) .... the job, we could share a flat again. And we could start by having a coffee while we (28 *begin*) .... to tell one another everything that (29 *happen*) .... to us in the past five years.

→ For more about tenses with *when* and *after*, see 42, 241 and 246.

past perfect progressive *she had been working too hard*

| + | I **had been working** etc | ? | **had** you **been working**? etc | - | she **had not been working** etc |

When we are talking about **a past time**, we can use the **past perfect progressive** to talk about **earlier situations** which had continued **up to that time**.

*All the roads were blocked: it **had been snowing** all night long.*
*After I **had been walking** for an hour, I decided to have a rest.*
*She got ill because she **had been working** too hard.*
*Rachel could see that the child **had been crying** for some time.*

1 **Grammar in a text. Complete the newspaper report with past perfect progressives. Choose verbs from the box.**

| drive   lie   repair   work |

John Latton, 39, an engineer at Felton Plastics in Upton, had a lucky escape after an accident on the A34 in the early hours of the morning. Mr Latton fell asleep while driving and crashed into a pile of sand left by workers who [1] .... the road.

When he left Felton Plastics at 3.00 this morning, Mr Latton

[2] .... for 72 hours without any sleep.

A passing motorist discovered the accident after the engineer [3] .... in his car with a broken leg for half an hour. Ambulance workers said that if Mr Latton [4] .... any faster his injuries might have been much worse.

2 **Read the text and answer the questions. Use past perfect progressives.**

On Tuesday afternoon, everyone in my family was very busy – except me. During the afternoon Helen repaired her car; Robert practised his karate; Kate did some gardening; Stephanie played tennis; Roger swam for half an hour; Rebecca went horse-riding; Philip painted the ceiling in his room light blue. I spent the afternoon sitting reading.

▶ Who had black grease on her hands at teatime? Why?
  Helen, because she had been repairing her car.
....

1 Who had dirt on her hands and knees? Why?
....

2 Who was wearing a short white skirt? Why?
....

3 Who was wearing a white jacket and trousers and a black belt? Why?
....

4 Who was wearing high boots and a hard hat? Why?
....

5 Whose hair had light blue streaks in it? Why?
....

6 Whose hair was all wet? Why?
....

In some answers, both contracted forms (for example *I'm, don't*) and full forms (for example *I am, do not*) are possible. Normally both are correct.

This is the first time etc

We use **perfect tenses** in sentences with *this/it/that is/was the first/second/third/only/best/worst* etc.

This is the first time that I've heard her sing.
(**NOT** ~~This is the first time that I hear her sing.~~)
This is the second time you've asked me the same question.
(**NOT** ~~This is the second time you ask~~ …)
That's the fifth cake you've eaten this morning.
It was the third time he had been in love that year.
(**NOT** ~~It was the third time he was in love~~ …)
It was one of the best books I had ever read.

1 **Complete the sentences correctly. Use verbs from the box.**

be   buy   drink   eat   feel ✓   have   make   say   see   see   sing

▶ This is the only time this week I ....*have felt*.............. happy.
1 This is the first time I .... this film.
2 That's the eighth time you .... that song today.
3 It was the third serious mistake he .... in his new job.
4 It was the best holiday I .... in my life.
5 It was the only time I .... ever .... her cry.
6 That's the tenth cup of coffee you .... since breakfast.
7 It was the first time all the family .... together since Sue's wedding.
8 This is the worst meal I .... this year.
9 'Excuse me.' 'That's the first thing you .... to me all day.'
10 These are the first clothes I .... myself since Christmas.

2 **Read the text and make sentences beginning *It was the first time* . . .**

John didn't enjoy his first week in the army. He had never been away from home before; he had never worn a uniform; he had never made his own bed; he had never cleaned his own boots; he had never fired a gun, and he hated the noise; he had never walked more than a mile.

▶ ...*It was the first time he had been away from home.*..
....
....
....
....
....

'I suggest you move. You won't be
the first dog I've kicked today.'

perfect tenses: more practice

1 **News and details. Put together sentences from the box to make news items. Choose the right tenses.**

> A light passenger plane (*crash*) in Surrey. ✓   Peter (*just offer*) me a new job!
> Five thousand fans (*be*) at the airport.   She (*be*) at a friend's house in Birmingham.
> According to eyewitnesses, the aircraft (*hit*) a tree while coming in to land. ✓
> Ana Gomez, of Peru, (*set*) a new record for the marathon.   He (*say*) I was just the person he needed.
> Novelist Maria Santiago (*marry*) actor Tony Delaney.   Police (*find*) missing schoolgirl Karen Allen.
> She (*cover*) the 42 km in just over 2 hours and 11 minutes.   The World Cup team (*arrive*) home.
> They (*fall*) just before reaching the summit of Mont Blanc (4,807 m).
> Two prisoners (*escape*) from Caernarvon high security prison.
> They (*meet*) while working on the screenplay for the film *Sun in the Morning*.
> They (*steal*) dustmen's uniforms and walked out through the main gate.
> Three climbers (*die*) in the Alps.

▶ *A light passenger plane has crashed in Surrey. According to eyewitnesses, the aircraft hit a tree while coming in to land.*

....
....
....
....
....
....
....
....
....
....
....
....
....
....
....

2 **GRAMMAR AND VOCABULARY: six games. Look at the pictures and say what the people have been playing. Use the verbs in the box; look them up in a dictionary if necessary.**

> badminton ✓   chess   darts   ice hockey   poker   polo

▶ *She has been playing badminton.*
1 ....
2 ....
3 ....
4 ....
5 ....

3 Time up to now, or not. Complete these sentences in any way you like.

1 I've often ....
2 I often .... when I was a child.
3 I've never ....
4 I never .... when I was a child.
5 I've .... times this year.
6 I .... times last year.

4 Grammar in a text. (Circle) the correct answers.

I[1] *know / have known* Adrian for a very long time – we[2] *are / have been* friends since our first day at school, thirty years[3] *ago / before / since*. He[4] *came / has come* round to see me last night to ask for my advice. His company[5] *did / has been doing* very well for the last few years, and they[6] *opened / have opened* several new offices. They[7] *just asked / have just asked* Adrian to move to Scotland, to run an office there. He[8] *didn't decide / hasn't decided* what to do yet. He doesn't really want to move: he[9] *never lived / has never lived* outside Manchester, and he[10] *bought / has bought* a new house there last year. But the new job would be interesting, and very well paid. We[11] *talked / have talked / have been talking* about it for a long time last night, but of course I couldn't tell him what to do.

5 Grammar in a text. Put in the correct forms.

Dear Eileen

Hope things are OK with you. The doctor (1 *come*) .... yesterday.
He (2 *not like*) .... my cough. I (3 *tell*) .... him, well,
I don't like it either. I (4 *lie*) .... in bed looking at the ceiling since
Tuesday, and believe me, I'm fed up with it. I (5 *never be*) ill
like this before – don't know what's happening to me. And the weather's terrible. It
(6 *rain*) .... all day, and I can't even have a cup of tea to cheer myself up,
because the milkman (7 *not come*) .... this morning. Don't know why –
I'm sure I (8 *pay*) .... his bill.
⠀⠀⠀Alice (9 *get*) .... married last week, so now all Mary's kids
(10 *leave*) .... home. She won't know what to do with herself, will she?
⠀⠀⠀Lucy Watson (11 *move*) .... to Doncaster. Since Fred
(12 *die*) .... she (13 *be*) .... all alone.
It (14 *be*) .... a heart attack, apparently. I'm sorry she
(15 *go*) .... – we (16 *be*) .... neighbours
(17 *since/for*) over thirty years, and she (18 *always be*) .... friendly
and ready to help out.
⠀⠀⠀Amy (19 *leave*) .... My cleaning lady, you remember? I'm glad.
She (20 *not be*) .... much use, and I (21 *not trust*) ....
her since the day when she (22 *break*) .... all those plates and
(23 *say*) .... it (24 *be*) .... the cat.
⠀⠀⠀There (25 *not be*) .... much change in the village. Some new people
(26 *take*) .... over the shop. They seem quite nice. Hope they're more
efficient than old Joe.
⠀⠀⠀No more news. Write when you've got the time.

Love Emma

6 DO IT YOURSELF **Are these rules true ('T') or false ('F')? (Two of rules 1–5 are true.)**
- ▶ Finished actions: always simple past. ...F.
- ▶ News: often present perfect. ...T.
1 Present perfect with words for finished time; simple past with words for unfinished time. ......
2 Present perfect with longer periods of time; simple past with shorter periods. ......
3 Finished actions with present results: usually present perfect. ......
4 Repeated actions: present perfect. ......
5 Situations continuing up to now: present perfect progressive (with most verbs). ......

7 Past perfect. **John loses things. Here are some of the problems he had on a visit to London. Complete the sentences using words from the box.**

address	appetite	glasses	key	luggage ✓	memory	money	ticket

- ▶ He couldn't change clothes at his hotel because ...*he had lost his luggage.*.......................................
1 He couldn't see very well because ....
2 He couldn't get into the theatre because ....
3 He couldn't buy another ticket because ....
4 He had trouble finding his hotel again because ....
5 He couldn't get into his hotel room because ....
6 He couldn't eat much in the hotel restaurant because ....
7 He didn't get home the next day because ....

8 DO IT YOURSELF **Look at the examples in Exercise 7. Which of rules 1–5 gives the best explanation for the use of the past perfect?**
1 We use the past perfect mostly in indirect speech.
2 We use the past perfect to show that a past action was completed.
3 We use the past perfect when we are already talking about the past, and want to talk about an earlier past.
4 We use the past perfect to talk about things that happened a very long time ago.
5 We use the past perfect to say why something happened.

9 Present perfect or simple past? **Circle the best verb forms in the cartoon captions. Can you make a present-tense sentence about the situation in the first cartoon?**

'First the good news. His temperature
went / has gone down.'

Present-tense sentence:

....

'Perhaps I could help you choose, sir –
what, exactly, *did you do / have you done* ?'

10 Internet exercise. **Use a search engine (e.g. Google) to see which of the following are more common. Then try the exercise again with some more verbs.**

has found it today   *number of hits ...*   has found it yesterday   *number of hits ...*
has seen it today   *number of hits ...*   has seen it yesterday   *number of hits ...*
has played today   *number of hits ...*   has played yesterday   *number of hits ...*

perfect tenses: revision test

1 **Put the time expressions into the sentences and choose the correct tenses.**

▶ I (*like*) sport. (*always*)
  I have always liked sport.
....

1 I (*spend*) three days in hospital. (*last month*)
....

2 I'm sorry for her. She (*have*) bad luck. (*all her life*)
....

3 I (*want*) to be a doctor. (*until I was fifteen*)
....

4 He (*be*) unemployed. (*ever since he left school*)
....

5 (*you live*) in this town? (*How long*)
....

6 I (*not learn*) much. (*in my last job*)
....

7 I (*not work*) very hard. (*when I was at university*)
....

8 Joe (*live*) in Durban for a year. (*before he got married*)
....

9 He was ill before Christmas, but he (*be*) fine. (*since then*)
....

10 I (*have*) trouble sleeping. (*all this week*)
....

11 I (*have*) trouble sleeping. (*all last week*)
....

12 I (*learn*) a lot. (*in this job*)
....

13 My boyfriend and I (*know*) each other. (*for ages*)
....

14 When I (*see*) her, I (*know*) that we (*meet*). (*before*)
....

15 I (*feel*) very tired, but I'm OK now. (*this morning*)
....

2 **Put the two sentences together, beginning with *after*.**

1 I wrote to my boyfriend. Then I watched television for an hour or so.
  After I .... boyfriend, I ....

2 Everybody had a chance to say what they thought. Then we took a vote.
....

3 I posted the letter. Then I felt much better about everything.
....

4 She stopped trying to lose weight. She looked much healthier.
....

5 He bought presents for everyone in his family. Then he bought something for himself as well.
....

3 **Correct the mistakes.**

▶ I've just ~~broke~~ a cup. ..*broken*..........................

1 The film has already startted. ....

2 I haven't spoke French for years. ....

3 I've been hopping to meet you for a long time. ....

4 I know Julia since 1996. ....

5 We are come to discuss something with you. ....

6 Shakespeare has written some great tragedies. ....

7 I couldn't get in because I lost my keys. ....

8 I'm studying physics for the last two years. ....

9 I asked her where she has been, but she said nothing. ....

10 You haven't drank your tea. ....

11 When have you left school? ....

12 I've had this sweater since years. ....

13 I've had a headache this morning, but it got better in the afternoon. ....

14 After I've finished the cooking I sat down for a rest. ....

15 The dog got out because I have forgotten to close the door. ....

4 **Imagine these sentences are spoken today. Read them and answer the questions.**

1 'How long has Naomi lived in Spain?' *Does Naomi still live in Spain?* ....

2 'George worked with me for two years.' *Does George still work with the speaker?* ....

3 'I had a headache all day.' *Has the speaker got a headache?* ....

4 'Pete phoned me this morning.' *Is it still morning?* ....

5 'Nobody's wished me a happy birthday.' *Is it still the speaker's birthday?* ....

6 'How long are you here for?' 'Since Monday.' *Is the answer correct?* ....

7 'Maggie Parsons has written six novels.' *Do we know whether Maggie Parsons is a living writer?*
....

8 'It's been a terrible day.' *Is today the 'terrible day'?* ....

9 'Everybody enjoyed the meal.' *Are they still eating?* ....

10 'Tuesday has been fine.' *Is it still Tuesday?* ....

11 'How long did Bill spend in Italy?' *Is Bill still in Italy?* ....

12 'I've been ill all week.' *Is the speaker still ill?* ....

5 **Put in the correct forms of the verbs (perfect or past, simple or progressive).**

Dear Jenny,

I hope everything's OK with you. I (▶ *go*) ..*went*.................... for another job
interview last week, but I (1 *not hear*) .... anything yet. The man
who interviewed me said that he (2 *receive*) .... 240 applications!
Do you know, I (3 *have*) .... nine job interviews since Christmas,
but no luck. It's really depressing. I (4 *try*) .... to get a job
(5 *since/for*) .... nearly a year now without success.

I (6 *see*) .... Sally a few weeks ago. She and Tom
(7 *just come back*) .... from a nice holiday in Tenerife. They went
to the same place that they (8 *go*) .... to before, and they had a
really good time, except that Tom (9 *lose*) .... all his documents
in the sea when they (10 *fish*) .... one day, and they had terrible
problems getting home.

Lots of love, Sue

In some answers, both contracted forms (for example *I'm*, *don't*) and full
forms (for example *I am*, *do not*) are possible. Normally both are correct.

PERFECT TENSES **69**

all past and perfect tenses: revision test

1 **Choose the best tenses (simple past, past progressive, present perfect, present perfect progressive, past perfect, past perfect progressive).**

1 Reports are coming in that a train .... near Birmingham. According to eyewitnesses, it .... a concrete block which somebody .... on the line. (*crash; hit; put*)

2 Halfway to the office Paul .... round and .... back home, because he .... to turn the gas off. (*turn; go; forget*)

3 I .... housework all day today. I .... every room in the house. (*do; clean*)

4 I .... in bed thinking about getting up when the doorbell .... (*lie; ring*)

5 It wasn't surprising that she .... getting toothache. She .... to the dentist for two years. (*start; not go*)

6 I .... a lot of bridge recently. (*play*)

7 When I .... home everybody .... TV. (*get; watch*)

8 We .... your mother for ages. (*not see*)

9 How long .... English? (*you learn*)

10 London .... a lot since we first .... to live here. (*change; come*)

11 'How many times .... this film?' 'This is the first time I .... it.' (*you see; see*)

12 'Who's that?' 'I .... him before in my life.' (*never see*)

13 I hear Joe .... married last summer. (*get*)

14 I .... where she .... her husband. (*often wonder; meet*)

15 .... Pam Marshall's latest book? (*you read*)

16 They .... a new fuel – it's half the price of petrol, and much cleaner. (*just discover*)

17 .... the storm last night? (*you hear*)

18 My sister .... married three times. (*be*)

19 While she .... on the phone the children .... fighting and .... a window. (*talk; start; break*)

20 He used to talk to us for hours about all the interesting things he .... in his life. (*do*)

21 You know, she .... looking at that picture for the last twenty minutes. (*stand*)

22 The old cross .... on top of the hill as long as anybody can remember. (*stand*)

23 I .... this job in January, and since then I .... most of my time travelling. (*get; spend*)

24 When I .... at school we all .... rugby. (*be; play*)

25 After he .... breakfast he .... down to write some letters. (*finish; sit*)

26 When I .... him he .... as a waiter for a year or so. (*meet; work*)

27 I .... to ski. (*never learn*)

28 .... in the bathroom yet? (*you finish*)

29 We .... in Scotland until I .... eighteen. (*live; be*)

30 She .... a hard life, but she's always smiling. (*have*)

In some answers, both contracted forms (for example *I'm*, *don't*) and full forms (for example *I am*, *do not*) are possible. Normally both are correct.

SECTION 6 modal verbs

GRAMMAR SUMMARY

| MODAL VERBS: | *can, could* | *may, might* | *shall, should* | *will, would* | *must* | *ought to* |

The **modal verbs** are a special group of **auxiliary verbs**. We use them **before other verbs** to express certain meanings – for example **permission, ability, possibility, certainty**.

Modals have **different grammar** from other verbs. For example, they have **no -s** on the third person singular: we say **he can**, NOT ~~he cans~~.

Have to, **be able to**, **used to**, **had better**, **be supposed to** and **needn't** are similar to modals in some ways, and they are included in this section.

For **will**, see pages 28–30.

Modal verbs can be used in a special structure with **have + past participle** (e.g **should have phoned**). This is used mainly to talk about possibilities in the past; the exact meaning depends on the particular modal.

'Should we walk upright? Should we continue to live in trees? Should we try to make things? Decisions, decisions!'

revise the basics: the grammar of modals

The 'modal auxiliary verbs' are *can*, *could*, *may*, *might*, *shall*, *should*, *will*, *would*, *must* and *ought*.
They are used **before other verbs**, and in **tags** and **short answers**.

'*You **can speak** Japanese, **can't you**?*' '*Yes, I **can**.*'
'*You **shouldn't be** here, **should you**?*' '*No, I **shouldn't**.*'

1 **DO IT YOURSELF** **Compare the modal verbs and the ordinary verbs in the examples, and answer the questions.**

MODAL VERBS	ORDINARY VERBS
I may see him.	*I hope to see him.*
He must be happy.	*He seems to be happy.*
Shall we stop?	*Do you want to stop?*
I can't sing.	*She doesn't like to sing.*
He ought to tell her.	*He plans to tell her.*

1 Which sort of infinitive is used after modal verbs? ....
2 Which is the exception? ....
3 What is special about the third person present (*he/she/it* ...) of modals? ....
4 What is special about the question and negative forms of modals? ....

2 **Use some of the infinitives from the box to complete the sentences.**

be   to be   do   to do   get   to get   go   to go   leave   to leave   make   to
make   move   to move   pass   to pass   phone   to phone   play   to play

1 Can you .... the piano?
2 She seems .... better today.
3 I want .... some shopping.
4 We may .... to France soon.
5 When will you .... school?
6 She hopes .... a new car.
7 Must you .... so much noise?
8 Could you .... the salt?
9 We ought .... Angela.
10 I'd like .... to another house.

3 **Make these sentences into questions, and change the pronouns as shown. Example:**

▶ I can swim. (*you*) *Can you swim?* ....
1 She can stay here. (*I*) ....
2 I must go. (*you*) ....
3 You may sit down. (*we*) ....
4 They can drive. (*she*) ....
5 He could do it. (*she*) ....
6 I would like to. (*you*) ....
7 They should pay now. (*he*) ....
8 You must change here. (*I*) ....

Modal auxiliary verbs have **no infinitives or participles**. Instead, we use other expressions like *be able to*, *have to*, *be allowed to*.

He'd like to **be able to** travel abroad more. (**NOT** ~~He'd like to can~~ …)
I've never **been able to** understand maths. (**NOT** ~~I've never could~~ …)
I'm sorry to **have to** tell you this … (**NOT** ~~I'm sorry to must~~ …)
We've **had to** get new shoes for both the kids. (**NOT** ~~We've must~~ …)
She has always **been allowed to** go out alone. (**NOT** ~~She has always could~~ …)

4 **Complete the sentences using expressions from the box (once or more than once).**

be able to	to be able to	been able to	been allowed to	have to	to have to	had to

1 One day, everybody will .... travel where they want.
2 I'm afraid you will .... work next weekend.
3 I would hate .... live in a big city.
4 I would have enjoyed the holiday more if I had .... speak Spanish.
5 I'd like .... ski better.
6 She's never .... spell properly.
7 I hate .... get up early.
8 We've .... move house twice this year.
9 I've never .... drive my father's car.
10 Will you .... come fishing next Saturday?

5 **Complete some of these sentences.**

1 I've never been able to ....
2 I'd like to be able to ....
3 One day, people will be able to ....
4 I wouldn't like to have to ....
5 I've always had to ....
6 I've never had to ....
7 When I am President of the World, people will have to ....
8 I've never been allowed to ....

6 **Choose the best word(s).**

1 .... you swim? (*may, can, shall*)
2 I really .... go now. (*shall, would, must*)
3 We .... see Ann tomorrow. (*might, ought, would*)
4 You .... to see the doctor. (*should, could, ought*)
5 I .... understand him. (*couldn't, mustn't, be able*)
6 You .... be here at exactly 10.00. Don't be late.
(*must, may, might*)
7 .... I carry your bag? (*might, will, can*)
8 It .... rain tomorrow. (*may, would, shall*)
9 It .... be 10 o'clock already!
(*might not, can't, oughtn't to*)
10 You .... be very tired after your journey.
(*would, must, can*)

7 **What do you think are the missing words in the cartoon caption?**

'But the good news is that you'll never
.... smoke,
drink or drive a car again.'

In some answers, both contracted forms (for example *I'm, don't*) and full
forms (for example *I am, do not*) are possible. Normally both are correct.

MODAL VERBS   **73**

revise the basics: *must, should* and *ought to*

Must *(not)* is used for **orders** and for **strong** suggestions, advice and opinions.
Should *(not)* is used for **less strong** suggestions, advice and opinions.

You must stop smoking or you'll die.   *I really think you should stop smoking.*
You must not park here.   *You shouldn't park here; somebody will steal your car.*
People must realise that the world is in trouble.   *People should do more to help others.*

Ought is similar to **should**, but is followed by **to**.

People ought to do more to help others.

1 **Put in the best word: *must* or *should*.**

1 You know, I think you .... take a holiday.
2 Tell Mark he .... tidy his room at once.
3 Visitors are reminded that they .... keep their bags with them.
4 I'm sorry, but you .... go. We don't want you here.
5 I really .... go on a diet. I'll start today!
6 I suppose I .... write to Aunt Rachel one of these days.
7 You absolutely .... check the tyres before you take the car out today.
8 All officers .... report to the Commanding Officer by midday.
9 You .... have your hair cut at least once a week.
10 I think everybody .... know two or more languages.

2 **Complete these sentences with your own ideas.**

1 People should ....
2 People shouldn't ....
3 Children should ....
4 Children shouldn't ....
5 Parents should ....
6 Parents shouldn't ....
7 Teachers ought to ....
8 Teachers oughtn't to ....
9 The government ....
10 I really must ....

We often use ***should*** in questions when we are wondering what to do.

Should *I change my job or stay where I am?*

3 **Write questions for people who don't know:**

▶ how much cheese to buy.   *How much cheese should I buy?*
1 whether to move to London.   ....
2 how long to wait.   ....
3 what to do at the weekend.   ....
4 where to park.   ....
5 when to pay the tax bill.   ....
6 whether to take a taxi.   ....

4 **Write some similar questions for yourself.**

▶   *Should I go on studying English?*
....
....
....
....
....
....

have to and *must*

Have (got) to is similar to **must**.

I **have to** finish this report before tomorrow.   OR   I **must** finish this report before tomorrow.
Do you **have to** make all that noise?   OR   **Must** you make all that noise?
We'**ve got to** check in before six o'clock.   OR   We **must** check in before six o'clock.

There is sometimes a small (and not very important) difference between **must** and **have (got) to**.
Must can be used especially to talk about the feelings and wishes of the speaker/hearer.
Have (got) to can be used especially to talk about obligations that come from somewhere else.
Compare:

I **must** stop smoking. (I want to.)
I'**ve got to** stop smoking – *doctor's* orders.
Must you wear those dirty jeans? (Is that what **you** want?)
Do you **have to** wear a tie at work? (Is there a **rule**?)
You **have to** drive on the left in England. (**MORE NATURAL THAN** ~~You must drive on the left~~ …)

1 **Choose the more natural form.**

1 I'm tired. I *must / have got to* go to bed early.
2 John *must / has to* go to school on Saturdays.
3 We *must / have to* get another dog soon.
4 'This is a great book.' 'I *must / have to* read it.'
5 Old cars *must / have to* pass a test every year to make sure they are safe.
6 We *must / have got to* go to London for a meeting tomorrow.
7 I think we *must / have to* pay in advance.
8 You really *must / have got to* visit us soon.
9 I *must / have got to* try to spend more time at home.
10 You *must / have got to* go through Carlisle on the way to Glasgow.

2 **Complete the sentences with expressions from the box and *must* or *have/has (got) to*.**

| do military service ✓ | do some shopping | get a haircut | give my love | hold a general election |
| pay | pay income tax | phone him | take more exercise | try to get | work |

▶ In some countries, men ..... *have (got) to do military service.* ....
1 I'm getting very unfit. I ....
2 I haven't heard anything from James for a long time. I ....
3 Nearly everybody ....
4 In Britain, we .... every five years or less.
5 You .... to Gareth when you see him.
6 Jack's really upset. He .... all of next weekend.
7 There's nothing to eat in the house. We really ....
8 You .... You're beginning to look very strange.
9 Children can get into the museum free, but adults ....
10 I'm getting very tired. I .... more sleep.

Must not and **do not have to** are very different. See page 76.

In some answers, both contracted forms (for example *I'm, don't*) and full forms (for example *I am, do not*) are possible. Normally both are correct.

MODAL VERBS   **75**

must not; do not have to; do not need to / needn't

We use *must not* in prohibitions (negative orders).
We use *do not have to*, *do not need to* (or *needn't*) to say that something is unnecessary.

Students must not leave bicycles in front of the library.
Passengers must not speak to the driver.
Friday's a holiday – I don't have to work. (**NOT** ~~I mustn't work.~~)
You needn't pay now – tomorrow's OK. (**NOT** ~~You mustn't pay now~~ …)

1 **Complete the sentences, using *must not / mustn't* or *do not / don't have to*.**

1   Campers .... play music after 10 p.m.
2   Students .... ask permission to stay out after midnight.
3   Bicycles .... be parked in the front courtyard.
4   Residents .... hang washing out of the windows.
5   British subjects .... get visas to travel in Europe.
6   Passengers .... lean out of the windows.
7   You .... pay for your tickets now.
8   It's rained a lot, so we .... water the garden.
9   You .... disturb your sister while she's working.
10 You .... knock before you come into my room.
11 We .... leave the windows open or the rain will come in.
12 You .... phone Karen now. Tomorrow will be OK.
13 You .... drive so fast – you'll have an accident.
14 We .... hurry. There's plenty of time.
15 I .... forget to send Pete a birthday card.

2 **Make sentences, using *mustn't* or *needn't* with the expressions from the box.**

> hit the ball before it bounces   hit your opponent below the belt
> lift the stick above your shoulder   move fast   look at other people's cards
> pass the ball forwards   run from one hole to the next
> start before the gun   touch the ball with your hands

1   In rugby ....
2   In tennis ....
3   In chess ....
4   In boxing ....
5   In a 100m race ....
6   In hockey ....
7   In golf ....
8   In soccer ....
9   In bridge ....

3 **Make six rules for your school, family or friends: three with *must not* and three with *do not need to* or *do not have to*.**

1   ....
2   ....
3   ....
4   ....
5   ....
6   ....

had better *You'd better take your umbrella.*

+	I **had better** go you **had better** go he/she/it **had better** go etc
−	I **had better not** go you **had better not** go he/she/it **had better not** go etc
	Contractions: *I'd better, you'd better* etc

I/you etc **had better** *do this* is **not past** or **comparative**. It means 'This is a **good thing** to do **now**.'
We use **had better** to give **strong advice** to people (including ourselves.)

You'd better stop that, young lady. (**NOT** ~~You've better~~ …)
You'd better take your coat.   *I'd better not stay any longer; I've got work to do.*

1 **Put the beginnings and ends together. Use *'d better* with the verbs in the box.**

do   not drink   give   go   invite   phone ✓   phone   remember   see   not sit   stop

0	My husband worries if I'm late.	A	I .... it. ......
1	This milk smells bad.	B	I 'd better phone him. ..*0*..
2	That chair looks very dirty.	C	We .... the doctor. ......
3	The baby's temperature is 40°.	D	We .... and get some. ......
4	You have to get up early tomorrow.	E	You .... to bed. ......
5	There's almost no petrol in the car.	F	You .... on it. ......
6	Sheila forgot my birthday last year.	G	We .... him round. ......
7	There's somebody at the door.	H	I .... some washing. ......
8	Helen needs her camera.	I	You .... it back to her. ......
9	We haven't got anything to wear.	J	I .... who it is. ......
10	We haven't seen John for ages.	K	She .... it this time. ......

We use both *had better* and *should* to say 'This is a good thing to do now.'
We use *should*, **BUT NOT** *had better*, to say 'This is a good thing to do in general.'

We're late (now). We'd better phone Mum. **OR** *We should phone Mum.*
You should always drive very carefully near schools. (**NOT** ~~You had better always drive~~ …)

2 **Write *'d better* where it's possible; in other places write *should*.**

▶ 'I can't move the fingers of my left hand.' 'You ..*'d better*........ see the doctor.'
▶ Everyone in the world ..*should*........ get enough food to eat.
1 If you don't like cats, you .... not come with us to Alice's house.
2 If you see an accident, you .... make a note of the time.
3 Oh, no, look – my car window's broken. I .... call the police.
4 Teachers .... mark homework and give it back as soon as possible.
5 The swimming pool closes in twenty minutes; we .... go in now.
6 People .... drive more slowly when it's raining.
7 Deborah's not well. I .... go and see her.
8 Governments .... listen to the people.
9 My trainers are falling to pieces. I .... get a new pair.
10 The boss is looking for you. You .... hide.

Had better is quite direct; it is **not** used in **polite requests**. Compare:

***Could you** help me if you've got time?* (**NOT** ~~You'd better help me.~~)   ***You'd better** help me or there'll be trouble.*

supposed to *You're supposed to start work at 8.30.*

We can use **be supposed** + **infinitive** to talk about **rules**: to say what people or things **should** do.

You're supposed to start work at 8.30 in the mornings.   *You're not supposed to park* on double yellow lines.

We can also use **be supposed** to talk about what people **believe** or **expect**.

This stuff is supposed to kill flies.   *He's supposed to be rich.*
She was supposed to be here an hour ago. Where is she?
That's a strange picture. What's it supposed to be?

1 **Complete the sentences with *(be) supposed to* and the expressions in the box.**

be ✓   be   come   cure headaches   do   go   go to church   have   pay for   phone   smoke

▶ Is this ...*supposed to be*... coffee? It tastes like dishwater.

1 Aspirins ....

2 Catholics .... on Sundays.

3 Wasn't Jack .... us today?

4 The computer .... an instruction manual, but I couldn't find it.

5 What am I .... with all this chicken salad?

6 You .... and see me yesterday.

7 You're not .... into the shower with shoes on.

8 You .... good at geography – where the hell are we?

9 You .... everything at the cash desk on the way out.

10 You're not .... in food shops.

2 **Write five things that you are supposed to do in your work or studies.**

....
....
....
....
....

3 **These are six children's drawings. What do you think they are supposed to be?**

1 It's supposed to be
   ....

2
   ....

3
   ....

4
   ....

5
   ....

6
   ....

must/can't: certainty *She must be in. He can't be hungry.*

We can use *must* to say that something *seems sure/certain*.

*Anna's gone to bed. She **must** be tired.* (= 'I am certain that she is tired.')
*Look at her clothes. She **must** have plenty of money.* (= 'I feel sure that she has plenty of money.')
*If A is bigger than B, and B is bigger than C, then A **must be** bigger than C.*

1 **Rewrite the sentences *in italics* with *must*.**

▶ Her light's on. *She's certainly in.* ...She must be in. ....

1 John's coming to see me. *I'm sure he wants something.* He ....
   ....

2 Listen to her accent. *I feel sure she's French.* ....

3 Look at all those books. *He certainly reads a lot.* ....

4 So you're studying politics. *I'm sure that's interesting.* ....

5 Are those his shoes? *He certainly has very big feet.* ....

6 Do you live in Barton? *You certainly know Paul Baker.* ....
   ....

7 Marie keeps crying. *I'm sure she has a problem.* ....

8 You believe what she says? *You're certainly crazy.* ....

9 They're always buying new cars. *I'm sure they're rich.* ....
   ....

10 He comes home late every night. *I'm sure he has another woman.* ....
   ....

The **negative** of *must* (to talk about **certainty**) is *can't*.

*It **can't** be true.* (= 'It's certainly not true.') (**NOT** ~~It mustn't be true.~~)
*'There's the doorbell. It must be Roger.' 'No, it **can't** be Roger – it's too early.'*
*She always wears old clothes. She **can't** have much money.*

2 **Rewrite the sentences *in italics* with *can't*.**

▶ Her light's out. *I'm sure she's not at home.* ...She can't be at home. ....

1 Listen to his accent. *He is certainly not American.* ....

2 He has a very expensive car. *I'm sure he's not a teacher.* ....

3 She's very bad-tempered. *I feel sure she doesn't have many friends.* ....
   ....

4 I filled up the car yesterday. *I'm sure we don't need petrol.* ....

5 He had lunch an hour ago. *He's not hungry: it's impossible.* ....

6 The cinema's half empty. *I'm sure the film isn't very good.* ....

7 You want to marry me? *You're not serious!* ....

8 You've already got 20 pairs of shoes. *I don't believe you want another pair.* ....
   ....

9 She looks very young. *It's not possible that she has six children.* ....

10 Why are you listening to that music? *I'm sure you don't like that rubbish.* ....

'She must be blind. She's smiling.'

In some answers, both contracted forms (for example *I'm, don't*) and full forms (for example *I am, do not*) are possible. Normally both are correct.

MODAL VERBS **79**

may and *might* *It may rain. It might even snow.*

We use **may** and **might** (but not usually *can*) to say that things are **possible** – perhaps they are true, or perhaps they will happen.

'Who's that?' 'I'm not sure. It **may** be Celia.' (**NOT** ~~It can be Celia.~~)
I **might** go and see Dad at the weekend.
The company **might** lose money this year.

To say that **perhaps** things are **not** true, or will **not** happen, we use *may/might not*.

I **may/might not** get that new job after all.

1 **Rewrite the sentences with *may (not)*.**
▶ Perhaps you're right. *You may be right.*
▶ Perhaps we won't see Bill. *We may not see Bill.*
1 Perhaps it won't snow. ....
2 Perhaps we'll get a dog. ....
3 Perhaps Joe is not well. ....
4 Perhaps Ruth needs money. ....
5 Perhaps the baby's sleepy. ....
6 Perhaps I won't move house. ....
7 Perhaps she's unhappy. ....
8 Perhaps he doesn't like you. ....
9 Perhaps she's not ready. ....
10 Perhaps I won't pay. ....

Might sometimes suggests a **smaller possibility**. Compare:

She **may** be at home. (perhaps a 50% chance)   Tina **might** be there too. (perhaps a smaller chance)
*According to the radio, it **may** rain today. It **might** even snow.*

Note the difference between *may/might not* and *can't*.

*The game **may/might not** finish before ten. (Perhaps it won't.)*
*The game **can't** finish before ten – it only started at 9.30. (It's not possible.)*

2 **Put in *may/might not* or *can't*.**
1 I'll go to the supermarket, but it .... be open.
2 Their car's not outside. They .... be at home; I'm not sure.
3 'Can I see you tomorrow?' 'Perhaps. I .... have time – I'll see.'
4 'You've won first prize in the lottery.' 'No, it .... be true!'
5 'They've found giraffes in Scotland.' 'That .... be right.'
6 We can try to see that play, but they .... have any tickets left.
7 He's got a strong French accent. He .... be English.
8 I .... pass the exam, but I'm hoping for the best.
9 I'm going to see my old primary school teacher tomorrow, but she .... remember me.
10 You .... want more to eat – you've just had an enormous meal.

We sometimes use *could* in the same way as *might*.

*The company **could** lose money this year.*   *It **could** rain today.*

NOTE: There is no contraction ~~mayn't.~~

revise the basics: permission, requests etc

We can **ask for permission** with *can, could* (more formal or polite) or *may* (very formal, less common).

Can I ask you a question?   *Could* I look at your newspaper?   *May* I sit here?

Can and *may* can also be used to **offer** to do things for people.

Can I get you a drink?   *May* I help you, sir?

1 Ask for permission with *can, could* or *may*.

▶ talk to you for a minute (*can*)   *Can I talk to you for a minute?*
1 leave early (*may*) ....
2 use your phone (*could*) ....
3 stop work now (*may*) ....
4 pay you tomorrow (*could*) ....
5 speak to Jane (*could*) ....
6 have a beer (*can*) ....
7 hang up your coat (*may*) ....
8 do your shopping (*can*) ....

We can **give** or **refuse** permission with *can't/cannot* or *may not*.

*You **can** use my car if you want to.*   *Visitors **may** park in Elm Road.*
*I'm sorry, you **can't** come in here.*   *Visitors **may not** park in front of the hospital.*

2 Give or refuse permission, using the words in the box.

come into	have	make	park ✓	ride	use

▶ you / here (*can*)   *You can park here.*
1 students / this lift (*may not*) ....
2 you / these tickets (*may*) ....
3 nobody / my horse (*can*) ....
4 you / my room (*can't*) ....
5 employees / personal phone calls (*may not*) ....

We can use *can* and *could* to **ask people to do** things.

Can you put the children to bed?   *Could* you help me for a few minutes?

3 Make sentences, using the words in the box.

luggage	supper ✓	the dogs	the TV	this letter	time to go

▶ could / tonight / you / cook / ?   *Could you cook supper tonight?*
1 translate / can / for me / you / ? ....
2 you / feed / could / ? ....
3 can / it's / you / tell me / when / ? ....
4 watch / you / for a minute / could / my / ? ....
5 switch on / you / can / ? ....

Could you possibly ...? and *I wonder if you could ...* are very polite.

Could you possibly help me?   *I wonder if you could* give me some advice?

In some answers, both contracted forms (for example *I'm, don't*) and full
forms (for example *I am, do not*) are possible. Normally both are correct.

MODAL VERBS **81**

shall in questions *What shall we do?*

1 Make sentences with *Shall I …?*

▶ put / the car / in the garage ? *Shall I put the car in the garage?* ....

▶ what / tell / Sandra ? *What shall I tell Sandra?* ....

1 where / put the coats ? ....

2 when / pay you ? ....

3 lock / the door ? ....

4 what time / come tomorrow ? ....

5 go / now ? ....

6 clean / the windows ? ....

7 how many potatoes / buy ? ....

8 when / come for the next lesson ? ....

9 what / buy / for lunch ? ....

10 get / your coat ? ....

2 Can you complete the sentences? (They are from a discussion about holiday plans.)
Use *shall we*.

▶ where? *Where shall we go?* ....

1 France or Scotland? ....

2 seaside or mountains? ....

3 when? ....

4 how long for? ....

5 fly? train? drive? ....

6 stay in one place or travel around? ....

7 hotel or camp? ....

8 what do with dogs? ....

9 take Granny? ....

10 go with the Jacksons? ....

WHAT SHALL I DO?

What shall I do
with all of your little possessions
now that you've gone?

The posters you left on your wall,
your five-year-old toys,
your comics and discs and
    computer games.
What shall I do with them all?

The medal you won
for the junior chemistry project
that you did with Samantha and John.
Shall I pack it and send it along?

Your football boots, baseball bats,
birthday cards, letters from friends,
your guitar with one string.
Shall I send them all on?

Now that your new life's begun,
what on earth shall we do
with your old one?
Shall I pack it all up
and send it along?

M.S.

can and *could* (ability): past and future

Future: We can use *can* if we are **deciding now** what to do in the future.
In other cases, we use *will be able to*.

*I **can** see you tomorrow morning for half an hour.*
*One day we **will be able** to live without wars.* (**NOT** ~~One day we can live~~ …)

① **Put in *can* or *can't* if possible; if not, use *will/won't be able to*.**

▶ I ....*can*............. pick it up tonight, if that's convenient.
▶ I think I ...*will be able to*...... speak English quite well in a few months.
1 'We need some more oil.' 'OK, I .... let you have some this week.'
2 'Dr Parker .... see you at twelve on Tuesday.' 'Thank you.'
3 She .... walk again in a few weeks.
4 Do you think one day people .... travel to the stars?
5 This week's no good, but I .... bring the car in next week.
6 In a few years, computers .... think better than we do.
7 I .... give you a lesson now, but I .... manage this evening
  if you like.
8 I'm free at the weekend, so the kids .... come round.
9 I'll post your letter, but the postman .... read the address.
10 We're busy this week, but we .... repair it by next Thursday.
11 I .... pay on Saturday – I promise.
12 Next year when you're 17, you .... leave school, but you ....
  to vote.

Past: We do **not** use *could* to say that we managed to do something **on one occasion**. Instead, we use,
for example, *managed to* or *succeeded in … ing*.

*I **managed to get** up early today.* (**NOT** ~~I could get up early today.~~)
*After six hours, **we succeeded in getting** to the top of the mountain.* (**NOT** ~~After six hours, we could get~~ …)
BUT: *She **could** read when she was four.* (Not one occasion.)
*He **couldn't** find the ticket office.* (He **didn't** manage it.)

② **Complete the sentences with *could*, *couldn't* or *managed to*.**

▶ 200 years ago, most people ...*could*............. ride a horse.
▶ At her third try, she ...*managed to*........ pass the driving test.
▶ I think I had the wrong key, because I ...*couldn't*............. open the door.
1 I .... speak French really well when I lived in Paris.
2 He .... repair the car, but it took him a long time.
3 At last I .... make her understand what I wanted.
4 We wanted to go to the opera, but we .... get tickets.
5 I .... swim across the river, but it was harder than I expected.
6 All three children .... ride as well as they .... walk.
7 Fortunately, I .... get her address from her office.
8 I don't know how the cat .... get through the window, but it did.
9 He .... already walk when he was ten months old.
10 After the accident, she somehow .... walk home.
11 It was my first marathon. It was too hard, and I .... finish.
12 He did no work at all. I don't know how he .... pass the exam.

→ For *could* meaning 'would be able to', see 257.

In some answers, both contracted forms (for example *I'm*, *don't*) and full
forms (for example *I am*, *do not*) are possible. Normally both are correct.

revise the basics: *used to*

I used to play tennis. I don't play now.

We use ***used to* + infinitive** for **finished habits and situations**: things that were true, but are not now.

She **used to live** in Liverpool.   ***Did* you *use to* play** football?

I **didn't use to like** her.   I **used not to like** her. (More formal.)

Used to … is **only past**. For present habits, we use the simple present tense.

My sister **plays tennis** occasionally. (NOT ~~My sister uses to play~~ …)

1 **Make sentences about past and present habits and situations.**

▶ Penny / play badminton / golf   *Penny used to play badminton. Now she plays golf.* ....

1 Anna / have lots of boyfriends / be married ....

2 John / study mathematics / physics ....

3 Mary / climb mountains / cycle ....

4 Joe / be a builder / driver ....

5 Gary / work in Germany / England ....

6 Claire / live in Scotland / Ireland ....

7 I / like meat / prefer fish ....

8 We / go to the cinema / watch TV ....

2 **Make sentences with *used to* and *didn't use to* about how people lived hundreds of years ago.**

▶ read or write   *Most people didn't use to read or write.* ....

1 travel / by horse ....

2 cook / on wood fires ....

3 live so long ....

4 fight / spears ....

5 hunt / bows and arrows ....

6 believe / ghosts and devils ....

7 be able / vote ....

8 think / earth was flat ....

9 have / bigger families ....

10 children / work ....

3 **Write some sentences about things that you *used to* or *didn't use to* do/think/believe when you were younger.**

....

....

....

....

....

will and *would*: typical behaviour *She will talk to herself.*

We can use *will* to talk about **habits** and **typical behaviour**.

She'll sit talking to herself for hours.   *If something breaks down and you kick it, it **will** often start working again.*

If we **stress *will***, it can sound **critical**.

*She **WILL** fall in love with the wrong people.*

Would is used to talk about the past.

*On Saturdays, when I was a child, we **would** all get up early and go fishing.*
*He was a nice boy, but he **WOULD** talk about himself all the time.*

1 **Complete the sentences with *will* + verbs from the box.**

| be   drive   fall   keep   listen   play   ring   talk   tell |

1 'Dad, I've broken my watch.' 'Well, you .... playing with it.'
2 That child's no trouble – he .... by himself for hours.
3 She's nice, but she .... about people behind their backs.
4 People .... to you if you listen to them.
5 If you drop toast, it .... butter side down every time.
6 If you're having a bath, the phone .... And if you answer it, it
   .... a wrong number.
7 He .... you one thing one minute and the opposite the next – he's crazy.
8 I'm not surprised you had an accident – you .... too fast.

2 **Complete the text with *would* + verbs from the box.**

| come   exchange   find   go   go   make   swim   skate   take |

When I was a child we lived by a lake. It was a beautiful place. On summer evenings we
[1] .... in the lake, or take a canoe out, and in winter we [2] ....
across to the other side. School was boring, but weekends were fun, especially when Dad was home.
Sometimes he [3] .... us fishing; or we [4] .... exploring in
the woods. We always got lost, but we [5] .... our way home again somehow. On
Sundays Mum [6] .... us pancakes for breakfast, and then we
[7] .... to the little village church for the Sunday service. We had a lot of relations
living in the same part of the country, and we saw a lot of them. At Christmas everybody
[8] .... to our house for dinner, and then we [9] .... presents.
It was a good time.

3 **Here are some laws of nature. Join the beginnings and the ends.**

0	After you have bought something,	A	it will. ......
1	If anything can go wrong,	B	somebody will. ......
2	If there are two good TV shows,	C	they will both be on at the same time. ......
3	If you explain so clearly that nobody can	D	will always move faster. ......
	misunderstand,	E	you'll never do enough. ......
4	If you throw something away,	F	will fall asleep first. ......
5	No matter how much you do,	G	you will find it somewhere else cheaper. ..0..
6	The one who snores	H	you'll need it the next day. ......
7	The other queue		

perfect modal verbs: *should have ...*

If somebody **didn't do** something that was important, we can say *he/she **should have done*** it.

*Julia **should have gone** to the doctor, but she forgot.*   *I **should have studied** harder at school.*

If somebody did something wrong, we can say *he/she **shouldn't have done*** it.

*You **shouldn't have told** the policeman that he was stupid.*

1 Complete the sentences with *should(n't) have*, using the verbs in the box.

| arrive   be   bring   bring   eat   go   lock   play   put   spend   tell ✓ |

▶ You ...*should have told*... me that you were coming.

1 He .... his car.

2 I .... so much.

3 You .... here at 2 o'clock.

4 He .... all his money on clothes.

5 She .... more sugar in.

6 I .... to bed so late last night.

7 We .... a map.

8 We .... poker with that nice man.

9 They .... at the station earlier.

10 I .... my umbrella.

perfect modal verbs: *may have …; must have …*

If we say something *may have happened*, we mean that **perhaps** it (has) happened.

*Suzy isn't answering the phone. She **may have gone out**. (= 'Perhaps she's gone out.')*

1 **Rewrite these sentences with *may have*.**

▶ Perhaps Shakespeare travelled in Italy.   *Shakespeare may have travelled in Italy.* ....

1 Perhaps she's broken her leg. ....

2 Perhaps I've lost my keys. ....

3 Perhaps Alice has gone back home. ....

4 Perhaps my great-grandfather was a soldier. ....

5 Perhaps I've found a new job. ....

6 Perhaps this house was a school once. ....

7 Perhaps I've made a mistake. ....

8 Perhaps we've taken the wrong road. ....

9 Perhaps I've caught a cold. ....

10 Perhaps life began on another planet. ....

If we say that something *must have happened*, we mean that it seems certain: we **feel sure** that it (has) happened. The opposite is *can't have*.

*She's late. She **must have missed the train**.   He **can't have gone away**. His car's still outside.*

2 **Rewrite the sentences *in italics* with *must have* or *can't have*.**

▶ The exam was easy. *I'm sure I've passed.*   *I must have passed.* ....

1 Her office is locked. *I'm sure she's gone home.* ....

2 I can't find my umbrella. *I feel sure I left it on the bus.* ....

3 Helen hasn't come. *I'm sure she's forgotten.* ....

4 The car isn't here. *I'm sure John has taken it.* ....

5 The fridge is empty. *Peter has certainly not been shopping.* ....

6 There's water everywhere. *It certainly rained in the night.* ....

7 She looks unhappy. *I guess she didn't get the job.* ....

8 The letters have gone. *Obviously Jenny has posted them.* ....

9 She's not speaking to me. *Clearly I've said the wrong thing.* ....

10 The flowers are dead. *Obviously you didn't water them.* ....

Note the difference between *must have …* and *had to …*

*Joe **must have gone** home. (= It seems certain that he has gone home.)*
*Joe **had to go** home. (= It was necessary for him to go home.)*

3 **Circle the best expression.**

1 Castles in the Middle Ages *must have been / had to be* cold places.

2 When I was a child, we *must have got / had to get* water from the village pump.

3 At my secondary school I *must have learnt / had to learn* Latin.

4 So you broke your leg skiing. That *must have been / had to be* terrible!

5 The kitchen window's broken. Those kids next door *had to do it / must have done it*.

6 In the army, we all *had to get up / must have got up* at 6.00 a.m.

7 I *had to go / must have gone* back to the house, because I'd forgotten my money.

8 We *had to call / must have called* our teachers 'Sir'.

9 I *had to show / must have shown* my passport four times at the airport.

10 There was a terrible storm in the night. You *must have heard it / had to hear it*!

In some answers, both contracted forms (for example *I'm*, *don't*) and full
forms (for example *I am*, *do not*) are possible. Normally both are correct.

perfect modal verbs: *could have ...; needn't have ...*

If somebody didn't do something that was possible, we can say *he/she* **could have done it**.

*I **could have gone** to university, but I didn't want to.*

1 Complete the sentences with *could have*, using words from the box.

| be | be | get | go | hit | lend | marry | phone | study | win |

1 Amy .... Ethan or Peter, but she didn't love either of them.
2 Why didn't you ask me for money? I .... you some.
3 I .... mathematics, but I decided to do languages instead.
4 Our team .... the match, but they didn't try hard enough.
5 The holiday was OK, but it .... better.
6 When she said that, I .... her.
7 Things were bad, but they .... much worse.
8 We .... to Paris last weekend, but we thought this weekend would be easier.
9 He .... the police, but he didn't want to cause trouble.
10 I .... a job in a bank, but I'm not very interested in money.

If we say that we **needn't have done something**, we mean that we did it, but it was unnecessary.

*I **needn't have cooked** all that food. Nobody was hungry.*

2 John took a lot of unnecessary things on holiday. Write sentences using *needn't have* with words in the box.

| HE TOOK: a camera   a Spanish dictionary   a swimsuit   a tennis racket   an alarm clock |
| books   climbing equipment   his driving licence   playing cards   running shoes   sunglasses |

▶ There was nothing interesting to photograph.   *He needn't have taken a camera.*
1 Nobody spoke Spanish. ....
2 It rained all the time. ....
3 There was nowhere to go running. ....
4 There was no swimming pool. ....
5 There were no mountains. ....
6 There was no tennis court. ....
7 Nobody wanted to play cards. ....
8 He didn't feel like reading. ....
9 There were no cars for hire. ....
10 The birds woke him up at 4.00 every morning. ....

NOTE the difference between *needn't have ...* and *didn't need to ...*

*We **needn't have hurried** – we got there much too early. (It was unnecessary to hurry, but we did.)*
*We **didn't need to hurry**; we had lots of time. (It was unnecessary to hurry, so we probably didn't.)*

modal verbs: more practice

1 **Mixed structures. Write sentences about yourself.**

▶ .....*I used to smoke*.......................... , but I don't any more. (*used to*)

1 .... , but I don't any more. (*used to*)

2 .... tomorrow. (*may*)

3 .... tomorrow. (*may not*)

4 .... last week. (*had to*)

5 .... one day. (*will be able to*)

6 .... (*will never be able to*)

2 **Mixed structures. What do you think? Put in *will*, *may*, *may not* or *won't*.**

1 I .... be very rich when I'm old.

2 It .... rain tomorrow.

3 There .... be a war next year.

4 Computers .... rule the world in year 2300.

5 Animals .... learn to speak one day.

6 I .... fall in love tomorrow.

7 Books .... disappear in 50 years.

8 Music .... very different in 100 years.

9 The world .... recognise my the ability very soon.

10 English .... get easier.

3 **Mixed structures. Write *It must be true*, *It may be true* or *It can't be true*.**

▶ There are people on other planets. .....*It may be true.*........................

1 There are plants on the moon. ....

2 Shakespeare interviewed Julius Caesar. ....

3 Some members of the government take drugs. ....

4 All English children can read. ....

5 It is raining somewhere in Africa at this moment. ....

6 Some people can see into the future. ....

7 There's a professor in Germany who speaks 500 languages. ....

8 The world's biggest man is 4m tall. ....

9 Plants can feel pain. ....

10 People who exercise live longer. ....

4 **GRAMMAR AND VOCABULARY: buying and paying**

Make sure you know the words in the box, and then use them in requests beginning *Can you ...* or *Can I ....*

bill	catalogue	contract	credit card	estimate	menu	price list	receipt

1 (*You have just paid a taxi driver.*) .... give me a .... ?

2 (*You have just sat down in a restaurant.*) .... bring me the .... ?

3 (*You are talking to a builder.*) .... give me an .... ?

4 (*You are in a car showroom and you want to know how much the cars cost.*) .... give me your .... ?

5 (*You have finished a meal in a restaurant.*) .... bring me the .... ?

6 (*You want to buy some things in a small shop.*) .... pay by .... ?

7 (*You are renting a car.*) .... explain this paragraph in the .... ?

8 (*You are telephoning a clothing company.*) .... send me your .... ?

5 *Must* (certainty). Read the text, look at the picture and complete the sentences with *must* or *may*.

A woman left her hotel room three days ago. Nobody has seen her since. The picture shows some things that the police have found in her room. What do they know about her?

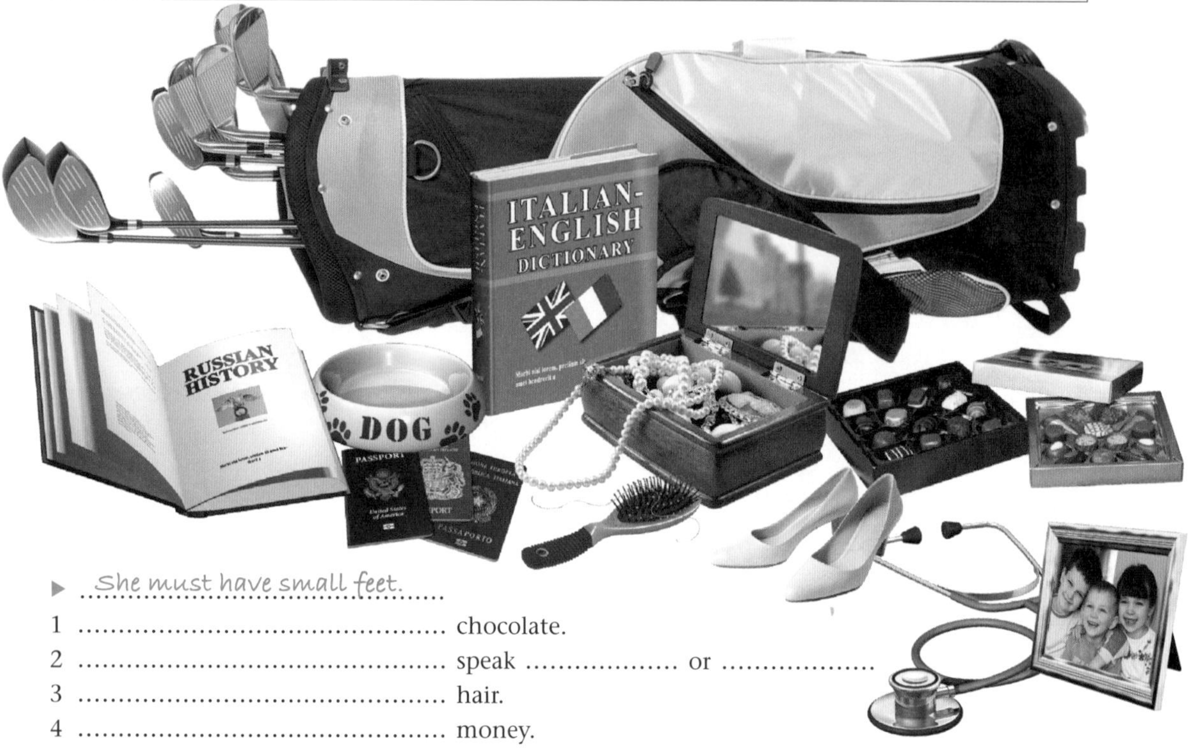

▶ She must have small feet.

1 .... chocolate.
2 .... speak .... or ....
3 .... hair.
4 .... money.
5 .... golf.
6 .... interested in ....
7 .... dog.
8 .... children.
9 .... doctor.
10 .... spy.

6 Grammar in a text. Complete the text with words from the box, using *used to* ...

buy   go   have   keep   look after   look at   live   play   stand   take

Recently we took our 15-year-old son Joe to the place in Paris where we
¹ .... when he was a baby. We showed him the house, with the balcony
where he ² .... and make speeches to imaginary crowds. Then we went
inside, and believe it or not, there was Mme Duchène, who ³ .... Joe when
we were working. She didn't look a day older. We couldn't get into the flat, but we saw the garden where
Joe ⁴ .... Then we visited the park where we
⁵ .... him for walks, the zoo where he ⁶ ....
the lions and tigers, and the lake where we ⁷ .... boating. Not much had
changed in the area: most of the shops were still there, including the wonderful old grocer's where
we ⁸ .... delicacies like cherries in brandy. But the friendly butcher who
⁹ .... the best pieces of meat for us was gone, and so was the restaurant with
the bad-tempered old waitress where we ¹⁰ .... Sunday lunch. I found it
strange to go back: it made me feel happy and sad at the same time. But Joe was delighted with the trip.

7 Perfect modals. Write sentences about yourself.

▶ ....I should have had a haircut.. yesterday. (*should have*)

1 .... yesterday, but I didn't. (*should have*)

2 .... last year, but I didn't. (*should have*)

3 .... yesterday, but I did. (*shouldn't have*)

4 .... last year, but I did. (*shouldn't have*)

5 .... last year, but I didn't. (*could have*)

6 ...., but I did. (*needn't have*)

8 Perfect modals. Complete the sentences with *should have ...* , *could have ...* , *may have ...* , *must have ...* or *can't have ...* . More than one answer may be possible.

▶ He ....should have paid......... me last week. (*pay*)

1 James .... to America. I saw him this morning. (*go*)

2 You .... somebody, driving like that. (*kill*)

3 'Where's Phil?' 'I don't know. He .... home.' (*go*)

4 'We went to Dublin for the weekend.' 'That .... a nice change.' (*be*)

5 If my parents hadn't been so poor, I .... to university. (*go*)

6 It's his fault she left him; he .... nicer to her. (*be*)

7 'We got lost in the mountains.' 'You fools – you .... a map.' (*take*)

8 The car's got a big dent in the side. Bernie .... an accident. (*have*)

9 Rob isn't here. He .... my message. (*get*)

10 'Who phoned?' 'She didn't give her name. It .... Yasmin.' (*be*)

9 ▮DO IT YOURSELF:▮ meanings of modals. What can these sentences mean?

▶ *I might phone you.*   **A** I managed to phone you.   Ⓑ Perhaps I'll phone you.   **C** Both.

▶ *She can drive.*   **A** She is able to drive.   **B** She has my permission to drive.   Ⓒ Both.

1 *You mustn't pay.*   **A** Don't pay.   **B** Don't pay if you don't want to.   **C** Both.

2 *You may have a holiday on Friday.*   **A** I'm giving you a holiday on Friday.
B Perhaps you'll have a holiday on Friday.   **C** Both

3 *She can't be a teacher.*   **A** She's not able to be a teacher.   **B** I'm certain she's not a teacher.   **C** Both.

4 *John may not be at home now.*   **A** John is certainly not at home now.
B Perhaps John is not at home now.   **C** Both.

5 *Theo should stop smoking.*   **A** Somebody has told Theo to stop smoking.
B I think it's best if Theo stops smoking.   **C** Both.

6 *Lucy had better go home.*   **A** It was important for Lucy to go home.
B It's important for Lucy to go home now.   **C** Both.

7 *We used to play a lot of tennis.*   **A** We played a lot of tennis but we don't any more.
B We played a lot of tennis and perhaps we still do.   **C** Both.

8 *He's supposed to speak German.*   **A** People believe he speaks German.
B Speaking German is part of his job.   **C** Both.

9 *She must have left.*   **A** It was necessary for her to leave.   **B** I'm certain that she has left.   **C** Both.

10 *You needn't have phoned.*   **A** You didn't phone because it was unnecessary.
B You phoned but it was unnecessary.   **C** Both.

10 Internet exercise. Use a search engine (e.g. Google) to find four simple sentences on the internet beginning *"We shouldn't have ..."* (put in a past participle). Write them out.

1 .... 3 ....

2 .... 4 ....

modal verbs: revision test

1 **Correct the mistakes.**

▶ It ~~mays~~ rain tomorrow. ...*may*...................

1 I don't can sing. ....

2 I would like to can travel more. ....

3 He should to work harder. ....

4 Could you telling me the time? ....

5 I must work last Saturday and Sunday. ....

6 One day everybody will can have enough to eat. ....

7 In this country, boys must not do military service. ....

8 That mustn't be Angela. She's in America. ....

9 You ought phone your sister. ....

10 I ran for the bus, and I could catch it. ....

2 **Choose the best form.**

1 We .... win, but I don't think there's much chance. **A** *may* **B** *might* **C** *both*

2 I .... ask you to help me later. **A** *may* **B** *can* **C** *both*

3 That .... be her daughter – they're nearly the same age. **A** *may not* **B** *can't* **C** *both*

4 We .... decide to go camping again at Easter. **A** *can* **B** *may* **C** *both*

5 There .... be enough room for everybody on the bus – we'll have to wait and see.
   A *may not* **B** *can't* **C** *both*

6 You .... get in without a ticket – not a chance. **A** *may not* **B** *can't* **C** *both*

7 You absolutely .... go and see Liz. **A** *should* **B** *must* **C** *both*

8 I think you .... have a cup of tea. **A** *should* **B** *must* **C** *both*

9 At what age .... you get a driving licence? **A** *can* **B** *may* **C** *both*

10 It took a long time, but I .... repair the car. **A** *could* **B** *managed to* **C** *both*

11 You .... show a passport to go from England to Scotland. **A** *must not* **B** *don't need to*
   C *both*

12 I .... see you at eight tomorrow. **A** *can* **B** *will be able to* **C** *both*

13 One day, everybody .... say what they like. **A** *can* **B** *will be able to* **C** *both*

14 She has new clothes every week. She .... have plenty of money.
   A *can* **B** *must* **C** *both*

15 When I was younger I .... sing quite well. **A** *could* **B** *was able to* **C** *both*

3 **Complete the sentences with *could have …*, *may (not) have …*, *should(n't) have …*,**
must have …*, *can't have …*, *had to …* or *needn't have …* . More than one answer may be possible.

▶ I ...*may have found*................... a new flat. I'll know tomorrow. (*find*)

1 I .... you, but I didn't have your number. (*phone*)

2 I .... so much garlic in the soup. (*put*)

3 If you needed money, you .... me. (*ask*)

4 When he said that to me I .... him. (*kill*)

5 'How are the builders getting on?' 'They .... by now. I'll go and see.'
   (*finish*)

6 'Kate isn't here.' 'Surely she .... – I reminded her yesterday.' (*forget*)

7 You .... eggs. We've got plenty. (*buy*)

8 They're not at home. They .... away for the weekend. (*go*)

9 She never got my letter. I .... it properly. (*address*)

10 I hadn't got enough money for the bus so I .... (*walk*)

In some answers, both contracted forms (for example *I'm*, *don't*) and full
forms (for example *I am*, *do not*) are possible. Normally both are correct.

SECTION 7 passives

GRAMMAR SUMMARY

When **A** does something to **B**, there are often two ways to talk about it: '**active**' and '**passive**'.

- We use **active** verbs if we want **A** to be the **subject**.
    *My sister **makes** these toys.   Two boys **stole** my car.*

- We use **passive** verbs if we want **B** to be the **subject**.
    *These toys **are made** by my sister.   My car **was stolen** by two boys.*

We make **passive verbs** with **be** (*am, are, is* etc) + **past participle** (*made, stolen* etc).
Passive verbs have the **same tenses** (simple present, present progressive, present perfect etc)
as **active** verbs.
For a list of active and passive tenses, see page 318.

Do you know? (Answers at the bottom of the page)

1 Which of these is used to look at stars?
A a telescope   B a microscope   C a stethoscope   D a kaleidoscope

2 Which animals are not found in Africa?
A lions   B camels   C jaguars   D elephants

3 Which game is played with a club?
A baseball   B golf   C tennis   D hockey

4 If you are fired, you:
A get very hot   B get excited   C die   D lose your job

5 Which of these was written by Shakespeare?
A Farewell My Lovely B The Bible   C Hamlet   D Bird-watching for
                                                                                                Beginners

6 Which Beatle was shot?
A John Lennon   B Ringo Starr   C George Harrison   D Paul McCartney

7 King Henry VIII:
A was married   B was sent to   C was sold to the Scots D was killed in
    six times   Australia   a flying accident

8 Which region of America was bought from France?
A Texas   B Uruguay   C Mexico   D Louisiana

'Bad news, Cromwell – you're being replaced by a machine.'

revise the basics: active and passive

When **A** does something to **B**, there are often two ways
  to talk about it: 'active' and 'passive'.
We use **active** verbs if we want **A** to be the **subject**.
We use **passive** verbs if we want **B** to be the **subject**.
We make **passive** verbs with *be* (*am, are, is* etc) + **past participle** (*cooked, seen* etc).

ACTIVE

A		B	
My sister	*makes*	*these toys.*	
Two boys	*stole*	*my car.*	
They	*sent*	*him*	*to America.*
The government	*will open*	*three new prisons*	*next year.*

PASSIVE

A		(by A)	
These toys	*are made*	*by my sister.*	
My car	*was stolen*	*by two boys.*	
He	*was sent*		*to America.*
Three new prisons	*will be opened*		*next year.*

Passive verbs have the **same tenses** (simple present, present progressive, present perfect etc) as **active** verbs. For a list of active and passive tenses, see page 318.

The subject of a passive verb corresponds to the object of an active verb.

	SUBJECT		**SUBJECT**
Passive:	This house *was built in 1486.*		German *is spoken in Austria.*
Active:	*They built* this house *in 1486.*		*Austrians speak* German *.*
	OBJECT		**OBJECT**

1 **Put the expressions from the box in the right places.**

> is made ✓   was made   had been made   was being made   has been made
> will be made   is being made

	ACTIVE	PASSIVE
SIMPLE PRESENT	makes	*is made* ....
PRESENT PROGRESSIVE	is making	....
FUTURE	will make	....
SIMPLE PAST	made	....
PAST PROGRESSIVE	was making	....
PRESENT PERFECT	has made	....
PAST PERFECT	had made	....

NOTE: Sometimes we make passives with *get* instead of *be*, especially in spoken English.

*I **get paid** on Fridays.*   *My window **got broken** by the wind.*

2 Make passive sentences.

▶ A Roman pavement ...*has just been found*........... under Oxford Street. (*just find*: present perfect)

1 Chinese .... in Singapore. (*speak*: simple present)

2 The Taj Mahal .... around 1640. (*build*: simple past)

3 The new hospital .... next year. (*open*: future)

4 She .... now. (*interview*: present progressive)

5 I realised I .... (*watch*: past progressive)

6 Who .... to Andy's party? (*invite*: present perfect)

7 He found that all his money .... (*steal*: past perfect)

8 Passengers .... not to speak to the driver. (*ask*: simple present)

9 The village church .... in a fire last year. (*destroy*: simple past)

10 You .... by Dr Capel. (*examine*: future)

3 Put in present progressive or past progressive verbs.

1 'Is my car ready?' 'It .... now.' (*repair*)

2 I kept looking round, because I thought I .... (*follow*)

3 We had to keep very quiet while the students .... (*examine*)

4 I can't use my office this week because it .... (*paint*)

5 'Where's Polly?' 'She .... for a new job.' (*interview*)

6 They say they'll put things right, but nothing .... (*do*)

7 I had to wait for a few minutes while the papers .... (*translate*)

8 Why do I always feel nervous while my passport .... ? (*check*)

4 Put in present perfect or past perfect verbs.

1 'Does everybody know?' 'No, Peter ....' (*not tell*)

2 I couldn't travel to America because my visa .... (*lose*)

3 They didn't give her the money that .... (*agree*)

4 I'm sorry, but next Tuesday's meeting .... (*cancel*)

5 I was shocked to hear that Sheila .... (*arrest*)

6 The Prime Minister .... in a car accident. (*hurt*)

7 According to the newspaper, a Roman statue .... in the Thames. (*find*)

8 When I arrived at the party, everything .... (*eat*)

With a passive, we only use **by** + **noun** if we need to say who does the action.

*This house was built in 1486 **by Sir John Latton**.*

My computer was made in China. (**NOT** … ~~by Chinese people.~~)

5 Cross out the expression *in italics* if you feel it gives no useful information.

▶ A 54-year-old accountant was arrested for drunk driving last night ~~*by the police*~~.

1 'Romeo and Juliet' was written *by Shakespeare*.

2 All of these birds have been seen in Britain *by people who watch birds*.

3 Everest was first climbed in 1953 *by mountain climbers*.

4 This house was built *by Frank Lloyd Wright*.

5 My sister's books have been translated into thirty languages *by translators*.

6 Sugar is made from sugar cane and sugar beet *by sugar companies*.

7 This letter wasn't written *by an English person*.

In some answers, both contracted forms (for example *I'm, don't*) and full
forms (for example *I am, do not*) are possible. Normally both are correct.

passive infinitives and -ing forms *to be seen; being seen*

> **PASSIVE INFINITIVES:** *(to) be watched, seen, made etc*
> **PASSIVE -ING FORMS:** *being watched, seen, made etc*

Many verbs are followed by infinitives or -ing forms (see pages 118 and 124).
These infinitives and -ing forms can be passive.

*I want **to be told** the truth.*   *Those people mustn't **be forgotten**.*
*I don't like **being ignored**.*   *She loves **being photographed**.*

Note the position of prepositions in these structures.

*I want **to be listened to**.*   *I don't like **being talked about** behind my back.*

(For more about prepositions with passives, see page 98.)

1 **Write sentences using *want* with passive infinitives.**

▶ 'Invite me!' He ....*wants to be invited.*............   5 'Please look at me!' He ....

1 'Remember me!' He ....   6 'Promise you won't forget me.'

2 'Respect me!' She ....   She doesn't ....

3 'Elect us!' They ....   7 'Don't talk about me.'

4 'I hope you'll listen to me.'   He ....

   She ....   8 'Don't pay me.' She ....

Modal verbs can be followed by **passive infinitives** (without *to*).

*This **mustn't be washed** in hot water.*   *The papers **can be sent** to my office.*

2 **Write sentences using modal verbs with passive infinitives (without *to*).**

▶ We mustn't forget them. ...*They mustn't be forgotten.*..

▶ We should put this in the fridge. ...*This should be put in the fridge.*.................

1 You can't criticise her. She ....

2 You mustn't fold this. This ....

3 You should keep this cool. ....

4 We ought to tell Ann. ....

5 They may invite him. ....

6 You can't send this through the post. ....

7 You should open this immediately. ....

8 You mustn't open this before Christmas. ....

3 **Write sentences beginning *I like / don't mind / don't like / hate*, with some of the verbs in the box. Use passive -ing forms.**

> admire   ask for money   correct   criticise   forget   ignore   interrupt   invite to parties
> kiss   laugh at   listen to   look at   photograph   shout at   talk about
> talk to (by strangers)   undervalue   wake up

▶ ...*I don't like being criticised. I don't mind being photographed.*..................

....

....

....

....

passives: verbs with two objects *Susan was given a prize.*

Verbs with two objects (see page 143) have **two** possible active and **passive** structures.

ACTIVE	PASSIVE
*They gave **Susan** a prize.*	***Susan** was given a prize.*
*They gave **a prize** to Susan.*	***A prize** was given to Susan.*

We choose the structure which fits best with what comes before and after (see page 143).
The structure with the **person** as subject (e.g. *Susan was given …*) is very common.

1 **Change the structure.**

▶ Nothing was sent to me. ....*I was sent nothing.*..

1 Papers were brought to us to sign. ....

2 A clock was given to Henry when he retired. ....

3 Stories were read to the children. ....

4 £5,000 is owed to me. ....

5 A new job has been offered to me. ....

6 French is taught to us by Mrs Lee. ....

7 A car has been lent to me for the week. ....

8 A full explanation was promised to us. ....

9 A lot of lies were told to me by the secretary. ....

10 Presents are often sent to me by my children. ....

2 **Make passive sentences. Use the words *in italics* as subjects and verbs.**

▶ Somebody sent application forms to *all the students*. (*send*)
....*All the students were sent application forms.*..

▶ Somebody sent *application forms* to all the students. (*send*)
....*Application forms were sent to all the students.*......................................

1 *All the passengers* received meal tickets. (*give*)
....

2 All the passengers received *meal tickets*. (*give*)
....

3 Ellen has seen *the plans for the new building*. (*show*)
....

4 *Ellen* has seen the plans for the new building. (*show*)
....

5 Someone has promised *all the office workers* a week's holiday. (*promise*)
....

6 Someone has promised all the office workers *a week's holiday*. (*promise*)
....

7 Someone sent *a bill for the repairs* to Laura. (*send*)
....

8 Someone sent a bill for the repairs to *Laura*. (*send*)
....

9 They did not explain *all the facts* to the police. (*not tell*)
....

10 They did not explain all the facts to *the police*. (*not tell*)
....

In some answers, both contracted forms (for example *I'm, don't*) and full
forms (for example *I am, do not*) are possible. Normally both are correct.

PASSIVES **97**

prepositions with passives *Ted likes being read to.*

In passive structures, **verb + preposition** groups **stay together**. Compare:

ACTIVE: *The doctors **operated on** her yesterday morning.*
PASSIVE: *She was **operated on** yesterday morning.*

1 Take words from each box to complete the sentences. More than one answer may be possible.

heard   looked   operated ✓   paid   played   read   sat   shouted   slept   spoken   talked

about   at   at   for   in   of   on ✓   on   to   to   with

▶ She was taken into hospital today, and she's going to be ..*operated on*.................................. tomorrow.
1 The children like to be .... when they're going to sleep.
2 I don't like being .... behind my back.
3 The new secretary's working very badly. He'll have to be ....
4 I don't think he came home last night. His bed hasn't been ....
5 That antique chair's not really meant to be ....
6 It's not really our house yet. It hasn't been ....
7 He left for America in 1980, and he hasn't been .... since.
8 The cat loves being ....
9 He's so shy: it even upsets him to be ....
10 Please talk calmly. I don't like being ....

To ask who did something in passive questions, we usually prefer *Who … by?*, especially in spoken English.

***Who** was the cathedral built **by**?*   ***Who** were you invited **by**?*

By whom …? is also possible, especially in writing.

2 Make ten questions from the following table.

Who was	electricity the film *The Birds* the novel *Anna Karenina* *Hamlet* *Happy Birthday to You* penicillin radio television the Eiffel Tower the Taj Mahal the Mona Lisa ('La Gioconda') the planet Neptune Antarctica the film *Casablanca*	built composed directed discovered invented painted written	by?

....
....
....
....
....
....
....
....
....
....

reasons for using passives

We choose **passive or active** so that we can **start the sentence** with the **thing or person** that we are **talking about.**

PASSIVE: *St Paul's Cathedral was built between 1675 and 1710. It …* (talking about the Cathedral)
PASSIVE: *St Paul's Cathedral was built by Christopher Wren. It …* (talking about the Cathedral)
ACTIVE: *Christopher Wren built St Paul's Cathedral. Then he …* (talking about Christopher Wren)

St Paul's Cathedral was built between 1675 and 1710.

Christopher Wren built St Paul's Cathedral.

1 Make active and passive sentences.

▶ Shakespeare / 'Hamlet' / 1601 / write
Write about Shakespeare. .....Shakespeare wrote 'Hamlet' in 1601.........................
Write about 'Hamlet'. ......'Hamlet' was written by Shakespeare in 1601.......

1 this sweater / Polly's mother / make
Write about Polly's mother. ....
Write about this sweater. ....

2 Carla / the electricity bill / last week / pay
Write about Carla. ....
Write about the electricity bill. ....

3 the first television / J. L. Baird / 1924 / build
Write about the first television. ....
Write about J. L. Baird. ....

We choose **passive or active** to **continue** talking about the **same thing** or **person.**

*Spanish is a useful language for travelling. **It** is spoken in most of Central and South America.*
(**BETTER THAN** *People speak it in most …*)
*We've got **two cats**. **They** catch a lot of mice.* (**BETTER THAN** *A lot of mice are caught by them.*)

2 Circle the best way to continue.

1 This ice cream has a very unusual taste.
   A I think someone makes it with coconut milk.   **B** I think it's made with coconut milk.
2 Rice is important in Cajun cooking.
   A People serve it with every meal.   **B** It's served with every meal.
3 Barry is very good to his parents.
   A He visits them two or three times a week.   **B** They are visited by him two or three times a week.
4 Luke Salvador is very popular at the moment.
   A They play his songs on the radio every day.   **B** His songs are played on the radio every day.
5 Alice is a very good poet.
   A She won a national poetry prize last year.   **B** A national poetry prize was won by her last year.

In some answers, both contracted forms (for example *I'm, don't*) and full forms (for example *I am, do not*) are possible. Normally both are correct.

PASSIVES **99**

passives: more practice

1 **Correct (✓) or not (✗)?**

1 Our house built in 1800. ......
2 You will be interviewed tomorrow. ......
3 I've been sent some money by Andy. ......
4 My room is been repainted. ......
5 She likes being looked at her. ......
6 My passport has been stolen last year. ......
7 These cars are making in Japan. ......

8 She was sorry because she hadn't been invited. ......
9 The toilets are cleaned every day by a cleaner. ......
10 I got up at 7.30. A cup of coffee was drunk by me at 8.00. ......

2 **Present perfect passives. You return to your old home town after fifty years, rich and famous. A lot of things are different. Make some sentences using words from the boxes and the present perfect passive.**

| Café Royal | houseboats | Super Cinema | new car park | new schools | old fire station |
| opera house | ring road | station | streets | statue of you | town centre | your house |

| build | modernise | put up in park | rebuild | widen |
| turn into casino / floating restaurants / museum / pedestrian area / supermarket |

The Café Royal has been turned into a casino.
....
....
....
....
....
....

3 **GRAMMAR AND VOCABULARY: ten adjectives. Complete the descriptions with verbs from the box.**

| blow up | break | drink | drop | eat | eat | find | handle | hear | see ✓ |
| read | trust | understand |

▶ invisible   can't ...be seen...
1 fragile   can easily .... ; mustn't ....
2 inaudible   can't ....
3 delicate   should .... carefully
4 unreliable   can't ....
5 illegible   can't ....
6 poisonous   mustn't .... **OR** ....
7 incomprehensible   can't ....
8 inedible   can't ....
9 available   can .... in the shops
10 inflatable   can ....

4 **Verbs with two objects. Complete these sentences any way you like.**

1 I was given .... for my last birthday.
2 I have often been given ....
3 I have never been given ....

5 Grammar in a text: verbs with two objects. Complete the text with expressions from the box.

> had been given   had been told   had never been taught   was given   was given
> was offered   was promised   was sent   was shown   wasn't being paid

I'll never forget my first day at that office, all those years ago. I ¹ .... to arrive at 8.30. but when I got there the whole place seemed to be empty. I didn't know what to do, because I ² .... no information about the building or where I was going to work, so I just waited around until some of the secretaries began to turn up. Finally I ³ .... a dirty little office on the fifth floor, where I ⁴ .... a desk in a corner. Nothing happened for an hour; then I ⁵ .... some letters to type on a computer by one of the senior secretaries. This wasn't very successful, because I ⁶ .... how to use a computer. (In the letter I ⁷ .... when I ⁸ .... the job, I ⁹ .... computer training, but they'd obviously forgotten about this.) By lunchtime things hadn't got any better, and I decided that I ¹⁰ .... enough to put up with this nonsense, so I walked out and didn't go back.

6 Grammar in a text: mixed passives. Complete the text with the correct passive forms.

King of the Dream Country

When I arrived in the Dream Country I (1 *take*) .... straight to the Palace. There I (2 *tell*) .... that I was the Great King who (3 *expect*) .... for many years. 'All your commands,' they said, '(4 *carry out*) .... immediately. Your most extravagant wishes (5 *fulfil*) ....'

I tried a small test. 'Bring me a monkey on a solid gold bicycle,' I said. A monkey on a solid gold bicycle (6 *bring*) .... at once. 'OK,' I said. 'I'll do it.' 'There is just one condition,' they said. 'For the next twelve months you will be all-powerful. But a year from today you (7 *sacrifice*) .... to the gods.' 'OK,' I said. 'No problem.'

I had a great time. Everything I wanted (8 *bring*) .... to me at once. I (9 *attend*) .... by beautiful women, I (10 *give*) .... delicious food and wine, and I (11 *dress*) .... in wonderful clothes and priceless jewellery. My favourite music (12 *play*) .... by the palace orchestra from morning to night. The whole country (13 *govern*) .... exactly as I commanded.

But time passed quickly. One day soldiers came to the Palace. 'Great King,' they said. 'The year is over. Today you (14 *sacrifice*) .... to the gods.' 'OK,' I said. 'No problem.'

With great ceremony I (15 *take*) .... to the temple at the top of the mountain. My clothes (16 *remove*) .... , and I (17 *make*) .... to lie on a massive stone altar. The High Priest stood over me with an enormous knife. 'Great King,' he said. 'Prepare (18 *sacrifice*) ....'

So I woke up. That fooled them.

(*Lovat McQueen*)

7 Internet exercise. Use a search engine (e.g. Google) to find five or more simple sentences beginning *"I have never been given"*. Write them out.

....
....
....
....
....

passives: revision test

① All these sentences have mistakes in. Write them correctly.

1 French taught in most schools in Britain.

   ....

2 A shower is had by me every morning.

   ....

3 The town hall is just been rebuilt.

   ....

4 I could see that the room hadn't cleaned for months.

   ....

5 Our bread is freshly baked every day by a baker.

   ....

6 Our car has been stolen last year.

   ....

7 Your car will be ready soon; it's repaired now.

   ....

8 I've been giving some beautiful flowers by my boyfriend.

   ....

9 These computers are making in Korea.

   ....

10 The work will being finish tomorrow.

   ....

② Put in the missing words (one or more).

1 He likes to .... listened ....
2 Your room .... still .... cleaned; it will be ready soon.
3 I was glad I .... been told everything.
4 Everybody has .... given a present.
5 This door can't .... opened.
6 I knew I .... being watched.
7 You .... definitely .... paid tomorrow.
8 English .... in a lot of countries.
9 .... you been given a cup of coffee?
10 'Invisible' means 'can't ....'.

③ Circle the best way to continue.

1 My friend Andrew takes photographs of animals and birds.
   A He sells them for a lot of money.   **B** They are sold by him for a lot of money.
2 George Yeo's new book is very good.
   A People bought 10,000 copies in the first week.   **B** 10,000 copies were bought in the first week.
3 This milk tastes funny.
   A I think someone has left it out of the fridge for too long.
   B I think it's been left out of the fridge for too long.
4 Zoë takes good care of her car.
   A She checks the oil and tyres every week.   **B** The oil and tyres are checked by her every week.
5 She lives in an old house.
   A Somebody built it in 1730.   **B** It was built in 1730.

In some answers, both contracted forms (for example *I'm*, *don't*) and full forms (for example *I am*, *do not*) are possible. Normally both are correct.

SECTION 8 questions and negatives

GRAMMAR SUMMARY

To make **questions**, we normally put an **auxiliary verb** (*be, have, can* etc) **before the subject**.
   The bus has left. → ***Has the bus** left?*   *She's crying.* → *Why **is she** crying?*

To make **negatives**, we put *not* or *n't* **after an auxiliary verb**.
   It is raining. → *It **is not** raining.*   *I could see.* → *I **couldn't** see.*

If there is **no other** auxiliary verb, we use *do*.
   I work in Sheffield. → *Where **do** you work?*   *He said 'No'.* → *What **did** he say?*
   She likes ice cream. → *She **doesn't** like ice cream.*

We do not use *do* when a **question word** is the **subject**.
   ***What** happened?* (NOT ~~*What did happen?*~~)

Prepositions often come **at the end** of questions.
   *What are you thinking **about**?*   *Where's she **from**?*

Negative questions can have two possible structures.
   Is she not ready? (very formal)   *Isn't she ready?* (informal)

No is used **before nouns** and *-ing* forms to mean '**not any**'.
   *There's **no bread** left.*   *NO SMOKING*

'Was the train very crowded, dear?'

'I married you for your money, Leonard. Where is it?'

revise the basics: questions

In questions, we normally put an **auxiliary verb** before the subject.

Have you seen Isabel? (NOT ~~You have seen Isabel?~~)   *When* **can I** pay? (NOT ~~When I can pay?~~)
Why **are those men** laughing? (NOT ~~Why those men are laughing?~~)

If there is **no other auxiliary**, we use *do*.

What **does 'gaunt'** mean? (NOT ~~What means 'gaunt'?~~)

We do **not** use *do* with **other auxiliaries** or with *be*.

Can you tell me the time? (NOT ~~Do you can … ?~~)   *Are you* tired?

After *do*, we use the **infinitive without** *to*.

What does she **want**? (NOT ~~What does she to want?~~ OR ~~What does she wants?~~)
Did you **go** out last night? (NOT ~~Did you went …?~~ OR ~~Did you to go …?~~)

❶ Correct the mistakes.

▶ How ~~you~~ pronounce 'write'? ...*do you*...........   6 Do you can speak Arabic? ....
1 She is happy? ....   7 What means 'vast'? ....
2 What he thinks? ....   8 Where you went? ....
3 Did you saw Max? ....   9 Why she is crying? ....
4 Where can I to sit down? ....   10 What I must to do now? ....
5 When the bus leaves? ....

We **only** put an **auxiliary verb** before the subject, **not the whole verb**.

Is your father coming tonight? (NOT ~~Is coming your father tonight?~~)
Where **are the President and his family** staying? (NOT ~~Where are staying … ?~~)

❷ Make questions.

▶ The 7.30 train for London leaves from platform 2.
   Does the 7.30 train for London leave from platform 2? ....

1 Jane and her mother will be staying in Ireland.
   Will ....

2 John and Susan want to play golf on Saturday.
   Do ....

3 The Sunday newspapers have arrived.
   Have...

4 The secretary from the accounts office has telephoned.
   Has ....

5 The big man with the grey beard said something.
   What...

6 Mrs Potter's two boys played football.
   When...

7 The people who were sitting at the back of the bus were singing.
   Why...

8 Sally's planted all those flowers that she bought.
   Where...

Note that *do* may come **twice** in questions: as an auxiliary verb and as a main verb.

What **does** your father **do**?   *What* **did** you **do** at university?

Common **question expressions before nouns**:
what colour, what size, what make of, what sort/kind/type of.

What colour eyes *has she got?* (**ALSO POSSIBLE**: *What colour are her eyes?*)
What size shoes *do you wear?*
What make of car *did you buy?*   **What sort of music** *do you like?*

Note that we usually ask *What time …?*, **NOT** *At what time …?*

What time *does the train get in?*

③ Complete the questions with a suitable expression.

▶ ....*What colour*... curtains shall we have in the kitchen?
1 .... jeans do you wear?
2 .... hair has the baby got?
3 .... books do you read?
4 .... mountain bike do you recommend?
5 .... food do you like?
6 .... shirt do you need?
7 .... TV is the best?
8 .... fridge shall we get?
9 .... books does she write?
10 .... is the concert?

Note the difference between *how?* and *what … like?*
We use *how?* mostly to ask about things that *change* – e.g. moods, health, work.
We use *what … like?* mostly to ask about things that **don't change** – e.g. people's character and appearance. Compare:

'How's Joe?' 'He's very well.'   'What's Joe like?' 'Tall, good-looking, a bit shy.'
'How does she seem today?' 'Much happier.'
'What does your sister look like?' 'Short, dark and cheerful-looking.'

④ Make questions with *How* or *What … like.*

▶ (*your flat?*) ....*'What's your flat like?'*........................... 'Small but very comfortable.'
1 (*the new teacher*) .... 'Not much good.'
2 (*your mother?*) .... 'Fine, thanks.'
3 (*work going?*) .... 'Not very well at the moment.'
4 (*business?*) .... 'Terrible.'
5 (*Anne's boyfriend?*) .... 'Not very nice.'
6 (*school?*) .... 'Much better now.'
7 (*Manchester?*) .... 'An interesting place.'
8 (*things at home?*) .... 'OK, I suppose.'
9 (*your village*) .... 'Very quiet.'
10 (*the neighbours*) .... 'A bit strange.'

In some answers, both contracted forms (for example *I'm, don't*) and full
forms (for example *I am, do not*) are possible. Normally both are correct.

question-word subjects *Who won? What happened?*

When *who* and *what* are **subjects**, we make questions **without** *do/does/did*. Compare:

'*Who*SUBJ won?' '*United*SUBJ won.' (**NOT** 'Who did win?')
'*Who*OBJ **did** you tell?' '*I told Anna*OBJ.'
'*What*SUBJ happened?' '*Something*SUBJ nice happened.' (**NOT** 'What did happen?')
'*What*OBJ **did** he say?' '*He said something*OBJ nice.'

The same thing happens when subjects begin with **which**, **what**, **whose** or **how much/many**.

Which team won? (**NOT** Which team did win?)   *What country hosted the 1928 Olympics?*
How many families live here? (**COMPARE** *How many families*OBJ **do** *you*SUBJ know?)
Whose child broke that window?

1 **Circle the correct form.**

▶ Who (works) / does work in that office?
▶ What *means catalyst*? / (*does catalyst mean* ?)
1 Who *played* / *did play* in goal?
2 What *caused* / *did cause* the explosion?
3 How many people *came* / *did come* to the party?
4 What sort of music *helps* / *does help* you to relax?

5 What *mean you*? / *do you mean*?
6 Who *told* / *did tell* you?
7 What *happened* / *did happen* to your arm?
8 Which car *costs* / *does cost* more?
9 What colours *suit* / *do suit* you best?
10 What *says the letter*? / *does the letter say*?

2 **Make questions. Ask about the words *in italics*.**

▶ (a) *Sam* loves computers.   (b) Sam loves *computers*.
　(a) *Who loves computers?*   (b) *What does Sam love?*

1 (a) Alice broke *her arm*.   (b) *Alice* broke her arm.
　...

2 (a) Paul found *a necklace*.   (b) *Paul* found a necklace.
　...

3 (a) The bomb destroyed *a school*.   (b) *The bomb* destroyed a school.
　...

4 (a) *Fred* lost the map.   (b) Fred lost *the map*.
　...

5 (a) Julie teaches *Japanese*.   (b) *Julie* teaches Japanese.
　...

6 (a) *His wife* prefers classical music.   (b) His wife prefers *classical* music.
　...

7 (a) Room 6 holds *300* people.   (b) *Room 6* holds 300 people.
　...

8 (a) *Her* baby keeps us awake at night.   (b) Her baby keep *us* awake at night.
　...

9 (a) *Sheila* can't wear red.   (b) Sheila can't wear *red*.
　...

10 (a) *Peter* caught the first train.   (b) Peter caught *the first* train.
　...

3 **Write five questions to test somebody's general knowledge.**

1 Who wrote .... ?
2 Who built .... ?
3 Who invented .... ?
4 Who discovered .... ?
5 Who said .... ?

prepositions in questions *What are you thinking about?*

Prepositions often come **at the end of questions**.
With whom … ?, For what … ? etc are unusual and very formal.
We usually prefer **Who … with?**, **What … for?** etc.

Who did you go **with**?   **What** did you say that **for**?

1 Write questions for these answers, using *'Who … ?'* or *'What … ?'*
 ▶ 'I went with my sister.' *'Who did you go with?'* ....
 1 'I'm thinking about my exams.' ....
 2 'I bought it from Janice.' ....
 3 'She sent it to the police.' ....
 4 'I'll carry it in a paper bag.' ....
 5 'You can eat it with a spoon.' ....
 6 'She hit him with her shoe.' ....
 7 'My father works for Shell Oil.' ....
 8 'I made it for you.' ....
 9 'The book's about Egypt.' ....
 10 'I was talking to Patrick.' ....

2 Write questions for these answers, using *'Who … ?'* or *'What … ?'*
 ▶ 'Soup.' (*starting*) *'What are you starting with?'* ....
 1 'A bus.' (*waiting*) ....
 2 'The future.' (*worried*) ....
 3 'Films.'(*talking*) ....
 4 'The manager.' (*want to speak*) ....
 5 'Universal Export.' (*work*) ....
 6 'A strange bird.' (*looking*) ....
 7 'My keys.' (*looking*) ....
 8 'Travel and music.' (*interested*) ....
 9 'My mother.' (*writing*) ....
 10 'Life.' (*thinking*) ....

In conversation, we often ask short questions with **Who/What/Where** + **preposition**.

'I'm going to France.' **'Who with?'**   *'We need to talk.'* **'What about?'**

3 Complete the conversations with two-word questions.
 ▶ 'I'm writing a poem.' *'What about?'* .... 'Lost love.'
 1 'I've had a strange letter.' .... 'My American friend.'
 2 'I've bought some chocolates.' .... 'You.'
 3 'We're thinking of moving.' .... 'Ireland.'
 4 'Joanne's in love again.' .... 'A policeman.'
 5 'Carola's got engaged.' .... 'To my cousin Robert.'
 6 'I'm really worried.' .... 'Everything.'
 7 'We went to Spain in May.' .... 'Harry and Lydia.'
 8 'I'm still waiting.' .... 'The phone call they promised two hours ago.'
 9 'I managed to open the lock.' .... 'A piece of bent wire.'
 10 'I've cleaned the sofa.' .... 'Furniture polish.'

In some answers, both contracted forms (for example *I'm*, *don't*) and full
forms (for example *I am*, *do not*) are possible. Normally both are correct.

QUESTIONS AND NEGATIVES **107**

revise the basics: negatives

To make **negative** verb forms, we put **not** or **n't** after **an auxiliary verb** or **be**. (Note: **won't** = 'will not').

*We **have not** forgotten.*   *She **can't** swim.*   *It **wasn't** raining.*   *I **won't** tell anybody.*

If there is **no other auxiliary**, we use **do**.

*I **don't** like the soup.* (NOT ~~I like not the soup.~~)

We do **not** use **do** with **other auxiliaries**.

*You **mustn't** worry.* (NOT ~~You don't must worry.~~)
*I **haven't** seen him.* (NOT ~~I don't have seen him.~~)

After **do**, we use the **infinitive without to**.

*I didn't **think**.* (NOT ~~I didn't to think / thinking / thought.~~)

1 **Correct these sentences by making them negative.**

▶ Karl Marx discovered America.   *Karl Marx didn't discover America.* ....

1 Shakespeare was French. ....

2 Austrians speak Japanese. ....

3 Roses are green. ....

4 Cats can fly. ....

5 George Washington lived in Russia. ....

6 Fridges run on petrol. ....

7 The sun goes round the earth. ....

8 Telescopes make things smaller. ....

9 There are seventeen players in a rugby team. ....

10 Bananas grow in Scotland. ....

In standard English, we do **not** use **not** or **do** with **other negative words** like *never, hardly, nothing*.
(But this is common in some English dialects.)

*He **never** works.* (NOT ~~He does never work.~~ OR ~~He doesn't never work.~~)
*It **hardly** matters.* (NOT ~~It doesn't hardly matter.~~)
*He said **nothing**.* (NOT ~~He didn't say nothing.~~)
*I've got **no** money.* (NOT ~~I haven't got no money.~~)

2 **Make the sentences negative.**

▶ I eat fish. (*not*) *I don't eat fish.* ....

▶ I eat fish. (*never*) *I never eat fish.* ....

▶ Somebody spoke. (*nobody*) *Nobody spoke.* ....

1 I like your new glasses. (*not*) ....

2 I understood. (*nothing*) ....

3 Something happened. (*nothing*) ....

4 Sally likes dancing. (*not*) ....

5 Somebody wants to sing. (*nobody*) ....

6 There's somewhere to sit down. (*nowhere*) ....

7 My mother drives fast. (*never*) ....

8 I go out. (*hardly*) ....

9 We'll get there. (*never*) ....

10 We'll get there. (*not*) ....

Note the **difference** between *not* and *no*.
We use *not* to make a word, expression or clause negative.

Not surprisingly, we missed the train. (NOT ~~No surprisingly~~ …)
*I can see you tomorrow, but **not** on Thursday.*   *I have **not** received his answer.*

We use *no* with a **noun** or *-ing* form to mean **'not any'** or **'not a/an'** (see page 171).

***No teachers** went on strike.* (= *There weren**'t any** teachers on strike.*)
*I've got **no Thursdays** free this term.* (= … **not any** Thursdays …)
*I telephoned, but there was **no answer**.* (= … **not an** answer.)
NO SMOKING

3 Put in *not* or *no*.

▸ We speak German in the office, but ....*not*...... at home.

▸ There's ...*no*........ parking in this street.

1 Sorry, I can't pay. I've got .... money.

2 She was .... able to understand him.

3 They had .... butter left in the shop.

4 They repaired my watch, but .... properly.

5 We've got .... time to talk now.

6 I can come round, but .... tonight.

7 They did .... want to help.

8 'Do you smoke?' '.............. usually.'

9 She's a woman with .... sense of humour.

10 .... MUSIC AFTER 10 O'CLOCK.

4 Correct the mistakes.

▸ We ~~not are~~ ready. ...*are not*...........

1 You don't must park here. ....

2 I understand not. ....

3 They didn't go nowhere. ....

4 We were no very happy. ....

5 I don't never eat meat. ....

6 We didn't waiting. ....

7 I don't hardly watch TV. ....

8 She not phoned. ....

9 I speak Arabic, but no well. ....

10 I didn't see nothing. ....

5 GRAMMAR AND VOCABULARY: **words for people who can't do things.**
Put the beginnings and ends together. Use a dictionary if necessary.

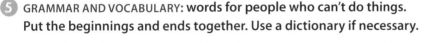

0 A blind person	A can't see. ...*O*...
1 Some disabled people	B can't hear well. ......
2 A deaf person	C can't read or write. ......
3 A tone-deaf person	D can't distinguish red and green. ......
4 Some colour-blind people	E can't distinguish musical notes. ......
5 An illiterate person	F can't move or work easily. ......

In some answers, both contracted forms (for example *I'm, don't*) and full
forms (for example *I am, do not*) are possible. Normally both are correct.

negative questions *Aren't you well?*

CONTRACTED (**CONVERSATIONAL**)	UNCONTRACTED (**FORMAL, UNUSUAL**)
n't **after auxiliary verb**	*not* **after subject**
Why isn't it ready yet? *Doesn't she know?*	*Why is it not ready yet?* *Does she not know?*

We say *aren't I?*, **NOT** ~~amn't I?~~

'**Aren't I** next?' 'No, I am.' (**BUT NOT** ~~I aren't next.~~)

1 **Make these questions more conversational.**

▶ Are you not well? ..*Aren't you well?*...

1 Can you not swim? ....

2 Do you not speak Spanish? ....

3 Were the shops not open? ....

4 Has Ann not arrived? ....

5 Did she not know him? ....

6 Why are you not working? ....

7 Has the postman not come? ....

8 Is your mother not at home? ....

9 Are you not ready yet? ....

10 Do they not understand? ....

We often use negative questions to **check that something has not happened, is not true** etc.
The meaning is like '**Is it true that … not … ?**'

Don't you feel well?   Oh dear. *Can't they come this evening?*

Negative questions can also express **surprise** that **something has not happened, is not happening** etc.

Hasn't the postman come yet?   *Didn't she tell you she was married?*

This may sound **critical**.

Can't you read? It says 'closed.'   *Don't you ever listen* to what I say?

2 **Use negative questions to confirm the following ideas.**

▶ It looks as if she can't swim. ..*Can't she swim?*......................................

1 It looks as if you don't believe me. ....

2 Is it true that she didn't pass the exam? ....

3 I believe you may not have paid for your ticket. ....

4 I think perhaps you didn't lock the door. ....

5 It seems as if you can't understand English. I said 'No'. ....
....

6 I'm afraid you don't like my cooking. ....

7 Perhaps you didn't get the letter I sent. ....

8 So you didn't enjoy the film? ....

9 Is it true that you and John aren't going to get married? ....
....

10 It seems that you don't want any more potatoes. ....
....

We can use negative questions in another way, to **make sure that something is true**.

Didn't you go and see Peter yesterday? How is he? (= 'I believe you went and saw Peter …')

3 **Make negative questions to make sure that these things are true.**

▶ I think you went to Scotland last week. _Didn't you go to Scotland last week?_ ....

1 I think you speak Arabic. ....

2 I think that's Bill over there. ....

3 I believe you studied at Oxford. ....

4 This is your coat, I think. ....

5 I think her mother is a doctor. ....

6 I thought Joe was at the party. ....

7 I think you're hot in that sweater. ....

8 I think you got a letter from Harry. ....

9 I believe they lost money last year. ....

10 She's Irish, surely? ....

We can use negative questions as **exclamations**.

Isn't it cold! **Doesn't your hair** look nice! **Weren't those children** noisy!

4 **Make exclamations.**

▶ It's surprising. _Isn't it surprising!_ .... 6 That film was terrible. ....

1 They're stupid. ....

2 She looks tired. .... 7 He's funny. ....

3 That child is dirty. .... 8 It's a pity. ....

.... 9 She complains. ....

4 It's hot. .... 10 Those flowers smell nice. ....

5 John works hard. ....

We can use negative questions in **polite invitations**.

Won't you come in? **Wouldn't you like** something to drink?

But we do **not** use negative questions to **ask people to do things for us**.

Can you help me? **You couldn't** help me, could you?
BUT NOT *Can't you* help me? (This sounds like a criticism.)

Notice how we use *Yes* and *No* in **answers to negative questions**.
'Yes' goes with or suggests an **affirmative** verb, and 'No' goes with or suggests a **negative** verb.

'Don't you like it?' *'Yes (I like it).'* *'Aren't you ready?'* *'No (I'm not ready).'*

5 **Add *Yes* or *No* to the answers.**

▶ 'Aren't you ready?' ' ...Yes...... , I am.'

1 'Don't you like her?' ' .... , I don't.'

2 'Can't you help me?' ' .... , I can't.'

3 'Isn't this nice?' ' .... , it is.'

4 'Hasn't she paid?' ' .... , she has.'

5 'Wasn't he at home?' ' .... , he was.'

6 'Didn't she phone?' ' .... , she didn't.'

7 'Isn't she coming?' ' .... , she isn't.'

8 'Aren't you tired?' ' .... , I am.'

9 'Didn't Max ask you?' ' .... , he did.'

10 'Can't you find your keys?' ' .... , I can't.'

'Haven't you brought any vegetables with it?'

In some answers, both contracted forms (for example *I'm*, *don't*) and full forms (for example *I am*, *do not*) are possible. Normally both are correct.

QUESTIONS AND NEGATIVES **111**

questions and negatives: more practice

1 **Question word subjects and objects. Complete the questions.**

▶ 'I saw some policemen.' 'How many ..*policemen did you see?*' ....

▶ 'One of these buses goes to York.' 'Which bus ..*goes to York?*' ....

1 'A lot of people voted against him.' 'How many people ....

2 'Jane bought the car.' 'Which car ....

3 'One of those houses belongs to my uncle.' 'Which house ....

4 'Roger owns a lot of horses.' 'How many horses ....

5 'Carl likes music.' 'What sort of music ....

6 'Some people like hunting.' 'What sort of people ....

7 'Somebody's dog dug up my roses last night.' 'Whose ....

8 'Mary writes books.' 'What sort ....

9 'We lost a lot of matches.' 'How many ....

10 'Some vegetables make me ill.' 'Which ....

2 **Mixed structures. Correct or not? Write 'Correct', or correct the mistake.**

▶ What did you say? ..*Correct.*..........   10 They arrived, but no in time. ....

▶ ~~Do you can~~ swim? ..*Can you*........   11 I didn't tell anybody. ....

1 'Can't you stop?' 'No, I can't.' ....   12 I hardly didn't go out for three months.

2 About what are you thinking? ....

3 I don't hardly ever go to London.   13 My parents never watch TV. ....

     ....   14 We had no food. ....

4 What colour of eyes has she got?   15 What time is starting your brother's football

     ....   match? ....

5 What sort of music do you like?   16 What did make that noise? ....

     ....   17 I didn't understand anything. ....

6 What is your boss like? ....   18 We can't never get tickets. ....

7 'Aren't you happy?' 'Yes, I'm not.'   19 It's hardly snowing. ....

     ....   20 What are all those people doing?

8 Aren't those flowers lovely! ....

9 How is your home town? ....

3 **GRAMMAR AND VOCABULARY: sharp tools. Write the questions, and choose the right answers from the box.**

axe ✓   breadknife   drill   hacksaw   lawnmower   pair of scissors   razor   saw

▶ cut down trees ..*What do you cut down trees with?*......   *An axe.*...........

1 cut metal   7

2 cut bread ....

3 make holes ....

4 shave ....

5 cut grass   6

6 cut wood ....

7 cut hair ....

     1   2   3   4   5

4 Grammar in a text. Read the text, and then write questions for the answers.

In a small village in North Yorkshire, there's a big old farmhouse where three families live together: Alice and George and their three children, Joe and Pam and their two children, and Sue and her baby daughter. The adults divide up the work between them. George does the cooking, Joe and Sue do most of the housework, Pam looks after the shopping and does the repairs, and Alice takes care of the garden. Alice, George and Sue go out to work; Joe works at home designing computer systems, and Pam, who is a painter, looks after the baby during the day. Two of the children go to school in the village, but the three oldest ones go by bus to the secondary school in the nearest town, ten miles away.

The three families get on well, and enjoy their way of life. There are a few difficulties, of course. Their biggest worry at the moment is money – one of the cars needs replacing, and the roof needs some expensive repairs. But this isn't too serious – the bank has agreed to a loan, which they expect to be able to pay back in three years. And they all say they would much rather go on living in their old farmhouse than move to a luxury flat in a big city.

▶ Two.   *How many children have Joe and Pam got?* ....
▶ The cooking.   *What does George do?* ....
1 In North Yorkshire.   ....
2 A big old farmhouse.   ....
3 Three.   ....
4 Sue has.   ....
5 The housework.   ....
6 The garden.   ....
7 At home.   ....
8 Computer systems.   ....
9 She's a painter.   ....
10 Two of them.   ....
11 By bus.   ....
12 In the nearest town.   ....

Read the text again and write questions for these answers.
1 George does.   ....
2 Joe and Sue.   ....
3 Pam does them.   ....
4 Alice.   ....
5 Money.   ....
6 One of the cars.   ....

5 Internet exercise: checking correctness. Use a search engine (e.g. Google) to see how many hits there are for these expressions.

"no ready"....................   "not ready"....................
"no here"....................   "not ready"....................
"no at home"....................   "not at home"....................
"no going"....................   "not going"....................
"no want"....................   "not want"....................
"no time"....................   "not time"....................
"no food"....................   "not food"....................
"no money"....................   "not money"....................

questions and negatives: revision test

1 **Make questions.**

▶ Lucy did something. (*what*) .....What did Lucy do?........................

1 Alex went home. (*why*) ....

2 Judy wrote something. (*what*) ....

3 Something happened. (*what*) ....

4 Somebody took the keys. (*who*) ....

5 Mike was making something. (*what*) ....

6 Carol passed her exam. (*how*) ....

7 Jenny arrived. (*what time*) ....

8 Something fell off the roof. (*what*) ....

9 Somebody shouted 'Help!'. (*who*) ....

10 The dog wants something. (*what*) ....

2 **Write 'Correct', or correct the mistake.**

▶ ~~Play you~~ tennis at weekends? .....Do you play.................

▶ Are you tired? ..Correct..........................

1 Will be there next week all the family? ....

2 What is your girlfriend like? ....

3 What does your little girl like? ....

4 About what is John talking? ....

5 'I've just been to Rome.' 'Who with?' ....

6 Are not you Peter Smith? ....

7 Alice doesn't hardly ever phone me. ....

8 'Can't you stop?' 'No, I can't.' ....

9 What are doing all the children? ....

10 What colour of hair has the baby got? ....

11 Will Jane and the girls come by bus? ....

12 'How is their new house?' 'Very small.' ....

13 What was your father talking about? ....

14 What do you do in the evenings? ....

15 They sent some money, but no enough. ....

16 What sort of films do you like? ....

17 Isn't her dress lovely! ....

18 'Aren't you happy?' 'Yes, I'm not.' ....

19 Who did you buy your car from? ....

20 What time did you get home at? ....

3 **Where do the missing words go?**

▶ Why∕you crying? (*are*)

1 What did you close the window? (*for*)

2 Why all the people in the class going to sleep? (*are*)

3 What you talking about? (*were*)

4 What time the tour of the City of London start? (*does*)

5 Who did you have lunch? (*with*)

6 Where you and your family going on holiday? (*are*)

7 What company do you work? (*for*)

8 'I've just got back.' 'Where?' (*from*)

9 'I'm reading a fascinating book.' 'What?' (*about*)

10 What did you mend the table? (*with*)

In some answers, both contracted forms (for example *I'm, don't*) and full forms (for example *I am, do not*) are possible. Normally both are correct.

SECTION 9 infinitives and -*ing* forms

GRAMMAR SUMMARY

> INFINITIVES: *(to) see, (to) go, (to) break* etc
> -*ING* FORMS (ALSO CALLED 'GERUNDS'): *seeing, going, breaking* etc

Infinitives often have *to* before them; but not always.
*I want **to go** home, but I can't **go** now.*

Negative infinitives are made with *not* (*to*).
*I told her **not to pay**.*

Besides ordinary infinitives, there are also **progressive**, **perfect** and **passive** infinitives.
*I'd like **to be lying** on the beach now.   You ought **to have told** me.*
*He can **be found** in the café most afternoons.*

We can use **infinitives** to say **why** we do things.
*I got up early **to say** goodbye to Miriam.*

We often use -*ing* forms as **subjects**.
***Smoking** is dangerous.* (More natural than *To smoke is dangerous.*)

If we use **infinitives** as **subjects**, we prefer a structure with *it*. (See page 147.)
*It's dangerous **to smoke**.*

After some verbs we use **infinitives**; after **others** we use -*ing* forms.
*I **expect to meet** John tomorrow.* (NOT *I expect meeting* …)
*I'll **finish painting** in a minute.* (NOT *I'll finish to paint* …)

We can use **infinitives** after some **adjectives** and **nouns**.
*We're **ready to stop**.   I'm **glad to be** here.   I've got **work to do**.*

After prepositions we use -*ing* forms, not infinitives.
*You can't live **without eating**.* (NOT … *without to eat.*)
*I usually watch TV **before going** to bed.* (NOT … *before to go to bed.*)

'There are three rules for writing the novel. Unfortunately, no one knows what they are.'
(*W Somerset Maugham*)

'Writing a book of poetry is like dropping a rose petal down the Grand Canyon and waiting for the echo.'
(*Don Marquis*)

'To be or not to be, that is the question.'
(*Shakespeare, 'Hamlet'*)

'Beethoven tells you what it's like to be Beethoven and Mozart tells you what it's like to be human. Bach tells you what it's like to be the universe.'
(*Douglas Adams*)

'Writing is easy; all you do is sit staring at a blank sheet of paper until the drops of blood form on your forehead.'
(*Gene Fowler*)

'A hen is only an egg's way of making another egg.'
(*Samuel Butler*)

'It's nice to get up in the morning, but it's nicer to stay in bed.'
(*Traditional*)

revise the basics: infinitive with and without *to*

We normally put *to* before an **infinitive**. Negative infinitives have *not to*.

*I want **to have** a rest.* (NOT ~~I want have a rest.~~)   *I decided **not to go** to Scotland.* (NOT … ~~to not go~~ …)

We use an **infinitive without *to*** after the auxiliary *do*.

*I didn't **know** her address.* (NOT ~~I didn't to know~~…)

And we use an **infinitive without *to*** after the modal verbs *can, could, may, might, must, shall, should, will* and *would*, and after *had better* and *needn't*. (**BUT NOTE** *ought to*).

***Could** you **help** me?* (NOT ~~Could you to help me?~~)   *You **should try** to forget about it.*

*'**Can** you **stay** for supper?' 'No, thanks, I'**d better** go home.'*   *You **needn't worry**.*   *We **ought to stop**.*

Note also the structure with *Why (not)* … ?

Why worry? ***Why not give*** *him socks for Christmas?*

① **Change the sentences as shown.**

▶ I ~~couldn't~~ understand the timetable. (*wasn't able*)   *I wasn't able to understand the timetable.*

1 It's important to eat enough. (*You should*) ....

2 I've decided not to have lunch. (*I won't*) ....

3 I'd like to go sailing this summer. (*I might*) ....

4 She will probably get married in June. (*She expects*) ....

5 I said I wouldn't tell her father. (*I agreed*) ....

6 It's necessary to make careful plans. (*We must*) ....

7 Perhaps he's ill. (*He seems*) ....

8 I want to change my job. (*I wish I could*) ....

9 I may come and see you next week. (*I hope*) ....

10 You don't need to apologise. (*You needn't*) ....

11 I thought 'I won't go back'. (*I decided*) ....

12 I will certainly pay you on Saturday. (*I promise*) ....

13 I couldn't find the ticket office. (*I didn't manage*) ....

14 This isn't a good time to go. (*I had better*) ....

15 She said she wouldn't see him again. (*She refused*) ....

16 I can play chess. (*I've learnt*) ....

② **Correct or not? Correct the mistakes or write 'Correct'.**

▶ Is it necessary ~~fill~~ in a form now?   *to fill*

▶ You ought to go home.   *Correct.*

1 I'd like know where she buys her clothes. ....

2 He seems be ill. ....

3 I promise to send you photos of the baby. ....

4 Try not to be late. ....

5 They will probably be back home in August. ....

6 You mustn't to expect too much. ....

7 It's important to learn to relax. ....

8 I want get a new bike. ....

9 You had better to think again. ....

10 John may phone this afternoon. ....

11 'I'm bored.' 'Why not to go and see Helen?' ....

12 I couldn't find the map. ....

13 I want study engineering. ....

14 We've decided to not go to Wales. ....

revise the basics: infinitive of purpose

We can use an **infinitive** to say **why** somebody does something.

*She sat down **to rest**.* (**NOT** ... ~~for rest.~~ **OR** ... ~~for resting.~~)

1 Write sentences to say why people go to the following places. Begin *You go ...*
   (Different answers are possible.)

▶ a library *You go to a library to borrow books.* ....

1 a bookshop ....

2 a bank ....

3 a cinema ....

4 a theatre ....

5 a swimming pool ....

6 a gym ....

7 a driving school ....

8 a station ....

9 an airport ....

10 a travel agent ....

11 a church ....

12 a football stadium ....

13 a post office ....

14 a restaurant ....

15 a supermarket ....

2 Write a sentence to say why you are learning English. (To get a better job? To study something
   else? To travel? To ... ?)

   ....

3 GRAMMAR AND VOCABULARY: cooking. Make sure you know the words in the box.
   Use a dictionary if necessary. Then complete the sentences.

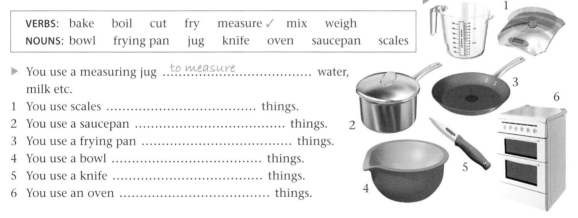

| **VERBS:** bake | boil | cut | fry | measure ✓ | mix | weigh |
| **NOUNS:** bowl | frying pan | jug | knife | oven | saucepan | scales |

▶ You use a measuring jug *to measure* .... water,
   milk etc.

1 You use scales .... things.

2 You use a saucepan .... things.

3 You use a frying pan .... things.

4 You use a bowl .... things.

5 You use a knife .... things.

6 You use an oven .... things.

In order to ... and *so as to ...* are common before *be, know* and *have*; and before other verbs in a more formal style.

*I got up early **in order to be** ready to leave at eight.*
*She studied English **in order to have** a better chance of getting a job.*
*I came to Britain **so as to know** more about British culture.*

In order and *so as* are very common before *not to.*

*I spoke quietly **so as not to** frighten her.* (**MORE NATURAL THAN** *I spoke quietly not to frighten her.*)

revise the basics: verb + infinitive or *-ing* form

Some **verbs** are followed by the **infinitives of other verbs**. Example: ***want***.

*I **want to play** in goal.* (**NOT** ~~I want playing in goal.~~)

Some **verbs** are followed by the *-ing* **forms of other verbs**. Example: ***enjoy***.

*I **enjoy playing** in goal.* (**NOT** ~~I enjoy to play in goal.~~)

(For spelling of *-ing* forms, see page 16.)

1 | **DO IT YOURSELF** Ten of these verbs are followed by infinitives and six are followed by *-ing* forms. Do you know which? Check in a good dictionary if necessary.

decide	expect	finish	give up	hope	keep (on)	learn	manage	mind	need
offer	practise	promise	seem	spend (time)	would like				

+ INFINITIVE: ....

....

+ -ING FORM: ....

2 Put in the correct forms of the verbs.

1 We expect .... from Sally soon. (*hear*)

2 I'll never learn .... properly. (*spell*)

3 I promise .... to you every week. (*write*)

4 I failed my driving test, because I didn't practise .... in traffic enough. (*drive*)

5 Your sister seems .... very upset. (*be*)

6 I've given up .... again. (*smoke*)

7 He spends ages .... on the phone. (*talk*)

8 When are you going to finish .... ? (*study*)

9 After 20 minutes I managed .... a taxi. (*find*)

10 I would like .... the manager, please. (*see*)

11 Would you mind .... the bread? (*pass*)

12 Do you enjoy .... that rubbish on TV? (*watch*)

13 Nobody offered .... when I was in trouble. (*help*)

14 Why does Caroline keep .... to herself? (*talk*)

15 We've decided .... at home next weekend. (*stay*)

16 I need .... to you for a few minutes. (*talk*)

After some verbs, we can use both infinitives and *-ing* forms, often with little or no difference of meaning.

*I like **walking** / **to walk** in the mountains.* (**BUT NOT** ~~I would like walking~~ ...)

3 | **DO IT YOURSELF** Which is correct – A, B or both? Check in a good dictionary.

▶ **A** I'm going to stop to work at 65. **B** I'm going to stop working at 65.

1 **A** I started to play the guitar when I was six. **B** I started playing the guitar when I was six.

2 **A** Ann loves to ride horses. **B** Ann loves riding horses.

3 **A** I have to go now. **B** I have going now.

4 **A** It began to rain on Monday afternoon. **B** It began raining on Monday afternoon.

5 **A** Would you mind to help me? **B** Would you mind helping me?

6 **A** Would you like to see my holiday photos? **B** Would you like seeing my holiday photos?

7 **A** We can't continue to lose money like this. **B** We can't continue losing money like this.

8 **A** Do you like to cook? **B** Do you like cooking?

9 **A** I hate to go to the dentist. **B** I hate going to the dentist.

10 **A** You had better go home now. **B** You had better going home now.

revise the basics: preposition + *-ing* form

We use *-ing* forms after **prepositions**.

*You can only live for a few days **without drinking**. (**NOT** … ~~without to drink.~~)*
*Teachers need to be good **at listening**.   I'm thinking **of changing** my job. (**NOT** ~~I'm thinking to change my job.~~)*

1 **Change the sentences, using prepositions and *-ing* forms.**

▶ I'm thinking that I might get married. (*thinking of*)
  I'm thinking of getting married.
....

1 I'm thinking that I might go to Australia. (*thinking of*)
....

2 Working with children interests me. (*interested in*)
....

3 I listen to her all day and I'm tired of it. (*tired of*)
....

4 She paints well. (*good at*)
....

5 I'm not a good listener. (*bad at*)
....

6 It was very kind of you to help me. (*Thank you for*)
....

7 I stayed in bed. I didn't go to work. (*instead of*)
....

8 You can't live if you don't eat. (*without*)
....

9 We said we might have a party. (*talk about*)
....

10 He passed the exam although he did no work. (*in spite of*)
....

2 **Write some sentences about yourself using prepositions and *-ing* forms.**

1 I'm thinking of ....
2 I've often thought of ....
3 I've never thought of ....
4 I'm quite good at ....
5 I'm not very good at ....
6 I'm bad at ....
7 I'm interested in ....
8 I'm not interested in ....
9 I couldn't live without ....
10 I could easily live without ....

'This one's for not asking, and this one's for not telling.'

In some answers, both contracted forms (for example *I'm, don't*) and full
forms (for example *I am, do not*) are possible. Normally both are correct.

INFINITIVES AND *-ING* FORMS **119**

more about infinitives: *to sit, to be sitting, ...*

There are **simple**, **progressive**, **perfect** and **passive** infinitives, with and without *to*.

SIMPLE:	*I want **to see** the manager.*	*It may **rain**.*
PROGRESSIVE:	*It's nice **to be sitting** here.*	*You must **be joking**.*
PERFECT:	*I'm glad **to have seen** her.*	*She could **have told** us.*
PASSIVE:	*She likes **to be liked**.*	*It will **be posted** today.*

There are also **perfect progressive** and **perfect passive** infinitives.

PERFECT PROGRESSIVE: *I'd like **to have been sitting** there when she walked in.*
PERFECT PASSIVE: *You could **have been killed**.*

Negative infinitives are made with ***not (to)***.

*Try **not to be** late.* (NOT ~~Try to don't be late.~~)
*I'm sorry **not to have phoned**.   You should **not worry**.*

1 **Put in the right kind of infinitive.**

1 I ought .... right now. (*work*)
2 Your watch will .... by Tuesday. (*repair*)
3 I'd like .... home early today. (*go*)
4 I'd like .... her face when she opened the letter. (*see*)
5 She must .... a shower – I can hear the water running. (*have*)
6 It's important .... to people. (*listen*)
7 She hopes .... for the national team. (*choose*)
8 Try .... back late. (*not be*)
9 You should .... me you were ill. (*tell*)
10 He doesn't like .... while he's working. (*interrupt*)

2 **Say what you think the woman in the pictures is doing.**
Begin *She could/may/must be ... ing* or *She seems to be ... ing*.

▶ ....*She seems to be cycling.*..................................   4 ....
1 ....   5 ....
2 ....   6 ....
3 ....   7 ....

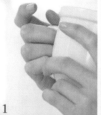

perfect infinitives: *to have gone* etc

Perfect infinitives have the same kind of meaning as **perfect** or **past** tenses.

*I'm glad **to have left** school.* (= '... that **I have left** school.')
*She was sorry **not to have seen** Bill.* (= '... that **she had not seen** Bill.')
*We hope **to have finished** the job soon.* (= '... that **we will have finished** ...')
*I seem **to have annoyed** Anne yesterday.* (= 'It seems that **I annoyed** ...')

1 **Rewrite these sentences using perfect infinitives.**

1 I'm glad I've met you.

....

2 I was sorry I had disturbed him.

....

3 I expect I'll have passed all my exams by June.

....

4 It seems that you made a mistake.
You seem ....

5 I'm happy that I've had a chance to talk to you.

....

6 I was disappointed that I had missed the party.

....

7 It seems that she's got lost.

....

8 She was pleased that she had found the house.

....

With ***was/were*, *would like*** and ***meant*, perfect infinitives** often refer to **unreal situations** that are the opposite of what really happened.

*He **was to have gone** to art college but he fell ill.* (He didn't go.)   *I **meant to have telephoned** but I forgot.*
*I'd **like to have been sitting there** when she walked in.* (I wasn't there.)

2 **Rewrite the sentences.**

▶ She didn't marry a friend of her parents. (*was to*)
  She was to have married a friend of her parents. ....

1 I didn't see his face when he realised what had happened. (*would like to*)

....

2 He didn't finish all his work by three o'clock. (*mean*)

....

3 We didn't spend a week skiing. (*were to*)

....

4 It wasn't the happiest week of my life. (*was to*)

....

5 She didn't say goodbye to everybody before she left. (*mean*)

....

6 I didn't live in the seventeenth century. (*would like*)

....

7 He didn't play in the Cup Final. (*was to*)

....

→ For perfect infinitives after modal verbs (e.g. *should have gone*), see pages 86–88.
→ For perfect infinitives in sentences with *if* (e.g. *would have gone*), see pages 258—259.

In some answers, both contracted forms (for example *I'm*, *don't*) and full forms (for example *I am*, *do not*) are possible. Normally both are correct.

INFINITIVES AND -*ING* FORMS **121**

to for whole infinitive *I'd like to. I don't want to.*

We can use *to* for the infinitive of a **repeated verb**, if the meaning is clear.

'Are you moving?' 'We hope to.' (= … *'We hope to move.'*)
'Come and dance.' 'I don't want to.'
I don't play tennis, but I used to.
'You made Anna cry.' 'I didn't mean to.'

1 **Complete the conversations with sentences from the boxes.**

> 'He seems to.'   'If you'd like to.'   'I'll try to, but I can't promise.'   'I'm sure she didn't mean to.' ✓
> 'No, but I used to.'   'Sorry, I forgot to.'   'Well, I'm starting to.'

▶ 'Alison really upset Granny.'   *'I'm sure she didn't mean to.'* ....
1 'Are you enjoying your new job?' ....
2 'Can I see you home?' ....
3 'Can you mend this by Tuesday?' ....
4 'Did you get my coat from the cleaner's?' ....
5 'Do you collect stamps?' ....
6 'Do you think he knows what he's doing?' ....

> but we can't afford to.   'I don't really want to – it's too cold.'
> 'I intend to. They make far too much noise'   'I'd like to, but I'm working late.'
> 'We don't need to – there's always plenty of room.'   'We'd love to.'   'Yes, she expects to.'

7 'Shall we go swimming?' ....
8 'Do you think she'll win?' ....
9 'How would you and Sue like to spend the weekend with us?'
  ....
10 'You ought to see the police about the people next door.'
  ....
11 'Do you want to come out with us tonight, Peter?
  ....
12 'Shall we book seats in advance?' ....
13 We'd like to move to a bigger house, ...

We **cannot** usually **drop** *to*.

'Come and have a drink.' 'I'd like to.' (**NOT** *I'd like.*)

But we can drop *to* in the expressions *if you like/ want, when you like/want* and *as you like*.

'Can I help?' 'If you like.'   *We'll stop when you want.*

'I can say we live in a fascist state if
I want to. It's a free country.'

-ing forms as subjects, objects etc *Smoking is bad for you*

We often use **-ing forms** as **subjects** – more often than infinitives.

Smoking is bad for you. (More natural than *To smoke is bad for you*.)

We can also use **-ing forms** as **complements** after *be*.

*My favourite activity is **reading**.*

An **-ing form** can have **its own object**.

Smoking cigarettes is bad for you.
*My favourite activity is **reading detective stories**.*

And we can use **-ing forms** as **objects after some verbs** (see page 118).

*I **hate packing**.   I **like watching** ice-hockey.*

① Complete the sentences with -ing forms of the verbs in the box.

answer	climb	drink	forget	hear	learn	lie	pay	say	ski	type	watch

1 .... too much alcohol is very bad for you.
2 I don't like .... bills.
3 He really enjoys .... his own voice.
4 What's wrong with .... in bed all day?
5 Her favourite sports are .... and .... mountains.

6 .... languages is hard work.
7 I hate .... goodbye.
8 .... is sometimes better than remembering.
9 .... animals can teach you a lot.
10 'What's your job?' ' .... the phone and .... letters.'

② Complete the sentence with -ing forms. (Write about yourself.)

My favourite activities are ....

We can use a **determiner** (e.g. *the, this, my*) or a **possessive** before an **-ing** form.

*the rebuilding of the cathedral   What's all **this shouting**?*
*Do you mind **my smoking**?   I don't like **his borrowing** my things without asking.*
John's leaving home upset everybody.

Object forms are possible instead of possessives, especially after a verb or preposition. They are **less formal**.

*I don't like **him borrowing** my things without asking.   She was upset about **him leaving** home.*

③ Make these sentences less formal.

▶ He does not like my asking him questions. *He doesn't like me asking him questions.* ....
1 Do you mind my giving you some advice? ....
2 I do not appreciate your shouting at me. ....
3 I could not understand Toby's wanting to pay for everybody. ....
....
4 What is the use of their asking all these questions? ....
....
5 The delay was caused by Peter's needing to see a doctor. ....
....
6 I was astonished at your expecting us to give you a room. ....
....
7 The holiday was ruined by Ann's having to go home early. ....
....
8 She cannot stand my telling her what to do. ....
....

In some answers, both contracted forms (for example *I'm, don't*) and full forms (for example *I am, do not*) are possible. Normally both are correct.   INFINITIVES AND *-ING* FORMS **123**

more about verb + infinitive or *-ing* form

After these verbs, we use the **infinitives of other verbs**:

agree	dare	fail	happen	plan	prepare	pretend	refuse	wish

*We all **agreed to meet** after the match.*   *If you **happen to see** John, give him my best wishes.*

1 **Rewrite the sentences.**

▶ We said we would wait for a few days. (*agree*)   ...We agreed to wait for a few days....

1 She was afraid to say anything. (*not dare*) ....

2 Columbus did not manage to reach India. (*fail*) ....

3 I saw Annie by chance while I was out shopping. (*happen*) ....
....

4 They are going to build two new hospitals here next year. (*plan*) ....
....

5 I'm getting ready to leave the country. (*prepare*) ....

6 He said he was rich, but it wasn't true. (*pretend*) ....

7 My uncle said he wouldn't lend me any money. (*refuse*) ....
....

8 I would like to see the manager. (*wish*) ....

After these verbs, we use the **-ing forms of other verbs**:

avoid	can't face	can't help	can't stand	deny	feel like	imagine	miss	postpone
put off	risk	succeed in	suggest	think of				

*I **can't face telling** the boss that I'm leaving.*   *Do you **feel like going** out tonight?*
*He's a bit strange, but you **can't help liking** him.*   **Imagine being** able to read minds!*
*I **succeeded in annoying** everybody.* (**NOT** I succeeded to annoy …)
*The doctor **suggested taking** a break from work.* (**NOT** … suggested to take …)
*We're **thinking of moving** to Scotland.* (**NOT** We're thinking to move …)

2 **Complete the sentences with verbs from the box. Use *-ing* forms.**

ask	be	cook	go to sleep	listen to	lose	make	pass	plan
see	spend	study	wake up	work				

1 I don't feel like .... this evening. Let's get a takeaway.

2 I just can't help .... in lectures.

3 Imagine .... married to her!

4 I'll miss .... with you when I change my job.

5 Don't put off .... the doctor. It could be something serious.

6 My brother succeeded in .... his driving test at the eighth attempt.

7 Try to avoid .... the whole house when you come in tonight, can you?

8 If you put your money in John's business, you'll risk .... everything.

9 Stay off the motorway and you'll avoid .... hours stuck in traffic.

10 Can you talk to Patrick? I just can't face .... his problems again.

11 I asked Peter for some advice, and he suggested .... you.

12 I'm thinking of .... Japanese.

13 All three men denied .... to rob the bank.

14 We'll postpone .... a decision until we know what Margaret thinks.

go … ing *She's gone shopping.*

We often use *go … ing* to talk about **sporting** and **leisure** activities (and shopping).

*Let's **go climbing** next weekend.   Did you **go dancing** last Saturday?*
*Are you **going shopping** tomorrow?*

Note the difference between *gone* (= 'still away') and *been* (= 'gone and come back').

*'Where's Alice?' 'She's **gone** shopping.'   'Sorry I'm late. I've **been** shopping.'*

1 Look at the pictures and write what you can do in the different places.

▶ *You can go shopping.*   1 ....   2 ....

3 ....   4 ....   5 ....   6 ....

2 GRAMMAR AND VOCABULARY: activities. Write sentences about yourself.
Use *go … ing* with some of the verbs from the box. Use a dictionary if necessary.

climb	canoe	dance	fish	ride	jog	ride	sail	shop	skate
ski	surf	swim	walk	wind-surf					

1 I often ....

2 I never ....

3 I've never been ....

4 I'd like to ....

5 I don't want to ....

6 Next weekend I might ....

-ing form and infinitive both possible

Some verbs can be followed by both *-ing* forms and infinitives, with different meanings.

1 **DO IT YOURSELF** *Remember, forget* and *regret.* **Look at the examples. Which structure is used to talk about things people did: *-ing* form or infinitive?** ....
Which is used to talk about things people are/were supposed to do? ....

*I still **remember buying** my first bicycle.* **Remember to lock** *the garage door tonight.*
*I'll never **forget meeting** the President.* *I **forgot to buy** the soap.*
*I **regret leaving** school last year.* *We **regret to say** that we are unable to help you.*

Complete sentences 1–5.

1 I remember .... to France when I was three. (*go*)
2 Don't forget .... to Aunt Stacie. (*write*)
3 I don't regret .... my job. (*change*)
4 Did you remember .... the garage bill? (*pay*)
5 We regret .... that the 9.20 train has been cancelled. (*announce*)

2 *Go on.* **Look at the examples. Which structure is used for a change to a new activity?**
.... **Which is used for continuation of an activity?** ....

*She **went on talking** about her illness for hours.* *Then **she went on to talk** about her other problems.*

Complete sentences 1–4.

1 I went on .... until I was tired out. (*run*)
2 They finished talking about money, and went on .... about women. (*talk*)
3 I got a maths diploma, and then went on .... engineering. (*study*)
4 She can happily go on .... the piano for hours. (*play*)

3 *Stop.* **Look at the examples. Which structure says that an activity stops?** ....
Which gives the reason for stopping? ....

*I've **stopped smoking**!* *I **stopped** for a few minutes **to rest**.*

Circle the correct forms.

1 My father says I've got to stop *to see / seeing* you.
2 Before you decide what to do, stop *to think / thinking* for a minute.
3 Stop *to talk / talking* and listen to me, please.
4 We stopped at Coventry *to have / having* a cup of coffee, and then drove straight to York.

4 *Like, love, hate* and *prefer.* **Look at the examples. Both structures can be used except – when?** ....

*Do you like **dancing / to dance**?* *Would you like **to dance**?*
*I don't get up on Sundays. I prefer **staying / to stay** in bed.* *'Can I give you a lift?' 'No, thanks. I would prefer **to walk**.'*
*I hate **criticising / to criticise** people.* *I would hate **to have** her job.*

Circle A, B or both.

1 **A** I'd like to reserve a table. **B** I'd like reserving a table.
2 **A** Most people like singing. **B** Most people like to sing.
3 **A** Would you prefer talking now? **B** Would you prefer to talk now?
4 **A** I don't mind cooking, but I prefer to eat. **B** I don't mind cooking, but I prefer eating.

5 *Allow* and *permit*. Look at the examples. Which structure do we use when there is no object? ....
When there is an object? ....

*We don't **allow/permit smoking**.*   *We don't **allow/permit people to smoke**.*

Circle the correct structures to complete sentences 1–4.

1 I don't allow anybody *to talk / talking* to me like that.
2 Do they allow *to park / parking* in this street?
3 They don't permit *to eat and drink / eating and drinking* in the theatre.
4 We will permit you *to stay / staying* for six months, but not *to work / working*.

6 *See*, *hear*, *watch* and *feel*. These can be followed by object + infinitive without *to*, or by object + *-ing* form. Look at the examples.
Which structure is used to talk about an action going on? ....
Which is used for a completed action? ....

*I **saw** her **pick up** the parcel, **open** it and **take** out a book.*
*I last **saw** him **walking** down the road towards the shops.*
*I **heard** her **play** Bach's A Minor concerto on the radio last night.*
*As we passed his house we **heard** him **practising** the violin.*

Complete the sentences.

1 I looked out of the window and saw a dog .... up my flowers. (*dig*)
2 Can you hear water .... somewhere? (*run*)
3 The police watched him .... the money and then arrested him. (*take*)
4 I didn't see the bomb, but I heard it .... (*explode*)
5 I can feel an insect .... up my leg. (*climb*)
6 I can hear children .... in the street. (*play*)

7 Choose the correct verb forms. (One question has two possible answers.)

1 Do you remember .... Susan last year? (*meet*)
2 Sorry – I forgot .... your letters. (*post*)
3 I regret .... her when she was ill. (*not visit*)
4 We discussed the budget and then went on .... about sales. (*talk*)
5 Do you want to go on .... English, or do you want to stop? (*learn*)
6 He doesn't allow us .... personal phone calls. (*make*)
7 The hospital only allows .... at weekends. (*visit*)
8 I like .... TV in the evenings. (*watch*)
9 Would you like .... the weekend with us? (*spend*)
10 Thanks – I'd love .... (*come*)
11 I saw John .... for a bus as I came home. (*wait*)
12 I heard you .... something – what was it? (*break*)
13 I can feel the rain .... down inside my clothes. (*run*)
14 We'll have to stop .... petrol soon. (*get*)
15 He stopped .... when he was sixty-five. (*work*)
16 I regret .... you that you have failed your examination. (*tell*)

verb + object + infinitive *He wants me to wash his socks.*

Some verbs can be followed by **object + infinitive**, for example *want*.

*He **wants me to wash** his socks.* (**NOT** *He wants that I wash his socks.*)

1 **Complete the sentences about Mary, using … *want(s) her to* … with words from the box. (Different answers are possible.)**

do something	buy her a car	buy him some new clothes	cook supper	go to church
leave her husband	pay his bill	pay taxes	take him for a walk	work harder

▶ *Everybody wants her to do something.* ....

1 Her boss ....

2 Her daughter ....

3 Her husband ....

4 Her mother ....

5 Her son ....

6 The butcher ....

7 The dog ....

8 The government ....

9 The priest ....

Other verbs that can be followed by **object + infinitive**:
advise, allow, ask, can't bear, cause, encourage, expect, forbid, force, get, help, invite, leave, mean, need, order, persuade, prefer, remind, teach, tell, warn, would like.

*I **expect Maggie to be** here soon.*   *We **need somebody to help** in the garden.*
*I **would prefer you not to use** my computer.*   *She **doesn't allow anybody to see** her room.*

2 **Change the sentences.**

▶ I told John, 'I think you should stop smoking.' (*advise*) ...*I advised John to stop smoking.*...........

1 They said we couldn't look at the house. (*didn't allow*)

....

2 I said to Jake, 'Please be more careful.' (*ask*)

....

3 She said to me, 'Do try the exam.' (*encourage*)

....

4 I think he'll come tomorrow. (*expect*)

....

5 I went away, so he had to solve the problem. (*I left …*)

....

6 Was it your idea that I should pay? (*Did you mean …*)

....

7 The captain told the men, 'Attack!' (*order*)

....

8 'Don't forget to buy coffee,' I told Sue. (*remind*)

....

9 She gave me cooking lessons. (*teach*)

....

10 Don't tell anybody. (*I would prefer …*)

....

Let and **make** are followed by **object + infinitive without to**.

*Don't **let me forget** to phone Jill.*   *His father **lets him do** what he likes.*
*The customs officer **made me open** all my bags.*   *You **make me laugh**.*

3 ***Let*** or ***make*?** **Make sentences beginning *Her parents let her …* or *Her parents made her …***

▶ stay up late   *Her parents let her stay up late.*
▶ help with the housework   *Her parents made her help with the housework.*
1 do the washing up   ....
2 clean up her room   ....
3 read what she liked   ....
4 iron her own clothes   ....
5 do her homework   ....
6 drink beer   ....
7 go to church   ....
8 have parties   ....
9 choose her own school   ....

5 **What did your parents *let / not let / make / not make* you do when you were young?**
1 ....
2 ....
3 ....
4 ....

6 **Complete one or more of these sentences.**
1 My parents want(ed) me to   ....
2 My parents don't / didn't want me
....
3 I would like my children   ....

7 **Complete the cartoon caption with the correct structure.**

'I'm not asking (*you serve*) .... me –
just to include me in your conversation.'

In some answers, both contracted forms (for example *I'm*, *don't*) and full
forms (for example *I am*, *do not*) are possible. Normally both are correct.

INFINITIVES AND *-ING* FORMS **129**

adjective + infinitive or *-ing* form *pleased to see* etc

Many **adjectives** can be followed by **infinitives**. This is common when we are talking about **feelings and reactions**.

*She was very **pleased to see** me.*   *I'm **sorry to disturb** you.*

1 DO IT YOURSELF **Thirteen of the adjectives in the box can be used in the sentence
I was … to see her. For example: *I was afraid to see her*. Which four cannot?**

afraid	anxious	fine	glad	happy	lazy	likely	lucky	ready	right	shocked
sorry	surprised	unusual	well	willing	wrong					

1 .... 　 2 .... 　 3 .... 　 4 ....

2 **Change the sentences, using adjective + infinitive.**

▶ I didn't want to open the door. I was afraid. *I was afraid to open the door.* ....

1 We got home. We were glad. ....

2 It's time to go. Are you ready? ....

3 We got tickets. We were lucky. ....

4 Lucy got a letter from Pete. She was surprised. ....
....

5 I heard about your accident. I was shocked. ....
....

6 I'll help you. I'll be happy to do so. ....

7 What about working at weekends? Are you willing? ....
....

8 You asked for my advice. You were right. ....

9 I believed what you said. I was wrong. ....

10 I'm late. I'm sorry. ....

Some other adjectives are followed by **preposition + *-ing* form**.

*I think Gomez is **capable of winning**.*   *I'm **bored with listening** to Eric's problems.*

3 **Make sentences with verbs from the box.**

▶ I have to work tonight. (*angry about*) *I'm angry about having to work tonight.* ....

1 Camels can go without water for a long time. (*capable of*) ....
....

2 I don't remember names easily. (*bad at*) ....

3 I go to business meetings. (*bored with*) ....

4 We're seeing our Greek friends next weekend. (*excited about*) ....
....

5 Anna has to do all the housework. (*annoyed at*) ....
....

6 I sit in the garden doing nothing. (*fond of*) ....

7 I see the same faces every day. (*fed up with*) ....
....

8 My brother works in a bank. (*tired of*) ....

9 Josh broke the speed limit. (*guilty of*) ....

noun + infinitive or -*ing* form *time to go; fear of flying*

> Some **nouns** can be followed by **infinitives**.
> Examples: *decision*, *need*, *plan*, *time*, *wish*.

*Who made the **decision to close** the factory?*   *Is there any **need to tell** Jessica?*
*I've made a **plan to save** money.*   *It's **time to go**.*   *I have no **wish to stay**.* (very formal)

> Other **nouns** can be followed by **preposition + -*ing***.
> Examples: *difficulty in*, *fear of*, *hope of*, *the idea of*, *the thought of*.

*I have **difficulty in staying** awake in lectures.* (**NOT** ~~I have difficulty to stay~~ …)
***Fear of flying** is very common.*   *I got there early in the **hope of finding** a seat.*
*I don't like the **idea of getting** old.* (**NOT** … ~~the idea to get old.~~)

1 (Circle) the correct form.

1 Has she told you about her decision *to go / of going* ?
2 I have difficulty *to read / in reading* quickly.
3 We have no hope *to arrive / of arriving* in time.
4 I hate the idea *to leave / of leaving* you.
5 There's no need *to reserve / of reserving* a table.
6 She has a plan *to spend / of spending* three years studying.
7 I won't get married: I dislike the thought *to lose / of losing* my freedom.
8 It's time *to get / for getting* ready.
9 I have no wish *to meet / of meeting* him again.

2 Complete the sentences with expressions from the box. Use infinitives or -*ing* forms, and put in prepositions where necessary.

> die   fly   get angry   get up   give   keep her temper   pass his exam ✓
> start a business   think before I speak

▶ Has your brother got any hope ...*of passing his exam?*..
1 I've made a decision ....
2 Does your fear .... stop you travelling?
3 Lucy has difficulty ....
4 She hated the thought .... without seeing the world.
5 Relax – there's no need ....
6 John and Maggie have a plan ....
7 It's time..
8 Who had the idea .... Peter a saxophone for Christmas?

---

some irrational **fears**, with their scientific names

fear of flying: *aviophobia*

fear of spiders: *arachnophobia*

fear of washing: *ablutophobia*

fear of being in high places: *acrophobia*

fear of open or crowded spaces:
  agoraphobia

fear of crossing the road: *agyrophobia*

fear of being in small closed spaces:
  claustrophobia

fear of getting old: *gerascophobia*

fear of being looked at: *scopophobia*

fear of being laughed at: *gelotophobia*

In some answers, both contracted forms (for example *I'm, don't*) and full forms (for example *I am, do not*) are possible. Normally both are correct.

INFINITIVES AND -*ING* FORMS **131**

more about noun/pronoun + infinitive *nothing to wear*

We can use **infinitives after nouns** to talk about things that we **can** or **must** do.

*I've got some **work to do** this evening.*   *Sorry – I haven't got any **food to offer** you.*

1 **Complete the sentences with the expressions from the boxes. Use infinitives.**

| clothes | complaint | information | letter | message | piece of music ✓ | potatoes |

| give | make | pass on | peel | practise ✓ | wash | write |

▶ I've got a really difficult ..*piece of music to practise*.. this week.
1 'Can I help with supper?' 'Yes, there are some ....'
2 I'd like to see the manager. I have a ....
3 I saw Angela, and she gave me a .... to Sarah.
4 I can't come out tonight. I've got an important ....
5 Every time I finish washing clothes, there are more ....
6 Have you got any new .... me about the conference dates?

We can use **infinitives with *to*** after words like *somebody, anything* and *nowhere*.

*Would you like **something to eat**?*   *I'm not going out; I haven't got **anything to wear**.*
*There's **nothing to drink** in the house.*   *Those people have **nowhere to go**.*

2 **Complete the sentences with *somebody* etc and the verbs *in italics*.**

▶ I looked out of the window, but there was (*see*) ..*nothing to see.*..........
1 I'm bored. There's (*do*) .... in this place.
2 Is there a chair free? I need (*sit*) ....
3 I couldn't find (*stay*) .... in the town.
4 I need (*help*) .... me with the accounts.
5 Can you wait a few minutes? I've got (*finish*) ....
6 Is there (*eat*) .... in the fridge?
7 The shops are empty – there's almost (*buy*) ....
8 I need (*read*) .... Have you got a newspaper?
9 'I don't understand what you want.' 'There's (*understand*) ....'
10 'I need (*sleep*) ....' 'You can use my bedroom.'

Tomorrow is another day

We couldn't get into our new home until the evening, because the previous owners had taken all day to move out. And when we finally did get in, there was so much to do: boxes to unpack, children and animals to feed, bedding to find and beds to make. And of course nobody could remember which boxes things had been packed in. When we'd finally got the children to bed, Jenny and I sat down and started making a list which just got longer and longer. The thing is, it wasn't really a 'new' home at all; it was an old house that had been neglected for years. There were five dirty rooms to clean up and decorate; windows to replace; plumbing, electrics and central heating to sort out; a whole lot of furniture to buy; and a real jungle of a garden to clear and plant. And for the kids: school and all the usual activities to organise. I looked at Jennie, she looked at me, I put the list down, I said 'Tomorrow is another day,' and we dragged ourselves off to bed.

(*James Eliot*)

for ... to ... *It's time for the postman to come.*

After an adjective or a noun, if an **infinitive** needs **its own subject** this is introduced by *for*. Compare:

Ann will be happy **to help** you.   Ann will be happy **for the children to help** you.
My idea was **to learn** Russian.   My idea was **for her to learn** Russian.

This structure is common after adjectives and nouns when we are talking about **possibility**, **necessity**, **importance** and **frequency**.

It's **impossible for Jane to get** here before Wednesday.
Is there any **need for Robert to work** this weekend?
I'm **anxious for everybody to say** what they think.
It's unusual **for foxes to come** so close to the house.

1 **Rewrite these sentences using *for ... to ...***

▶ She can't come. (*it's impossible*)
   It's impossible for her to come.

1 The meeting needn't start before eight. (*There's no need*)
   ....

2 The postman ought to come. (*It's time*)
   ....

3 He's not usually late. (*It's unusual for him*)
   ....

4 I want the children to go to a good school. (*I'm anxious*)
   ....

5 John shouldn't go to Australia. (*It's a bad idea*)
   ....

6 Tanya shouldn't change her job just now. (*It would be a mistake*)
   ....

7 Can Paul come to the meeting? (*Is it possible*)
   ....

8 The car really should have regular services. (*It's important*)
   ....

9 He normally stays up late on Saturdays. (*It's normal*)
   ....

10 I'd be happy if you took a holiday. (*I'd be happy for*)
   ....

2 **Give your opinions about teachers. Write sentences beginning *It's very important*, *It's important*, *It's not very important* or *It's unnecessary*. Use *for ... to ...***

▶ (*know their subject*) *It's very important for teachers to know their subject.* ....
1 (*be able to dance*) ....
2 (*be good listeners*) ....
3 (*be able to draw*) ....
4 (*speak clearly*) ....
5 (*like people*) ....
6 (*be good-looking*) ....
7 (*be patient*) ....
8 (*have lots of energy*) ....
9 (*have a good sense of humour*) ....

In some answers, both contracted forms (for example *I'm*, *don't*) and full
forms (for example *I am*, *do not*) are possible. Normally both are correct.

INFINITIVES AND -*ING* FORMS **133**

more about adjective + infinitive *easy to please* etc

After some adjectives, we can use an **infinitive** to mean **'for people to …'**.

*She's **easy to amuse**.* (= 'She's easy for people to amuse', 'People can amuse her easily.')
*Just open the packet, and it's **ready to eat**.*

Other adjectives like this: *difficult, hard, impossible, good, nice, interesting.*

① **Make some sentences from the table.**

English Chinese small children silver boiled eggs lobster maths modern music *etc (your ideas)*	is/are	easy hard difficult nice impossible good interesting boring	to	please amuse understand clean listen to watch cook eat drink read learn *etc (your ideas)*

▶ ....Small children are easy to amuse. ....
....
....
....
....
....
....
....
....

② **GRAMMAR AND VOCABULARY: school subjects**

Make sure you know the words in the box. Use a dictionary if necessary. Then write five or more sentences to say what you think about some of the subjects.

biology   chemistry   English   geography   history   literature mathematics / maths (singular)   philosophy

1 .... is easy to learn.
2 .... is hard to learn.
3 .... is easy to understand.
4 .... is difficult to understand.
5 .... is interesting to study.
6 ....
7 ....
8 ....

before, after, since, by and for + -ing

After *before*, *after* and *since*, we can use **subject + verb** or an *-ing* form.

*I usually read the paper **before** I go to work OR **before** going to work.*
*Zoë always felt better **after** she had talked to Pete OR **after** talking to Pete.*
*Stephen has changed a lot **since** he got married OR **since** getting married.*

1 Rewrite the expressions *in italics*, using *-ing* forms.

▶ Jack usually has a cup of hot milk *before he goes to bed*.   *before going to bed* ....

1 I always wash my hair *after I swim*. ....

2 *Since she passed her exam*, Cynthia has seemed much happier. ....

3 We always phone Aunt Jane *before we visit her*. ....

4 My grandmother was never really well *after she broke her leg*. ....

5 *Before he crashed his car*, Luke always drove too fast. ....

6 Emma's bought a lot of new clothes *since she got her new job*. ....

2 Complete this sentence about yourself.

After leaving school, I ....

We use *by … ing* to say **how** – by what **method** or **means** – we do something.

*You can find out somebody's phone number **by looking** in the directory.*
*He made his money **by buying** and selling houses.*

3 Find the answers in the box; write them with *by … ing*.

| look in a dictionary   oil it   play loud music   rob a bank   stroke it ✓ |
| switch on the ignition   take an aspirin   use an extinguisher |

▶ How do you make a cat happy?   *By stroking it.* ....

1 How do you start a car? ....

2 How can you annoy your neighbours? ....

3 How can you get money fast? ....

4 How do you stop a door squeaking? ....

5 How do you find out what a word means? ....

6 How can you cure a headache? ....

7 How can you put a fire out? ....

We use *for … ing* to give the **purpose** of something – to say what it is used for.

*I've bought some special glue **for mending** broken glass.*
*'What's that funny knife **for**?' 'Opening letters.'*

4 Write sentences to say what these things are for: a telephone, a paperclip, soap,
a saucepan, a knife, money, a hairbrush, a pen, a bag.

A telephone is for talking to people who are a long way away. ....
....
....
....
....
....

In some answers, both contracted forms (for example *I'm, don't*) and full
forms (for example *I am, do not*) are possible. Normally both are correct.

to ...ing *I look forward to seeing you.*

The **preposition** *to* is followed by an *-ing* form.

*I look forward **to your letter** / **to hearing** from you.* (*To* is a preposition used after *look forward* – it can be followed by a noun or an *-ing* form.)

Compare:

*I **hope to hear** from you.* (*To* is part of the infinitive after *hope*, not a preposition – it couldn't be followed by a noun. You couldn't say ~~I hope to your letter.~~)

Other expressions followed by *to … ing*: **be/get used to**, **object to**.

*If you come to England you'll soon **get used to driving** on the left.*
*I **object to** strangers **telephoning** me.*

1 DO IT YOURSELF **Choose the best explanation of each expression.**

1 **I look forward to seeing you.**
   A It gives me pleasure to think that I will see you.   B I know I will see you.   C I hope I will see you.

2 **I'm used to driving in London.**
   A I drive in London regularly.   B In the past, I drove in London regularly.
   C I have driven in London so often that it seems easy and natural.

3 **I object to paying good money for badly made products.**
   A This often happens to me.   B I am not pleased when this happens.   C I try to stop this happening.

2 **These are sentences taken from real conversations. Complete them with verbs from the box, using *to … ing*.**

come   deal   get up   go away   have   pay   receive   see   sleep   walk

1 Aren't you used .... this far?
2 I look forward .... your comments.
3 I'm not sure where to turn. I'm not used .... this way.
4 Starting at half four's no problem. I'm used .... early.
5 I object .... for it. It should be free.
6 I look forward .... you again.
7 Sean's used .... with difficult kids.
8 I'll never get used .... on the floor.
9 If you're used .... money, it's hard to be without it.
10 I'm not looking forward .... in six months' time.

3 **Write two things that you're *used to doing*, two things that you're *not used to doing*, two things that you *look forward to doing*, two things that you *don't look forward to doing*, and two things that you *object to doing*.**

....
....
....
....
....
....
....
....

→ For *used to* + infinitive (e.g. *I **used to be** shy when I was younger*), see page 84.

infinitives and *-ing* forms: more practice

1 Kinds of infinitive. **Choose the right kind of infinitive.**

1 I would like .... on the beach right now. (*to lie, to be lying, to have lain*)
2 Her office is locked. She must .... home. (*go, be going, have gone*)
3 I don't like .... for money by strangers. (*to ask, to be asking, to be asked*)
4 I want .... a holiday next week. (*to take, to be taking, to have taken*)
5 I'm so pleased .... your family last weekend. (*to meet, to have met, to be met*)
6 You seem .... everything I said. (*to misunderstand, to have misunderstood, to be misunderstood*)
7 Your car will .... by Tuesday. (*repair, be repairing, be repaired*)
8 I meant .... the painting this morning. (*to be finished, to have finished, to be finishing*)
9 You should .... us you were in London. (*tell, be telling, have told*)
10 I'd love .... his face when he opened the letter. (*to see, to have seen, to be seeing*)

2 Preposition + *-ing*. **Make ten or more sentences from the table.**

Are you interested		answering that child's questions
I got the money		changing her job, but I don't think she will
I've been much happier	about	coming to Greece with us?
I like to sit and read the paper	as well as	convincing the police that she was not a burglar
He passed his exams	at	cooking
I apologise	besides	disturbing you
I like walking	for	eating
I sometimes dream	in	having time to read all my books
I'm fed up	in spite of	moving to Canada
I'm not capable	instead of	not doing any work
I'm tired	by	playing football
She succeeded	of	selling things
She talks	since	staying at home?
This key is	with	leaving home
Always look in the mirror	without	telling me the truth
Thank you	before	understanding this – it's too difficult
You can't live	after	unlocking the windows
We're thinking		driving off
Why don't you come out with us		getting home in the evening

▶ *Are you interested in coming to Greece with us?* ....
....
....
....
....
....
....
....
....
....

In some answers, both contracted forms (for example *I'm, don't*) and full forms (for example *I am, do not*) are possible. Normally both are correct.

INFINITIVES AND -*ING* FORMS 137

3 *To used for whole infinitive.* Write your own answers to the following questions, using *I'd love to, I'd like to, I wouldn't like to* or *I'd hate to.*

1 Would you like to go to the moon? ....
2 Would you like to have ten children? ....
3 Would you like to live on a boat? ....
4 Would you like to spend your life travelling? ....
5 Would you like to be a bird? ....
6 Would you like to be President of your country? ....
7 Would you like to be a professional singer? ....
8 Would you like to be rich and famous? ....
9 Would you like to be able to read people's minds? ....
10 Would you like to work in a bank? ....

4 **Adjective + infinitive.** Make sentences with the infinitives of verbs from the box.

| clean   climb   dislike   eat   find   find   open   pronounce   remember ✓ |
| understand   wear |

▶ My phone number / easy   *My phone number is easy to remember.* ....
1 Their house / hard ....
2 Grammar / sometimes difficult ....
3 That mountain / impossible ....
4 This shirt / nice ....
5 The word 'sixth' / hard ....
6 This furniture / easy ....
7 My uncle / impossible ....
8 Those apples / not good ....
9 Good restaurants / not easy ....
10 The front door / difficult ....

5 **Mixed structures.** Correct or not? Correct the mistakes or write 'Correct'.

▶ I agreed ~~paying~~ in advance.   *..to pay.....*
▶ He never stops talking about himself.
   .Correct..
1 She's strange, but you can't help liking her.
   ....
2 I was glad seeing Joe yesterday. ....
3 I suggested to meet on Friday. ....
4 Sophie's not capable of telling a lie. ....
5 Did you succeed to get your visa? ....
6 I'll never forget meeting the Prince. ....
7 I hate the thought to get old. ....
8 I'm very sorry telling you this. ....
9 Can you hear the rain fall on the roof?
   ....

10 They don't allow smoking here. ....
11 I have difficulty in understanding her.
   ....
12 I'm tired to cook every evening. ....
13 They refused paying for my taxi. ....
14 I don't feel like to work today. ....
15 Can you imagine being a bird? ....
16 I've got a lot of letters for writing. ....
17 We're thinking to go to Italy in June.
   ....
18 Everybody was surprised to see us. ....
19 Do you mind my smoking? ....
20 I look forward to seeing you soon. ....

6 **Complete the sentences with your own ideas.**

▶ I would like ...*everybody*...... to ...*sing all the time.*...
1 I would like .... to ....
2 I don't want .... to ....
3 I would hate .... to ....

7 Grammar in a text. Complete the poem with the infinitives of the verbs in the box.

| ask go go keep stop watch |

STOPPING BY WOODS ON A SNOWY EVENING

Whose woods these are I think I know.
His house is in the village though;
He will not see me stopping here
¹ .... his woods fill up with snow.

My little horse must think it queer
² .... without a farmhouse near
Between the woods and frozen lake
The darkest evening of the year.

He gives his harness bells a shake
³ .... if there is some mistake.
The only other sound's the sweep
Of easy wind and downy flake.

The woods are lovely, dark and deep.
But I have promises ⁴ ....,
And miles ⁵ .... before I sleep,
And miles ⁶ .... before I sleep.

(*Robert Frost*)

8 Choose the correct forms to complete the cartoon captions.

'I don't want *to go / going* to their party and *have / having* a good time. I don't enjoy *to have / having* a good time.'

'He has nothing *to do / to be done*. All his batteries have run down.'

9 Internet exercise. Use a search engine (e.g. Google) to find five simple sentences beginning "We want people to". Write them below.

....
....
....
....
....

infinitives and *-ing* forms: revision test

1 **Circle the correct form.**

▶ I'm no good *to sing* / (*at singing*).

1 Jane's fed up *to cook* / *with cooking*.

2 Do you feel like *go* / *going* / *to go* for a walk?

3 It's time *to stop* / *for stopping* work.

4 I'm planning *to sell* / *selling* / *for selling* my house soon.

5 We're thinking *to travel* / *of travelling* round Europe by bus.

6 I hate the idea *to go* / *of going* to the dentist.

7 We all agreed *to help Andy* / *helping Andy*.

8 If you happen *to see* / *seeing* Anna, give her my best wishes.

9 They succeeded *to climb* / *climbing* / *in climbing* the mountain at the third attempt.

10 I sometimes dream *to fly* / *of fly* / *of flying*.

11 Nobody wants *you lose* / *you to lose* / *that you lose* your job.

12 'Come here!' 'I don't *want* / *want to*.'

13 I wish *to see* / *seeing* the manager.

14 We're all tired *to study* / *of studying*.

15 Their house is *easy to find* / *easy to find it* / *easy finding*.

16 We're all looking forward *to see* / *to seeing* / *seeing* our families again.

17 You can't live without *eat* / *to eat* / *eating*.

18 I always put off *to go* / *going* to bed.

19 My father is always glad *to help* / *helping* / *at helping*.

20 I'm just not capable *to draw* / *to drawing* / *drawing* / *of drawing*.

2 **Which continuation is correct – A, B or both?**

▶ I like **A** to play golf. **B** playing golf. (**C**) both

▶ We hope (**A**) to see you soon. **B** seeing you soon. **C** both

1 I always have a cup of tea **A** before I go to bed. **B** before going to bed. **C** both

2 Please remember **A** to buy milk. **B** buying milk. **C** both

3 She learnt English mostly **A** by talk to people. **B** by talking to people. **C** both

4 I want **A** everybody to be here tomorrow. **B** everybody is here tomorrow. **C** both

5 I'll never forget **A** to have met you. **B** meeting you. **C** both

6 What would you like **A** to do now? **B** to be doing now? **C** both

7 I'm sorry **A** to be woken you up. **B** to have woken you up. **C** both

8 It's important **A** to tell everybody. **B** for you to tell everybody. **C** both

9 Please tell that child to stop **A** to scream. **B** screaming. **C** both

10 We visited Cambridge and then went on **A** to see Oxford. **B** seeing Oxford. **C** both

11 Would you like **A** dancing? **B** to dance? **C** both

12 I feel much better since **A** I talked to Roger. **B** talking to Roger. **C** both

13 What on earth is that? It's **A** for to clean leather. **B** for cleaning leather. **C** both

14 I don't remember **A** to have learnt to read. **B** learning to read. **C** both

15 She refused **A** to let me pay. **B** letting me pay. **C** both

16 Do you mind **A** me using your phone? **B** my using your phone? **C** both

17 It's impossible **A** John gets here in time. **B** for John to get here in time. **C** both

18 You were right **A** to go to the police. **B** going to the police. **C** both

19 May I suggest **A** to take a short break? **B** taking a short break? **C** both

20 I was very surprised **A** to see you here. **B** seeing you here. **C** both

In some answers, both contracted forms (for example *I'm, don't*) and full forms (for example *I am, do not*) are possible. Normally both are correct.

SECTION 10 various structures with verbs

GRAMMAR SUMMARY

Several different structures are practised in this section:

- **imperatives**
  Write your address here.

- *let's*
  Let's go and see Fred.

- **verbs with two objects**
  *Can you **send me the details**?*

- **causative structures with** *have* **and** *get*
  *I must **have my watch repaired**.*   *We need to **get the curtains cleaned**.*

- **exclamations**
  What a fool!   *How strange!*   *Isn't she sweet!*

- **emphatic** *do*
  *You **do** look nice.*   ***Do** sit down.*   *I said I was going to win, and I **did** win.*

- **structures with preparatory** *it* **and** *what*
  ***It's** strange that she hasn't phoned.*   ***It's** not tea I want, it's coffee.*
  ***What** I need is a drink.*

- **phrasal verbs**
  *My car has **broken down**.*

Note that we introduce phrasal verbs, but we do not give long lists of them. We think it's best to learn phrasal verbs like other words, one at a time as they are needed. In our opinion grouping them together, as some grammars do, only causes confusion.

For prepositional verbs, see pages 298–299.

'When it is not necessary to change, it is necessary not to change.'

(*Lucius Cary*)

'It was such a lovely day I thought it was a pity to get up.'

(*W Somerset Maugham*)

'It's easy to see the faults in people I know; it is hardest to see the good, especially when the good isn't there.'

(*Will Cuppy*)

'Anybody who has ever struggled with poverty knows how extremely expensive it is to be poor.'

(*James Baldwin*)

'It is impossible to enjoy idling thoroughly unless one has plenty of work to do.'

(*Jerome K Jerome*)

revise the basics: imperatives; *let's*

We use **imperatives** to tell people what to do, advise them, encourage them etc. Imperatives look the same as **infinitives without to**.

Look in the mirror before you drive off.   *Try again.*   *Have some more tea.*

Negative imperatives begin with *do not/don't*. (Note: these can be used before *be*.)

Please do not lean out of the window.   *Don't worry.*   *Don't be silly!*

Note the position of *always* and *never* before imperatives.

Always try to tell the truth. (**NOT** ~~Try always~~ ...)   *Never do that again.*

1 **Choose the best way of completing each sentence.**

▶ (*Always add*) / *Never add* salt to potatoes when you cook them.
1 *Always check* / *Check always* the tyres before you drive a car.
2 *Believe* / *Don't believe* everything that people say.
3 *Always cook* / *Never cook* chicken when it's frozen.
4 *Wait* / *Don't wait* more than fifteen minutes for somebody who's late.
5 *Always unplug* / *Unplug always* electrical appliances before repairing them.
6 *Count* / *Don't count* your change after buying something.
7 *Always put off* / *Never put off* till tomorrow what you can do today.
8 *Always say* / *Never say* 'I will love you for ever'.
9 *Be not* / *Don't be* afraid.

We can use *let's* (or *let us* – very formal) + **infinitive without to** to make **suggestions** or give **orders** to a group that **includes the speaker**.

Let's have a drink.   *Let's stay in this evening.*

The normal **negative** is *Let's not* ... ; *Don't let's* ... is informal; *Let us not* is very formal.

Let's not tell Granny what happened.

2 **Write the suggestions, using *Let's (not)*.**

▶ .....Let's go swimming.....................
1 ....
2 ....
3 ....
4 ....
5 ....

6 ....
7 ....
8 ....
9 ....
10 ....

Note also the common expressions *let me see* and *let me think*.

*So what time will I get there? **Let me see** – suppose I start at half past six ...*
*What am I going to wear? **Let me think** – it's too cold for the black dress ...*

revise the basics: verbs with two objects

COMMON VERBS WITH TWO OBJECTS:
bring buy cost get give leave lend make offer owe pass pay play promise read refuse send show sing take teach tell wish write

Many verbs can have **two objects** – one direct and one indirect. Usually the **indirect object refers** to a **person**, and this often **comes first**.

*He gave **his wife a camera**.   I wish **you a Merry Christmas**.*

If we put the **indirect object last**, we use a preposition (usually **to** or **for**).

*I passed my licence **to the policeman**.   Mum bought the ice cream **for you**, not for me.*

1 Change the structure.

▶ I gave my sister some flowers. *I gave some flowers to my sister.*

▶ Let me make you some tea. *Let me make some tea for you.*

1 Could you send me the bill? ....

2 I've bought a present for you. ....

3 Leave me some potatoes. ....

4 I lent Henry £5 yesterday. ....

5 Show Granny your picture. ....

6 Read the letter to me, will you? ....

7 She teaches adults French. ....

8 I took the report to Mrs Samuels. ....

9 Would you get me a beer? ....

10 We owe £20,000 to the bank. ....

11 I offered the class free tickets. ....

12 I wrote a letter to the doctor. ....

13 Sing the children a song. ....

14 Can you bring the newspaper to me? ....

15 Pay Mrs Jones €200, please. ....

2 Write about yourself: complete the sentences, using two objects.

▶ *I would like to send my mother some flowers.*

1 I would like to buy ....

2 I never lend ....

3 I must write ....

4 I think it's difficult to teach ....

5 Nobody has ever given ....

Explain, say, suggest and *describe* do **not** have the **indirect object first**.

*Can you **explain the plan** to us?* (**NOT** ~~Can you explain us the plan?~~)
*I've come to **say goodbye** to you.* (**NOT** … ~~to say you goodbye.~~)
*I suggested **a new method** to her.* (**NOT** ~~I suggested her a new method.~~)
*Describe **your wife** to me.* (**NOT** ~~Describe me your wife.~~)

Ronald Searle

'Get me the Zoo, please,
Miss Winterton.'

In some answers, both contracted forms (for example *I'm*, *don't*) and full forms (for example *I am*, *do not*) are possible. Normally both are correct.

VARIOUS STRUCTURES WITH VERBS **143**

revise the basics: causative *have* and *get*

Have/Get something done: arrange for something to be done.

*I must **have my watch repaired**.   We need to **get the curtains cleaned**.*

1 GRAMMAR AND VOCABULARY: doing things to things. Make sentences using *have* or *get* + object + the past participles in the box. Use a dictionary to help you.

changed	cleaned	cut ✓	print	put in	redecorated	repaired	reproofed
re-strung	serviced	sharpened	unblocked	valued			

▶ When did you last (*your hair*)?
   When did you last have/get your hair cut?

1 It would be nice to (*some more electric sockets*).

2 We (*our knives*) once a year.

3 We're going to (*the roof*) next summer.

4 I must (*my jacket*). And I'd better (*my raincoat*).

5 'Do we need to (*the car*)?' 'Well, we ought to (*the oil*).'

6 When she (*her jewellery*), she found it wasn't actually worth much.

7 You need to (*your tennis racket*).

8 Shall we (*the kitchen*), or shall we do it ourselves?

9 I need to (*some business cards*)

10 The water isn't running away. We must (*the drains*)

2 John has a lot of problems. Why does he have them? Use *He hasn't had ...*

▶ His hair is much too long.   *He hasn't had it cut.*
1 His raincoat doesn't keep him dry.
2 His clothes are dirty.
3 His car's running very badly.
4 His knives won't cut.
5 His roof has got holes in.
6 The rooms in his flat are dark and dirty.
7 He can't see through the windows.

exclamations *How beautiful! What a surprise!*

Exclamations with *how* and *what* are constructed differently.

HOW + ADJECTIVE	WHAT (+ ADJECTIVE) + NOUN
How beautiful!	What a beautiful day!
How stupid!	What a fool!
How strange they are!	What strange people they are!

We do not drop articles after *What*.

What a stupid idea! (**NOT** ~~What stupid idea!~~)

1 **Change the sentences into exclamations with *how* or *what*.**

▶ That's a strange picture. *..........What a strange..........*
..picture!..

▶ That's interesting. *.....How interesting!.........*

1 Those are beautiful flowers. ....
....

2 That's a nuisance. ....

3 That's terrible. ....

4 It's boring. ....

5 That's a stupid hat. ....

6 He's a star. ....

2 **DO IT YOURSELF** **In exclamations with verbs, what is the order of the following?**

A expression with *how/what*   **B** verb   **C** subject

Look at the examples and complete the rule.

How beautiful she is! (**NOT** ~~How she is beautiful!~~)
How hard he works! (**NOT** ~~How he works hard!~~)
What a lot of languages your sister speaks!

RULE FOR WORD ORDER IN EXCLAMATIONS WITH VERBS

1	2	3

3 **Change the sentences into exclamations with *how* or *what* and verbs.**

▶ Those children are noisy. *How noisy those children are!*
....

▶ You've got big eyes, grandmother. *What big eyes you've got, grandmother!*
....

1 He cooks well. ....

2 We were wrong. ....

3 He talks a lot of nonsense. ....

4 She wears funny clothes. ....

5 She plays badly. ....

6 I was a fool. ....

We can use **negative questions** (see page 111) as exclamations.

Isn't she beautiful!   **Doesn't he** work hard!   **Wasn't it** a surprise!

4 **Change the sentences from Exercise 3 into exclamations with negative questions.**

▶ *Aren't those children noisy!*
....

▶ *Haven't you got big eyes, grandmother!*
....

1 ....

2 ....

3 ....

4 ....

5 ....

6 ....

do: emphatic auxiliary *You do look nice.*

Emotive emphasis: we can use *do* to make an expression **sound stronger**. *Do be* is possible in imperatives.

*You **do** look nice today!*   *I **did** enjoy our talk.*   ***Do** sit down.*   ***Do** be careful.*

1 **Complete the sentences with expressions from the box, and make them more emphatic by using *do/does/did*.**

a lot   early tonight   cooking   disturbing you   ill ✓   John my love   the party with you   hairstyle

▶ I feel   *I do feel ill.* ....
1 I agree ....
2 I apologise for ....
3 I hate ....
4 Peter enjoyed ....

5 Alice talks ....
6 Be home ....
7 Give ....
8 I like your ....

Contrastive emphasis: we can use *do* to show a **contrast** – between false and true, appearance and reality, or a general statement and an exception.

*She thinks I don't love her, but I **do** love her.*
*It looks easy, but it **does** need quite a bit of practice.*
*There wasn't much time for shopping, but I **did** buy a couple of shirts.*

We can also use *do* to compare what is **expected** with what actually **happens**.

*I said I was going to win, and I **did** win.*

2 **These sentences and conversations have the wrong ends. Sort them out, and add *do/does/did* to express contrast.**

▶ I've forgotten her name,   but I know something about life.
  I've forgotten her name, but I do remember it began with a B ....

1 I'll be ready in a minute,   ~~but I remember it began with a B.~~
  ....

2 'You don't love me.'   They said eight o'clock, didn't they?
  ....

3 I may not be educated,   'I love you.'
  ....

4 She doesn't really like sport,   she gave me her phone number.
  ....

5 Although she didn't say much,   but I iron my own trousers.
  ....

6 I'm not sure she'll be there,   but I have to make a phone call.
  ....

7 My wife does the housework,   and she had a broken finger.
  ....

8 I made her go to the doctor's,   but if you see her give her my love.
  ....

9 It's a small house,   but she plays a bit of tennis sometimes.
  ....

10 There's nobody at home.   but it has a nice big kitchen.
  ....

it: preparatory subject *It's nice to talk to you.*

When the subject of a sentence is an infinitive or a clause, we generally use *it* as a **preparatory subject**, and put the infinitive or clause later.

*It's nice **to talk** to you.* (More natural than *To talk to you is nice.*)
*It was surprising **that she didn't come back.***

1 **Rewrite these sentences with *It …* to make them more natural.**

▶ To book early is important.
   It is important to book early.

1 To speak languages in your head is easy.

2 To hear her talk like that annoys me.

3 To get from here to York takes four hours.

4 To get upset about small things is silly.

5 To get up in the morning is nice, but to stay in bed is nicer.

6 To watch him makes me tired.

7 To hear her complaining upsets me.

8 To say no to people is hard.

2 **Put the sentences together using *It … that …***

▶ He wasn't there. This surprised me.
   It surprised me that he wasn't there.

1 Everybody should say what they think. This is necessary.

2 She's got some money saved. This is a good thing.

3 He's got long hair. This doesn't bother me.

4 John never talked to her. This worried her.

5 She should be told immediately. This is essential.

6 He didn't remember my name. This was strange.

7 He can't come. This is a pity.

8 The children should get to bed early. This is important.

9 Wolves attack people. This is not true.

10 She kept stealing from shops. This shocked me.

emphasis with *it* and *what* *It's not tea that I want.*

We can **emphasise** a part of a sentence by using the structure *It is/was … that*. Compare:

The secretary sent Jake the photos yesterday.
It was the secretary that/who sent Jake the photos yesterday. (not the boss)
It was Jake that the secretary sent the photos to yesterday. (not Bill)
It was the photos that the secretary sent Jake yesterday. (not the drawings)
It was yesterday that the secretary sent Jake the photos. (not last week)

1 **Change these sentences to emphasise each part in turn.**

1 Sarah hid Dad's shoes this morning.

....

....

....

2 Maria married Harry last week.

....

....

....

3 Carl broke the kitchen window today.

....

....

....

4 Mark met Cathy in Germany in 2002.

....

....

....

....

2 **Change these sentences using *It's / It was …***

▶ I don't want tea, I want coffee.   *It's not tea that I want, it's coffee.*
▶ They didn't arrest Tara, they arrested Louise.   *It wasn't Tara that they arrested, it was Louise.*
1 He doesn't speak Greek, he speaks Dutch. ....
2 I don't love you, I love Peter. ....
3 Carol isn't the boss, Sandra is. ....
4 I don't hate the music, I hate the words. ....
5 I didn't lose my glasses, I lost my keys. ....
6 Ryan isn't getting married, Clive is. ....
7 I didn't see Judy, I saw Jill. ....
8 He's not studying maths, he's studying physics. ....
9 Max isn't crazy, you are. ....
10 You don't need a nail, you need a screw. ....

Note the use of pronouns and verbs in this structure in informal and formal styles.

INFORMAL	FORMAL
*It's **me that's** responsible.*	*It is **I who am** responsible.*
*It's **you that's** in the wrong.*	*It is **you who are** in the wrong.*

Another way of emphasising is to use a structure with **what** (='the thing(s) that'). Compare:

The wind keeps me awake.   **What** keeps me awake **is the wind**.

I need **a change.**   **What I need is a change.** (OR **A change is what** *I need*.)

We can use **all** (**that**) (meaning '**the only thing that**') in the same way as *what*.

All *I need is a home somewhere.*   **All** *I did was touch him.*

3 **Change the sentences so as to emphasise the words** *in italics*. **Begin** *What ....*

▶ He wants a *motorbike*.   *What he wants is a motorbike.*

1 *Her rudeness* shocked me.   ....

2 I need *a drink*.   ....

3 I like *her sense of humour*.   ....

4 I hate *his jealousy*.   ....

5 *Cycling* keeps me fit.   ....

6 *The travelling* makes the job interesting.   ....

7 I want *five minutes' rest*.   ....

8 I found *something very strange*.   ....

9 *The weather* stopped us.   ....

10 I don't understand *why she stays with him*.   ....

4 **Complete these sentences about yourself.**

1 All I need is ....

2 All I want is ....

3 What I really like is ....

4 What I really hate is ....

5 What I want to know is ....

'I've already met the tall, dark man.
What I'd like to know is, where is he now?'

In some answers, both contracted forms (for example *I'm, don't*) and full
forms (for example *I am, do not*) are possible. Normally both are correct.

VARIOUS STRUCTURES WITH VERBS **149**

phrasal verbs *Look out! I'll think it over.*

English has a large number of **phrasal verbs**, made up of a **verb** and a **small word (adverb particle)** like *at*, *in*, *on*, *up*, *down*, *away*, *out*. The adverb particles are not the same as prepositions (though some of them have the same form). Phrasal verbs are very common in an **informal** style.

1 **Match the phrasal verbs with the more formal one-word verbs from the box.**

| arrive   awake   consider   continue   disintegrate   explode ✓   leave   postpone |
| return   return   rise |

blow up ...*explode*...   break up ....   come back ....   get up ....
go away ....   go on ....   put off ....   turn up ....
send back ....   think over ....   wake up ....

Adverb particles can have various meanings. *Up* often means 'completely'.

*I'll cut **up** the wood.*   *Let's clean **up** the house.*   *Fill **up** your glass.*   *I tore **up** her letter.*

2 **Look at the adverb particles in the following sentences, and choose the best meaning from the box for each one.**

| away   completely ✓   further   further   higher   louder   quieter   on paper |
| to various people   working   not working |

▶ Can you cut up the onions? ...*completely*.....   6 I've sent out the invitations. ....
1 He drove off. ....   7 Go on. ....
2 Write it down. ....   8 Prices are going up. ....
3 The heater's off. ....   9 Is the printer on? ....
4 Turn the radio down. ....   10 Who turned the music up? ....
5 Drive on. ....

3 **Here are some sentences from conversations. Complete the phrasal verbs with words from the boxes.**

| back   off   over   up   up   up |

1 He turned .... two hours late and then expected me to fix lunch for him.
2 'Are you coming tomorrow?' 'Not sure. I'll think it ....'
3 I'm going to send these shirts .... They're all too big.
4 You know what they say. Never do today what you can put .... till tomorrow.
5 It would be nice if that kid cleaned .... his room sometimes. Just once a week would do.
6 'You wash .... the plates and I'll dry.' 'No, I'll wash and you dry.'

| bring   cut   look   pick   switch   switch   take |

7 I'll .... you up about 8.00 and we'll go straight on to Holly's, OK?
8 OK, you can have the car, but please .... it back in one piece.
9 'It's too hot.' 'Well, you could .... off your coat.'
10 'What does *precipitation* mean?' 'No idea. .... it up.'
11 When I get home I just .... off my brain and .... on the TV.
12 You can .... up the onions. If I do, it makes me cry.

Adverb particles can usually go **before** or **after noun objects**.

*Fill **in this form**.* OR *Fill **this form in**.*
*I'm going to **put on a sweater**.* OR *I'm going to **put a sweater on**.*
*Did you **throw away the newspapers**?* OR *Did you **throw the newspapers away**?*

But an adverb particle must go **after a pronoun object**.

*Fill **it in**.* (NOT ~~Fill in it.~~)   *I threw **them away**.* (NOT ~~I threw away them.~~)

4 **Change the sentences twice.**

▶ I put on my raincoat.
I put my raincoat on.   I put it on.

▶ I cleaned up the kitchen.
I cleaned the kitchen up.   I cleaned it up.

1 Could you turn off the radio?

2 I'll throw away these old plates.

3 Do take off your coat.

4 Please write down my address.

5 Get Mary to fill in this form.

6 I'll switch off all the lights.

7 We'd better put off the next meeting.

8 We'll have to give back the money.

9 I'll think over your suggestion.

10 I couldn't put down the book, it was so interesting.

time to *tidy up*

Every now and then you decide it's time to tidy up, don't you? Because you just can't find anything. So you pick up all the stuff that's been lying around on the floor since Adam was a lad. You throw out the old magazines that you're never going to read again. You give back the books and music that you borrowed from the people upstairs when you were all much younger. You take down your old posters and put up the new ones you bought three years ago to replace them. You sort out the papers on your desk, arrange some of them in systematic-looking piles, and throw away the others. Finally you put on some relaxing music, pour yourself a drink, and sit back with a feeling of satisfaction. A good job done. Only one small problem, which you slowly discover over the next few days: you just can't find anything. ❄

In some answers, both contracted forms (for example *I'm*, *don't*) and full forms (for example *I am*, *do not*) are possible. Normally both are correct.

VARIOUS STRUCTURES WITH VERBS **151**

various structures with verbs: more practice

1 Emphatic *do*. Complete the sentences using words from the box. Use *do/does/did* twice in each sentence.

| a lot a lot against Britain against China bacteria beer English films ✓ fly |
| Japanese mice money plays ✓ potatoes run fast smell taste viruses |

▶ (*Shakespeare / make / write*) Shakespeare didn't make films, but he did write plays.
1 (*Scottish people / speak*) ....
2 (*In England / snow / rain*) ....
3 (*Banks / sell / lend*) ....
4 (*Napoleon / fight*) ....
5 (*Cats / eat*) ....
6 (*Blue cheese / good*) ....
7 (*Antibiotics / kill*) ....
8 (*Ostriches*) ....

2 Preparatory *it*. What do you think? What is important in a relationship (for example with a boyfriend or girlfriend, wife or husband)? Use the expressions in the box to give your opinions.

| I think it's (very) important to …   I don't think it's (very) important to … |
| I think it's (very) important not to …   I (don't) think it's necessary to … |

▶ do everything together I don't think it's important to do everything together.
1 always tell the truth ....
2 always be polite ....
3 say nice things about the other person ....
4 give presents ....
5 listen a lot ....
6 criticise ....
7 have the same interests as the other person ....
8 think about the other person's needs ....
9 think about your own needs ....
10 spend plenty of time alone ....

3 Phrasal verbs. Choose a phrasal verb from the box for each meaning.
Use a dictionary if necessary.

| break off break up give out go on pull down put off take off think over |
| turn up wake up ✓ warm up wash up work out |

awake ..wake up........   arrive ....   calculate ....
clean (cups, plates etc) ....   consider ....
continue ....   demolish ....   destroy ....
distribute ....   heat ....   pause ....
postpone ....   remove (clothes) ....

4 Phrasal verbs. **What can you do in these situations? Write answers using words and expressions from the two boxes**.

cool	cut ✓	look	send	switch	throw	tidy	warm	write

away	back	down	down	off	up ✓	up	up	up

▶ You need an onion to be in small pieces. ..*Cut it up.*.....................
1 Your soup is cold ....
2 The bookshop has sent you the wrong books. ....
3 It's important not to forget some phone numbers. ....
4 You don't understand a word. ....
5 Your bedroom is a mess. ....
6 You don't like the TV programme. ....
7 The bathwater is too hot. ....
8 The tomatoes in the fridge have gone bad. ....

5 Various structures. **Correct or not? Correct the mistakes or write 'Correct'.**

▶ I switched ~~off it~~. ..*it off*.............
▶ I must have my watch repaired. ..*Correct.*.......
1 Think always before you speak. ....
2 Don't be stupid! ....
3 How nice is the weather! ....
4 Isn't she beautiful! ....

5 How he works hard! ....
6 I'm going to put on a coat. ....
7 What good idea! ....
8 Is strange that she isn't here. ....
9 Get your hair cut. ....
10 Do be careful! ....

6 Emphasis with *it*. **Change these sentences using *It's / It was ...***

▶ I don't need food, I need sleep.
   ..*It's not food that I need, it's sleep.*...
1 He doesn't play the violin, he plays the guitar.
   ....
2 I didn't buy a sweater, I bought jeans.
   ....
3 Andy isn't the captain, Pete is.
   ....
4 I don't speak German, I speak Dutch.
   ....
5 I didn't break a cup, I broke a glass.
   ....

7 Internet exercise. **Use a search engine (e.g. Google) to find simple sentences beginning *I do like, I do think, I do feel* and *We do need*.**

....
....
....
....

various structures with verbs: revision test

1 **Put in the missing words.**

1 I didn't see Alice, but I .... see her brother.

2 .... is not necessary to book in advance.

3 Can you cut .... the vegetables?

4 I'll .... up the dishes if you dry them.

5 This programme's rubbish. Do switch it ....

6 Move to London? What .... terrible idea!

7 You'd better .... your hair cut.

8 .... nice her hair looks!

9 It's not grammar .... causes me trouble; it's pronunciation.

10 She thinks I don't care about her, but I .... care.

2 **Choose the correct form(s): A, B, C or more than one.**

▶ **A** Don't worry.   **B** Worry not.

▶ **A** Come in.   **B** Do come in.

1 **A** Don't let's wait.   **B** Let's not wait.   **C** Let's wait not.

2 **A** Never lend money to strangers.   **B** Lend never money to strangers.

3 **A** I sent my sister an email.   **B** I sent an email to my sister.

4 **A** How it's cold!   **B** How cold it is!   **C** How cold is it!

5 **A** How they're playing well!   **B** How well they're playing!   **C** How well are they playing!

6 **A** Doesn't she talk fast!   **B** Does not she talk fast!   **C** Does she not talk fast!

7 **A** Can you explain me this word?   **B** Can you explain this word to me?

8 **A** It's important to eat properly.   **B** It's important eat properly.

9 **A** I cut up the potatoes.   **B** I cut the potatoes up.

10 **A** I think you're wrong.   **B** I do think you're wrong.

3 **These sentences all have mistakes in. Rewrite them correctly.**

1 Let's don't go out this evening.

....

2 This coat's dirty; I must have cleaned it.

....

3 The eggs were all bad, so I threw away them.

....

4 Can I put out our meeting till next week?

....

5 What I need now, it's a drink.

....

6 It's not important have a perfect pronunciation.

....

7 Can you say me your name?

....

8 What beautiful garden!

....

9 Lock always the door at night.

....

10 I always have cut my hair at the same place.

....

In some answers, both contracted forms (for example *I'm, don't*) and full forms (for example *I am, do not*) are possible. Normally both are correct.

SECTION 11 articles: *a/an* and *the*

GRAMMAR SUMMARY

A/An shows that we are talking about **one person or thing**. We often use *a/an*:

- in **descriptions**
  *She's **a** kind woman.*   *He's got **an** interesting face.*

- when we say **what something is**, or what somebody's **job** is.
  *This is **an** earring.*   *She's **a** farmer.*

The usually means 'You know which one(s) I'm talking about'.
  *Can I use **the** bathroom?* (The hearer knows that this means 'your bathroom'.)

Nouns used **without articles** often have a special meaning.
  I'm interested in birds. (This means 'all birds'.)

Most Western European languages have articles. So if you speak (for example) French, German, Spanish or Greek, you will not have too many problems with *a/an* and *the*: they are used mostly in the same way as your articles. There are a few differences: see pages 156, 157, 160, 162, 163. If you speak a non-Western-European language (for example Russian, Polish, Arabic, Chinese, Japanese), you may find articles more difficult. In that case, study all of this Section.

> *'Writing about art is like dancing about architecture.'*
> (*Anonymous*)

> 'An optimist is someone who thinks the future is uncertain.'
> (*Anonymous*)

> 'A woman without a man is like a fish without a bicycle.'
> (*Attributed to Gloria Steinem*)

> *'Treat a work of art like a prince: let it speak to you first.'*
> (*Attributed to Arthur Schopenhauer*)

> 'A diplomat is a person who can tell you to go to hell in such a way that you actually look forward to the trip.'
> (*Caskie Stinnett*)

> *'The happiest time of anyone's life is just after the first divorce.'*
> (*John Kenneth Galbraith*)

> 'I always pass on good advice. It is the only thing to do with it. It is never any use to oneself.'
> (*Oscar Wilde*)

> 'Equality is a lie – women are better.'
> (*Anonymous*)

> 'An accountant is a man who is hired to explain that you didn't make the money you did.'
> (*Anonymous*)

revise the basics: *a/an* and *one*

We use *a* **before a consonant** and *an* **before a vowel.**
But it depends on the **pronunciation** of the following word, not the spelling.

a dog *a hat* *a one-pound coin* (/ə ˈwʌn … /) *a union* (/ə ˈjuːnɪən/)

an orange *an uncle* *an hour* (/ən ˈaʊə/) *an MP* (/ən em ˈpiː/)

1 *A* or *an*?

1 .... elephant
2 .... university
3 .... umbrella
4 .... ticket
5 .... VIP
6 .... honest man
7 .... half-hour lesson
8 .... one-hour lesson
9 .... useful book
10 .... SOS
11 .... X-ray
12 .... European
13 .... hand
14 .... underpass
15 .... unit
16 .... CD
17 .... exam
18 .... school

'Good morning, Mr Dolby. It's 5.15 a.m., and this is radio station WJRM. If you name the next tune you will win a ride on an elephant and two tickets to a rock concert!'

We use **one**, not *a/an*:
● in contrast with *another* or *other(s)*
● in the expression *one day*
● with *hundred* and *thousand* when we want to sound **precise** (see page 325)
● in expressions like *only one* and *just one*.

One girl wanted to go out, but *the others* wanted to stay at home.
One day I'll take you to meet my family.
'How many are there? About a hundred?' 'Exactly *one* hundred and three.'
We've got plenty of sausages, but *only one* egg.

2 *A/An* or *one*?

¹ .... day last year – it was ² .... very hot afternoon in June – I was hurrying to get home. I was about ³ .... hour late – well, to be precise, exactly ⁴ .... hour and ten minutes: I had missed my train. Anyway, there was ⁵ .... woman standing under the trees, and there were several children with her. I saw ⁶ .... child clearly – she was ⁷ .... lovely dark-haired girl – but I only heard the others. Suddenly ⁸ .... strange thing happened. The girl took some stones out of her pocket, and threw ⁹ .... stone after another into the air.

revise the basics: *a/an* *She's a farmer. He's got a long nose.*

We use *a/an* to say **what job** a person does, **what kind of thing** somebody or something is, or **what** something is **used as**. *A/An* has **no plural**.

She's **a farmer**.   They're **farmers**.
He worked as **a taxi-driver**.   They worked as **taxi-drivers**.
Don't use the plate as **an ashtray**.   Don't use the plates as **ashtrays**.

1 Say what these people's jobs are, using the words in the box.

builder   conductor ✓   doctor   gardener   hairdresser
lorry driver   mechanic   musician   photographer   scientist

▶ ..... *is a conductor.* .....
1 ....
2 ....
3 ....
4 ....
5 ....
6 ....
7 ....
8 ....
9 ....

We use *a/an* in **singular descriptions**.

She's got **a** small nose. (**NOT** … *the small nose.*)
He's got **an** interesting face. (**NOT** … *the interesting face.*)

2 Write sentences beginning *He's/She's got* to describe the people in the pictures, using some of the expressions from the box.

big moustache   big mouth   big smile   long beard   long neck   long nose
loud voice   small moustache   small mouth   small nose ✓

▶ ..... *She's got a small nose.* .....
1 ....
2 ....
3 ....
4 ....
5 ....
6 ....
7 ....
8 ....
9 ....

In some answers, both contracted forms (for example *I'm, don't*) and full forms (for example *I am, do not*) are possible. Normally both are correct.

ARTICLES: *A/AN* AND *THE* **157**

revise the basics: *a/an* *A spider has eight legs.*
A man called.

A/An can mean **'any example** of something'.

A spider has eight legs.   Have you got **an Italian dictionary**?

1 GRAMMAR AND VOCABULARY: getting information through the eyes. Complete the sentences with words from the box. Use *a/an*. Use a dictionary if necessary.

| barometer   compass   lens   magnifying glass ✓   microscope |
| mirror   screen   speedometer   telescope   thermometer   torch |

▶ ..*A magnifying glass*.... makes things look bigger.

1 .... makes things look nearer.

2 .... bends light.

3 .... tells you the air pressure.

4 .... tells you where north is.

5 .... makes things look much bigger.

6 .... reflects light.

7 .... shows how fast you are going.

8 .... shows the temperature.

9 .... displays the picture on a computer or TV.

10 .... shines light on things.

A/An can mean **'a particular one'** (if you don't say **exactly who or which**).

A man called while you were out.   James married **a doctor**.   I've bought **a new bike**.

2 Complete these sentences in any way you like.

There's a/an .... in my pocket/handbag.

In my town, there's a big ....

If you see a/an .... you'll have good/bad luck.

I recently bought a/an ....

I've got a beautiful ....

If I look out of the window I can see a/an ....

I was once bitten by a/an ....

Yesterday I ate a/an ....

For my last birthday, ... gave me a/an ....

My .... is married to a/an ....

NOTE

We don't use *a/an* with **uncountable** nouns. (NOT *a rain*)

We don't use *a/an* with **possessives**. (NOT *a my friend*)

After **kind of** or **sort of**, *a/an* is usually **dropped**: a kind of tree (NOT *a kind of a tree*)

In **exclamations** with **what**, *a/an* is **not dropped**. What a pity! (NOT *What pity!*)

A/An usually comes **after quite, rather** and **such**: *quite/rather/such a* nice day.

In the **plural**, we use **no article** or **some** (see page 170), not *a/an*.

*They both married **doctors**.   **Some men** called.*

---

revise the basics: *the* *Please close the door.*

The means 'you know **which (one/ones)** I mean'.

*I bought a TV and a radio, but **the radio** didn't work.*
(= the radio I just told you about – you know which one.)
***The women** over there work with my sister.*
(= the women I'm showing you – you know which ones.)
*Please close **the door**.* (You can see which one.)
*He's been to **the North Pole**.* (It's obvious which – there's only one.)

We often use *the* with *only* and with **superlatives**.

*She's **the only** woman for me.*   *It's **the best** restaurant in town.*

1 Put in *the* if the speaker and hearer probably know exactly which (one/ones).
   Put in *a/an* if not.

1 Who opened .... window?
2 She lives in .... centre of Glasgow.
3 I'd like .... glass of water.
4 My sister is married to .... farmer.
5 .... man in .... next flat is French.
6 He's .... oldest child in .... school.
7 Who's .... girl by .... piano?
8 There's .... strange man in .... garden. What's he doing there?
9 Today is .... only day that I'm free.
10 'Which coat is yours?' '............... red one.'

2 Put in *the* or *a/an*.

'Do you see ¹ .... man standing near ² .... door? He works as ³ .... assistant
in ⁴ .... same shop as I do. Well. I saw him the other day and he was driving ⁵ ....
big red Porsche. And do you see ⁶ .... expensive clothes he's wearing? Where does he get
⁷ .... money to pay for it all? ⁸ .... month ago he hadn't got ⁹ .... penny.
I told you about ¹⁰ .... burglary that we had at ¹¹ .... shop, didn't I? Do you think
I should go to ¹² .... police?'

3 Imagine that you are talking to a friend in your school classroom or your usual workplace.
   If you say the following expressions, will he/she know which one(s) you probably mean?
   If not, add some words so that he/she will know which one(s).

▶ the teacher / the boss *OK*...................   6 the bus ....
▶ the window *the window on the right*....   7 the house ....
1 the light ....   8 the post office ....
2 the lights ....   9 the station ....
3 the ceiling ....   10 the President ....
4 the floor ....   11 the government ....
5 the place ....   12 the restaurant ....

In some answers, both contracted forms (for example *I'm*, *don't*) and full
forms (for example *I am*, *do not*) are possible. Normally both are correct.

ARTICLES: *A/AN* AND *THE* **159**

revise the basics: generalisations without *the* *I like music.*

> *The* does **not** mean 'all'.
> We **do not use** *the* in **generalisations** with plural and uncountable nouns. Compare:
>
> | | |
> |---|---|
> | *I like* **music**. (**NOT** … ~~the music.~~) | *Can you turn off* **the music**? |
> | *She's very interested in* **nature**. | *What is* **the nature** *of his illness?* |
> | *People have to live in* **society**. | *I've joined* **the Poetry Society**. |
> | ***Books** are expensive.* | *Put* **the books** *on the table.* |

① **Put *the* or – (= no article) in each blank.**

There must be something wrong with me. ¹ .... people usually think that ² .... babies are sweet and ³ .... teenagers are annoying. Not me. I think ⁴ .... babies are boring. For me, ⁵ .... children start being interesting at ⁶ .... age when you can understand ⁷ .... things that they say. But ⁸ .... years that I like best are ⁹ .... period between ages thirteen and twenty. Oh, it's difficult at times, but I still prefer talking about ¹⁰ .... life with a teenager to cleaning a baby's bottom.

> We **do not** normally use *the* in **generalisations** with plural and uncountable nouns, even if there is an **adjective before the noun**.
>
> *She's studying* **Chinese history**. (**NOT** … ~~the Chinese history.~~)   *He collects* **antique clocks**.
>
> But we use *the* when a description with *of* follows the noun.
>
> *She's studying* **the history of China**.

② **Use some adjectives from the box, or other adjectives, to write true (or false!) sentences about yourself. Don't use *the*.**

air	casual	classical	detective	foggy	formal	historical	Italian
loud	really hot	pop	quiet	romantic	spicy	stormy	train

1 I (don't) like eating .... food.
2 I can't stand listening to .... music.
3 I love .... music.
4 I hate .... weather.
5 I love .... weather.
6 I (don't) like wearing .... clothes.
7 I (don't) like .... people.
8 I (don't) like .... travel.
9 I (don't) like reading .... novels.
10 I often/sometimes/never go for .... walks.

> 'Never lend books, for no one ever returns them; the only books I have in my library are the books that other people have lent me.'
> (*Anatole France*)

> 'I would give anything to hear and to love music, but do the best I can, it is just noise and nothing more.'
> (*Catherine the Great of Russia*)

> 'Classical music is the kind we keep thinking will turn into a tune.'
> (*Kin Hubbard*)

> 'Without music, life would be a mistake.'
> (*Nietzsche*)

> 'I don't know anything about music – in my line you don't have to.'
> (*Elvis Presley*)

> 'Give me books, fruit, French wine and fine weather and a little music out of doors, played by somebody I do not know.'
> (*John Keats*)

the in generalisations *Who invented the telescope?*

We can use *the* in generalisations with **singular countable nouns**, to talk about a whole class of things.
This is common in scientific and technical language.

*Who invented **the telescope**?*   ***The tiger** is in danger of dying out.*
*I can't play **the piano**.*   *I hate **the telephone**.*

1 **Complete the sentences with the words from the box. Use *the*.**

ballpoint pen	camera	computer	dog	novel	ostrich ✓	train
violin	whale	wheel	wolf	X-ray machine		

▶ Some birds can't fly – for example, ...*the ostrich.*..........

1 Before people invented ...., they couldn't transport heavy loads easily.

2 In its early years, ... wasn't thought to be good reading for young ladies.

3 Scientific calculations were much slower before the invention of ....

4 .... is one of the hardest instruments to play.

5 What did people write with before ....?

6 Is .... descended from ....?

7 What can we do to save .... from dying out?

8 .... is a valuable tool for doctors, but it has its dangers as well.

9 In the 19th century, ... revolutionised travel.

10 Has .... made portrait-painting unnecessary?

2 **GRAMMAR AND VOCABULARY: musical instruments. Put in the correct instruments from the box. Use a dictionary if necessary.**

cello	guitar	harp	organ	piano	saxophone	trumpet	violin

1 It has four strings. You put one end under your chin and play it with a bow. ....

2 Children often learn this instrument. It has 36 black keys and 52 white keys. ....

3 It has six strings. You hold it in front of your body; it can be played with both hands.
....

4 A big one can have 46 or 47 strings, stands on the floor, and is played with both hands.
....

5 It has four strings. You put one end on the floor and play it with a bow. ....

6 This is a wind instrument, often played by jazz musicians. It was invented by Adolphe Sax in 1841.
....

7 This is a very big wind instrument often found in churches, played with the hands and feet.
....

8 A wind instrument made of metal, widely used in traditional jazz. ....

Some other common general expressions with *the*: *the sea, the mountains, the town, the country, the cinema, the theatre.*

*I love **the sea**.*   *Do you like living in **the country**?*   *I never go to **the cinema** or **the theatre**.*

3 **Give your answers to these questions.**

1 Which do you prefer for a holiday: the sea or the mountains? ....

2 Which do you go to more often: the cinema or the theatre? ....

3 Where would you prefer to live: the town or the country? ....

In some answers, both contracted forms (for example *I'm, don't*) and full
forms (for example *I am, do not*) are possible. Normally both are correct.
ARTICLES: *A/AN* AND *THE* **161**

place names *Lake Superior; the Atlantic*

PLACE NAMES WITH NO ARTICLE:

continents, most countries	*Africa, Germany, Peru* (**BUT** *The Netherlands*)
states, counties etc	*Texas, Oxfordshire, Normandy*
towns	*Ottawa, Prague, Sydney* (**BUT** *The Hague*)
most streets	*Fifth Avenue, Westgate Street*
lakes, most mountains	*Lake Superior, Everest, Mont Blanc*
town + building	*Oxford University, York Airport, Reading Station*

PLACE NAMES WITH *THE*:

seas, rivers, deserts	*the Atlantic, the Thames, the Sahara*
mountain and island groups	*the Alps, the Himalayas, the West Indies*
name includes common noun	*the Czech* **Republic**, *the United* **States**, *the Far* **East**
most buildings	*the British Museum, the Ritz, the Playhouse*

1 **Circle the correct expression.**

▶ We went on a boat trip on the *(Mississippi)/ Lake Superior.*

▶ They're hoping to drive across *(Africa)/ Sahara.*

1 My brother works in *China / People's Republic of China.*

2 There are four countries in the *Great Britain / United Kingdom.*

3 We're going on holiday to the *South America / Republic of Ireland.*

4 Here's a photo of Annie and me in *USA / Oxford Street.*

5 I've never been to *Netherlands / Norway.*

6 Joe has a small farm near the *Marseille / Mediterranean.*

7 There are a lot of European immigrants in the *USA / America.*

8 This is a piece of rock from the *Himalayas / Mount Everest.*

9 Our hotel is just opposite the *Ritz / Victoria Station.*

10 From the plane window we had a wonderful view of *River Rhine / Mont Blanc.*

2 **Put in *the* or – (= no article).**

▶	..the.... British Museum		10	.... River Seine
▶	..–....... Canterbury Cathedral		11	.... Victoria Street
1	.... California		12	.... Rocky Mountains
2	.... Mount Kilimanjaro		13	.... Berlin
3	.... Lake Garda		14	.... Morocco
4	.... Australia		15	.... Pacific Ocean
5	.... National Gallery		16	.... Apollo Theatre
6	.... Hilton Hotel		17	.... Cambridge Town Hall
7	.... Three Dragons Restaurant		18	.... White House
8	.... Geneva Airport		19	.... Yorkshire
9	.... Dominican Republic		20	.... Gobi Desert

3 **Write the English names of five places you have been to, and five places you would like to go to. Use a dictionary if necessary.**

I have been to: ....

....

I would like to go to: ....

....

other special cases *in prison; She became Queen.*

Some common expression with **no article** after a **preposition**:

to/at/from school/university/college	to/in/out of church/prison/hospital/bed

to/at/from school/university/college   to/in/out of church/prison/hospital/bed
at home   to/at/from work   on holiday
by car/bus/bicycle/plane/train/underground/boat   on foot

*She's **in prison**.* (She's a prisoner.)   *She works as a cook **in the prison**.*
*You should be **in bed**.* (resting)   *I found chewing gum **in the bed** again.*

1 **Choose a word or expression for each blank, and add a preposition.**

> bed   bicycle   bus   bus   church   foot   holiday   home   home
> prison   school   underground   university   work

1 'How do you usually go to the shops?' 'Oh, I usually go ...., but sometimes if I have a lot to carry I go ....'
2 After a hard day ...., my mother used to come home and go .... to rest for half an hour before making supper.
3 Children go .... to learn to read and write.
4 Does your family usually go away .... or do you stay ....?
5 When Juliet was studying ...., she broke her leg and had to stay .... for two weeks.
6 My aunt goes .... every morning and twice on Sundays.
7 If you're travelling across London, it's much faster ...., but you can see more ....
8 Another way of getting across London is ...., but it's quite dangerous.
9 My friend George spent three months .... for something that he didn't do.

Some other expressions with **no article**:

*He was **elected President**.*   *She **became Queen**.*   *They **made** her **Manager**.*
*What's on **TV**?*   *Let's watch **television**.*   (BUT on **the radio**, listen to **the radio**)

Note that we do not usually drop articles after *with, without, as* or *what*.
Note also: **the** same, on **the** right/left, **a** hundred/thousand.

*You can't eat soup **with a** fork.* (**NOT** … ~~with fork.~~)
*I had to do the translation **without a** dictionary.* (**NOT** … ~~without dictionary.~~)
*I worked **as a** guide last summer.* (**NOT** … ~~as guide~~ …)
***What a** surprise!* (**NOT** ~~What surprise!~~)
*Most of the government ministers went to **the same** school.* (**NOT** … ~~to same school~~ …)
*'Where are the toilets?' 'Over there on **the right**.'*   *I've just planted **a hundred** tulips.*

2 **Put in *a/an, the* or – (= no article).**

1 They appointed him .... General Manager at the age of 23.
2 You can't go there without .... visa.
3 'What's for lunch?' '.............. same as yesterday.'
4 There's absolutely nothing on .... TV this evening.
5 What .... strange haircut!
6 Please don't use your plate as .... ashtray.
7 Did you hear the weather forecast on .... radio this morning?
8 'I'm trying to learn .... thousand new words every month.' 'Good luck.'
9 I don't like writing with .... pencil.
10 They didn't elect him .... Chairman – he gave himself the job.

In some answers, both contracted forms (for example *I'm, don't*) and full forms (for example *I am, do not*) are possible. Normally both are correct.

ARTICLES: *A/AN* AND *THE* **163**

articles: more practice

1 Mixed article uses. Correct or not? Correct the mistakes or write 'Correct'.

▶ I really like ~~the Indian food~~. ..*Indian food*..

▶ I'm learning the violin. ..*Correct.*..

1 The life is sometimes difficult. ....

2 You can't go out in the rain without a coat! ....

3 I go to cinema two or three times a week. ....

4 We always go to mountains on holiday. ....

5 Do your children go to the school on Saturdays? ....

6 I'll see you at Dragon Restaurant at 8.00. ....

7 I climbed the Mont Blanc last year. ....

8 Do you think Foster will be elected the President? ....

9 Ann's interested in sport and nature. ....

10 About a hundred people came to the festival. ....

2 Mixed article uses. Complete the quotations with *a, an, the* or – (= no article).

1 When I was born, I was so surprised that I couldn't talk for .... year and .... half. (*Gracie Allen*)

2 California is .... great place – if you happen to be .... orange. (*F Allen*)

3 Never put anything on .... paper, my boy, and never trust .... man with .... small black moustache. (*P G Wodehouse*)

4 .... dog is .... only thing on earth that loves you more than you love yourself. (*Josh Billings*)

5 .... Americans like .... fat books and .... thin women. (*Russell Baker*)

6 .... actor's .... guy who, if you ain't talking about him, ain't listening. (*Attributed to Marlon Brando*)

7 .... death is .... nature's way of telling you to slow down. (*Anonymous*)

8 .... diplomacy is the art of saying 'nice doggie!' until you can find .... stone. (*Wynn Catlin*)

9 .... birds do it; .... bees do it; even .... educated fleas do it. Let's do it. Let's fall in .... love. (*Cole Porter*)

10 I love acting. It is so much more real than .... life. (*Oscar Wilde*)

11 Nothing's illegal if .... hundred businessmen decide to do it, and that's true anywhere in .... world. (*Andrew Young*)

12 Remember that as .... teenager you are at .... last stage in your life when you will be happy to hear that .... phone is for you. (*Fran Lebowitz*)

13 Save .... water, shower with .... friend. (*Anonymous*)

14 When I was .... boy of fourteen, my father was so ignorant I could hardly stand to have .... old man around. But when I got to be twenty-one, I was astonished at how much he had learned in seven years. (*Mark Twain*)

15 A banker is .... man who lends you .... umbrella when .... weather is fair, and takes it away from you when it rains. (*Anonymous*)

3 Place names. See if you can make sentences using some of the words and expressions from the box.

Anna	to college	by train	the Pacific	Oxford	Prison
Paul	in prison	by car	Everest	Edinburgh	Town Hall
the President	at dinner	by plane	the Alps	Cardiff	Airport
I	to work	on foot	the North Sea	Ottawa	Station
All of us	home	by bike	Lake Superior	Sydney	
It's easy	at work	by bus	The Hague	Boston	

Anna often goes to work on foot if the weather's fine.
I went to Edinburgh Prison by bike.
It's not easy to go by plane from Cardiff Airport to Ottawa.
....
....
....
....
....
....
....
....
....

4 Internet exercise: *the* in generalisations. Use the internet (if necessary) to complete the following sentences.

1 Miles Davis and Louis Armstrong both played ....
2 Pablo Casals and Mstislav Rostropovich both played ....
3 Andres Segovia played ....
4 Niccolò Paganini played ....
5 Chopin wrote music for ....
6 .... invented the Snugli® baby carrier.
7 .... was the first scientist to use the telescope.
8 .... invented the windscreen (windshield) wiper.
9 .... invented the computer language Cobol.
10 .... invented the telephone.

5 Complete the cartoon captions with *a*, *an*, *the* or –.

'One night you'll get me out of .... bed and it really will be .... burglar.'

'For heaven's sake, Harry! Can't you just relax and enjoy .... art, ... music, ... religion, ... literature, ... drama and .... history, without trying to tie it all together?'

articles: revision test

1 Put in *a* or *an*.

1 .... uncle
2 .... X-ray
3 .... union
4 .... bus
5 .... hour

6 .... half-hour break
7 .... one-hour break
8 .... hole
9 .... useful idea
10 .... student

2 Put in *a/an* or *one*.

1 It happened .... afternoon last summer.
2 Could I have .... knife?
3 The journey lasts exactly .... hour.
4 Only .... person was late.
5 It was .... cold day.

6 If it's not .... problem, it's another.
7 I'm going to put on .... sweater.
8 He went out wearing .... sock.
9 I've got to make .... phone call.
10 I booked .... room, not two.

3 Put in *a/an, the* or –.

1 Have you seen .... small blue bag anywhere around?
2 Can you lock .... front door when you go out?
3 She's interested in .... art and .... African history.
4 May I use .... bathroom?
5 What's that black stuff on .... floor?
6 Is there .... post office near here?
7 I'll meet you at 8.00 outside .... station.
8 I'll drive you to .... airport. What time is .... plane?
9 .... people are more interesting than .... grammar.
10 I've had .... interesting idea.
11 My brother is married to .... doctor.
12 You've got .... nice smile.
13 .... woman in .... next office comes from New York.
14 I work in .... centre of Birmingham.
15 Do you like .... Chinese food?
16 I'm learning .... guitar.
17 My youngest brother is .... engineer.
18 I don't know how we managed before .... computer was invented.
19 What's on .... TV this evening?
20 You can't get in here without .... ticket.

4 Put in *the* or –.

1 .... Ritz Hotel
2 .... Oxford Street
3 .... Czech Republic
4 .... Cambridge University
5 .... Lake Geneva
6 .... Mount Everest
7 .... North Sea
8 .... Wales
9 .... Washington
10 .... Eiffel Tower

11 .... Smithsonian Museum
12 .... New Theatre
13 .... Dublin Airport
14 .... Atacama Desert
15 .... River Nile
16 .... Great Pyramid
17 .... Netherlands
18 .... Hague
19 .... Alps
20 .... Yorkshire

In some answers, both contracted forms (for example *I'm, don't*) and full forms (for example *I am, do not*) are possible. Normally both are correct.

SECTION 12 determiners

GRAMMAR SUMMARY

> this, that, these, those   some, any, no   all, each, every   both, either, neither
> much, many, a little, a few   enough   too much/many   less, least   more, most
> a lot, lots   which, what   (articles a/an, possessives my, your etc)

Determiners are words that come at the beginning of noun phrases, before adjectives.
Determiners help to show **which** or **how much/many** we are talking about.

   this small dog   *some* new suggestions   *all* Scottish towns   *enough* time

Most determiners are explained and practised in this section (together with other uses of *too* and *enough*).
Articles have a separate section on pages 155–166. Possessive determiners are explained together
with pronouns on pages 189–191.

'Yes, of course it's important enough
to disturb him.'

'Straighten your tie, Stephen. The world is
already filled with enough disorder.'

revise the basics: *this, that, these, those*

1 **DO IT YOURSELF** Study the examples, and think about the difference between *this/these* and *that/those*.

Come and look at this picture.	*What's that on the roof?*
This isn't a very good party.	*He's ill. That's why he's away.*
Do you like this music?	*Stop that noise!*
Listen – this will make you laugh.	*Thanks – that was a great meal.*
(on the phone) This is Emma.	*(on the phone) Who's that?*
This is my friend Paula.	*I didn't like those stories he told.*
These shoes are hurting my feet.	*Do you remember those people we met in Edinburgh?*
These grapes are really sweet.	

2 **DO IT YOURSELF** Look at the examples again. Which words and expressions in the box go with *this/these*, and which go with *that/those*?

finished	happening now	said before	just about to start	here	near	over there
distant	unwanted					

THIS/THESE: ....

THAT/THOSE: ....

3 Put in *this/that/these/those*.

1 Why am I living in .... country?
2 Get me .... box from the table.
3 Ugh – .... potatoes taste burnt!
4 What was .... noise?
5 Who are .... people over there?
6 Come .... way, please.
7 Isn't .... weather great?
8 Did you hear .... explosions in the night?
9 Tell her to stop .... shouting.
10 .... was a great party – thanks.
11 Who said .... ?
12 Why did she marry .... idiot?
13 Do it .... way, not like ....
14 Listen – you're not going to believe ....
15 Look at .... earrings. Jamie gave them to me.

4 *This* or *that*?

'My wife told me to carry *this/that*.'

revise the basics: *some* and *any*

> *Some* means 'a certain (not large) number or amount of'.
>
> We use *some* mostly in **affirmative** (➕) sentences.
> We also use *some* in **questions** when we **expect** or **invite** people to say **'Yes'**
> (for example, in **requests** and **offers**).
>
> ✓ ✓ ✓ ✓ ✓
> ✓   SOME   ✓
> ✓ ✓ ✓ ✓ ✓

She's got some interesting ideas.   *There's some mud on the carpet.*
'Could I have some coffee?' 'Sure. And would you like some biscuits?'

> We use *any* instead of *some* in **negative** sentences,
> in most **questions**, and with *if*.
>
> ✗ ✗ ✗ ✗ ✗ ✗
> ✗   ANY   ?
> ? ? ? ? ? ?

Do you know any good jokes?   *He hasn't got any money.*   *If you find any mistakes, please tell me.*

> The difference between *somebody/anybody, someone/anyone, something/anything* etc is the same as
> the difference between *some* and *any*.

There's somebody outside.   *Would you like something to drink?*
Does anybody understand this?   *She didn't say anything.*

① **Put in *some, any, somebody, anybody, something* or *anything*.**

1 I can't find .... butter, but we've got
   .... margarine.
2 Did you meet .... interesting at the party?
3 Emma has got .... old pictures of the house.
4 Can I offer you .... wine?
5 Do you know .... German?
6 Helen brought me .... beautiful roses.
7 Is there .... I can do?
8 There's .... waiting to see you.
9 I haven't got .... to wear.
10 Shall we listen to .... music?
11 If you have .... problems, just
    phone me.
12 Have you got .... children?
13 Would you like .... to help you?
14 There aren't .... buses on Sunday.

> We use *any* with words like *never, hardly, without, refuse, doubt* (which have a **negative kind of meaning**).
>
> *She never has any fun.*   *We got there without any difficulty.*   *I refuse to give him any help.*

② **Here are some sentences with *any*. Which word in each sentence gives the 'negative kind of meaning'?**

▶ He (never) listens to anyone.
▶ We've (hardly) got any cat food.
1 The baby refuses to eat anything.
2 I doubt if you'll find any bread now.
3 There was hardly anybody in town.
4 You never get any sense out of her.
5 You seldom hear any birds here.
6 I left the house without any money.

③ **Choose the right word.**

1 Have you got *some / any* time free on Wednesday afternoon?
2 There's *something /anything* strange about the way Pete's acting today.
3 Nobody can find out *something / anything* about when the exams will be.
4 Is there *something / anything* we should bring to the meeting?
5 Shall I bring you *something /anything* to read while you wait?
6 Do you know if *some / any* of the Morrises are coming on Sunday?
7 Can I get you *some / any* coffee? I've just made *some / any*.
8 She refuses to have *something / anything* to do with her family now.
9 If there's *some / any* soup left, could you put it in the fridge, please?
10 I doubt if there's *something / anything* we can do now.

In some answers, both contracted forms (for example *I'm, don't*) and full
forms (for example *I am, do not*) are possible. Normally both are correct.

some/any or no article *Have some toast. I don't like toast.*

We use *some* and *any* to talk about **limited numbers or quantities**. Compare:

LIMITED NUMBERS/QUANTITIES	NOT LIMITED
'Have some toast.' ('one or two pieces')	*'No thanks. I don't like toast.'* ('toast in general')
I need some new clothes.	*She always wears nice clothes.*
Is there any water in the fridge?	*Is there water on the moon?*

We **don't** normally use *some* in **descriptions**.

*She's got **black hair**.* (NOT ~~She's got some black hair.~~)

We **don't** use *some* when we say **what people/things are**.

*Andy and John are **students**.* (NOT ~~Andy and John are some students.~~)

1 **Join the beginnings and ends.**

▶	'What are those?'	A	'Chocolates.' ..*o*..
1	'What did she give you?'	B	any money with you? ......
2	Cheese is made from	C	some milk in my coffee? ......
3	Could I have	D	'Some chocolates.' ......
4	Why does she always talk about	E	milk. ......
5	Have you got	F	money? ......
6	Her children are both	G	air. ......
7	In the pub we met	H	students. ......
8	Let me show you	I	good photos. ......
9	Open the window and let in	J	some fresh air. ......
10	This camera takes	K	some photos of the children. ......
11	You can't live without	L	some students. ......

2 **GRAMMAR AND VOCABULARY: buying food**

**A man went shopping and bought some food. Complete the sentences.
Learn the words for food. Use a dictionary if necessary.**

- ▶ *grapes* ➕ He bought some grapes, because he likes ..*grapes.*..................
- ▶ *cheese* ➖ He didn't buy ..*any cheese*.......... because he doesn't like cheese.
- 1 *mustard* ➕ He bought some mustard, because he likes ....
- 2 *mushrooms* ➕ He bought .... because he likes ....
- 3 *carrots* ➖ He didn't buy any carrots, because he doesn't like ....
- 4 *vinegar* ➖ ....
- 5 *rice* ➕ ....
- 6 *pepper* ➖ ....
- 7 *cornflakes* ➕ ....
- 8 *oil* ➖ ....

any, *not any*, *no* and *none*

No is a more emphatic way of saying '**not a**' or '**not any**'. Note the sentence structure.

*Sorry, I've got **no** time.* (**NOT** … ~~I haven't got no time.~~)
*There were **no** letters for you this morning.*

At the beginning of a sentence, *no* is almost always used.

No cigarette is completely harmless. (**NOT** ~~Not any cigarette~~ …)
No tourists ever come to our village.

1 Change *not … any* to *no*, or *no* to *not … any*.

▶ I haven't got any American friends. *I've got no American friends.* ....
▶ There's no bread. *There isn't any bread.* ....
1 She speaks no German.   She doesn't ....
2 He's written no letters to her. ....
3 We don't get any rain here. ....
4 There isn't any post on Sundays. ....
5 She hasn't got any brothers or sisters. ....

Before *of*, or without a noun, we use *none*, not *no* (often with a singular verb).

None of his friends likes his wife. (**NOT** ~~No of his friends~~ …)   *There's **none** in the house.*

2 Put in *no* or *none*.

▶ ...*None*.... of these telephones works.
▶ I had ...*no*........ difficulty understanding her.
1 'How many children has he got?' ....
2 There are .... trains after midnight.
3 Did you buy milk? There's .... in the fridge.
4 .... of us can play the piano.
5 There are .... palm trees in Antarctica, and there are .... in Greenland.

Nobody, *nothing* etc are used in the same way as *no*.

Nobody loves me.   *I've got absolutely **nothing** to say.*

3 Put in *no*, *none* or *nobody*,

1 'Why can't I have toast for breakfast?' 'Because there's .... bread.'
2 'My students expect me to know everything.' '.................. knows everything.'
3 .... newspaper tells the whole truth.
4 'What were your photos like?' 'I'm afraid .... of them came out.'
5 'Do you think he's honest?' '.................. politician is completely honest.'
6 .... of the people there remembered seeing anything unusual.
7 I've got .... patience with people like her.
8 There's .... I can talk to in this place.
9 .... of you care what I think.
10 He had .... money, ... job and .... place to live.

In conversation, we often make short incomplete sentences with *any* and *no*.

*'Can you help me?' 'Sorry, **no** time.'*   *'**Any** letters for me?' 'Yes.'*

4 Make short questions (❓) or negative sentences (➖).

▶ *news* ❓ ...*Any news?*.........
▶ *'It's dark.' 'Electricity'* ➖ ...*No electricity.*......
1 *Sorry, milk* ➖ ....
2 *phone calls for me* ❓ ....
3 *more money* ➖ ....
4 *problems today* ❓ ....

In some answers, both contracted forms (for example *I'm*, *don't*) and full forms (for example *I am*, *do not*) are possible. Normally both are correct.

any = 'one or another – it's not important which'

We can use *any* to mean 'one or another – **it's not important which'**.
With this meaning, *any* is common in **affirmative** (➕) sentences.

*'When shall I come and see you?' 'It doesn't matter – **any** time.'*
*'What newspaper do you want?' 'I don't mind. **Any** paper is OK.'*

In negative sentences, we can use *just any* to make this meaning clear.

*I don't do **just any** work: I choose jobs that interest me.*

1 **Complete each sentence with *any* and a word from the box.**

bank   boy   bus   colour   day   doctor ✓   problems   question   supermarket

▶ ...*Any doctor*................... will tell you to stop smoking.
1 He gets angry with .... who talks to his girlfriend.
2 'Would you like red, blue, ...?' 'It doesn't matter. .... is OK.'
3 You can get this kind of rice in ....
4 I think she knows everything. She can answer .... you ask.
5 If you have ...., come and ask me for help.
6 'When shall we meet?' 'I don't mind. .... this week.'
7 'Where can I change money?' 'In ....'
8 You can't take just .... – you need a 4 or a 16.

We can use *anybody*, *anything* and *anywhere* to mean '**it's not important who/what/where'**.

*It's easy. **Anybody** can do it.*   *That dog eats **anything** – meat, bread, shoes, ...*
*'Where shall I sit?' '**Anywhere** you like.'*   *She doesn't go out with **just anybody**.*

2 **Put the beginnings and ends together and put in *anybody*, *anything* or *anywhere*.**

▶ It's not hard to dance.	A 'I don't mind. I'm so hungry I'll eat ....' ......
1 'Where would you like to live?'	B 'It's true. Ask ....' ......
2 'What would you like for lunch?'	C 'Yes. Put it .... you like.' ......
3 'I don't believe you.'	D ...*Anybody*... can do it. ..*0*..
4 'Can I park the car behind your house?'	E He can play ....
5 Joe's a brilliant pianist.	F ' .... in America.' ......

Any is **not negative** – it is the opposite of *no* or *not any*. Compare:

*That's easy: **anybody** can do it.*   *That's too hard: **nobody** can do it.*
*I'm really hungry – I'll eat **anything**.*   *I'm not hungry – I **don't** want **anything**.*

3 **Circle the best word or expression in each sentence.**
1 *Any / No* doctor can tell you if you've got flu.
2 *Any / No* doctor can tell you exactly how long you're going to live.
3 Just say *anything / nothing*, so we can see if the microphone works.
4 If the police arrest you, say *anything / nothing* until your lawyer gets there.
5 What do you mean, music? I *can't hear / can hear* any music.
6 You can hear *any / no* kind of music you like at the Reading Festival.
7 Anna's very secretive: she talks to *anybody / nobody* about her problems.
8 Jim tells his problems to *anybody / nobody* who will listen.

revise the basics: *much, many, a lot (of)*

We use *much* with **singular** (uncountable) nouns and *many* with **plurals**.

*How **much time** have we got?*   *How **many tickets** do we need?*

Much and *many* are most common in **questions** and **negatives**. In informal **affirmative** (⊞) sentences, we generally prefer *a lot (of)*, *lots (of)* or *plenty (of)*. These can be used with both uncountables and plurals.

*'Do you have **much** trouble with English?' 'I don't have **much** trouble speaking, but I have **lots of** difficulty writing.'*
(**NOT** … ~~much difficulty~~ …)

*'Are there **many** opera houses in London?' 'Not **many**, but **a lot of** theatres and **plenty of** cinemas.'*
(**NOT** … ~~many theatres and many cinemas.~~)

1 Write at least ten sentences about yourself. What have you got *not much, not many, a lot / lots of, or plenty of* … ? Use the words in the box, or other words if you prefer.

| ambition | books | confidence | cousins | energy | free time | ideas | nice clothes |
| old friends | problems | work to do |

▶ *I haven't got much ambition.* ....
▶ *I've got lots of ideas.* ....
1 ....
2 ....
3 ....
4 ....
5 ....
6 ....
7 ....
8 ....
9 ....
10 ....

After *so*, *as* and *too*, *much* and *many* are normal in **affirmative** sentences.

*That child makes **so much** noise!*   *Take **as much** time as you like.*   *There are **too many** people here.*

2 Put in *much/many* with *so, as, too*.

1 It was nice to have .... time to talk to you.
2 Are there .... chairs as people?
3 You can never have .... love.
4 I don't have .... friends as you.
5 She's got .... relatives!
6 Get .... tickets as you can.

In a **formal** style, *many* and *much* are more common in affirmative sentences.

***Many** commentators have already thrown **much** darkness on this subject, and it is probable that if this continues we shall soon know nothing at all about it.*   (Mark Twain)

→ For *of* with *much* and *many*, see page 184.

In some answers, both contracted forms (for example *I'm, don't*) and full forms (for example *I am, do not*) are possible. Normally both are correct.

DETERMINERS **173**

revise the basics: *enough, too* and *too much*

1 **DO IT YOURSELF** **Look at the examples.**

This isn't **hot enough.** (NOT ... ~~enough hot.~~)   *Am I going* **fast enough?**
There is never **enough time.**   *Have you got* **enough rice?**

Now choose the correct forms of the rules.

Enough normally comes *before / after* an adjective or adverb.
Enough normally comes *before / after* a noun.

2 **Put in words from the box together with *enough*.**

| big   champagne   clever   confidence   good ✓   hard   money   time   friends   old |

▶ In art the best is ..*good enough.*...... (*Goethe*)
1 There was .... to give everybody a glass.
2 This town isn't .... for both of us.
3 I never had .... when I was young: now I never have ....
4 Susie hasn't got .... to play football with.
5 Daniel's not .... to travel by himself.
6 If you work .... , you don't have to be very intelligent.
7 She was .... to do anything she wanted, but she didn't have ....
   to try.

3 **DO IT YOURSELF** *Too much/many* or *too*? Look at the examples and complete the rules.**
Examples

He's **too old.** (NOT ... ~~too much old.~~)   *She's driving* **too fast.**
My problem is **too much work** *and* **too many late nights.**

Rules

Before an adjective without a noun, or an adverb, we use ....
Before a noun (with or without an adjective), we use ....

4 **Invent answers to the questions, using *too, too much* or *too many*.**
▶ Why did Jack leave his car at the pub and take a taxi home? (*beer*)
   He'd drunk too much beer.
1 Why did they drive to the cinema in two cars? (*people*)
   ....
2 Can you understand what he's saying? (*quickly*)
   ....
3 Why didn't Joanna stop for lunch yesterday? (*busy*)
   ....
4 Why don't we go to the Caribbean for our holiday? (*expensive*)
   ....
5 Why don't you let the children cycle to school? (*traffic*)
   ....
6 What went wrong in your exam? (*slowly*)
   ....
7 Why did you have the phone installed in the other room? (*noise*)
   ....

⑤ Write descriptions for the pictures using *not enough* or *too much/many*.

1 .... 2 .... 3 .... 4 ....

5 .... 6 .... 7 .... 8 ....

We can use **infinitive** structures with *enough* and *too*.

*She's old **enough to vote**.*   *I'm **too tired to go out** tonight.*

A structure with ***for* + object + infinitive** is also possible.

*It's not warm enough **for me to swim**.*   *The box was too heavy **for us to lift**.*

We can drop ***for* + object**.

*It's not warm enough **to swim**.*   *The box was too heavy **to lift**.*

⑥ Complete the sentences with *enough* or *too*.

▶ Sally's not .....*old enough to take*..... the dog for a walk. (*old / take*)

▶ The food was .....*too spicy for the children to eat.*..... (*spicy / children / eat*)

1 There's someone in the garden, but I can't see .... if it's Emma. (*well / decide*)

2 I'll work on this tomorrow – I'm .... it tonight. (*tired / think about*)

3 I don't understand Arabic .... to Egyptian radio. (*well / listen*)

4 I'm not .... the piano. (*strong / move*)

5 I was .... on the lecture. (*bored / concentrate*)

6 They were speaking .... what they were saying. (*quietly / me / hear*)

7 Near some beaches the sea's not .... in. (*clean / people / swim*)

8 The room was .... anything. (*dark / us / see*)

9 He drove .... him. (*fast / police / catch*)

10 This shirt isn't .... (*clean / wear*)

In some answers, both contracted forms (for example *I'm, don't*) and full forms (for example *I am, do not*) are possible. Normally both are correct.

revise the basics: *(a) little, (a) few*

> *(A) little* is used with **singular** (uncountable) nouns and *(a) few* with **plurals**.

*We've got **a little coffee** left, and **a few biscuits** – not really enough if your mother's coming.*

1 Write *little* or *few*.

1 There is .... friendship in the world, and least of all between equals. (*Francis Bacon*)
2 A .... learning is a dangerous thing. (*Alexander Pope*)
3 Men of .... words are the best men. (*William Shakespeare, Henry V*)
4 Never in the field of human conflict was so much owed by so many to so .... (*Winston Churchill*)
5 Never before have we had so .... time in which to do so much. (*Franklin Roosevelt*)
6 A country having a .... inflation is like a woman being a little pregnant. (*Leon Henderson*)
7 Death is one of the .... things that can be done as easily lying down. (*Woody Allen*)
8 .... people can be happy unless they hate some other person, nation or creed. (*Bertrand Russell*)

> *Little* and *few* are rather **negative**: they mean '**not much/many**'.
> *A little* and *a few* are more **positive**: their meaning is more like '**some**'.

*Cactuses need **little water**.*
*Give the roses **a little water** every day.*
*His ideas are very difficult, and **few people** understand them.*
*His ideas are very difficult, but **a few people** understand them.*

2 *Little* or *a little*? *Few* or *a few*?

1 There is .... use trying to change her mind.
2 Could you possibly give me .... help?
3 .... teenagers in the village could read.
4 Slowly, ... children began coming to school.
5 I only need .... minutes to get ready.
6 She only wanted .... love, ... kindness.
7 Nadia drank .... coffee and no alcohol.
8 Unfortunately, he had .... friends.

> *Little* and *few* (without *a*) are rather **formal**; in a **conversational** style we more often say *only a little/few* or *not much/many*.

*Cactuses **only** need **a little** water.*   *Not many people understand his ideas.*

3 Rewrite these sentences in a more conversational style.

▶ I have little time. *I've only got a little time.* **OR** *I haven't got much time.*
1 We have few friends. ....
2 There is little that I can do for you. ....
3 Few people wanted to help her. ....
4 They had little money, but they were pretty happy. ....
5 Few children are as difficult as Robert. ....
6 I dislike few people. ....
7 My father does little exercise. ....
8 I need little sleep. ....
9 Vermeer painted few pictures. ....
10 I speak little Japanese. ....

less and *least*, *fewer* and *fewest*

Less and *fewer* are **comparative** (see page 228): they are the opposite of *more*.
Least and *fewest* are **superlative** (see page 228): they are the opposite of *most*.
Less and *least* are used with **singular** (uncountable) nouns.
Fewer and *fewest* are used with **plural** nouns.

*I've got **less money** than I thought.*
*Of all my friends, Jake does the **least work**.*
*There were **fewer problems** than we expected.*
*Mandy was the person who made the **fewest mistakes** in the translation exam.*

1 Write *less / the least / fewer / the fewest*.

1 Of all British cars, this one uses .... petrol. It also needs .... repairs.
2 .... girls than boys do mathematics at university. This may be because girls get ....
encouragement to study maths at school.
3 As the years went by, they had .... things to say, and .... interest in talking
to each other.
4 Do you want more time and .... money, or more money and .... time?
5 Liz is very clever, but she has got .... self-confidence of anyone I know.
6 I've had .... days off work of anybody in the office.
7 There are .... apples on the trees this year.
8 I earn .... money in our family, and my brother earns the most.
9 Annie always has .... things to say, but what she does say is usually interesting.
10 Now that we've got two children we've got much .... spare time than we used to have.

Less and *least* can also be used with **adjectives** and **adverbs**.

*Amy's **less shy** than Jessica.*   *It was the **least successful** party we'd given.*
*He drives **less carefully** than I expected.*

2 Complete the sentences with *less* or *the least* and some of the words from the box
(or other words if you prefer).

| boring confident confidently dangerous easily fluently important intelligent |
| interesting optimistic pessimistic politely prosperous quickly religious selfish |
| shy shyly worried |

1 I feel .... about the future than I did a year ago.
2 My mother/father/brother/sister is/was .... person you can imagine.
3 I spoke English .... a year ago than I do today.
4 I think this country is .... than it was a year ago.
5 People from the north of my country speak .... than people from the south.
6 My home town is .... place I know.
7 Most of my friends are .... than I am.
8 Some people say that money is the .... thing in life, but I'm not so sure.
9 I think TV gets .... late at night.
10 .... intelligent people often think they are the most intelligent.

Many people use *less* with plurals (e.g. *There were **less problems** than we expected*). This is also correct,
but some people think it isn't (including some teachers and examiners), so be careful!

revise the basics: *all*

All can go **with a noun** or **with a verb**.

All the rooms cost the same.   The rooms **all cost** the same.   **All cats** climb trees.   Cats **all climb** trees.

1 Change the sentences.

▶ ~~All the family got flu.~~ ~~The family all got flu.~~ ....

▶ ~~The trains all stop at York.~~ ~~All the trains stop at York.~~ ....

1 All the marketing people like Oliver. ....

2 Our children all speak French. ....

3 The tourists all went back home. ....

4 All these cars cost too much. ....

5 All meetings take too long ....

6 My friends all thought I was crazy. ....

7 All my old friends live a long way away. ....

8 The classes all started late. ....

Note the **word order** when *all* goes **with a verb**. *All* goes:

● **before one-word verbs**

*Our children **all speak** French.   The papers **all arrived** yesterday.   We **all went** home.*

● **after auxiliary verbs** (*will, have, can* etc) and **after** *are* and *were*.

*Our children **can all speak** French. (**NOT** …all can speak French.)*
*The papers **have all** arrived.   We **were all** tired. (**NOT** We all were tired.)*

2 Put *all* in the right place with the verb.

▶ Babies ...all... cry .... sometimes.

▶ Our visitors .... have ...all... gone home.

▶ The apples .... are ...all... bad.

1 The museums .... close .... on Tuesdays.

2 The interviews .... will .... start .... next week.

3 We .... stopped .... for a rest.

4 Your clothes .... are .... ready.

5 We .... went .... to Paris for Easter.

6 Sorry, the buses .... have .... left.

7 These children .... can .... speak .... English.

8 The apples .... have .... gone .... bad.

3 GRAMMAR AND VOCABULARY. Cities and countries. Which one is different? Write sentences using the expressions in the box. Use an internet search engine if you need help.

| Asia   Australia ✓   China   England   Europe   German-speaking countries |
| Italy ✓   South America   the United States   seaports |

▶ Rome, Florence, Milan, Paris ~~They are all in Italy except Paris.~~ ....

▶ Sydney, Seoul, Brisbane, Canberra ~~They are all in Australia except Seoul.~~ ....

1 Melbourne, Tokyo, Beijing, Delhi ....

2 Beijing, Shanghai, Delhi, Hong Kong ....

3 Japan, Austria, the Czech Republic, Poland ....

4 Oxford, London, Birmingham, Edinburgh ....

5 Vienna, Berlin, Zurich, Athens ....

6 Rio, Mexico City, Buenos Aires, Lima ....

7 Chicago, Boston, Toronto, Los Angeles ....

8 Copenhagen, Rio, Madrid, Genoa ....

revise the basics: *all, every, everybody, everything*

We can use *all* with **plural** nouns and verbs. We use *every* with **singular** nouns and verbs.

All birds lay eggs.   *Every bird lays eggs.* (NOT ~~Every birds lay eggs.~~)

We can use other determiners (*the, my, this* etc) after *all*, but not after *every*.

All the shops were closed.   *Every shop was closed.* (NOT ~~Every the shop ...~~)

① Rewrite the sentences with *every*.

▶ All the players were tired.   *Every player was tired.*
1 Not all birds can fly. ....
2 I've read all the newspapers. ....
3 Please listen to all the words. ....
4 All the roads were under water. ....
5 All languages are difficult in one way or another. ....
6 All London trains are cancelled today. ....
7 The police have interviewed all the employees. ....
8 All the plates are dirty. ....
9 Not all changes are good. ....
10 All the computers are down today. ....

We **don't** normally use *all* without a noun to mean **'everybody'**.

Everybody was tired. (NOT ~~All were tired.~~)

② Put in *all* or *everybody*.

1 .... women become like their mothers. That is their tragedy. No man does. That's his. (*Oscar Wilde*)
2 In the future, ... will be famous for fifteen minutes. (*Andy Warhol*)
3 .... human beings are born free and equal in dignity and rights. (*Universal Declaration of Human Rights*)
4 I am free of .... prejudices – I hate .... equally. (*W C Fields*)
5 He who praises .... praises nobody. (*Samuel Johnson*)
6 Justice is open to .... people in the same way as the Ritz Hotel. (*Judge Sturgess*)

We can use *all* to mean **'everything'** or **'the only thing'**, but only with a **relative clause** (*all that* ...).

She gave me all/everything (that) she had.   *All (that) I want is a place of my own.*
The thieves took everything. (NOT ~~The thieves took all.~~)

③ Put in *all* if possible; if not, put in *everything*.

1 .... I need to make a comedy is a park, a policeman and a pretty girl. (*Charlie Chaplin*)
2 I hurry to laugh at ...., for fear of having to cry. (*Beaumarchais*)
3 I can resist .... except temptation. (*Oscar Wilde*)
4 .... I want is a room somewhere. (*My Fair Lady*)
5 You can only have power over people so long as you don't take .... away from them. (*Solzhenitsyn*)
6 They say .... in the world is good for something. (*John Dryden*)
7 [A cynic] knows the price of .... and the value of nothing. (*Oscar Wilde*)
8 Life is like nothing, because it is .... (*William Golding*)
9 .... I want is you. (*song title*)

In some answers, both contracted forms (for example *I'm, don't*) and full forms (for example *I am, do not*) are possible. Normally both are correct.

DETERMINERS **179**

every and *each*; *every one*

Every and *each* mean the same. They are both used with **singular** nouns and verbs.
Every is more common.

Every/Each day **brings** *a new problem.*

We use *every* for **three or more**. We use *each* for **two or more**.

She had a ring on every finger.   *She had a bag in each hand.* (**NOT** … ~~in every hand.~~)

1 Right or wrong? Correct the mistakes or write 'Correct'.

▶ You get more beautiful every day.   ...*Correct*...........
▶ I paid separately for each ~~books~~.   ..*book*..............
1 Every passenger have to show his or her passport.   ....
2 There's a mistake in each line.   ....
3 Cars are parked on every side of the road.   ....
4 Every children are different.   ....
5 Please say each word slowly and clearly.   ....
6 The doctor made him sit down and looked into every ear.   ....

We often prefer *each* when we want to say that things are **separate** or **different**. Compare:

*We asked every politician **the same** question.*   *Each politician gave a **different** answer.*

2 Both answers are correct, but one is a little better. Which?

▶ I work *each* / (*every*) month except August.
1 *Each / Every* day is new and different.
2 Not *each / every* Canadian speaks English.
3 I looked for my keys in *each / every* pocket, one after the other.
4 She wrote a different personal message on *each / every* card.
5 The doctor examined *each / every* patient very carefully.
6 *Each / Every* house in this village looks the same.
7 But inside, *each / every* house is quite different.

Before *of* (see page 184), or with **no noun**, we use *every one*, not *every*.

*She knows **every one of** her students by name.* (**NOT** … ~~every of her students~~ …)
*He's got hundreds of books, and he's read **every one**.* (**NOT** … ~~he's read every.~~)

3 Put in *every* or *every one*.

1 .... of these oranges is bad.
2 I learnt Latin for seven years at school, but I've forgotten .... word.
3 'Can I have one of those chocolates?' 'Sorry, I've eaten ....'
4 .... of his teachers said he was stupid; but he did well in .... of his exams.
5 When the soldiers left the town they burnt down .... house.
6 The questions were easy: I could answer ....
7 We've won .... match so far this year.
8 .... of my friends has got more money than me.

both, either and *neither*

We use *both*, *either* and *neither* to talk about **two** people or things.
Both (● + ● = 'one and the other') has a **plural** noun.
Either (● / ● = 'one or the other') has a **singular** noun.
Neither (✖ ✖ = 'not either, not one and not the other') has a **singular** noun.

'Do you speak French or Spanish?' 'I speak **both** languages.'
'Which one is easier for you?' '**Either** language is OK.'
'How about writing?' 'No, I can't write very well in **either** language.'
'And your wife?' 'No, she speaks **neither** language.'

1 Put in *both*, *either* or *neither*.

1 .... sisters are studying engineering.
2 'Do you want to come round tomorrow or Friday?' ' .... day is fine.'
3 'Do you like Brussels and Amsterdam?' 'I don't know .... city.'
4 Use .... hands to carry the vase – it's heavy.
5 .... films looked interesting, but .... was much good, in fact.
6 .... her sons studied physics, but .... boy works in science.
7 .... shirt would look good on you. Why don't you buy one of them?
8 I don't like .... camera. And .... cameras are very expensive.
9 He's a good player, and he can kick equally well with .... foot.
10 'Which car can I take?' 'You can take .... car. .... cars are full of petrol.'
11 I'm busy on .... the next two Tuesdays.
12 I paid for .... tickets – yours and mine.

2 *Both hands/feet/eyes* or *either hand/foot/eye*?

▶ You can pick up a small chair with ...*either hand.*...................
▶ To move a table you probably need ...*both hands.*...................
1 You play a piano with ....
2 You need .... and .... to play an organ.
3 You can kick a football with ....
4 You can hold a fork in ....
5 You can turn a key with ....
6 It's easier to make a bed if you use ....
7 People usually watch TV with .... open.
8 You can look through a telescope with ....
9 I can write with ...., equally badly.
10 When you're walking, you never have .... off the ground.

> 'Hold a true friend with both hands.'
> (*Nigerian proverb*)

> 'To love and be loved is to feel the sun from both sides.'
> (*David Viscott*)

> 'My candle burns at both ends.
> It will not last the night.
> But ah, my foes, and oh, my friends –
> It gives a lovely light.'
> (*Edna St Vincent Millay*)

In some answers, both contracted forms (for example *I'm, don't*) and full forms (for example *I am, do not*) are possible. Normally both are correct.

which? and what?

We ask *which?* when there is a **limited choice**.

We ask *what?* when there is a **wide choice**.

Which size do you want – small, medium or large?

What is your shoe size?

Sometimes both are possible.

Which/What day next week can you come and see us?

1 **Which** or *what?*

1 We've got red wine and white – .... will you have?
2 .... books did you read for last year's English class?
3 .... was your favourite subject at primary school?
4 .... English king had six wives?
5 .... 's your name?
6 .... hand do you write with?
7 .... kind of car have you got?
8 I'm going to buy a new carpet. .... colour should I get?
9 .... party do you think will win the election?
10 .... subject do you prefer, chemistry or physics?

'We have high quality and low prices. Which do you want?'

Before *of* and *one*, we can use **which** but not *what*.

Which of the countries in Europe have you visited? (**NOT** ~~What of … ?~~)
Look at all those stars. **Which one** is the nearest? (**NOT** ~~What one … ?~~)

When there is no noun, we use *who* for people, not *which*. Compare:

Which boxer won?   **Who** won? (**NOT** ~~Which won?~~)

2 **Which**, *what* or **who?**

1 .... of the books on the list have you already read?
2 There are two coats on the bed. .... one is yours?
3 I really don't know .... earrings to wear with this dress.
4 .... time shall we meet tomorrow?
5 .... of your brothers is the one who works in Paris?
6 .... got the job, Andy or Liz?
7 .... language do you speak at home?
8 I don't remember .... of your parents plays the piano.
9 .... gave you that – John or Alex?
10 I can come to your place, or we can meet at mine. .... is best for you?

other(s) and *another*

> When *other* is used **before a plural noun**, it does **not** have **-s**.
> When *other* is used **without a noun**, it has **-s** in the plural. Compare:
>
> *Tell the **other** people.* (**NOT** … *the others people.*)   *Tell the **others**.*
> *Can you show me some **other** shoes?*   *Can you show me some **others**?*

1 **Write *other* or *others*.**

1 I could see Karima and Nedjma at their desks – but where were the ……………… ?
2 Long after all the ……………… cars had left, Dawson's BMW was still there.
3 I'll phone all the ……………… if you'll phone Ted and Lucy, OK?
4 I can play the Sonata in C, but not any of the ………………
5 Do you know any ……………… people who might have a reason to do this?
6 This doesn't suit me. Have you got any ……………… colours?
7 Some metals are magnetic and ……………… aren't.
8 The police arrested Jane, Fred and two ………………
9 I wish that girl would play more with ……………… children.
10 Gerald Durrell wrote a book called 'My Family and ……………… Animals'.

> We can use *another* (one word) to mean '**one more**'. But with uncountables and plurals, we do not generally use *other* to mean 'more'. Compare:
>
> *Have **another** potato.* (**NOT** … *an other potato.*)
> *Have some **more** meat.* (**NOT** … *other meat.*)
> *We need **more** cups.*

2 **Write expressions with *another* or with *more*.**

▶ English *more English*
▶ book *another book*
▶ eggs *more eggs*
1 clothes ………………………………
2 friends ………………………………
3 child ………………………………
4 hour ………………………………
5 mile ………………………………
6 sleep ………………………………

7 job ………………………………
8 possibilities ………………………………
9 money ………………………………
10 time ………………………………
11 freedom ………………………………
12 holidays ………………………………
13 problem ………………………………
14 question ………………………………
15 tickets ………………………………

> We can use *another* + *few* or *another* + *a number* with a **plural** noun.
>
> *Let's wait **another few minutes**.* (= '… a few more minutes.')
> *The job will take **another ten days**.* (= '… ten more days.')

3 **Change the expressions to use *another*.**

▶ three more pages *another three pages* ………………
1 a few more days ………………………………………
2 a hundred more pounds ………………………………………
3 twenty more miles ………………………………………
4 a few more mistakes ………………………………………
5 a million more dollars ………………………………………

In some answers, both contracted forms (for example *I'm*, *don't*) and full forms (for example *I am*, *do not*) are possible. Normally both are correct.

DETERMINERS **183**

determiners and *of* *most people; most of us*

We use **determiners** (*some, any, much, many, more, most, few, enough* etc) with *of* before **other determiners** (*the, this, my* etc) and before personal pronouns (*it, us* etc).

DETERMINER + *OF*	DETERMINER WITHOUT *OF*
• before *the*: *some of the matches we played*	*some matches* (**NOT** ~~some of matches~~)
• before *this* etc: *more of that coffee*	*more coffee* *I'll have more.*
• before *my* etc: *most of our meals*	*most meals* *I cook most.*
• before *it, us* etc: *enough of it* *most of them*	*enough water* *most elections*

The same thing happens with **numbers** one, two etc.

two of the dogs *four of my friends*	*two dogs* *four friends*

Before *of* we use **every one**, not *every*, and **none**, not *no*.

every one of the dogs *none of my friends*	*every dog* *no friend*

1 **Put in *of* or nothing (–).**

Dear Phil,

Well, some [1] .... our luggage has arrived, so things could be worse. I've got the books and papers, but I've lost most [2] .... my clothes. I haven't got any [3] .... socks at all, and I'll have to buy some more [4] .... jeans, but at least I've got enough [5] .... underwear for the week. (They don't sell it here. I don't think they wear it.) I'm going to buy a few [6] .... those woollen shirts that you like, and one [7] .... the big coats that we looked at. They've got no [8] .... shoes in my size, unfortunately, and none [9] .... the jackets suit me. Anyway, I'm not alone. Every one [10] .... us has lost something – in fact, three [11] .... people have got no [12] .... luggage at all. Well, as they say, into each [13] .... life a little [14] .... rain must fall. See you on the 17th.

Andy

Note the difference between **most people** (talking about people in general) and **most of the people** (talking about particular people).

Most people *want to have children.*   **Most of the people** *I know live in the country.*

2 **Put in *most people* or *most of the people*.**

1 .... enjoy talking about themselves.
2 .... who wanted to see the match were disappointed.
3 I know .... in our street.
4 .... like dancing.
5 I think fishing for sport is wrong, but .... would disagree.
6 .... on the train were going on holiday.
7 He gets on with ....
8 .... at the party were friends of Jan's.
9 .... I work with live in London.
10 .... would like more money and less work.

NOTE: we often drop *of* after *all* and *both*. **After *a lot / lots / plenty*** we **always** use *of* with a noun or pronoun (see page 173).

all (of) *my problems*   **both (of)** *her brothers*   **a lot of** *good ideas* (**NOT** ~~a lot good ideas~~)

determiners: more practice

1 Mixed structures. (Circle) the correct forms.

1 This car hardly uses *petrol / some petrol / any petrol / no petrol*.
2 Could you lend me *money / some money / any money* for a few days?
3 I have never told *someone / anyone* about your past.
4 Helen can ride a bike without *some / any* help now.
5 You've got *pretty toes / some pretty toes*.
6 I understood *little / a little* of the lecture, but not very much.
7 She was sad because she had *few / a few* friends.
8 Of all the children, Billy is *the less / the least* trouble.
9 I don't know where the *other / others* people went.
10 Not every *bear / bears* can climb trees.
11 Her children *all have left / have all left / have left all* home.
12 We *are all / all are* ready.
13 She had a rose behind *every / each* ear, and one in her teeth.
14 'Monday or Tuesday?' 'Both / Either days are OK.'
15 *Which / What* language do they speak in Azerbaijan?

2 *Any* = 'one or another'. Answer the questions using *any*.

1 Where can you get: a plane ticket? ......*any travel agent's*......................
  petrol? ....
  dog food? ....
  stamps? ....
  running shoes? ....
  a dictionary? ....

2 Who can give you advice on: English pronunciation? ....
  getting a divorce? ....
  paying your taxes? ....
  problems with your camera? ....
  milking cows? ....

3 Mixed structures. Correct the mistakes. (One of sentences 1–15 is correct.)

▶ I haven't got ~~some~~ money. ...*any*...........................
▶ Everybody was late. ...*Correct.*........................
1 Not anybody wrote to me last week. ....
2 None her friends helped her. ....
3 She talks so fast that anybody can understand her. ....
4 I have much free time. ....
5 You're walking too much slowly. We'll be late. ....
6 Have we got enough of chairs for everybody? ....
7 This soup isn't enough warm. ....
8 'Did you find any mushrooms?' 'Yes, a lot of.' ....
9 We found the place without no difficulty. ....
10 We'll be here for another six days. ....
11 The plan was complicated, but all understood. ....
12 Nobody played well, but Joe was the less bad. ....
13 She showed me two sweaters, but I didn't like neither. ....
14 Would you like other meat, or have you got enough? ....
15 I learnt French at school, but I've forgotten all. ....

In some answers, both contracted forms (for example *I'm, don't*) and full
forms (for example *I am, do not*) are possible. Normally both are correct.

DETERMINERS **185**

4 *No etc. Write sensible answers. Use no, none, nothing, and nobody.*

▶ 'Why can't you take me to school in the car today?' ..*Because I've got no time.*..................

1 'Can you ask someone in your family to help you with your French?'

....

2 'How many of your brothers are married?'

....

3 'Jeremy says his father speaks seventy-six languages.'

....

4 'Do we have to go out tonight? Can't we eat at home?'

....

5 'Do you think I could ask you for a cup of coffee?'

....

6 'Why don't you phone home to find out if your letter's arrived?'

....

7 'If you're bored, why don't you go to the cinema?'

....

8 'Why didn't you buy any flowers?'

....

9 'Why didn't you join in the conversation last night?'

....

5 **Grammar in a text: formality. Choose a phrase from each pair in the box to write a) a formal text and b) an informal text.**

> Few people learn foreign languages perfectly / Not many people learn foreign languages perfectly
> when they're grown up. / as adults.   The majority of us / Most of us
> make many mistakes / make a lot of mistakes   when we are speaking / when we're speaking
> another language. / another language.   It's best / The best policy is
> to aim for a reasonable level of accuracy, / to try to get most things right,
> but not to be too perfectionist. / but not to be too perfectionist.
> A lot of common mistakes / Many common mistakes   have little effect / don't have much effect
> on communication. / on communication.

A) FORMAL: Few..

....

....

....

B) INFORMAL: ....

....

....

....

6 **Internet exercise. Use a search engine (e.g. Google) to find simple sentences that begin as follows. Write the sentences.**

1 "All we want is"   ....

2 "All they asked for was"   ....

3 "All she said was"   ....

4 "All I can do is"   ....

5 "All you need is"   ....

7 Mixed structures. **Use six of the expressions in the box to complete the four cartoon captions. Which caption goes with which cartoon?**

| any | any | any of | anybody | anything | anywhere | less | less of | nothing |

1 'Oh, he's right here beside me making his "I don't want to go .... with ....
at .... time" face.' *Cartoon* ......

2 'Girls, girls, a little .... noise, please.' *Cartoon* ......

3 'I suppose you've brought me here to tell me you haven't got .... money.' *Cartoon* ......

4 'It's your birthday? Cook .... you like for supper.' *Cartoon* ......

determiners: revision test

1 **Choose the correct words to complete the sentences. More than one answer may be possible.**

▶ Come here and look at ..*this*.... (*this / that*)

▶ Would you like ..*some/any*...... more juice? (*some / any*)

1 John passed .... his exams last year. (*none / none of / any of / no of*)

2 My father won't lend money to .... (*anybody / nobody*)

3 There hasn't been .... this year. (*rain enough / enough rain*)

4 .... my friends live in London. (*Most / Most of*)

5 Rashpal's got .... hair. (*beautiful / some beautiful*)

6 There's .... money in my bank account. (*any / none / no*)

7 I'll be home in .... hours. (*another two / other two / two other*)

8 That child hardly eats .... (*anything / nothing / something*)

9 Those people have .... money. (*much / a lot / a lot of / lots of*)

10 I bought the .... expensive bike. (*less / least*)

11 Are you ....? (*enough warm / warm enough*)

12 She walked out without .... explanation. (*any / no*)

13 .... her children is happily married. (*Every / Every one / Every one of / Every of*)

14 I answered .... letter myself. (*every / each*)

15 We .... ready in time. (*all were / were all*)

16 .... could speak French except Denise. (*All / Everybody*)

17 I can write with .... hand. (*every / each / either*)

18 There's .... ice cream in the fridge, if you'd like some. (*little / a little / few / a few*)

19 I think the children .... home. (*all have gone / have all gone*)

20 You're talking .... fast – I can't understand. (*too / too much*)

2 **Right or wrong? Correct the mistakes or write 'Correct'.**

▶ I don't want ~~some~~ help, thanks. ..*any*.............................

▶ I've got some nice American friends. ..*Correct*.......................

1 Who's this man over there talking to Anna? ....

2 I've hardly got no time these days. ....

3 Mark and Joanna are here, but where are the others? ....

4 We all will be on holiday next week. ....

5 Not every birds can fly. ....

6 Not all birds can fly. ....

7 What leg hurts – the left or the right? ....

8 Sally got a lot presents for her birthday. ....

9 She gave me a lot of information, but I don't remember all. ....

10 You can have either room – they're both free. ....

11 All I want is a quiet life. ....

12 We understood a little, because he had a really bad accent. ....

13 This was terrible music. Please don't play it again. ....

14 The plates are all dirty. ....

15 All the plates are dirty. ....

16 'Would you like other coffee?' 'No, thanks. I've had enough.' ....

17 I don't think there are enough of rooms for everybody. ....

18 I've got so much to do, and so little time! ....

19 She has to eat food without no salt. ....

20 Can you just wait another five minutes? ....

In some answers, both contracted forms (for example *I'm, don't*) and full forms (for example *I am, do not*) are possible. Normally both are correct.

SECTION 13 personal pronouns and possessives

GRAMMAR SUMMARY

> *I, you, he, she, it, we, you, they   me, you, him, her, it, us, you, them*
> *my, your, his, her, its, our, your, their   mine, yours, his, hers, ours, yours, theirs*
> *myself, yourself, himself, herself, itself, ourselves, yourselves, themselves   each other*

We use **pronouns** when it is **not necessary**, or not possible, to use a **more exact** noun phrase.
*Jake emailed me yesterday. **He** said …*
(The speaker uses the personal pronoun *he* because it is not necessary to repeat 'Jake'.)
*Karen talks about **herself** all the time.*
(It is unnecessary to repeat 'Karen'.)

In this section we explain uses of **personal pronouns** (*I, me, you* etc), **possessives**
(*my, your* etc and *mine, yours* etc), **reflexives** (*myself, yourself* etc) and *each other*.

'I used to do it all myself, but now I
have my lawyers handle it.'

'For your first effort you should write
about something you understand.
Don't write about yourself.'

revise the basics: *I, me, my, mine* etc

1 **Complete the table.**

I	me	my	mine
	you		
he		his	
			hers
	it		–
		our	
			yours
they			

2 **Correct the mistakes.**

▶ I ~~her haven't phoned~~ yet.   *haven't phoned her* ....

1   Our house is a lot older than their.   ....

2   There are 30 miles to the nearest hospital.   ....

3   'What's Annie's address?' 'Have forgotten.'   ....

4   Darren and Cindy are interesting. But theirs parents!   ....

5   I told they to go home.   ....

6   I bought my ticket, but I didn't have enough money for your.   ....

7   John and her mother are on holiday.   ....

8   We are Tuesday.   ....

9   That's not my coat – this is the mine.   ....

10   Is that yours bike?   ....

11   Is December 1st today.   ....

12   'Is the pie OK?' 'Yes, I like.'   ....

3 **Put in a personal pronoun (*me, you* etc) or a possessive (*my, your* etc or *mine, yours* etc).**

▶ ...*It*........ is five o'clock.

1   I don't like .... and he doesn't like ....

2   I can't find .... keys. Can I borrow ....?

3   That girl keeps losing .... shoes.

4   Peter's coming this evening with .... three sisters.

5   I think her job is more interesting than ...., but she thinks .... is more interesting than ....

6   Mary's mother's really nice, but I don't like .... father much.

7   We've invited Jan and Peter to dinner twice, but .... have never invited .... back.

8   How far is .... to Paris from here?

9   I bought some chops for supper, but I left .... on the bus.

10   That car has got something wrong with .... steering.

4 **Put in *its, it's, whose* or *who's.***

1   I like your dog. What's .... name?

2   .... is that car? .... parked in front of my garage.

3   Do you know the woman .... talking to Elizabeth?

4   The company's in trouble. .... closing three of .... factories.

possessives *a friend of mine   Anne broke her arm.*

We **don't** put **possessives** immediately **after articles** or **after** *this/that* etc. Instead, we use the structure
a/this etc … *of mine/yours* etc.

She's *a friend of mine*. (NOT ~~She's a my friend.~~)
How's *that brother of yours*? (NOT ~~How's that your brother?~~)

1 **Use this structure to join the ideas.**

▶ that + your smelly dog   *that smelly dog of yours* ....
1 these + our silly cats   ....
2 that + her unemployed brother   ....
3 another + my good friend   ....
4 a + my brilliant idea   ....
5 these + his stupid plans   ....
6 those + your old books   ....
7 some + his distant relations   ....
8 a + her beautiful cousin   ....
9 this + your wonderful news   ....
10 that + our lazy son   ....

We often use **possessives** with **parts of the body** and **clothes**.

Anne broke *her* arm skiing. (NOT ~~Anne broke the arm skiing.~~)
He stood there, *his* eyes closed and *his* hands in *his* pockets.

2 **Put in one of the words from the box with a suitable possessive.**

coats   eyes   foot   head   lips   mouth   raincoat   shoes   sweater   tail

1 It's cold. I'm going to put .... on.
2 Helen dropped a heavy bag on .... yesterday, and she can't walk.
3 That dog's hurt ....
4 They took off .... and gave them to the waiter.
5 Look at the weather – and I've forgotten .... again.
6 I'll tell you everything if you promise to keep .... shut.
7 'You didn't write anything down.' 'It's all in ....'
8 'How do you know he's lying?' ' .... are moving.'
9 Don't come into the house with .... all wet.
10 Please open .... and look at me.

We often use *the* instead of a possessive in expressions with **prepositions**, especially when we talk about
common kinds of **pain** and **physical contact**, and when the possessor has already been mentioned.

*He's got a pain **in the chest**.*   *She hit **me on the head**.*   *I looked **him in the eye**.*

We use **possessives** with *own*.

my own room / a room of my own (NOT ~~an own room~~)

personal pronouns *'Who's that?' 'It's me.'*

After *be*, we usually use object pronouns: *me, him* etc. (*I, he* etc are possible, but they are very formal and unusual in modern English.)

'Who's that?' 'It's me.' (**NOT NORMALLY** *'It is I.'*)   *'Where's Maggie?' 'That's her over there.'*

In **short answers** we can use *me, him* etc (informal) or *I, he* etc **with a verb** (more formal). The same thing happens after *as* and *than*.

INFORMAL	MORE FORMAL
'I'm thirsty.' 'Me too.' (**NOT** *I too.*)	*'I'm thirsty.' 'I am too.' / 'So am I.'*
'Who's paying?' 'Her.'	*'Who's paying?' 'She is.'* (**NOT** *She.*)
*I've got the same number **as him**.*	*I've got the same number **as he has**.*
*She gets paid more **than me**.*	*She gets paid more **than I do**.*

1 Complete these informal sentences with suitable pronouns.

1 'Who knows where the key is?' 'Only ...., and I'm not telling you.'
2 'I haven't met Mark yet – is .... here?' 'That's .... over there.'
3 'I've had enough of this party.' '............ too.'
4 'Who bought these flowers?' 'It was .... I thought you'd like them.'
5 He's faster than ...., but I'm stronger than ....
6 John's two years younger than Alice, but ....'s nearly as tall as ....
7 'Who said that?' 'It was .... – the man in glasses.'
8 You've got almost the same colour eyes as ...., but mine are smaller.
9 You may be older than ...., but I don't have to do what you say.
10 'Which is Mario's wife?' 'That must be .... just getting out of the car.'

2 Change these to make them more formal or less formal.

▶ I live in the same street as him.
   I live in the same street as he does.

1 Anne's got the same car as me.
2 They've been here longer than us.
3 I'm much taller than him.
4 'He's going to Mexico.' 'Me too.'
5 'Who said that?' 'Her.'
6 We are not as old as they are.
7 He had a bigger meal than I did.
8 I am not as quick as she is.
9 'We are from York.' 'So am I.'
10 'Who wants a drink?' 'I do.'

We generally use *who* as both **subject** and **object**. *Whom* is unusual, especially in questions, except in a formal style. (For *whom* in relative clauses, see page 269.)

Who *do you want to see?* (More natural than *Whom do you want to see?*)

We use *it* to refer to *nothing*, *everything*, *something* and *anything*.
We also use *it* when we answer questions about **who people are.**

Nothing *is ever the way you expect* ***it*** *to be.*
'Who's the woman in red?' *'**It**'s Clara Lewis.'* (**NOT** ~~'She's Clara Lewis.'~~)

People generally use *he* and *she* for **their cats, dogs, horses** etc; some people use *she* for **their cars, motorbikes** and **boats. Countries** are usually *it*.

You can take my horse, but don't ride ***him*** *on the main road –* ***he****'s a bit nervous.*
'How's the car?' *'**She**'s running beautifully.'*
Britain imports more than ***it*** *exports.*

3 **Put in a suitable pronoun.**

1 'What's your cat's name?' 'Annie. .... understands everything we say.'
2 Thailand is quite unusual: .... has never been ruled by another country.
3 'Do you know who the managing director is?' '............... Rose Berczuk.'
4 Come and have a ride in my new sports car. .... runs beautifully – like a bird.
5 Nothing happened while I was away, did ....?
6 .... did you have lunch with?
7 'Who's that on the phone?' '...............'s your father.'
8 Australia doesn't accept as many immigrants as .... used to.
9 I don't know .... she's going out with now.
10 Everything always happens when you don't want .... to.

'I don't know anybody
who says "It is I".'

'Me?'

reflexives *She taught herself to play the guitar.*

| myself | yourself | himself | itself | ourselves | yourselves | themselves |

We use **reflexives** when the **object** is the same person/thing as the **subject**.

*I cut **myself** shaving this morning.* (**NOT** ~~I cut me~~ ...)
*He tried to kill **himself**.* (Different from *He tried to kill **him**.*)
*The lights switch **themselves** on at night.*

1 **Put in *myself, yourself* etc or *me, you* etc.**

1 Mary bought a book and taught .... to play the guitar.
2 June can't afford to buy .... a new car, so her dad's going to buy one for ....
3 The computer will turn .... off if you don't use it.
4 We looked at .... in the mirror to check our make-up.
5 Don't pay any attention to .... – he always complains.
6 How much time do you give .... to drive to work?
7 He talks about .... all the time.
8 Who gave .... those lovely flowers?
9 It hurt .... when I realised Kim wasn't going to phone me.
10 John fell and hurt .... yesterday.

We can also use **reflexives** to **emphasise** the **subject** or **object** – to say 'that person/thing and nobody/nothing else'.

*It's best if you do it **yourself**.*   *I'll see the President **himself** if necessary.*
*The house **itself** is nice, but the garden's small.*

2 **Put in suitable reflexives.**

1 No one is going to help us, so we'll have to do it ....
2 Veronica always cuts her hair ...., and it always looks great.
3 Robert .... is quite friendly, but the rest of his family are very cold.
4 Did you know that the Morrises built their house ....?
5 I don't trust anyone else to do my accounts; I always do them ....
6 I got to see the gardens, but the palace .... was closed.
7 I had a phone call from the President .... At least, he said he was the President.
8 Children, you'll have to cook supper .... this evening. We're going out.
9 My mother's 83, but she does all the gardening ....
10 George, I haven't got time to fix your bike, you'll have to do it ....

Note the difference between *-selves* and *each other* / *one another*.

*They are looking at **themselves**.*   *They are looking at **each other** / **one another**.*

3 *Each other* **or** *-selves*?

1 Hilary and Jenny write to .... every week.
2 Agnes and Gemma have bought .... a flat in Rome.
3 Do you and your wife tell .... everything?
4 You will all need photos of .... for your membership cards.
5 We've promised .... to telephone if one of us is going to be late home.
6 Can you stop those children hitting ....?
7 We've decided to give .... a really nice holiday this year.
8 Some people only think about ....
9 Cats spend a lot of time washing .... They're very clean animals.
10 Don't invite Louise and Karen together – they hate ....

4 Put in *myself* etc, *each other* or *me, you* etc.

1 We decided to keep most of the fruit for ....
2 Before leaving Eric's office the robbers tied .... up and pulled out all the phone wires.
3 Christine and I always take .... to lunch on our birthdays.
4 Mum, please don't help me – I'd rather do it ....
5 Did you ask Alice whether her brother had phoned .... yet?
6 Don't just stand there shouting at .... – do something!
7 I've just got up – can I phone you back when I've made .... a cup of tea?
8 I've never met John, but we've been writing to .... for over a year now.
9 The necklace .... wouldn't normally be valuable, but it belonged to Queen Elizabeth I, so it will certainly bring a very high price.
10 When babies first start to feed ...., they usually make a big mess.
11 You can't be sure that she got the message unless you told her ....
12 Your teenage children want to be independent – but they expect .... to be ready to help .... whenever they ask you to.

Common expressions with reflexives:
behave yourself   enjoy yourself   help yourself (= 'take what you want')   make yourself at home
by oneself (= 'alone', 'without help')

Verbs normally used without reflexives:
wash, shave, dress, feel, hurry

---

5 Complete the sentences with the words from the box, with or without a reflexive.

behave	by	dress	enjoy	feel	help	hurry	make	shave	washes

1 Children, if you don't .... you'll got straight to bed without any supper.
2 Harry started to .... when he was 16.
3 Hi, Petra. Come in and .... at home.
4 'Can I have something to drink?' 'Sure. ....'
5 'We're off on holiday tomorrow.' 'Are you? Well, ...'
6 Please .... We're very late.
7 I .... ill. Do you think I should see the doctor?
8 I can't do this .... Can you help me?
9 That boy's neck is really dirty. I don't think he ever ....
10 I don't usually .... when I get up. I stay in pyjamas until after breakfast.

Own replaces possessive reflexives: *my own* room (**NOT** ~~myself's room~~).

you, *one* and *they* *You can't learn French in a month.*

You and **one** can mean **'people in general'** (including the **speaker** and **hearer**). *One* is more formal than *you*.

You/One *can't learn French in a month.*
You *dial* / **One** *dials 999 in an emergency.*

One has a possessive **one's**.

One's *own problems always seem important.*

To talk about people **not including the speaker/hearer**, we use *they* or a **passive**.

They speak *English in this shop.*   **English is spoken** *in this shop.*
(**NOT** ~~One speaks English in this shop.~~)

① **Complete the sentences using the expressions in the box. Begin *You can't*.**

at age 15   from Birmingham to Canberra   if you get up late   if you're bad at maths
in a cold climate   in your sleep   with a fork   without a passport   without a ticket ✓
without an appointment   without breaking eggs

▶ travel by train .....You can't travel by train without a ticket.....................................
1 get into the US ....
2 fly directly ....
3 be a physicist ....
4 grow oranges ....
5 get a driving licence ....
6 eat soup ....
7 see animals in the forest ....
8 learn languages ....
9 see the Director ....
10 make an omelette ....

② **Make the sentences in Exercise 1 more formal, changing *you* to *one* and *your* to *one's*.**

1 ....
2 ....
3 ....
4 ....
5 ....
6 ....
7 ....
8 ....
9 ....
10 ....

'Diplomacy – the patriotic art of lying for one's country.'
(*Ambrose Bierce*)

'I was [judged] in my absence and sentenced to death in my absence, so I said they could shoot me in my absence.'
(*Brendan Behan*)

'You can get much further with a kind word and a gun than you can with a kind word alone.'
(*Al Capone*)

'Knowing what you cannot do is more important than knowing what you can do.'
(*Lucille Ball*)

'You cannot feed the hungry on statistics.'
(*David, Earl Lloyd George*)

'Britain would be a great country if only you could roof it over.'
(*Anonymous*)

They (informal) can mean **'the people around'** or **'the authorities'**, **'the government'**.

They don't like strangers around here.   *They* say she's pregnant again.
They're always digging up the roads.   *They* don't care about old people.

3 Put in *you*, *your*, *they* or *them*.

' 1 ....'ve
put the price of
stamps up again.'

'Oh, 2 ....
haven't, have 3 ....?
4 .... seem to do it more and more
often. 5 .... can't buy more than a few
stamps at a time, or else 6 .... have to
buy extra 1p stamps to add to all
7 .... letters when the prices
go up again'

'I know. And it's got so
expensive! Nowadays 8 .... think
twice before 9 .... write a letter.
Of course 10 ....'ve got special
rates for businesses – it's only ordinary
people that pay
the extra.'

'I know. It makes
11 .... wonder
why we keep electing
12 ....'

We can also use *they*, *them* and *their(s)* to refer to a **singular indefinite person** – for example,
after *somebody*, *anybody*, *nobody*, *who*, *a person*.

Somebody phoned and said **they** wanted to see you.
If *anybody* calls, tell **them** I'm out.
Who's forgotten **their** umbrella?

4 *They/them/their/theirs* or another pronoun?
1   Someone's left me a note, but .... haven't signed it.
2   The person who phoned wouldn't give .... name.
3   Nobody in the club has paid .... annual subscription yet.
4   I can't help anybody unless .... bring all the right documents with ....
5   If I find out who's made this mess in the kitchen, I'll kill ....
6   Judy says somebody's stolen .... lecture notes.
7   Some idiot has taken my bag and left me .... !
8   If anybody can fill in this form, ...'re brighter than me.
9   Nobody will believe me unless I show .... the picture.
10   That woman I was talking to had .... car stolen yesterday.

'No one can make you feel
inferior without your consent.'
(*Eleanor Roosevelt*)

'Watermelon – it's a good fruit. You eat,
you drink, you wash your face.'
(*Enrico Caruso*)

'If the child possesses the
nationality or citizenship of
another country, they may
lose this when they get a
British passport.'
(*Passport application form*)

'I hate to spread rumours,
but what else can one do
with them?'
(*Amanda Lear*)

personal pronouns and possessives: more practice

1 **Mixed structures. Choose the correct form.**

1 Seven o'clock. .... time to get up. (*Its, It's*)
2 Everybody put on .... coats and went out. (*the, their*)
3 'Which is Dr Packer?' 'That's .... at the bar.' (*he, him*)
4 We decided to give .... a holiday in Wales. (*us, ourselves*)
5 '.............. the woman in blue?' '.............. Professor Archer.' (*Whose, Who's; It's, Its, She's*)
6 ....! We're going to be late. (*Hurry, Hurry yourself*)
7 That horse has got something wrong with .... eye. (*its, it's*)
8 Do you know .... bike that is by the gate? (*whose, who's*)
9 My brother's a lot older than .... (*I, me*)
10 I hope you .... on holiday next week. (*enjoy, enjoy yourselves*)

2 **Mixed structures. Correct the mistakes or write 'Correct'.**

▶ I cut ~~me~~ shaving this morning. ....*myself*............
▶ It's Tuesday. ....*Correct.*..................
1 Alex is a good friend of mine. ....
2 Everybody was late except me. ....
3 We write to ourselves every week. ....
4 Somebody's taken my coat instead of theirs. ....
5 It's nice if a child can have an own room. ....
6 'Nice cakes.' 'I made them myself.' ....
7 'Who said that?' 'Not me. It was her.' ....
8 'I'm cold.' 'I too.' ....
9 Come in and make you at home. ....
10 It's raining. You'd better take the raincoat. ....

3 **Structures with *than* and *as*. Write six sentences comparing yourself and a relative or friend. Use *than me/him* or *as me/him*.**

▶ ....*My brother's much taller than me.   I don't work as hard as him.*....................
1 ....
2 ....
3 ....
4 ....
5 ....
6 ....

4 **Structures with *than* and *as*. Now make your six sentences more formal.**

▶ ....*My brother's much taller than I am.   I don't work as hard as he does.*....................
1 ....
2 ....
3 ....
4 ....
5 ....
6 ....

5 *You* meaning 'people in general'. Write six things that you can do in a railway station, or six things that you can't do in a bank.

▶ ...You can have a party in a railway station. You can't play football in a bank...........

1 ....

2 ....

3 ....

4 ....

5 ....

6 ....

6 Grammar in a text. Complete the text with words from the box. Use a dictionary if necessary.

balance build dive give put throw throw tie use wrap

A BRICK CAN BE REALLY USEFUL

You can ¹ .... it at somebody you don't like. You can ² .... it on your head to practise walking elegantly. In the mountains, you can ³ .... it in your friend's backpack to slow him down. If you want to take out a bad tooth, you can ⁴ .... it to the tooth and then drop it. You can throw it into a swimming pool and ⁵ .... for it. You can ⁶ .... it as a door stop. If you haven't got any friends, you can ⁷ .... it a name, and it can be your friend. You can ⁸ .... it in pretty paper and give it as a present to somebody you hate. You can ⁹ .... it through a window if you want to break into a house. If you find some more, you can ¹⁰ .... a house with it.

7 Internet exercise. Use a search engine (e.g. Google) to find five interesting sentences with "*each other*".

1 ....

2 ....

3 ....

4 ....

5 ....

8 Mixed structures. Choose some of the words from the box to complete the cartoon captions.

its it's her herself our ours we you you

'Have .... any
"Do it .... " books?'

' .... just natural, that's all.
.... love ....
because you're ...., like the car.'

personal pronouns and possessives: revision test

1 One mistake has been corrected in the table. Can you find the other five?

me	me	my	mine	myself
you	your	your	yours	yourself
he	him	his	his	himself
she	her	hers	hers	herself
it	it	~~it's~~ *its*	–	itself
we	us	our	ours	ourselves
you	you	your	yours	yourselves
they	them	their	their	theirselves

2 Choose the right words.

1 'Is this Alice's book or *your / yours*, do you know?' 'It's *her / hers*.'
2 '*Who's / Whose* car is that in the drive?' 'I don't know – not *our / ours*.'
3 Take *your / yours* feet off the table. *It's / Its* legs aren't very strong.
4 John's coming with *his / her* sister and Catherine's bringing *his / her* brother.
5 Christopher and Patricia never cut the grass in *their / theirs* garden.
6 The Whartons are spending August in *our / ours* flat, and we're borrowing *their / theirs*.
7 That's *my / mine* coat, and the scarf is *my / mine* too.
8 They're both talking at the same time, and not listening to *each other / themselves* at all.
9 I don't *feel / feel myself* very well today.
10 She loves to look at *her / herself* in the mirror.
11 I'm not as clever as *he / he is*.
12 Don't just stand there with *the / your* mouth open.
13 I'd like to have *an / my* own flat.
14 My parents don't understand me, and sometimes I don't understand *me / myself*.
15 'Who broke that glass?' 'It was *he / him*.'

3 Correct the mistakes or write 'Correct'.

▶ It's January 10th. ...*Correct.*...........
▶ I'm looking for Mrs Armstrong. Is that ~~she~~? ...*her*...........
1 You can't buy stamps in a bank. ....
2 Whose the man in the blue suit? ....
3 Anna's sister is a lot younger than she. ....
4 One cannot buy stamps in a bank ....
5 Let's go out and buy us a nice meal. ....
6 I bought this car from a my friend. ....
7 They say Peter's lost his job. ....
8 'I'm getting tired.' 'Me too.' ....
9 Hurry yourself. It's time to get the bus. ....
10 Somebody phoned, but they didn't leave their name. ....
11 I think that cat has hurt its foot. ....
12 You didn't shave yourself this morning, did you? ....
13 That's a very original jacket. Did you make it yourself? ....
14 Everybody understood except I. ....
15 What's that brother of yours doing these days? ....

In some answers, both contracted forms (for example *I'm, don't*) and full forms (for example *I am, do not*) are possible. Normally both are correct.

SECTION 14 nouns

GRAMMAR SUMMARY

English nouns can be **countable** (we can say *two dogs*) or **uncountable** (we can't say ~~two waters~~).
Countable nouns have **plurals** (*dogs*), and we can use *a/an* with them (*a dog, an apology*).
Uncountable nouns have **no plurals**, and we **can't** use *a/an* before them.

Some English uncountable nouns are countable in some other languages (like *information*).

We can join two nouns:

- with a **possessive *'s or s'*** (for example *my **sister's** car, my **parents'** neighbours*).
- with a **preposition** (for example *the **top of the** hill*).
- directly one after the other (for example *orange juice, a flower shop*).

Usually, an idea can be expressed in only one of these ways, and it is often difficult to know which is correct. The rules on pages 207–210 will help, but there are exceptions – this is a difficult point of grammar.

NEW **Christmas range**
New Christmas range now available in store and online

save 20% **Garden buildings**
Save 20% off over 150 garden buildings. Web exclusive price only

save 1/3 off **Selected bathroom collections**
Save one third off selected bathroom collections

save 15% **All Venture integrated kitchen appliances**
Save 15% off Venture integrated kitchen appliances

save 1/3 off **Wright and Miller kitchen furniture**
Save one third off Wright & Miller kitchen doors, drawer fronts & cabinets

revise the basics: countable and uncountable nouns

Countable nouns have **plurals**, and **can** be used with *a/an*.

a chair – chairs   *a house – houses*   *an idea – ideas*

Uncountable nouns have **no plurals**, and **cannot** normally be used with *a/an*. Examples: *air, water, sand, intelligence, English, weather.*

*Can you open a window? I need **air**.* (NOT *… an air* OR *… airs*)
*She speaks good **English**.* (NOT *… a good English.*)
*It's terrible **weather**.* (NOT *… a terrible weather.*)

1 **Can you divide these words into uncountable and countable?**

book, cup, dust, flour, flower, happiness, knowledge, love, milk, meat, mountain, music, oil, piano, rain, river, snow, song, table, wall

COUNTABLE: ....
....

UNCOUNTABLE: ....
....

Some nouns can be **countable** or **uncountable**, with **different meanings**.

Paper is made from wood.   *I'm going out to buy **a paper**.* (= 'a newspaper')
*Did you remember to buy **coffee**?   I'll have **a** (cup of) **coffee**, please.*
*My mother never drinks **wine**.   Spain produces some wonderful **wines**.* (= 'kinds of wine')

2 **Uncountable, singular countable (with *a/an*) or plural? Complete the sentences.**

1 Could you pass me ....? (*glass*)
2 This table is made of .... (*glass*)
3 I need a piece of .... (*wood*)
4 The house was near .... (*wood*)
5 She looked at him with .... (*pity*)
6 It's .... Anne isn't here. (*pity*)
7 .... goes so quickly. (*time*)

8 She phoned six .... yesterday. (*time*)
9 Three ...., please. (*beer*)
10 .... makes you fat. (*beer*)
11 He hasn't got much .... (*experience*)
12 It was .... I won't forget. (*experience*)
13 There's .... in the garden. (*chicken*)
14 Do you want .... or beef? (*chicken*)

The following words are normally **uncountable** in English (but **countable** in some other languages).
They are normally only **singular**. We can use *some* with them, but **not *a/an*.** (NOT *a travel, an information*)

advice   baggage   bread   furniture   hair   information   knowledge   luck
luggage   news   research   spaghetti (and *macaroni* etc)   *travel   work*

*I need **some information**.   This **bread is** too expensive.*
*Her **hair is** very long.   **Travel teaches** you a lot.*

3 **Put *a* with the countable nouns and *some* with the uncountable nouns.**

.... baggage .... bread .... bus .... dishwasher .... furniture
.... holiday .... house .... luck .... knowledge
.... magazine .... problem .... research .... table .... travel
.... work

more about countable and uncountable nouns

Sometimes uncountable and countable nouns have **similar meanings**.

food – a meal   *clothing – a coat*   *crockery – a plate*

1 Can you put these words in pairs (one uncountable, one countable) expressing similar ideas?

> accommodation ✓   advertisement   luggage   bread   cars   dollar   fact   flat ✓
> furniture   information   job   journey   loaf   money   publicity   suitcase   table
> traffic   travel   work

accommodation, a flat ....

....

....

....

2 GRAMMAR AND VOCABULARY: fixed expressions. The nouns in the box are normally uncountable. They can be made countable by adding other words. Use a dictionary or the internet to find out which words go with which.

> advice ✓   bread   chess   chocolate   grass   lightning   luck   news   soap   thunder

a piece or word of ...*advice*............   a blade of ....

an item or a piece of ....   a bar of .... **OR** ....

a flash of ....   a loaf of ....

a stroke of ....   a game of ....

a clap of ....

3 Choose the correct form of the caption for each cartoon.

'*An advice,* / *A word of advice,* / *Some advices*, Arthur: no-one ever solved his problems by running away.'

'Doesn't it make you sick? Our *baggage has* / *baggages have* been sent to Jupiter.'

With a few uncountable nouns referring to **emotional** and **mental** activity, we use *a/an* when there is an **adjective** or other description.

*a **love** of music*   *an excellent **knowledge** of German*   *a good **education***

In some answers, both contracted forms (for example *I'm*, *don't*) and full forms (for example *I am*, *do not*) are possible. Normally both are correct.

NOUNS **203**

revise the basics: how to spell plurals

1 **DO IT YOURSELF** Look at the words in the box and answer the questions.

babies	books	boys	buses	buzzes	cars	chairs	cities	dishes	echoes
Eskimos	foxes	gases	heroes	holidays	kilos	ladies	lorries	matches	monkeys
photos	pianos	potatoes	quizzes	radios	shops	tables	taxes	times	tomatoes
watches	ways	wishes	zoos						

1 What is the most common way of making the plurals of nouns?

....

2 How do we make the plurals of words ending in **consonant** (*b, t, d* etc) + **-y**?

....

3 How do we make the plurals of words ending in **vowel** (*a, e, o, u*) + **-y**?

....

4 After which letters and groups of letters do we add **-es** to the singular?

....

5 Four common words ending in -*o* have plurals in -*es*. Can you remember which they are without looking? ....

2 Write the plurals of these nouns.

address .... box .... brush ....
computer .... desk .... face ....
guy .... list .... loss ....
mess .... patch .... patio ....
peach .... play .... poppy ....
reply .... toy .... tree ....
witch .... worry ....

3 Write six sentences, using at least two plurals from Exercise 1 in each.

Foxes don't like tomatoes.
....
....
....
....
....
....
....

One potatoe, two potatoes

IN JUNE 1992, US Vice-President Dan Quayle visited a school class in New Jersey while the children were having a spelling competition. When 12-year-old William Figueroa wrote the word potato correctly on the blackboard, Quayle told him he should add an e. William became a schoolchildren's national hero (without an e) and appeared on television; the Vice-President became an international laughing-stock as echoes (with an e) of his mistake went round the world.

plurals of nouns: special cases *aircraft, sheep, arms*

1 Here are seven groups of nouns. Look in the box and find two more nouns to add
to each group. Use a dictionary to help you if necessary.

| aircraft   crisis   dozen   mathematics   means   mouse   news   police   scissors |
| sheep   shelf   thousand   tooth   wolf |

1 COUNTABLE NOUNS WITH SINGULAR (AND PLURAL) IN -*s*
series   crossroads   analysis – analyses   .... – ....

2 NOUNS WITH SINGULAR AND PLURAL THE SAME
trout   deer   fish   salmon   ....

3 NOUNS THAT HAVE A PLURAL WITHOUT -*s* AFTER A NUMBER
hundred (e.g. *two hundred*)   million   ....

4 NOUNS WITH SINGULAR IN -*f(e)*, PLURAL IN -*ves*
calf – calves   half   knife   leaf   life   loaf   self   thief   wife
.... – .... – ....

5 NOUNS WITH IRREGULAR PLURALS
child – children   criterion – criteria   foot – feet   fungus – fungi   goose – geese
man – men   medium – media   ox – oxen   penny – pence   phenomenon – phenomena
woman – women   .... – .... – ....

6 UNCOUNTABLE SINGULAR NOUNS ENDING IN -*s* (NORMALLY NO PLURAL)
athletics   billiards   economics   gymnastics   measles   physics   politics
....

7 PLURAL NOUNS WITH NO SINGULAR
arms   belongings   cattle   clothes   congratulations   contents   earnings
goods   outskirts   people   remains   surroundings   thanks   troops   trousers
....

deer

fish

In some answers, both contracted forms (for example *I'm, don't*) and full
forms (for example *I am, do not*) are possible. Normally both are correct.

NOUNS **205**

mixed singular and plural *My family are angry with me.*

Singular nouns for **groups** of people often have **plural verbs and pronouns** in British English, especially when we are talking about personal kinds of action. Compare:

*My **family are** very angry with me: **they** think I should go to university.*
*The average **family has** 3.5 members: **it** is much smaller than in 1900.*
*The **team are** going to lose again. **They're** useless.*
*A cricket **team is** made up of eleven players, including **its** captain.*

1 Choose the best expressions from the box to complete the sentences.

class is	club has	orchestra is	school has	staff do
class are	club have	orchestra are	school have	staff does

1a In England, a state .... to give time to religious education.
1b My daughter's .... decided to hold their sports day next Saturday.
2a The .... given £5,000 to charity this year.
2b The .... fifty per cent more members than a year ago.
3a The .... not like the new manager.
3b The .... not need to be increased.
4a Jane's .... in Room 6.
4b Our .... planning a party.
5a The .... just tuning up – let's hurry in.
5b An .... composed of string, wind, and percussion instruments.

The following **singular expressions** can be followed by **plural nouns and verbs**:
a number of   the majority of   a couple of   a group of   a lot of   the rest of

***A number of** us **are** worried about it.* (**NOT** ~~A number of us is ...~~)
***The majority of** teachers **disagree**.*
*There are **a couple** of children outside.*   ***The rest of** the members **are** ill.*

Some **plural expressions** (names of quantities, and expressions joined by *and*) have **singular verbs**.

***Ten pounds is** too much to pay.*   ***The United States is** smaller than Canada.*   ***Fish and chips costs** £8.*

2 Choose the right verb.

1 A number of people *has / have* complained about the noise.
2 Do you think three pounds *is / are* a big enough tip?
3 Hamburger and chips *is / are* not a very healthy lunch.
4 In the latest rail union vote, the majority *has / have* voted to go on strike; the rest of the members *is / are* expected to support the strike fairly solidly.
5 Two kilos *is / are* pretty small for a newborn baby.
6 Our teenage son thinks there *is / are* a number of good reasons for staying up late and having a good time.
7 A couple of dangerous-looking men *is / are* waiting for you outside.
8 Six weeks *is / are* a long time to wait for news of your family.
9 The majority of the children's parents *is / are* unemployed.
10 A lot of shops *is / are* opening on Sundays now.
11 The United States *has / have* serious economic problems.
12 Tom and Rosie were late, but the rest of us *was / were* on time.
13 *Is / Are* bacon and eggs what you usually eat for breakfast?
14 We've just learnt that a couple of our club members *has / have* been chosen for the national team.

revise the basics: possessive 's

SINGULAR noun(s) + **'s:**   my **mother's** car   **Sarah and Henry's** house (NOT ~~Sarah's and Henry's house~~)
PLURAL noun + **':**   my **parents'** home
IRREGULAR plural + **'s:**   the **children's** names

1 **Make possessive forms from the expressions in List 1, to combine with expressions from List 2. Make fifteen combinations.**

> **LIST 1**   your sister   Jonathan   Emily and Claire   those women   my teachers
> Katie   our dog   Simon and Jill   most people   doctors

> **LIST 2**   address   car/cars   ideas   health   legs   father/fathers   nose/noses
> clothes   education   fear of heights

▶ *your sister's address* ....
▶ *my teachers' clothes* ....
1 ....
2 ....
3 ....
4 ....
5 ....
6 ....
7 ....

8 ....
9 ....
10 ....
11 ....
12 ....
13 ....
14 ....
15 ....

Possessives usually **replace articles** before nouns. We can say **the** car or **Sue's** car, but not ~~Sue's the car~~ or ~~the Sue's car~~.
But a possessive word can have its own article: **the boss's** car.
NOTE ALSO: that car of Sue's; a friend of Joe's (like a friend of mine – see page 191).

2 **Right or wrong? Correct the mistakes or write 'Correct'.**

▶ my ~~mothers~~ car   *mother's* ....
▶ Anna's sister.   *Correct.* ....
1 Is this the teacher's pen? ....
2 Are you the Al's daughter? ....
3 Do you know Lesley's last name? ....
4 Here's the Barry's address. ....
5 Here's my parents' address. ....
6 It was the school's responsibility. ....
7 What's the Wilsons' number? ....
8 That's an old habit of Marion's. ....
9 It's a crazy idea of Alice. ....
10 Where is that brother of Carol? ....

'I laid 67,000 eggs last year, and
if I don't receive a Mother's Day
card there'll be trouble.'

NOTE: We spent the evening **at Cathy's.** (='... at Cathy's house.')

She's at **the hairdresser's.**   I bought it at **Harrod's.**

In some answers, both contracted forms (for example I'm, don't) and full
forms (for example I am, do not) are possible. Normally both are correct.

NOUNS **207**

possessive *'s* or *of* ... *my father's name; the name of the book*

We use the **possessive *'s*** structure especially when the first noun is the name of a **person**, **group of people**, **organisation**, **country** or **animal**.
In other cases we generally prefer a structure with *of*. Compare:

my **father's** name	the name **of the book**
the **firm's** structure	the structure **of plastic**
America's influence	the influence **of alcohol**
the **dog's** head	the head **of the bed**

We also use the **possessive *'s*** structure with common **'time when'** expressions, and in expressions of **measurement of time**.

today's paper	**tomorrow's** weather	**yesterday's** news
a month's holiday	**three hours'** delay	

1 Join the expressions in the box to make expressions with possessive *'s* or *'*, or with *of*.

> the club + its monthly meeting ✓   his parents + their car ✓   the world + its end ✓
> Angela + her leg   the trees + their highest branches   my suitcase + its lock
> your dog + its mouth   the bank + its branch in Paris   your office + its floor
> the river + its mouth   my family + its name   the town + its atmosphere
> our company + its best sales manager   the police force + its main problem
> next week + its timetable   last night + its party   today + its news

▶ the club's monthly meeting
▶ his parents' car
▶ the end of the world

2 Make two noun groups from each set of words.

▶ file: your secretary, legal documents: *your secretary's file, the file of legal documents*
1 story: Helen, the French Revolution
2 bed: the stream, the patient
3 policy: full employment, the company
4 style: my favourite author, the 1930s
5 place: language education, women
6 ideas: modern physics, my son
7 rules: the club, football
8 view: the committee, the lake
9 head: the cat, the queue
10 arm: the chair, John

revise the basics: noun + noun

We often put one noun in front of another. The **first noun** is rather like an **adjective**, and is usually **singular**, even if the meaning is plural.

a *horse* race (a kind of race)   a *race* horse (a kind of horse)
a *shoe* shop (**NOT** ~~a shoes shop~~)   a *Lancashire* man
a *ten-mile* walk (**NOT** ~~a ten-miles walk~~)

Articles belonging to the **first noun** are **dropped** in this structure. *Officers in **the army** = **army** officers*, **NOT** ~~the army officers~~.

1 Match the expressions on the left with their meanings on the right.

0	coffee table	A	shoe made of leather ......
1	chocolate milk	B	book describing cases ......
2	milk chocolate	C	chocolate made with milk ......
3	book case	D	leather for making shoes ......
4	case book	E	drawing done in ink ......
5	leather shoe	F	garden with flowers in ......
6	shoe leather	G	ink used for drawing ......
7	flower garden	H	milk flavoured with chocolate ......
8	garden flower	I	piece of furniture for books ......
9	ink drawing	J	flower that grows in gardens ......
10	drawing ink	K	table for coffee ..*0*..

2 What do you call these?

1 a shop that sells music ....
2 a man from Birmingham ....
3 a frame for a picture ....
4 tea made from mint ....
5 the clock in the station ....
6 a rocket that goes into space ....
   ....
7 a factory that makes biscuits ....
   ....
8 powder made from soap ....

9 furniture for the garden ....
10 a sign in the road ....
11 a brush for teeth ....
12 programmes about wildlife ....
    ....
13 a bottle for wine ....
14 a play produced by a school ....
    ....
15 a paper that is sold in the evening ....
    ....

3 Put these words into pairs to make noun + noun expressions. Change plural to singular if necessary.

antique   bicycle   bus   cowboy   door   film   grapes   juice   kitchen   map
newspapers   publisher   race   roads   shop   station

....
....
....
....

Note the difference between, for example, *a water bottle* (a bottle for water, which may be full or empty) and *a bottle of water* (a bottle with water in).

In some answers, both contracted forms (for example *I'm*, *don't*) and full forms (for example *I am*, *do not*) are possible. Normally both are correct.

NOUNS **209**

noun + noun or preposition *road signs; signs of anger*

We use the **noun + noun structure** for **well-known** everyday combinations.
To talk about things that **do not go together** so often, we usually prefer a structure with a **preposition**.
Compare:

a war film   *a film about a dog* (**NOT** ~~a dog film~~)
a history book   *a book about violins* (**NOT** ~~a violin book~~)
a postman   *a man from the bank* (**NOT** ~~a bank man~~)
road signs   *signs of anger* (**NOT** ~~anger signs~~)
a corner table   *the girl in the corner* (**NOT** ~~the corner girl~~)

1 **Eight of these ideas can naturally be expressed by 'noun + noun'. Which are they? Rewrite them.**

1 a cake made of chocolate ....
2 a child in the garden ....
3 a cupboard in the kitchen ....
4 a box for matches ....
5 paste for cleaning teeth ....
6 discussions about furniture ....
7 the door to the kitchen ....
8 a bottle designed for wine ....
9 a timetable of trains ....
10 a book about the moon ....
11 chairs for the garden ....
12 a man with a hat ....

2 **Look at the labels. Can you think of five more names of food that use the noun + noun structure?**

1 ....
2 ....
3 ....
4 ....
5 ....

Newspaper headlines often save space by using the noun + noun structure instead of the preposition structure.
Strings of three or four nouns are common.

**Channel ferry safety drill
leaves 18 injured**

Decision day
in rail dispute

Football club burglars
cut home phones

one(s) *a big one with cream*

> We use *one(s)* to avoid repeating a countable noun.

*'What sort of **cake** would you like?'* *'A big **one** with cream.'*
*I'd like some **shoes** like the **ones** in the window.*
*'Could you lend me a **pen**?'* *'Sorry, I haven't got **one**.'*

> We **don't** use *one* for an **uncountable** noun.

*We haven't got fresh **cream**. Would you like **tinned**?* (**NOT** *… tinned one.*)

1 **Put in words and expressions from the box with or without *one(s)*.**

| Chinese   cold   long sunny   new   red woollen ✓   sharp   small metal |
| solid practical   that I've read   unsweetened orange   white cotton |

▶ 'What colour cardigans would you like to see?' '.. Red woollen ones ...., please.'

1 There's my suitcase, the ....!

2 I've lost my jacket. It's a ....

3 'What kind of juice is that?' '......................................'

4 I've got too many books. I'm giving away the ....

5 She doesn't sell used cars, only ....

6 'What sort of holiday are you having this year?' 'A ....'

7 This isn't Thai food, it's ....

8 I don't want pretty shoes, but ....

9 Hand me a knife, will you – a ....

10 Don't wash this in warm water. Use ....

> If there is **no adjective**, we do **not** use *a* with *one*.

'What sort of cake would you like?' *'**One** with cream.'* (**NOT** *'A one …'*)

> We use *some/any* without *ones*. We use *mine* etc **instead of** *my one* etc.

*'Could you lend me some **stamps**?'* *'I haven't got **any**.'* (**NOT** *'… any ones.'*)
'Which car shall we take?' *'**Mine**.'* (**NOT** *'My one.'*)

2 **Put in *one*, *some*, *any* or *mine/yours* etc.**

1 'What sort of job would you like to do?' '.................. where I travel a lot.'

2 I haven't got a train timetable, but ask Adrian – he may have ....

3 'Is that your car or Anna's?' '.................. – Anna hasn't got a car.'

4 There aren't any matches here, but there may be .... in the kitchen.

5 I need a watch – .... with an alarm.

6 'Where are the forks?' 'Oh, no! We didn't bring ....!'

7 Barry has put his name on this book, but Liz says it's ....

8 If you haven't got enough plates, I'll be happy to bring ....

3 **Give your own answers to the questions. Use *one*.**

1 What sort of car would you like? ....

2 What sort of house would you like? ....

3 What sort of garden would you like? ....

4 What sort of job would you like? ....

In some answers, both contracted forms (for example *I'm*, *don't*) and full
forms (for example *I am*, *do not*) are possible. Normally both are correct.

NOUNS **211**

nouns: more practice

1 Irregular plurals. See if you can remember the plurals of these nouns.

criterion ....   fish ....   thief ....

fungus ....   phenomenon ....   series ....

analysis ....   tomato ....   goose ....

2 No singular; no plural. Seven of these nouns are normally singular with no plural; seven are plural with no singular; seven are normal. Write 'S', 'P' or 'N'.

athletics ..S..   belongings ..P..   end ..N..   billiards ......   cattle ......   clothes ......
congratulations ......   economics ......   exam ......   glass ......   gymnastics ......   hand ......
idea ......   meal ......   measles ......   paper ......   physics ......   research ......   scissors ......
thanks ......   trousers ......

3 Mixed singular and plural. Choose the best forms.

1 The missing group of climbers *has / have* radioed to say that they are safe.
2 A number of people *has / have* written to Professor Taylor to show their support for his plan.
3 Ten euros *is / are* a lot to pay for one coffee.
4 Fish and chips *is / are* a traditional British supper.
5 Most of the people here *agrees / agree* with me.
6 A couple of policemen *is / are* outside and *wants / want* to speak to you.
7 A rugby union team *has / have* fifteen players.
8 My family *thinks / think* I'm crazy.
9 Eight months *is / are* a long time to wait for a visa.
10 The majority of us *wants / want* a change of government.

4 Mixed structures Choose the correct forms.

1 I'd like *one / a one* with long sleeves.
2 Have you got a *bus timetable? / timetable of buses?*
3 Do you know *school's / the school's* phone number?
4 Here's a photo of *Mark's / Mark* and Sylvia's baby.
5 I'm reading a *Napoleon book. / book about Napoleon.*
6 I can hear *the postman's van. / the van of the postman.*
7 She's *a John's friend. / a friend of John. / a friend of John's.*
8 Please don't put your cup on *the chair's arm / the arm of the chair.*
9 There was an empty *wine bottle / wine's bottle / bottle of wine* under his bed.
10 That was a really good idea of *Maggie. / Maggie's.*

5 Noun + noun and possessives Choose the correct forms of the cartoon captions.

'Fear? He doesn't know *the meaning of the word. / the word's meaning.*'

'Right , Mr Wilson. I have here *your tests' results. / the results of your tests.*'

6 GRAMMAR AND VOCABULARY: words beginning with *sun*. Complete the sentences with the words in the box (use a dictionary if necessary). There is one expression too many – it doesn't exist!

sunburn	suncream	sundial	sunfall	sunflowers
sunglasses	sunrise	sunset	sunspots	sunstroke suntan

1 Let's just sit here and look at the .... until it gets dark.
2 Those .... are taller than I am.
3 If you don't put on more ...., you'll get ....
4 John got .... during the race. He's been taken to hospital.
5 Apparently there are more .... than usual every eleven years.
6 I've lost my .... Have you seen them anywhere?
7 That's not a real .... She puts it on out of a bottle.
8 Do you think that .... tells the right time?
9 What time is .... tomorrow morning?

7 Grammar in a text. Complete the news story with expressions from the box. Don't forget to add '*s* or '.

a man	children	girls	Josie and Cara	local people	the other children
the shopkeeper	their grandmother ✓	their grandparents			

Police looking for two young girls

The two girls disappeared from ▶ *their grandmother's* ..... garden in Ilkley yesterday evening. Josie and Cara Sharp, aged 7 and 9, were staying at [1] ....
house for a week. They were in Ilkley for a [2] .... theatre course. The police have asked the course teachers for [3] .... names and addresses, and they have also put [4] .... photos on local television. The two [5] .... mother, Mrs Jenna Sharp, has appeared on TV as well. A shopkeeper thinks she saw Josie and Cara getting into [6] .... car; police officers have asked for [7] .... help with a photofit picture of the man. The police have also got [8] .... help in looking for the girls near the town.

8 Internet exercise. Put '✓' against the expressions that you think are more common. Then use a search engine (e.g. Google) to see how many hits you get for each.

EXPRESSION	HITS
"office door" ✓	553,000
"chocolate biscuit"	
"furniture garden"	
"car door"	
"garden flower"	
"food dog"	

EXPRESSION	HITS
"door office"	9,300
"biscuit chocolate"	
"garden furniture"	
"door car"	
"flower garden"	
"dog food"	

nouns: revision test

1 **Put *a/an* before the countable nouns, and *some* before the uncountables.**

.... advice   .... artist   .... bread   .... company

.... curtain   .... furniture   .... information   .... job

.... joke   .... journey   .... money   .... publicity

.... traffic   .... train   .... travel

2 **Write the plurals.**

baby ...*babies*...   boy ....   bus ....   city ....

crossroads ....   deer ....   echo ....   loaf ....

gas ....   half ....   kilo ....   monkey ....

phenomenon ....   piano ....   series ....   watch ....

3 **What do you call these?**

1 a shop that sells flowers. ....

2 juice made from raspberries ....

3 a brush for shoes ....

4 a radio in a car ....

5 a paper that you buy in the morning ....

6 bottles for water ....

7 poison for rats ....

8 exams in universities ....

9 a factory that makes marmalade ....

10 a cupboard in a bathroom ....

4 **Right or wrong? Correct the mistakes or write 'Correct'.**

▶ Are those ~~Johns'~~ glasses? ...*John's*...

▶ I need some advice. ...*Correct.*...

1 I'm going to buy some new furnitures. ....

2 Athletics are my favourite kind of sport. ....

3 Mr Parker's cattle have got out again. ....

4 My family are planning to move to Scotland. ....

5 The majority of the voters wants a change. ....

6 The United States are having serious economic problems. ....

7 Those keys are yours. My ones are on the kitchen table. ....

8 I'd really like some juice of fruit. ....

9 Do you know the basketball's rules? ....

10 I've lost Sue and Andy's phone number. ....

11 I need some cooking apples – six big ones, please. ....

12 We haven't got any more cat food. ....

13 What have you done with the bottle of the baby? ....

14 We haven't got any black tea, but I've got green one. ....

15 Jack is a brilliant tennis table player. ....

16 Are you the Maria's sister? ....

17 Sam is a good friend of mine. ....

18 The policeman wanted an information about Harry. ....

19 I thought it was chocolate, but it was a bar of soap. ....

20 This old jeans is falling to pieces. It's time to buy a new one. ....

In some answers, both contracted forms (for example *I'm*, *don't*) and full forms (for example *I am*, *do not*) are possible. Normally both are correct.

SECTION 15 adjectives and adverbs

GRAMMAR SUMMARY

Adjectives are words like *easy*, *slow*, *sorry*, *important*. They can go **before nouns**, or **after some verbs** (e.g. *be, seem, look, appear, smell, taste*). Some kinds of adjective normally go before others (e.g. opinion before description).

   an **interesting old** cathedral

The exact rules are complicated (and not very important).

Adverbs are words like *easily*, *slowly*, *yesterday*, *there*. Different kinds of adverb go in different positions, for example with the verb, or at the end of a sentence.

   Harry **often goes** to Denmark.   I**'ve never seen** a rhinoceros.   You **are probably** right.
   I **only play** tennis with Gary.   The team played **badly last night**.

Some words (e.g. *fast*, *loud*, *daily*) can be **both adjectives and adverbs**.

Many **adverbs** end in *-ly* (e.g. *carefully*). But a few words ending in *-ly* are **adjectives** (e.g. *friendly*).

'If a thing is worth doing,
   it is worth doing well.'
(*Traditional*)

'If a thing is worth doing,
   it is worth doing badly.'
(*G K Chesterton*)

'Speak softly and carry a big stick.'
(*President Theodore Roosevelt*)

'Power tends to corrupt and
absolute power corrupts absolutely.'
(*Lord Acton*)

'[You are] incredibly, inordinately,
devastatingly, immortally, calamitously,
hearteningly, adorably beautiful.'

(*The poet Rupert Brooke to the
actress Cathleen Nesbitt*)

revise the basics: adjectives, adverbs of manner

ADJECTIVES: *kind, shy, cold, angry, wonderful, bad, unusual, mad*
ADVERBS OF MANNER: *kindly, shyly, coldly, angrily, wonderfully, badly, unusually, madly*

We use **adjectives** after **some verbs**, to say how something **is, seems, becomes, looks, feels, sounds, tastes** or **smells.**

*She **is kind**.   She **seems/appears** shy.   It's **getting cold**.*
*He **felt angry** (**NOT** He felt angrily.)   That **smells wonderful**.*

We use **adverbs of manner** with other verbs to say how something **happens** or **is done.**

*She **spoke kindly** but **shyly**. (**NOT** She spoke kind …)   He **answered** me **coldly**.   He **closed** the door **angrily**.*

1 Complete the sentences with words from the box.

> beautiful   beautifully   calm   calmly   slow   slowly   terrible   terribly
> unhappy   unhappily

1 I suppose I should be nervous, but I've never felt so .... in my life.
2 'I suppose we'll never see each other again,' she said ....
3 The house is small and rather simple, but Anne has decorated it ....
4 This soup tastes ....
5 He spoke very ...., but she heard every word like a shout.
6 The train was very ....; perhaps they were working on the line.
7 This is a .... house. I enjoy looking at it every time I walk past.
8 The team played .... last Saturday.
9 Time seemed to go so .... When would he arrive?
10 He looks really .... I wonder what's wrong.

We also use **adverbs before adjectives, past participles, other adverbs** and **prepositional expressions.**

*It's **terribly cold**. (**NOT** … terrible cold.)   This is very **badly cooked**.*
*You're driving **unusually fast**.   He was **madly in love** with her.*

2 Choose the right word.

1 Angela is *amazing / amazingly* good with animals.
2 As soon as I saw him I was *sure / surely* he had been drinking.
3 Do you think that's a *real / really* diamond in her ring?
4 I read an *amazing / amazingly* thing in the newspaper this morning.
5 One leg of the chair was *slight / slightly* damaged.
6 The door was *bad / badly* painted.
7 The food was *wonderful / wonderfully*, but the service was *awful / awfully*.
8 The room is *clever / cleverly* organised so three of us can work there.
9 We're all *complete / completely* on your side.
10 He's acted *unbelievable / unbelievably* stupidly in the past year.

Some verbs are used with both adjectives and adverbs, with different meanings.

*You **look angry**. (= 'You seem angry.')   He **looked angrily** at the manager. (= 'He turned his eyes …')*
*His plan **appeared impossible**. (= 'His plan seemed …')*
*She **suddenly appeared** in the window. (= 'She was visible …')*

interested and *interesting* etc

Interested, *bored*, *excited* etc say **how people feel**.
Interesting, *boring*, *exciting* etc describe **the people or things that cause the feelings.**

I was very interested in the lesson. (**NOT** ~~I was very interesting ...~~)
His lessons are always interesting. (**NOT** ~~His lessons are ... interested.~~)
Do you ever get bored at work?   *My job's pretty boring.*

1 **Complete the words.**

1 I was surpris.......... to see Ann there.
2 It was surpris.......... to see her.
3 I find this work very tir.......... .
4 It makes me tir.......... .
5 Her exam results were disappoint.......... .
6 She was pretty disappoint..........
7 She was excit.......... about her new job.
8 It was an excit.......... new challenge.
9 We were shock........ to hear about
   your brother.
10 The news was really shock.......... .
11 This explanation is very confus.......... .
12 Reading it, I got confus.......... .
13 I get annoy.......... when people
    break promises.
14 It's annoy.......... when that happens.

2 **Look at the cartoon.**
Who is boring – the host or the visitors?

....

'No really, your husband's right, it is late and we must go.'

3 **GRAMMAR AND VOCABULARY: specialists. What are the people interested in?**
Make sentences with words from the two boxes. Use a dictionary if necessary.

| astronomer ✓ | botanist | cook | doctor | explorer | fashion designer |
| geographer | historian | linguist | mathematician | zoologist | |

| animals | clothes | food | languages | medicine | numbers | places |
| plants | the past | the stars ✓ | unknown places | | | |

▶ *An astronomer is interested in the stars.*...

1 ....
2 ....
3 ....
4 ....
5 ....
6 ....
7 ....
8 ....
9 ....
10 ....

In some answers, both contracted forms (for example *I'm*, *don't*) and full
forms (for example *I am*, *do not*) are possible. Normally both are correct.

ADJECTIVES AND ADVERBS **217**

adjectives without nouns *in the country of the blind*

We can use **the + adjective** (without a noun) to talk about some **social groups**.

the young	the old	the rich	the poor	the sick	the disabled	the blind	the deaf
the mentally ill	the homeless	the unemployed	the dead				

These expressions are **plural**: *the blind* means 'blind people'. Compare:

*I'm collecting money for **the blind**.*
*Do you know **the blind person** next door?* (**NOT** … ~~the blind next door?~~)
*I met **a blind man** on the train.* (**NOT**… ~~a blind~~ …)

We can't use all adjectives in this way: we don't normally talk about *the foreign* or *the greedy*, for example.

1 **Complete the sentences with expressions from the box.**

the blind	the dead	the living	the living	the old	the poor
the poor	the rich	the rich	the young	the young	

1 In the country of .... the one-eyed man is king. (*Anonymous*)
2 Love, like youth, is wasted on .... (*Sammy Cahn*)
3 When the rich make war on each other, it's .... who die. (*Jean-Paul Sartre*)
4 It's all that .... can do for ...., to shock them and keep them up to date. (*George Bernard Shaw*)
5 'Let me tell you about .... They are different from you and me.'
  'Yes, they have more money.' (*F Scott Fitzgerald and Ernest Hemingway*)
6 We owe respect to the dead; to .... we owe only truth. (*Voltaire*)
7 .... have more children, but .... have more relatives. (*Anonymous*)
8 Pray for .... and fight like hell for ....
  (*Mother Jones*)

The structure is also used with the following **nationality words**: *Dutch, English, French, Irish, Spanish, Welsh.*

***The Welsh** have a very old literary tradition.*
BUT: *I like **the Welshman** who works in the garage.* (**NOT** … ~~the Welsh~~ …)

2 **Test your knowledge. Put in *Dutch, English, French, Irish* or *Welsh*.**

1 The .... have produced great painters, and are good at building canals.
2 The .... are great musicians, and produce a famous beer called 'Guinness'.
3 The .... have also produced great painters, and make wonderful wine.
4 The .... are good at rugby. They have their own language, and call their country 'Cwmru'.
5 'Continentals think life is a game. The .... think cricket is a game.' (*George Mikes*)

NOTE: Most other nationality words are nouns, not adjectives.

***The Brazilians** speak Portuguese.* (**NOT** ~~The Brazilian~~ …)

order of adjectives *a terrible little boy; old and grey*

This is a complicated (and not very important) point of grammar. The following rules have exceptions. Words for **colour**, **origin/place**, **material** and **purpose** go in that order. Other adjectives come before these.

	OTHER	COLOUR	ORIGIN/PLACE	MATERIAL	PURPOSE	
	old	red	Spanish	leather	riding	boots
a	funny	brown	German		beer	mug

1 **Here are descriptions from a newspaper, a journal, a biography and a novel.**
   Rewrite each description in the right order.

▶ club: jazz, local ....*local jazz club*.................................... (place before purpose)

1 buildings: modern, industrial ....

2 dress: evening, silk, red ....

3 eyes: narrow, colourless ....

4 trunks: black, swimming, nylon ....

5 frame: gold, flat ....

6 tie: blue, woollen ....

7 jacket: short, leather ....

8 boots: French, ski ....

Opinions often come **before descriptions**.

	OPINION	DESCRIPTION	
	funny	old	buildings
a	terrible	little	boy
	nice	new	clothes

2 **Rewrite these descriptions in the right order.**

▶ books: old, terrible ....*terrible old books*.......................... (opinion + description)

1 city: Belgian, beautiful, little ....

2 dinner: excellent, cold ....

3 furniture: old, lovely ....

4 ideas: strange, new ....

5 university: grey, concrete, depressing ....

We use **and** with adjectives that refer to **different parts** of something. Compare:

a long green dress (**NOT** *a long and green dress*)   *a long green and black dress*

When adjectives come **after a verb**, we usually put **and** before the last.

*He was tall, dark **and handsome**.*   *I'm cold, tired **and hungry**.*

3 **Rewrite the words *in italics*, adding *and* if necessary.**

▶ The brick was *rough/pink*. ....*rough and pink*....   4 The sea was *cold/rough*. ....

▶ a *narrow/brown* room ....*narrow, brown*....   5 The church was *old/ugly*. ....

1 *hot/breezy* weather ....   6 a *quiet/tense* woman ....

2 *untidy/red* hair ....   7 *yellow/grey* sand ....

3 The man was *young/bearded*. ....   8 The badges were *red/blue*. ....

First, next and **last** usually come **before numbers**.

*the **first three** weeks* (**NOT** *the three first weeks*)   *my **last two** holidays*

adverbs with the verb *I can never wake up in time.*

Adverbs that go **with the verb** include words expressing **frequency** (e.g. *always*, *often*, *usually*, *never*) and **certainty** (e.g. *definitely probably*). Note the exact position:

AFTER AM/ARE/IS/WAS/WERE

*You **are usually** right.*
*It **was certainly** cold.*

AFTER AUXILIARY VERBS

*She **has probably** forgotten.*
*I **can never** wake up in time.*

BEFORE OTHER VERBS

*He **always forgot** my birthday.*
*I **often get** headaches.*

NOT BETWEEN VERB AND OBJECT

He forgot always my birthday.
I get often headaches.

1 Make ten sentences about yourself and people you know, from the box.

I am .... is ....are	always usually often sometimes not often occasionally never	happy late tired friendly bad-tempered depressed worried in love in trouble etc

▶ My father is often bad-tempered.

1 ....
2 ....
3 ....
4 ....
5 ....
6 ....
7 ....
8 ....
9 ....
10 ....

2 Make ten sentences beginning *I have often/never …*

▶ I have often been to America.   I have never seen an opera.

1 ....
2 ....
3 ....
4 ....
5 ....
6 ....
7 ....
8 ....
9 ....
10 ....

③ Say how often you do some of the following things.

stay in bed late	have bad dreams	eat chocolate	get headaches	play tennis	read poetry

fall in love   go to concerts   play the piano   forget people's names   go to the cinema

cook   go to the doctor   write letters   go skiing   go swimming   get depressed   feel happy

▶ *I sometimes stay in bed late.   I don't often go to the doctor.* ....

1 ....

2 ....

3 ....

4 ....

5 ....

6 ....

7 ....

8 ....

9 ....

10 ....

④ These sentences are all taken from real recorded conversations. Can you put the adverbs in the right places?

▶ You are∕here when something happens. (*usually*)

1 Her mum cooks a meal in the evenings. (*always*)

2 We book that April holiday in January. (*usually*)

3 They think that we have got bread. (*probably*)

4 You should look where you're going. (*always*)

5 She is going to stay overnight. (*probably*)

6 Chocolate cakes are the best. (*definitely*)

7 I will be able to get it cheaper. (*probably*)

8 I have had an illness in my life. (*never*)

9 We saw sweets in those days. (*never*)

10 I remember buying some. (*definitely*)

11 Do you read upside down? (*usually*)

12 I can manage to get there. (*usually*)

13 She has done that before. (*never*)

14 Something is burning. (*definitely*)

15 She has been nervous. (*always*)

16 I feel cold in your house. (*never*)

17 They were against me. (*always*)

18 We are going to win. (*definitely*)

19 February is the worst. (*usually*)

20 It is very difficult. (*sometimes*)

21 I buy them in boxes. (*always*)

22 I have tried to find it. (*often*)

23 They are fighting. (*always*)

24 She saw this ghost. (*often*)

25 You are right. (*probably*)

'You never tell me you hate me any more.'

If there is more than one auxiliary verb, adverbs of **frequency** and **certainty** usually go **after the first auxiliary**.

*The roof **has never been** repaired.   I **will definitely be** seeing him tonight.*

Adverbs go **before** or **after** *not*, depending on the meaning. Compare:

*It's **definitely not** raining.   She's **not often** late.*

In some answers, both contracted forms (for example *I'm, don't*) and full forms (for example *I am, do not*) are possible. Normally both are correct.

ADJECTIVES AND ADVERBS **221**

even and *only*; end-position adverbs

Even and **only** can go **just before** the words that they emphasise.

He plays tennis **even in the rain.**   They've lived here **only a few weeks.**
He eats anything – **even raw potatoes.**   **Only you** could do a thing like that.

But they most often go **with the verb** when they focus on words later in the sentence.

He **even plays** tennis in the rain.   They**'ve only lived** here for a few weeks.
He's rude to everybody. He**'s even** rude to me. (**NOT** ~~Even he's rude to me.~~)
I **only liked** the first part of the concert.

1 **Put in *even* or *only*.**

▶ She talks to her brother. (*only*) ....*She only talks to her brother.*...............

1 He sings in his sleep. (*even*) ....

2 I am doing this because I love you. (*only*) ....

3 She gets up at six on Sundays. (*even*) ....

4 He wears a suit on holiday. (*even*) ....

5 She ate a piece of dry toast. (*only*) ....

6 I can play very easy music. (*only*) ....

7 He can't write his own name. (*even*) ....

8 They make you pay for a carrier bag. (*even*) ....

9 I'm sorry. I was trying to help. (*only*) ....

10 You can ski there in summer. (*even*) ....

At the end of a sentence we often put words and expressions which say **how, where** and **when.**
They most often go **in that order.**

She sang **very well at the concert last night.**   The children were playing **quietly in the garden.**
He works **in the garage on Tuesdays.**   (**NOT** … ~~on Tuesdays in the garage.~~)
He's working **there now.**   Let's go **to bed early.** (**NOT** … ~~early to bed.~~)

We do **not** normally put adverbs **between a verb and its object.**

You speak **English very well.** (**NOT** ~~You speak very well English.~~)
Can you repair **my watch now?** (**NOT** ~~Can you repair now my watch?~~)

2 **Put the words in brackets into the sentences (not before the verb).**

▶ I work/at night. (*best*)

1 I don't think she plays tennis. (*very well*)

2 He always moves very slowly. (*in the morning*)

3 She was crying in her room. (*quietly*)

4 We talked about it briefly. (*at lunchtime*)

5 I'm going to break the eggs into the bowl. (*carefully*)

6 Ann works at the village shop. (*on Saturdays*)

7 I paid at once. (*the bill*)

8 She speaks Japanese. (*fluently*)

9 I can't explain my feelings. (*clearly*)

10 The team played yesterday. (*brilliantly*)

11 I think we'd better open the parcel. (*now*)

12 I always worked at school. (*very hard*)

13 She practises the piano here. (*every evening*)

14 He read every word. (*slowly*)

15 Put the butter in the fridge. (*at once*)

After verbs of **movement**, the order can be different: we most often put an **expression of place first.**

He **went upstairs quietly.**

confusing adjectives and adverbs: *fast, hard, late ...*

Some words can be **both adjectives** and **adverbs**.

*If you've got a **fast** car, why don't you drive **fast**?*

More examples:

daily	early	hard	late	loud*	monthly	weekly	well	yearly

1 **Put in suitable words.**

1 It's getting .... , so I'm going to stop work.
2 *The Times* is a .... paper (but it isn't published on Sundays).
3 The postman's .... I wasn't expecting him for another hour.
4 She speaks English very .... She must have spent time in an English-speaking country.
5 We usually have .... meetings, but there were only two in September.
6 Don't talk so .... It hurts my head.
7 If you want me to work .... , you'll have to pay me more.
8 Fresh milk is delivered .... to the local shops.
9 I'm sorry I'm .... My train arrived very ....
10 I can't stand .... noises.
11 She's becoming very .... to live with.
12 'How are you?' 'Very .... , thanks.'
13 I get paid .... , on the 30th or 31st.
14 Please try to come home .... for once.

Some words that end in *-ly* are **adjectives**, not **adverbs**.

*She's a very **friendly** person.*
*She always speaks in a **friendly** way.* (**BUT NOT** ~~She always speaks friendly.~~)

More examples:

cowardly	deadly	likely	lively	lonely	lovely	silly	ugly

2 **Put in suitable words.**

1 Curare is a .... poison.
2 I don't think rain is very .... today.
3 What .... flowers!
4 Why does he wear such a .... hat?
5 She was .... , so she got herself a dog.
6 This music is really depressing. Can you put on something more ....?
7 He was too .... to tell the boss he was leaving.
8 Cinderella was beautiful, but she had two .... sisters.

3 **Choose one or more words from Exercises 1 and 2 to go in each blank.**

▶ *weekly, monthly* .... magazines
1 .... expressions
2 .... phone calls
3 .... music
4 She sings too ....
5 He visits us ....
6 .... things to say
7 .... faces

8 very .... to rain
9 .... flowers
10 I feel very ....
11 We left ....
12 trying ....
13 a .... illness
14 .... work
15 a .... life

*Loudly is also possible, especially in a formal style.

In some answers, both contracted forms (for example *I'm, don't*) and full forms (for example *I am, do not*) are possible. Normally both are correct.

ADJECTIVES AND ADVERBS **223**

adjectives and adverbs: more practice

1 **Adjective or adverb? Put in the correct word.**

1 I haven't got much money. If I travel this year, I'll have to do it .... (*cheap / cheaply*)
2 I felt her arm .... to see if any bones were broken. (*gentle / gently*)
3 Her hair is so .... – like a baby's hair. (*soft / softly*)
4 Mary doesn't speak very .... I often have trouble understanding her. (*clear / clearly*)
5 You're looking very .... today. (*happy / happily*)
6 I'm sorry, but you're .... wrong. (*complete / completely*)
7 He may appear .... , but in fact he's .... intelligent. (*stupid / stupidly; extreme / extremely*)
8 That fish smells .... (*bad / badly*)
9 Please carry this very .... (*careful / carefully*)
10 John was in an accident yesterday, but he wasn't .... hurt. (*bad / badly*)

2 **Mixed structures. Right or wrong? Correct the mistakes or write 'Correct'.**

▶ Please don't drive so ~~fastly~~. ..*fast*..............
▶ I'm not well today. ..*Correct.*..........
1 She spoke to me very cold. ....
2 The soup tastes wonderfully. ....
3 The play was brilliantly performed. ....
4 I feel lonely these days. ....
5 There's a deaf in the downstairs flat. ....
6 You speak very well Japanese. ....
7 The secretary always smiles at me very friendly. ....
8 Don't talk so loud – I'm not deaf. ....
9 He always wears blue old jeans. ....
10 I was very boring in the maths lesson today. ....
11 My mother usually is very cheerful. ....
12 The choir sang last night in the church beautifully. ....
13 Botanists are interesting in plants. ....
14 I have never seen a ghost. ....
15 John works for the British Association of Teachers of the Deaf. ....

3 **Focusing adverbs. Complete the sentences with expressions from the box. Put in *only* or *even*.**

| brush their teeth   for a few minutes   on Sundays   really understands me ✓   she likes rats |
| watch tennis   the cat thinks   the clock   the guides got lost |

▶ My mother ..*Only my mother really understands me.*......
1 I work every day, ...
2 They do everything together. They .... together.
3 She likes all animals. ....
4 Everybody thinks you're wrong. .... you're wrong.
5 Everything went quiet. .... broke the silence.
6 You can borrow it, but ....
7 They all got lost in the fog. ....
8 I don't like sport much. I .... sometimes.

4 GRAMMAR AND VOCABULARY: personality. Choose one word from each pair in the box to complete the definitions. Use a dictionary if necessary.

> bad-tempered / good-tempered   generous / mean
> hard-working / lazy   open / reserved   optimistic / pessimistic
> patient / impatient   practical / not practical   shy / self-confident
> slow-thinking / quick-thinking   sociable / unsociable

1 An .... person doesn't like waiting.
2 A .... person easily gets angry.
3 A .... person is good at making and mending things.
4 A .... person doesn't like giving.
5 A .... person often doesn't like to be talked to or looked at.
6 A .... person likes parties.
7 A .... person doesn't like to talk about him/herself.
8 A .... person doesn't like work.
9 An .... person thinks that things will probably be all right.
10 A .... person can soon find solutions to problems.

5 GRAMMAR AND VOCABULARY: personality. Use some of the words from Exercise 4 to describe yourself or another person you know. Useful words: *very, quite, not very, not at all*.

> ► I'm patient, quite generous, very hard-working, not at all practical,
> quite reserved, very unsociable and quite pessimistic.
> ....
> ....

6 DO IT YOURSELF position of adverbs. Two of these rules are wrong. Which?

A Adverbs like *often*, *sometimes* or *probably* go after *am, are, is, was, were*.
B Adverbs like *often*, *sometimes* or *probably* go after auxiliary verbs.
C All adverbs can go between the verb and the object.
D Expressions of place usually go before expressions of time.
E Short adverbs go earlier in the sentence than long ones.

  Wrong rules: ...... and ......

7 Confusing adjectives and adverbs. Choose the best words to complete the quotations.

1 'Say it *loud / hard / friendly*, I'm Black and proud.' (*Title of song by James Brown*)
2 'Once the toothpaste is out of the tube, it's awfully *fast / silly / hard* to get it back in.' (*H R Haldeman*)
3 'People tell me there are a lot of guys like me, which doesn't explain why I'm *lovely / lonely / lively*.' (*Mort Sahl*)
4 'Give us this day our *daily / weekly / friendly* bread.' (*The Lord's Prayer*)
5 'The universe is not hostile, nor is it *lonely / silly / friendly*. It is simply indifferent.' (*J B Holmes*)
6 'It is better to be beautiful than to be good. But ... it is better to be good than to be *loud / ugly / lovely*.' (*Oscar Wilde*)

8 Internet exercise. Circle the expression from each pair that you think is more common. Check with a search engine (e.g. Google).

"red old" / "old red"   "new blue" / "blue new"   "shiny leather " / "leather shiny"
"interesting little" / "little interesting"   "large concrete" / "concrete large"

adjectives and adverbs: revision test

1 **Write the sentences with the adverbs in the correct positions.**

1 That girl spends hours in the bathroom. (*always*)

....

2 I have been to Jamaica. (*never*)

....

3 We got home very late. (*last night*)

....

4 Somebody was trying to open the door. (*definitely*)

....

5 He puts tomato ketchup on cornflakes. (*even*)

....

6 Life is hard. (*sometimes*)

....

7 I know some French, and I speak Russian. (*very badly*)

....

8 We have been invited to Jamie's parties. (*never*)

....

9 Alice needs somebody to help her. (*probably*)

....

10 The water was too cold for swimming. (*usually*)

....

2 **Right or wrong? Correct the mistakes or write 'Correct'.**

▶ She works too ~~hardly~~. ....*hard*...............

▶ I'm terribly happy. ....*Correct.*............

1 I'm collecting money for the blind. ....

2 Jake always is so optimistic. ....

3 'Hi!', she said friendly. ....

4 I'm really not interesting in that woman's problems. ....

5 Alex has never been to my house. ....

6 The thieves took even my old clothes. ....

7 Your hair looks beautifully. ....

8 The work isn't complete finished. ....

9 I only believe half of what he says. ....

10 Please put the glasses away careful. ....

11 Lucy seems very intelligently. ....

12 Where's your old big car? ....

13 I have weekly guitar lessons. ....

14 The team played yesterday very well. ....

15 I like your new and black dress. ....

In some answers, both contracted forms (for example *I'm, don't*) and full forms (for example *I am, do not*) are possible. Normally both are correct.

SECTION 16 comparison

GRAMMAR SUMMARY

We can **compare** people and things with each other using *as … as, -er than* or *more … than*.
> You're **as silly as** me.   Luke's **younger than** me.
> The second problem was much **more difficult than** the other three.

We can use **the -est** or **the most** to compare people and things with **all of their group**.
> Carl is **the fastest of the young sprinters**.   Ramona is **the most sociable person in the class**.

We use **-er** and **-est** with **shorter adjectives** and some **short adverbs**. We use *more* and *most* with **other adjectives and adverbs**.

Double comparatives
> It's getting **colder and colder**.   The children are **more and more difficult** these days.

the … the …
> **The more** money she has, **the more** she wants.
> **The warmer** it gets, **the happier** I am.

Some colourful and unusual comparisons:

as slow as a broken down snail

as dirty as a dustbin lid

as thick as two short planks (= 'stupid')

as black as two o'clock in the morning

as ugly as home-made soap

as happy as a dog with two tails

as poor as a church mouse

as crooked as a dog's hind leg

as crooked as a barrel of fish hooks

as nervous as a brick wall

as brave as the first man who ate an oyster

as cold as an ex-wife's heart

as big as the little end of nothing

as welcome as a wet shoe

as noisy as two skeletons dancing
  on a tin roof

as dark as the inside of a wolf

as scarce as hen's teeth

as exciting as watching paint dry

> ### Why study?
>
> *The more I study, the more I know.*
> *The more I know, the more I forget.*
> *The more I forget, the less I know.*
> *So why study?*

revise the basics: comparative and superlative adjectives

forms

more/most beautiful	more/most careful	more/most distant	more/most intelligent	
easier, easiest	faster, fastest	happier, happiest	later, latest	nicer, nicest	older, oldest

Comparative adjectives are forms like *younger*, *more expensive*.
Superlative adjectives are forms like *youngest*, *most expensive*.

1 **DO IT YOURSELF** **Look at the examples at the top of the page, and then complete rules 1–5 from the box.**

put *more* and *most* in front.   put *more* and *most* in front.   add -*r*, -*st*.
add -*er*, -*est*.   change *y* to *i* and add -*er*, -*est*.

To make the comparative and superlative of:
1 one-syllable adjectives ending in -*e*, ...
2 other one-syllable adjectives, ...
3 two-syllable adjectives ending in -*y*, ...
4 other two-syllable adjectives, ...
5 longer adjectives, ...

2 **DO IT YOURSELF** **doubling. Look at the examples in the box and choose the correct way of completing the rule.**

bigger	fatter	hottest	longest	oldest	meaner	plainer	shortest	sweeter	thinnest

Before -*er* and -*est*, we double the last letter of …
1 all adjectives.
2 adjectives that have three letters.
3 adjectives that have one vowel.
4 adjectives that end in one vowel + one consonant.
5 adjectives that end in one consonant.
6 adjectives that end in -*g* or -*t*.

3 **Write the comparatives and superlatives.**

1 boring ....
2 cheap ....
3 fine ....
4 funny ....
5 green ....
6 handsome ....
7 hard ....

8 interesting ....
9 lazy ....
10 nervous ....
11 sad ....
12 silly ....
13 slim ....
14 wet ....

A few words have irregular comparatives and superlatives.

| good – better – best | bad – worse – worst | far – farther/further – farthest/furthest |
| old – older/elder – oldest/eldest | little – less – least | much/many – more – most |

Farther/further and ***farthest/furthest*** are both used to talk about **distance**.
We use ***further*** to mean 'additional' in some expressions. (**NOT** *farther*)

*She lives three miles **farther/further** away from the office than I do.*
further education   ***further*** information   ***further*** discussion

Elder and ***eldest*** are used with *brother, sister, son, daughter, grandson, granddaughter*.

*John's my **elder** brother. (I have one brother older than me.)*
*Sarah's my **eldest** sister. (I have more than one sister.)*

4 Complete the sentences with irregular comparatives.

1 'My computer keeps crashing.' 'Get a ………………………………… computer.'
2 'Why did your song win the competition?' 'It was the ………………………………'
3 It takes me the longest to get to work because my house is the ………………………………… from here.
4 My cold was getting ………………………………, so I went home.
5 I used most of the old apples, but I had to throw away the three …………………………………
6 Megan was born in 1990. Her sisters Sarah and Rachel were born in 1992 and 1993. So Megan is Sarah's ………………………………… sister, and she's Rachel's …………………………………
7 Jacob and Ryan were born in 1991 and 1994. So Jacob is Ryan's ………………………………… brother.
8 The doctors don't know what's wrong, so they're going to do ………………………………… tests.
9 I took the job that paid the ………………………………… money for the ………………………………… work.
10 We've got ………………………………… money than Andy and Tara, but we're happier. Maybe.
11 It's a nicer drive if you go there through the mountains, but it's much …………………………………

using comparatives and superlatives

We use a **comparative** (with *than*) to compare **one** person, thing, action or group with another person, thing etc. We use a **superlative** to compare **one** person, thing etc with the **whole group** that he/she/it belongs to.

Mary's **taller** than **her three sisters**.   Mary's **the tallest of the four girls**.
Your accent is **worse** than **mine**.   Your accent is **the worst in the class**.

Before a superlative we normally use *the* or a **possessive**.

the best singer   *my* oldest friend   *John's* most attractive quality

5 Compare hotels. Here are some facts about three hotels. Write at least ten sentences.

	HOTEL X	HOTEL Y	HOTEL Z
expensive?	£££££	£££	£
comfortable?	🛏🛏🛏	🛏🛏🛏🛏🛏	🛏
efficient?	★★	★★★	★★★★★
friendly?	☹	☺☺☺☺☺	☺☺☺☺
convenient?	city centre	middle of nowhere	two miles out

Hotel Y is more expensive than Hotel Z. Hotel X is the most expensive of the three hotels.
....
....
....
....
....
....
....
....
....
....

Some people use a **comparative** instead of a superlative when the **whole group** has **two members**.

*I like them both, but Sally's the **nicer/nicest** of **the two**.*
*You can have **the bigger/biggest steak** if you like – I'm not very hungry.*

In some answers, both contracted forms (for example *I'm*, *don't*) and full forms (for example *I am*, *do not*) are possible. Normally both are correct.

revise the basics: comparative and superlative adverbs

Comparative and superlative adverbs normally have *more* and *most*. We can put *the* before superlative adverbs, but we often leave it out.

*Could you drive **more slowly**?* (**NOT** … ~~slowlier?~~)
*French is the language he speaks **(the) most easily**.*

The following adverbs have *-er, -est* like adjectives: *early, fast, hard, late, near, soon.*
Better, best, worse and *worst* can be used as adverbs.

1 **Complete the sentences with the comparatives or superlatives of words from the box.**

beautifully   clearly   early   fast   fluently   hard   late   peacefully

1 If we don't walk ...., we'll never arrive on time.
2 She sings .... than anyone else I've ever heard.
3 Andy's the most intelligent, but Sue works ....
4 Eight is late – could you possibly get here any ....?
5 Of all the children, Helen writes ....
6 I would sleep .... if I weren't worried about Tom.
7 For the 10.20 train, ... we can leave home is 10.
8 Mark speaks French .... of all the boys in his class.

2 **Write sentences with comparative and superlative adverbs about people you know (family, friends, …). For example, who sings best, sings worst, cooks better than you, cooks worse than you, can run fastest, gets up earliest, goes to bed later than you, works hardest?**

Carlos sings best in my family.   Kenji speaks English better than me.
....
....
....
....
....
....
....

3 **Complete the captions with comparative adverbs.**

A She ought to drive ....   B He ought to drive ....

as … as *as many people as possible*

We use **as … as** to say that people or things are **equal** in some way.

She's **as tall as** her brother.   Is it **as good as** you expected?   She speaks French **as well as** the rest of us.

After **not**, we can use **so … as** instead of *as … as*.

He's **not so/as** successful as his father.

Other useful structures: **as much/many as**, **the same as**.

I haven't got **as much** time **as** I thought.   We need **as many** people **as possible**.
She earns **twice as much** money **as me / as I do**.
He went to **the same** school **as me / as I did**. (NOT … ~~to (a) same school~~ …)

1 Look at the information about Jake and Susie, and then write sentences comparing
   them using *as … as*, *not so/as … as* and *the same … as*.

	JAKE	SUSIE
UNIVERSITY	Manchester	Liverpool
SCHOOL	Leeds H.S.	Leeds H.S.
HEIGHT	1.92 m	1.70 m
WEIGHT	87 kg	56 kg
JOB	accountant	accountant
BORN: WHEN? WHERE?	27.7.84 Leeds	31.3.84 Leeds
SALARY	£26,000	£52,000
WORKS FOR	IBM	Rolls Royce
HOLIDAY	5 weeks	3 weeks
ADDRESS	3 Ross Street, Manchester	8 Ross Street, Manchester
CHILDREN	2	1
LANGUAGES	Fluent French, some German	Fluent French, fluent German
READING	Newspapers	Newspapers, magazines, non-fiction

Susie went to the same school as Jake.
Jake's not as old as her.
....
....
....
....

2 Here are the beginnings of some traditional expressions with *as … as*.
   See how many you can put together correctly from the box.

| a beetroot   a mouse   grass   the grave   the hills   ice ✓ |
| iron   night   a pancake   a picture   a rake   a sheet |

▶ as cold *as ice.*

1 as black ....
2 as flat ....
3 as green ....
4 as hard ....
5 as old ....

6 as pretty ....
7 as quiet ....
   OR ....
8 as red ....
9 as thin ....
10 as white ....

'How d'you mean I'm as fit as a
man of thirty – I **am** thirty!'

In some answers, both contracted forms (for example *I'm*, *don't*) and full
forms (for example *I am*, *do not*) are possible. Normally both are correct.

COMPARISON **231**

more on comparatives *taller and taller; the more the better*

We can use **double comparatives** to say that things are **changing**.

*We went **more and more slowly**.* (**NOT** … ~~more slowly and more slowly.~~)
*It's getting **colder and colder**.*

① **Look at the pictures and complete the sentences.**

1   2   3   4

5   6   7

1 She's driving ....
2 She's getting ....
3 It's getting ....
4 The maths lessons are getting ....
5 That cat's getting ....
6 I'm getting ....
7 Bread's getting ....

② **Complete the sentences with *is /are getting* and double comparatives of words from the box.**

bad   boring   dangerous ✓   difficult   expensive   good   hard   long   young

▶ My mother's driving *is getting more and more dangerous* .... as the years go by.
1 My daughter's maths homework .... to understand.
2 Jeremy's doing well. His piano playing ....
3 It seems as if police officers ....
4 My temper ....
5 It .... to find time for everything you want to do.
6 Professional tennis .... to watch.
7 Restaurants ....
8 School holidays ....

We can use **the … the** with **comparatives** to say that things **change or vary together**. Note the word order.

The older I get, **the happier** I am. (**NOT** ~~Older I get, more I am happy.~~)
The more dangerous it is, **the more** I like it. (**NOT** ~~The more it is dangerous~~ …)
The more money he has, **the more** useless things he buys. (**NOT** ~~The more he has money~~ …)
'Can I invite some friends over?' 'Sure. **The more the better.**'

③ **Complete the sentences with expressions from the box. Use *the … the*.**
(Different answers are possible.)

faster/louder	longer/more	more/angrier	more/less	more/less
more/more	older/darker	older/more ✓	warmer/more	

▶ ....The older.......... Mark gets, ...the more.............. he looks like his grandfather.
1 .... he talked, ... I listened.
2 .... I live here, ... I like it.
3 .... it got, ... time we spent on the beach.
4 .... I get to know you, ... I understand you.
5 .... money he lost, ... it made him.
6 .... he drove, ... he laughed.
7 .... clothes she buys, ... clothes she wants to buy.
8 .... I get, ... my hair gets.

Before comparatives, we can use *much, far, very much, a little, a bit* (informal), *a lot/lots* (informal), *any, no* and *even*.

He's **much/far older** than her. (**NOT** ~~He's very older~~…)   She's **very much happier** in the new job.
I feel **a little / a bit better**.   These grapes are **a lot sweeter** than the others.
The train's **no quicker** than the bus.   You look **even more beautiful** than usual.

④ **Compare some of the things in the box. Use *much / very much / far / a little / a bit / a lot / even / no / any*.**

the Taj Mahal	the Great Pyramid	the White House	a Ferrari	a Ford	a Volvo

the Amazon   the Thames   the Rhône   a pen   a typewriter   a computer   a dog
a cat   a parrot   a horse   living in the country   living in the city   the Mediterranean
the Atlantic   Europe   Africa   Asia   North America   South America   you
your mother/father/friend/boss/teacher

▶ ...The Taj Mahal is much older than the White House.........

In some answers, both contracted forms (for example *I'm, don't*) and full
forms (for example *I am, do not*) are possible. Normally both are correct.

more about superlatives *the best player of us all*

After superlatives, we often use *of*.

It was the **most successful of** his early plays.   She's the **best** player **of** us all.
The **nicest** moment **of** the day.

But we do **not** use *of* with a **singular word for a place or group**.

I'm the happiest man **in the world**. (**NOT** ... ~~of the world.~~)   She's the best player **in the team**.

1 *Of* or *in* after a superlative?

▶ the most interesting ...of...... all the
   suggestions
▶ the most experienced general ...in......
   the Army
1 the most famous actor .... them all
2 the best restaurant .... Rome
3 the most expensive .... the books
   I bought
4 the worst student .... the class

5 the highest mountain .... Europe
6 the oldest person .... my family
7 the most frightening .... the four men
8 the shortest day .... the year
9 the most comfortable chair ....
   the office
10 the most valuable .... the paintings
   in the gallery

2 Write sentences with superlatives.

▶ Where I live, August / quiet month / year *Where I live, August is the quietest month of the year.*
▶ Which / high mountain / Africa / ? *Which is the highest mountain in Africa?*
1 Who / young / your three sisters / ? ....
2 Which / cheap / these three jackets / ? ....
3 For a time, my grandfather / famous footballer / country ....
   ....
4 Cassie and Louise / fast swimmers / team ....
5 When I was a child, I / tall boy / my class ....
6 For me, the early morning / good time / day ....
   ....
7 Andy is very quiet, but he / interesting person / the group ....
   ....

We normally use *the* before a **superlative** when we are comparing one person/thing/group with others.

It's **the longest day** of the year.   This winter is **the coldest** in living memory.

But we do **not** use *the* when we are comparing somebody or something with him/her/itself in other situations.

He's **nicest** when he's had a few drinks. (**NOT** ~~He's the nicest when~~ ...)   England is **best** in spring.

3 Invent suitable beginnings for these sentences. *The* or not?

▶ *The weather is usually* .... worst in February.
▶ *Kathleen Ferrier was the* .... best singer of her generation.
1 .... most beautiful city in my country.
2 .... most dangerous when they're hungry.
3 .... best modern writer.
4 .... most interesting person I've ever met.
5 .... quietest in the early morning.
6 .... most efficient way to learn a language.
7 .... most comfortable when there aren't too many people around.

like and *as*; *so* and *such*

We can use *like* and *as* to say that things are **similar**.
Like is a **preposition**, used before a **noun or pronoun**.
As is a **conjunction**, used before **subject + verb** or a **prepositional** expression.

*He runs **like the wind**.*   *She looks **like me**.*
*Nobody knows her **as I do**.*   *On Friday, **as on Monday**, we meet at eight.*

Note the common expressions *__as I said__, __as you know__, __as you see__, __as usual__*.

1 *Like* or *as*?

1 He died .... he lived, fighting.
2 Being in love is .... an illness.
3 It's mended, ... you can see.
4 In Paris, ... in Rome, traffic is heavy.
5 His eyes are .... knives.
6 My brother isn't at all .... me.
7 She left .... she came, silently.
8 You're shy, ... me.
9 Your smile is .... your sister's.
10 .... I said, you're too late.

In informal speech (but not writing), many people use *like* as a conjunction.

*Nobody loves you **like I do**.*   ***Like I said**, she wasn't there.*

To talk about **jobs**, **functions** etc, we use *as*, not *like*.

*He's working **as a waiter**.* (**NOT** ~~He's working like a waiter.~~)   *I used my shoe **as a hammer**.*

Compare:

***As your brother**, I must warn you to be careful.* (I am your brother.)
***Like your brother**, I must warn you …* (We both warn you.)

We use *so* before an **adjective** (without a noun), or an **adverb**.
We use *such* before (**adjective +) noun**. *A/An* comes **after** *such*.

*She's **so babyish**.*   *I'm **so hungry** that I could eat a horse.*
*… your country, which is **so beautiful**.* (**NOT** … ~~your so beautiful country.~~)
*I wish you wouldn't drive **so fast**.*
*She's **such a baby**.*   *I didn't know you had **such nice friends**.*
*It was **such a comfortable** bed that I went straight to sleep.*

2 Put in *such* or *so*.

1 The weather was .... cold that all the football matches were cancelled.
2 The book was .... boring that I stopped reading it.
3 It was .... a good film that I went to see it three times.
4 They've got .... a nice house that I always love staying there.
5 It was .... a hot day that nobody could do any work.
6 Their garden is .... beautiful!
7 His voice is .... pleasant that I could listen to him all day.
8 I don't know why she talks in .... a loud voice.
9 The canteen served .... bad food that nobody could eat it.
10 The case was .... heavy that I couldn't lift it.

In some answers, both contracted forms (for example *I'm*, *don't*) and full
forms (for example *I am*, *do not*) are possible. Normally both are correct.

comparison: more practice

1 **Forms. Write the comparatives and superlatives.**

active .....*more active, most active*.....   bad ....

clean ....   dirty ....

famous ....

far .... OR ....

fit ....   green ....

happy ....   lazy ....

modern ....   nice ....

red ....   short ....

slim ....   sweet ....

tall ....   thin ....

tiring ....   white ....

2 **Mixed structures. Right or wrong? Correct the mistakes or write 'Correct'.**

▶ The weather's ~~gooder~~ today.   *better* ....

▶ I feel much happier now.   *Correct.*.........................

1 My feet are cold like ice.   ....

2 You're the strangest man of the world.   ....

3 Ann's more late than usual.   ....

4 This shirt's not so expensive as the others.   ....

5 More I learn, more I forget.   ....

6 We need to ask further questions.   ....

7 It's getting more warm and more warm.   ....

8 The more he has money, the more he spends.   ....

9 Pete's the fastest swimmer in the team.   ....

10 I feel the same like you.   ....

11 The older I get, the less I know.   ....

12 Britain is the nicest in April.   ....

13 I worked like a tourist guide for a year.   ....

14 The work's getting more and more boring.   ....

15 I got there earlier that the others.   ....

3 **Comparisons. Make two sentences for each item.**

▶ a tiger / large / a leopard   large / of all the big cats / ?
 A tiger is larger than a leopard.   Is it the largest of all the big cats?.........................

1 this box / strong / that one / ?   strong / you've got / ?
 ....

2 Alistair / tall / anyone else / the team   tall / the team
 ....

3 the state of Alaska / big / any of the other states / the US   big / the US
 ....

4 this wine / expensive / that one   expensive / in the world
 ....

5 Max's party / good / Rob's party   good / I've ever been to
 ....

6 this job / bad / my last one   bad / I've ever had
 ....

4 *The ... the ...* **Circular situations: make sentences like the one in the example.**

▶ He drives fast; he gets nervous.
The faster he drives, the more nervous he gets. And the more nervous he gets, the faster he drives.

1 He eats ice cream; he gets fat.
The more ice cream ....

2 He reads; he forgets.
....

3 She ignores him; he loves her.
....

4 She buys shoes; she wants shoes. (*Mind the word order.*)
....

5 We spend money; we have friends.
....

6 I sleep; I'm tired.
....

5 **Grammar in a text. Put in the superlatives of the words in the box.**

fast	fast	high	large	large	long	long	long	small	tall

The ¹ .... man in medical history was Robert Pershing Wadlow (US). When he was measured in 1940 he was 2.72 m tall.

The world's ² .... hair measured 5.62 m in 2004. It belonged to Xie Qiuping (China), who had been growing her hair since 1973, from the age of 13.

The ³ .... ski lesson was given to 594 skiers by Hansjürg Gredig at Sarn-Heinzenberg, Switzerland, on 23 February 2008. The 16-minute lesson extended over 1,300 metres. There were extra instructors for every 20-30 people to help them follow the lesson correctly.

The ⁴ .... windsurfing journey was made by Flavio Jardim and Diogo Guerreiro. They went from Chui to Oiapoque on the Brazilian Coast (8,120 km) between May 2004 and July 2005.

The ⁵ .... motorised sofa was driven at 148 km/h in 2007 by Marek Turowski (UK).

The ⁶ .... time for a hundred-metre barefoot sprint on ice is 17.35 sec. The record was set by Nico Surings in Eindhoven, Netherlands, in December 2006.

The world's ⁷ .... ruby measures 130 x 138 x 145 mm and weighs 8184 g. It belongs to a Chinese jewellery company.

The ⁸ .... ears on a dog belong to Tigger, a bloodhound, owned by a couple in Illinois. The ears measured 34.9 cm (right) and 34.2 cm (left) in September 2004.

The world's ⁹ .... jump by a pig is 70 cm. It was made by a Japanese pig called Kotetsu in 2004.

The ¹⁰ .... dog measured in 2005 was a female chihuahua who lived in Florida. She was 15.2 cm long.

(*information from Guinness Book of World Records website*)

6 **Internet exercise. Get some information about world records from the internet and complete these sentences.**

1 The oldest ....
2 The biggest ....
3 The fastest ....
4 The longest ....
5 The heaviest ....

comparison: revision test

1 **Write the comparatives and superlatives.**

boring	....	bright	....
cheap	....	clean	....
distant	....	exciting	....
far	....	fit	....
funny	....	honest	....
lazy	....	nice	....
plain	....	safe	....
short	....	slim	....
thin	....	well	....
wet	....		

2 **Choose the right words.**

1 I've got three sisters. Jane's the *older / elder / eldest*.

2 Do you feel better *that / than / as* yesterday?

3 Your dress is *same as / the same as / the same like* mine.

4 The doctors are going to do *further / farther / furthest / farthest* tests.

5 This hotel is *worse / the worse / worst / the worst* I've ever stayed in.

6 I've got *a more easy / an easier* job this week.

7 I always feel *best / the best* about 11 o'clock in the morning.

8 Karen's working *as / like* a secretary at the moment.

9 Rebecca is *the more / the most / more / most* remarkable singer I've ever heard.

10 *More / The more / The most* I listen to him, *more / the more* bored I get.

3 **Right or wrong? Correct the mistakes or write 'Correct'.**

▶ The weather's getting ~~badder~~. ...*worse*...............................

▶ The train's even later than usual. ...*Correct.*........................

1 Real life is stranger as novels or films. ....

2 He's the fastest man of the world this year. ....

3 The older I get, the less hair I have. ....

4 Holidays are becoming more and more cheap. ....

5 I'll see you this evening like usual. ....

6 The more he gets tired, the more mistakes he makes. ....

7 My father is a lot older than my mother. ....

8 Did you receive any farther information?. ....

9 The ticket wasn't as expensive as I expected. ....

10 This shirt's not so expensive as the others. ....

11 His heart is cold like ice. ....

12 I'm getting more bored and more bored. ....

13 They say it's the best restaurant of the world. ....

14 Tolstoy is the more famous Russian novelist. ....

15 He's definitely nicest when he's asleep. ....

In some answers, both contracted forms (for example *I'm*, *don't*) and full forms (for example *I am*, *do not*) are possible. Normally both are correct.

SECTION 17 conjunctions

GRAMMAR SUMMARY

after	*although*	*and*	*as if*	*as long as*	*as soon as*	*because*	*before*	*but*		*provided that*

so   *so that*   *until*   *when*   *while*   *both … and*   *either … or*   *neither … nor*

(For *if*, see Section 18.)

We use **conjunctions** to **join sentences** together.

*I rang John **because** I didn't know what to do.*   *We came home **after** the shops closed.*

*She can take my bike **as long as** she brings it back this evening.*

Some conjunctions (and the words that follow them) can go in **two places**.

*I told him **as soon as** I knew.*   ***As soon as** I knew, I told him.*

We use **present** tenses to talk about the **future** with time-conjunctions.

*I'll wait here **until** the office **opens**.*

We can use **perfect** tenses with time conjunctions to express **completion**.

*Traffic will be easier **after** they**'ve built** the new road.*

***As soon as** I **had checked in**, I phoned Pat and Alice to fix a meeting.*

After some conjunctions, *-ing* forms can be used.

*Always look in the mirror **before driving** off.*

● I rang John ๒   **because**   ๑ I didn't know what to do. ●

As soon as   ๑ I had checked in.   ●

๑ I phoned Pat and Alice. ●

● We came home ๒   **after**   ๑ the shops closed. ●

● I'll wait here ๒   **until**   ๑ the office opens. ●

revise the basics: use and position of conjunctions

Conjunctions join clauses into sentences. Examples: *but, because, while, if.*

*She was poor **but** she was honest.*   *I went to bed **because** I was tired.*
*Can you watch the kids **while** I'm out?*   *I'll do it **if** I can.*

1 **DO IT YOURSELF** **Which of the words could come just before '... she went home'?**
Those words are conjunctions. The others are not.

after ...Yes.....   all ...No......   although ....   and ....   as ....   at ....
because ....   before ....   by ....   if ....   or ....   since ....
so ....   that ....   this ....   under ....   unless ....   until ....
when ....   whether ....   with ....

Some conjunctions and their clauses can go either **first** or **last** in a sentence.
We often use a **comma** (,) when the conjunction and its clause are **first** in the sentence.

If you need help, come and see me.   *Come and see me if you need help.*

2 **Write the sentences with the clauses *in italics* first, when this is possible.**

1   I'll come round to your place *after I've finished work.*
....

2   Let's have a weekend in the country *when the weather gets better.*
....

3   You ought to see Paula *before you go back to Canada.*
....

4   I'm quite sure *that she's telling the truth.*
....

5   I enjoyed the lecture, *although I didn't understand everything.*
....

6   Your train leaves in half an hour, *so you'd better hurry.*
....

One conjunction is enough to join **two clauses** – we do not normally use two conjunctions.

Although she was tired, she went to work.   *She was tired, **but** she went to work.*
(**BUT NOT** *Although she was tired, but she went to work.*)
As you know, I work very hard.   *You know **that** I work very hard.*
(**BUT NOT** *As you know, that I work very hard.*)

3 **Put in a conjunction or nothing (–).**

▶   Although he was very bad-tempered, ... everybody liked him. (*but / –*)
▶   He was very bad-tempered, ...but..... everybody liked him. (*but / –*)
1   Always brush your teeth .... you have a meal. (*after / –*)
2   As Liz told you, ... her mother went back home last week. (*that / –*)
3   Because I knew her family, ... I tried to help her. (*so / –*)
4   Don't do that again .... I'll hit you. (*or / –*)
5   Emily explained .... her mother left for Berlin last Friday. (*that / –*)
6   I was sorry for her, ... I did what I could for her. (*so / –*)
7   If you do that again, ... I'll call the police. (*and / –*)
8   There'll be trouble .... he stops that. (*unless / –*)

revise the basics: present for future *I'll tell you when I know.*

If the time is made clear once in a sentence, this may be enough. So **tenses** are **simplified** after many **conjunctions**. For example, we often use **present tenses** instead of *will* after *when*, *before*, *after*, *until*, *as soon as* and *if*.

*I'll tell you **when** I **know** myself.*   *I'll see you **before** I **go**.*
*Let's go out **after** the rain **stops**.*   *You won't get in **until** you **buy** a ticket.*
*I know she'll phone **as soon as** I **go** to bed.*   ***If** you **hold** it like that, it'll break.*

1 **Put in the correct verb form: present tense or *will* … .**

1 When I .... time, I .... to her. (*have; write*)

2 .... here until the plane .... off? (*you stay; take*)

3 As soon as I ...., I .... you. (*arrive; phone*)

4 If you .... there first, keep a seat for me. (*get*)

5 I .... you again when I .... next in London. (*see; be*)

6 I .... the window as soon as it .... raining. (*open; stop*)

7 You can borrow my coat if you .... it back. (*bring*)

8 I .... here until you .... time to answer my question. (*wait; have*)

9 After you .... university, you .... time to travel a bit. (*finish; have*)

10 It .... dark before we .... home. (*be; get*)

2 **Look at Bill and Ann's summer dates and complete the conversation.**

> **BILL AND ANN'S SUMMER DATES**
>
> The children will get out of school at midday on July 8th. ✓
> Bill's brother will be in England from July 12th to July 14th.
> Bill and Ann's new car will be ready on July 17th.
> Eric will go back to work on July 20th.
> Ann's father will go into hospital on July 25th.

BILL: Let's go to Eric's from the 4th to the 30th.
ANN: No, we can't leave until the 8th. The children, remember?
BILL: OK. We'll leave as soon as the children ▶ ..get........................... out of school.
ANN: That won't work, because we'll have to be here while ¹ ....
BILL: Then we'll go from the 15th to the 30th.
ANN: No, we'll have to be back before ² .... on the 25th.
BILL: OK. The 15th to the 24th it is.
ANN: Well, in that case, let's wait until ³ .... on the 17th.
BILL: The 17th to the 24th. Right.
ANN: But we can't stay with Eric after ⁴ ....
BILL: Fine. The 17th to the 20th.
ANN: No, because …

If and **when** can be followed by **will** in **indirect** and **direct questions**.

*I don't know **if** I'll be there.*   *They haven't said **when** it'll be ready.*
***When** will I **see** you again?*

We can also use **will** after **if** in **polite requests**.

*If you **will** just come this way …*

In some answers, both contracted forms (for example *I'm, don't*) and full forms (for example *I am, do not*) are possible. Normally both are correct.

using certain conjunctions: *so that, as long as, until* etc

Do you know how to use these conjunctions: *so that* (purpose), *while* (contrast), *as long as / provided (that)*, *until, as if/though*?

*Let's start now, **so that** we're sure to have enough time.*
*You can go out **as long as** (OR **provided / provided that**) you tell us where you're going.*
*The summers here are wet, **while** the winters are very dry.*
*I'll look after the kids **until** you get back.*
*I feel **as if** (OR **as though**) I'm getting a cold.*

In a **formal** style, *whereas* can be used in the same way as *while*.

*Sound travels at 330 metres per second, **whereas** light travels at 300,000 kilometres per second.*

In an **informal** style, *like* is often used in the same way as *as if*.

*I feel **like** I'm getting a cold.*

1 **Choose the best conjunctions.**

1   You can have my bike .... you bring it back tomorrow. (*as long as, until, while*)
2   I'm staying here .... I get my money back. (*as long as, until, as if*)
3   I put the light on .... I could see where I was going. (*so that, as if, while*)
4   Joe was short and dark, ... his sister was the exact opposite. (*provided that, so that, while*)
5   You look .... you've seen a ghost. (*as long as, so that, as if*)
6   He won't get any money .... he finishes the work properly. (*as long as, until, while*)
7   It looks .... it's going to rain. (*as if, whereas, provided that*)
8   You can cancel the ticket .... you tell the airline 48 hours in advance. (*while, until, provided that*)
9   I'm going to the bank now, ... I'll have enough money for shopping. (*until, so that, as long as*)
10   .... I think his novels are good, his poetry is not so impressive. (*until, as if, whereas*)

2 **Put in *as long as* or *so that*.**

1   He went to Switzerland .... he could learn French.
2   I don't mind you singing .... you do it quietly.
3   We moved the piano .... there would be room for the Christmas tree.
4   We'll play tennis .... it doesn't rain.
5   We'll come back this afternoon .... that's OK with you.
6   I put another blanket on the bed .... I would be warm enough.

3 **Rewrite these sentences, beginning *While* ...**

▶   It was sunny, but there was a cold wind.   *While it was sunny, there was a cold wind.*
1   She's very clever, but she's got no common sense at all.
    ....
2   I know how you feel, but I think you're making a mistake.
    ....
3   The job's well paid, but it's deadly boring.
    ....
4   I'm interested in economics, but I wouldn't want to work in a bank.
    ....
5   The hotel was nice, but it was a long way from the beach.
    ....

4 Write sentences about the pictures, beginning *He/She/It looks as if …* Use expressions from the box to help you.

| been painting | going swimming ✓ | going to rain | got a cold | had bad news |
| had good news | lost something | seen a ghost |

► *She looks as if she's going swimming.*
1 ....
2 ....
3 ....
4 ....
5 ....
6 ....
7 ....

Because (conjunction) and *because of* (preposition) are **different**.

*We stayed in **because it was raining**.   We stayed in **because of the rain**.*
*He was able to go to university **because his uncle helped him / because of his uncle's help**.*

Although (conjunction) and *in spite of* (preposition) are **different**.

*We went out, **although it was raining**.   We went out **in spite of the rain**.*
*I got the job, **although my English was bad / in spite of my bad English**.*

5 GRAMMAR AND VOCABULARY: related nouns, verbs and adjectives.
The words in the boxes are all nouns. Make sure you know them. Use a dictionary if necessary. Then change the sentences.

| heat | hunger | illness ✓ | rain | snow ✓ | unhappiness |

► We drove slowly because it was snowing. ....*because of the snow.* ....
► Although she was ill, she went on working. ...*In spite of her illness, ...* ....
1 Because I was unhappy, I didn't want to see anybody. ....
2 Although she was hungry, she didn't eat anything. ....
3 We had to drink a lot because it was hot. ....
4 We had to stop playing because it was raining. ....

| cold | interest (in something) | thirst | tiredness | work |

5 She kept all the windows open, although it was cold. ....
6 I couldn't go away last week because I was working. ....
7 Although he was interested in the lesson, he went to sleep. ....
8 I couldn't understand her because I was tired. ....
9 Although I was thirsty, I didn't drink anything. ....

In some answers, both contracted forms (for example *I'm, don't*) and full forms (for example *I am, do not*) are possible. Normally both are correct.

CONJUNCTIONS **243**

leaving out *that* *She knew I was right.*

We often **leave out** the conjunction *that* in an informal style. This happens mostly **after very common verbs and adjectives.**

She **knew (that)** *I was right.*   *I'm* **glad (that)** *you're better.*

1 **Complete the sentences with beginnings from the box.**

Did you know	He suggested	I believe	I expect	I heard
I'm glad	It's funny	Tell me	Were you surprised	You knew

1 .... he didn't say hello to you.
2 .... I phoned you?
3 .... I wouldn't forget your birthday.
4 .... there were mice in the cellar?
5 .... this is your coat.
6 .... we might like to go skiing with him.
7 .... we've had this talk.
8 .... you love me.
9 .... you'd got a new job.
10 .... you've seen this already.

We can also **leave out** *that*, in an informal style, after *so, such, now, provided*.

Come in quietly **so (that)** *she doesn't hear you.*
It was **such** *a shock* **(that)** *I didn't know what to say.*
Now (that) *you're in London we'll see more of you.*
You can use my bike **provided (that)** *you clean it afterwards.*

2 **Put in the right conjunction, with *that* if the sentence is formal, and without *that* if it is informal.**

▶ ...Now that... the plans have been approved, the company will be able to begin construction.
▶ ...Now... Alan's arrived, we can start supper.

1 He may use the firm's car .... he pays for all petrol used.
2 I left the bedroom door open .... I'd hear the phone.
3 .... she's sixteen she thinks she can do what she likes.
4 It was .... a serious operation .... she was not expected to live.
5 Closed-circuit television was installed .... everybody would be able to watch the performance.
6 You can go out .... you're back in time to give me a hand with the cooking.
7 .... the new managers have taken over we expect the company to become profitable in the very near future.
8 I'll tell you everything, ... you don't tell Maggie.
9 He shut himself in the bathroom .... he wouldn't have to help with the housework.
10 .... the exams are over I'm going to enjoy myself.

both ... and; (n)either ... (n)or

These expressions can **join nouns**, **verbs** or **other** kinds of expression.

She plays **both** *tennis* **and** *badminton.*   *He* **both** *sings* **and** *dances.*
The place **both** *depressed me* **and** *made me want to go home.*
Their kid's name is **either** *James* **or** *Charlie – I forget which.*
We can **either** *eat in* **or** *go out to a restaurant.*
That's **neither** *interesting* **nor** *true.*   **Neither** *Sue* **nor** *Ann was there.*

1 **Join the sentences with *both ... and*, *either ... or* or *neither ... nor*.**

▶ He repairs cars. He repairs motorbikes.
He repairs both cars and motorbikes.

1 He doesn't speak English. He doesn't speak French.
....

2 It was Tuesday. It was Wednesday. I'm not sure.
....

3 I don't like her. I don't dislike her.
....

4 You're not right. You're not wrong.
....

5 I admire him. I distrust him.
....

6 He lied to us. He made a mistake. I don't know which.
....

7 Paul is on holiday. Sally is on holiday.
....

8 The secretary did not have the file. The accountant did not have the file.
....

9 The play was funny. The play was shocking.
....

10 He collects paintings. He collects jewellery.
....

2 **Write some sentences about people in history or fiction (the ones in the box or others) using *both ... and* or *neither ... nor*.**

Cinderella	Cleopatra	Dickens	Helen of Troy	J F Kennedy
Julius Caesar	Queen Victoria	Shakespeare	Sitting Bull	

▶ *Neither Julius Caesar nor Queen Victoria had a TV.* ....
....
....
....
....

3 **Write some sentences about yourself (true or not).**

1 I can both ....
2 I can neither ....
3 I like both ....
4 I don't like either ....
5 I haven't got either ....
6 ....

In some answers, both contracted forms (for example *I'm, don't*) and full
forms (for example *I am, do not*) are possible. Normally both are correct.

CONJUNCTIONS **245**

perfect for completion *when I've finished*

With **time conjunctions**, we can use a **present perfect** tense to express **completion** in the **future**.

*I'll have lunch **when I've finished** these letters.*
*Traffic will be easier **after** they**'ve built** the new road.*
***As soon as** Annie**'s gone** back home we'll have a party.*

1 **Change the sentences to emphasise the idea of completion.**

▶ I'll come and see you when I finish work.
  I'll come and see you when I've finished work.
  ....

1 When I finish my exams I'm going to sleep for a week.
  ....

2 I'll go shopping as soon as it stops raining.
  ....

3 After I do the washing up I'm going to have a bath.
  ....

4 I'll phone Sally when I find her number.
  ....

5 Let's wait here until Peter arrives.
  ....

6 When I finish the report I'll ask you to read it.
  ....

We can use a **past perfect** with time conjunctions in a similar way: to show that something was **completely finished** before something else happened.

***After** he **had painted** the kitchen and bathroom, he decided to have a rest.*
***As soon as** I **had checked in**, I phoned Pat and Alice to fix a meeting.*
*We couldn't get into the office **until** the cleaners **had finished**.*

2 **Make sentences using the past perfect.**

▶ 1. Jack finished his lunch.   2. He sat down to watch a film. (*when*)
  When Jack had finished his lunch, he sat down to watch a film.
  ....

▶ 2. I went on a trip round America.   1. I finished my exams. (*after*)
  I went on a trip round America after I had finished my exams.
  ....

1 1. He tried on six pairs of shoes.   2. He decided he liked the first ones best. (*after*)
  ....

2 1. Mary did all the shopping.   2. She took a short walk round the park. (*when*)
  ....

3 1. I washed and dried the last plate.   2. Paul came in and offered to help. (*as soon as*)
  ....

4 2. He went to the café in the square for a cup of coffee.   1. He said goodbye to the visitors. (*after*)
  ....

5 2. I ate all the dark chocolate.   1. I ate all the milk chocolate. (*when*)
  ....

6 2. Peter didn't start his karate training.   1. He phoned his mother. (*until*)
  ....

tenses with *since* and *for* ... *since we were students*

Sentences with *since* usually have a **perfect** tense. But **past tenses** are possible in the **time expression after since**. Compare:

I've known her since 2005.   I've known her since we were students.

① Choose the right tenses.

1 It *is / was / has been* snowing since I *have got up / got up*.
2 Things *have been / were* difficult since Carol *has lost / lost* her job.
3 Since Jake *has taken up / took up* the trumpet, nobody *has / has had / had* any peace.
4 He *has been / was* quite different since he *has got / got* married.
5 Since she *has gone / went* to live in France we *haven't heard / didn't hear* anything from her.
6 He *has been / was* strange ever since he *has had / had* the accident.
7 I *haven't seen / didn't see* Cassie since she *has come / came* back from America.
8 Since I *have met / met* Harry, life *has been / was* much more interesting.
9 *We've lost / We lost* touch with each other since we *have left / left* school.
10 What *have you been / were you* doing since *I've last seen / I last saw* you?

② Complete one or more of the sentences.

1 Things have been much better since I ....
2 Things have been much worse since I ....
3 Things have been very different since I ....

A **present tense** is sometimes used in the main clause to talk about **changes**.
Note also the structure **It is ... since ...**

*She **looks** quite different since her illness.   It's **a long time since** lunch.*

**③ Complete the sentences with some or all of the ends from the box.
(Different answers are possible.)**

he had a job he shaved off his beard I met her, but it seems like years	
she stopped going out with Pete we got our own flat we last had a proper talk	

1 He looks much younger since ....
2 It's nearly three years since ....
3 It's only a week since ....
4 It's too long ....
5 She's a lot happier ....
6 Things are better ....

Sentences with *for* have a **perfect** tense when the meaning is **'time up to now'**, but other tenses are used with other meanings.

I've known her for ages.   I was in that school for three years.
She's staying for another week.   He'll be in hospital for a month.

In some answers, both contracted forms (for example *I'm, don't*) and full forms (for example *I am, do not*) are possible. Normally both are correct.

CONJUNCTIONS **247**

conjunction + *-ing* or *-ed* *after talking to you; until cooked*

Some conjunctions can introduce **clauses** made with *-ing* forms. This is common with *after*, *before*, *when*, *while* and *since*. These *-ing* clauses are a little more **formal** than clauses with **subject + verb**.

After talking to you I felt better. (More formal than *After I talked to you …*)
*Look in the mirror **before driving off**.*

① **Put in suitable conjunctions.**

1 I usually have a snack .... going to bed.
2 He had a heart attack .... watching a baseball game.
3 .... spending all that money on shoes I'd better not buy anything else.
4 Use damp string .... tying up parcels; when it dries it shrinks and gets tight.
5 How many jobs have you had .... leaving school?
6 We went for a walk .... leaving for the airport.
7 Put this on .... shaving and you'll smell wonderful.
8 I haven't heard anything from her .... getting that letter last month.
9 I often listen to music .... working.
10 Always wear goggles .... working with metal.

② **Complete the sentences with suitable conjunctions and the *-ing* forms of verbs from the box.**

| come | drive | eat | exercise | fail | return | talk | travel |

1 Don't go swimming immediately ....
2 Have a rest every hour or so ....
3 He has been terribly depressed .... the exam.
4 I had a word with the secretary .... to the manager.
5 I often solve problems in my head .... at the gym.
6 .... back from America we haven't even had time to unpack.
7 A few days .... from holiday he began to feel ill
8 She always gets nervous .... by air.

A few conjunctions (e.g. *until*, *when*, *if*) can be used with *past participles* instead of full verbs.

*Leave in oven **until cooked**.*   ***When questioned**, he denied everything.*
If given time, I can usually remember people's names.

③ **Rewrite the sentences with conjunction + past participle.**

▶ When he was arrested, he was carrying a loaded shotgun.
  When arrested, he was carrying a loaded shotgun.

1 The parcel will arrive within 24 hours if it is sent by express delivery.
....

2 Warm slowly until it is completely melted.
....

3 Guarantee: your money back if you are not satisfied.
....

4 When he was examined, he was found to have a fractured skull.
....

5 Stir the sugar until it is dissolved.
....

It is possible to have *-ing* and *-ed* **clauses without conjunctions**. These are usually rather formal.

Putting down my book, I went over to the phone.
It rained for two weeks, **completely ruining our holiday**.
Having failed to persuade John, I tried his brother. (= 'As I had failed …')
Used economically, a tin will last for weeks. (= 'If it is used economically …')
Not knowing what to do next, I sat down to think. (= 'As I didn't know …')

① **Rewrite the sentences, changing the words *in italics* and using *-ing* or *-ed* clauses without conjunctions.**

1 *As he had left* school at twelve, he had no qualifications.
   Having ....

2 *If it is fried* in butter and sprinkled with lemon juice, it tastes delicious.
   ....

3 *She walked* over to her desk and picked up a paper.
   ....

4 The water came into the houses, *and flooded* the downstairs rooms.
   ....

5 *As I knew* his tastes, I took him a large box of expensive chocolates.
   ....

6 *He put on* his coat *and* went out.
   ....

7 A lorry broke down in Bond Street, *and caused* a massive traffic jam.
   ....

8 *As I didn't want* to frighten her, I phoned before I went round.
   ....

9 *If it is sent* first class, it should arrive tomorrow.
   ....

10 At 3 a.m. Simon came in, *and woke* everybody in the house.
   ....

② **Grammar in a text. Complete the text with *-ing* or *-ed* forms of words from the box.**

| feel | find | fix | give up | invest | look at | pull | take care of | turn away |

We talked for a little but,[1].......................... I was getting
nowhere, I went out onto the beach and stood
[2]..........................the sea. Why was I still with this man? I had been
with him for five years now, looking after him, [3]..........................
him out of depression after depression, [4]..........................ways to
give him back his self-respect, and [5]........... all the hope I had of a life
of my own. And for what purpose? Love? What did that mean? I had
perhaps thirty years of life left. [6]..........................carefully, those
years could bring me great happiness. Did I want to spend them
[7].......................... a self-centred bad-tempered fool?
[8]..........................from the sea, I looked up at the sky and once
again asked my question: 'What is love? And is it worth the trouble?'
No answer, as usual. [9]..........................a smile on my face, I went
back in and poured us both a drink.

In some answers, both contracted forms (for example *I'm*, *don't*) and full
forms (for example *I am*, *do not*) are possible. Normally both are correct.

CONJUNCTIONS **249**

conjunctions: more practice

1 **Mixed structures. Which is/are correct? Choose A, B or both.**

▶ (A) I know you're right. (B) I know that you're right.

▶ (A) I'll see you when you get back.   B I'll see you when you'll get back.

1 A Picking up his bag, he went downstairs.   B He picked up his bag and went downstairs.

2 A I haven't seen her since we left Paris.   B I haven't seen her since we've left Paris.

3 A After I'd been to the bank, I paid Jeff.   B After going to the bank, I paid Jeff.

4 A When I finished work, I went home.   B When I'd finished work, I went home.

5 A He'll wait until it will be too late.   B He'll wait until it's too late.

6 A I got up early so I could see the sunrise.   B I got up early so that I could see the sunrise.

7 A Although she was ill, but she went shopping.   B Although she was ill, she went shopping.

8 A He should try again when he'll be older.   B He should try again when he's older.

9 A Before going home, I rang Mark.   B Before go home, I rang Mark.

10 A You'll know as soon as I know.   B You'll know as soon as I'll know.

11 A We stopped playing because the rain.   B We stopped playing because of the rain.

12 A Both she can dance and sing.   B She can both dance and sing.

13 A Because it was Sunday, so we all got up late.   B Because it was Sunday, we all got up late.

14 A Taken once a day, these pills will change your life.   B If they are taken once a day, these pills will change your life.

15 A I got lost although I had a good map.   B I got lost in spite my good map.

2 **Perfect for completion. Put the sentences together with present perfect or past perfect tenses.**

▶ I'll do the washing up. Then I'll make the beds. (*when*)
When I've done the washing up, I'll make the beds.

▶ Jane finished her dinner. Then she sat down to watch TV. (*when*)
When Jane had finished her dinner, she sat down to watch TV.

▶ David phoned his girlfriend. Before that he did his piano practice. (*after*)
David phoned his girlfriend after he had done his piano practice.

1 George ate all the chocolate biscuits. Then he started eating the lemon ones. (*when*)
....

2 I turned off the lights in the office. Then I locked the door and left. (*after*)
....

3 You'll finish with the newspaper. I'll read it. (*when*)
....

4 Zach had a long hot shower. Before that he did his exercises. (*after*)
....

5 I'll tell Jackie the good news. I'll go to bed. (*as soon as*)
....

6 I'll stay by his bed. He'll go to sleep. (*until*)
....

7 The opera started. Mike went to sleep. (*as soon as*)
....

8 I locked the door. I realised the children were still outside. (*after*)
....

9 Deborah will leave school. She's going straight into an office job. (*when*)
....

10 They watched me. I went out of the door. (*until*)
....

3 Mixed structures. All these sentences are wrong. Correct the mistakes.

▶ Because it was late, ~~went home.~~ .....*I went home.*.......

1 I liked her in spite of she was bad-tempered. ....

2 I haven't spoken to Angela since we've had that argument. ....

3 Although it was expensive, but he bought it. ....

4 I want to get home before it'll start raining. ....

5 He can neither sing neither play anything. ....

6 I don't like to go to the gym after eaten. ....

7 Because you were so nice to me, so here are some flowers for you. ....

8 As soon as I have told her my plans she started laughing. ....

9 When you've finished work, I take you for a drink. ....

10 We had a good time in spite the weather. ....

4 Grammar in a text. Complete the text with conjunctions from the boxes.

although	because of	if	provided	so that	until	while

HOLIDAY PLANS

Everything was OK ^{1} .... we started talking about holidays. Then it got difficult. The problem was, ^{2} .... John and I wanted to go to the Alps ^{3} .... we could do some climbing, Jenny just wanted to spend two weeks lying on the beach. I said I didn't mind spending a week at the seaside ^{4} .... we could go to the mountains after that. But John said he couldn't go to the seaside ^{5} .... his allergy to sand and salt. Jenny said that ^{6} .... most of us wanted to go to the mountains, she would go along with the majority, ^{7} .... personally she hated mountains.

after	as long as	either	or	so that

Carola said that she didn't mind where we went ^{8} .... she didn't have to do any cooking. Then Mark said something very unpleasant. ^{9} .... Carola had stopped crying, Jenny said, 'Well, what about two weeks in Rome?' and everybody else started shouting, 'Are you crazy? Rome in August. 35 degrees.' etc etc. When they had all finished shouting I said I'd make a cup of tea ^{10} .... we could all calm down a little. Jenny said she would prefer coffee, and John said he could only drink ^{11} .... decaf ^{12} .... water, and Carola said she would like fruit juice.

after	although	in spite of	provided

^{13} .... I was beginning to get a little cross by this time, I kept my temper ^{14} .... everything. I just asked politely if they thought I was running a hotel. Then Jenny said something very unpleasant, and Carola said she thought she would have a lovely holiday ^{15} .... she didn't have to go with any of us, and John threw a book at her, and Carola hit John with a flower vase, and everything became extremely confused. ^{16} .... the police had left, we decided to put off a decision about holidays for a day or two.

5 Internet exercise. Use a search engine (e.g. Google) to find interesting expressions beginning as follows. Write them down.

"in spite of" ....

....

"as long as you don't" ....

....

"so that we can" ....

....

conjunctions: revision test

① Change the structure, but not the meaning.

▶ I filled in the form. Then I posted it. (*when*)
When I had filled in the form, I posted it.
....

1 We stopped playing because it was raining. (*because of*)
....

2 We drove as fast as we could, but we got there late. (*although*)
....

3 They went on climbing although it was snowing. (*in spite of*)
....

4 We hadn't got much money, so we went on a camping holiday. (*because*)
....

5 He got the job although he had poor qualifications. (*in spite of*)
....

6 I finished the shopping. Then I took the car in for a service. (*when*)
....

7 She has not come to see me. She has not answered my emails. (*neither ... nor*)
....

8 He went over to his desk. He picked up a small black book. (*going*)
....

9 The film was interesting, but it was much too long. (*while*)
....

10 Everybody felt sleepy because of the heat. (*because*)
....

② Choose the right word(s) to complete the sentence.

▶ I'll tell you as soon ..as....... I know. (*as, that, –*)
▶ I couldn't find the house because ..⁻..... it was so dark. (*that, of, –*)
1 You can get a cheap ticket .... you pay in advance. (*as long as, until, while*)
2 Karen's staying in New York .... she passes her exams. (*as long as, until, whereas*)
3 I'd better phone my parents .... they know what's happening. (*so that, that, as*)
4 You can stay in the country for three months .... you don't take a job. (*provided, whereas, as if*)
5 .... the food wasn't bad, the service was terrible. (*As long as, So that, While*)
6 You look as .... you've had bad news. (*if, like, –*)
7 Although I spoke some German, ... I couldn't understand what they were saying. (*so, but, –*)
8 I went into the house .... there was nobody there. (*although, in spite of, –*)
9 I like to relax for an hour after .... to the gym. (*go, going, gone*)
10 I haven't seen Oliver since we .... to Scotland together. (*went, have been, were*)

③ Right or wrong? Correct the mistakes or write 'Correct'.

▶ He couldn't walk ~~because~~ his bad knee. *because of* ....
▶ We enjoyed the holiday in spite of the weather. *Correct.* ....
1 We need to get home before it'll get dark. ....
2 When I had told him everything, I felt better. ....
3 As soon as I'll have finished this job, I'm going home. ....
4 You can either come with me or walk home. ....
5 Since Joanne went to America, the house has been very quiet. ....

In some answers, both contracted forms (for example *I'm*, *don't*) and full forms (for example *I am*, *do not*) are possible. Normally both are correct.

SECTION 18 *if* etc

GRAMMAR SUMMARY

In sentences with *if*, **most tenses** are possible.

*He certainly **won't come** tomorrow if he **came** yesterday.*   *If that **was** John, why **didn't** he **say** hello?*
*If you**'ve been** to Rome, I suppose you**'ve seen** the Colosseum.*   *Metals **expand** if you **heat** them.*
*If you**'re** happy, I**'m** happy.*

Note the following **three important structures**:

- **present tenses for future:**
  With *if* (and many other conjunctions) we use **present** tenses to talk about the **future**.
  *I'll tell you if I **get** any news.* (**NOT** ... ~~if I will get any news.~~)

- ***if* + past, ... *would* ...**
  We can use **past** tenses with *if* to show that we feel something is **not real** or **not probable** now.
  (We normally use *would* in the other part of the sentence.)
  *If I **spoke** Arabic, I **would go** and work in Egypt.*

- ***if* + past perfect, ... *would have* ...**
  To talk about **unreal past events** – situations that did not happen – we use *if* + **past perfect**.
  (We normally use *would have* + **past participle** in the other part of the sentence.)
  *If I **had taken** Mary's advice, I **would have been** in deep trouble.*

These three structures are often called 'first', 'second' and 'third conditional'.
The structure with two present tenses (e.g. *If you're happy, I'm happy*) is sometimes called
'zero conditional', for no very good reason.

We can use *unless* to mean 'if not', 'except if'.
*You can't work here **unless** you belong to the union.* (= '... if you don't belong to the union.')

Note the difference between *in case* and *if*.
*I'll take my raincoat **in case** it rains.* (= ... because it might rain.)
*I'll put my raincoat on **if** it rains.*

Past tenses can be used to talk about the **present** or **future** not only after *if*, but also after ***it's time***
and ***would rather*** (= 'would prefer').
***It's time** you **went** home.*
*I'm busy today. **I'd rather** we **had** the meeting tomorrow.*

'If we had some eggs we
could have bacon and eggs
if we had some bacon.'
(*old army joke*)

'Look, I should sit down if I were you. Have you got a
drink? Now it's nothing to worry about, really it isn't...'

revise the basics: ordinary tense use

If can be used with the **same tenses** as **most conjunctions**.

*If you **didn't do** much maths at school, you'**ll find** economics difficult.*
*If that **was** John, why **didn't** he say hello?   Metals **expand** if you **heat** them.*

An *if-clause* can come at the **beginning** or **end** of a sentence. When it comes first, it is often separated by a **comma (,)** in writing.

If you have any problems, telephone 4966498.
Telephone 4966498 if you have any problems.

1 **Complete the sentences with expressions from the box.**

> I never get anything done   I'm sure I can't   say you're with me
> she was lying   we can catch the early train   you don't know what's going on?
> you park near the station   you want to learn a musical instrument
> you won't need to do it again   you're not feeling up to it

1 If anybody asks you what you're doing, ...
2 How can you make decisions if ....
3 If you did the test last week, ...
4 If I don't get up till nine, ...
5 If John couldn't fix the computer yesterday, ...
6 If she said she didn't know me, ...
7 The shops are easy to get to if ....
8 We don't have to go out if ....
9 If you're ready before eight, ...
10 You have to practise if ....

After *if*, we normally use a **present tense** to talk about the **future**. (This happens after most conjunctions.)

*If I **have** enough time tomorrow, I'll come and see you. (NOT If I will have …)*
*I'll give her your love if I **see** her. (NOT … if I will see her.)*
If it's fine tomorrow, I'm going to paint the windows.

2 **Put in the correct tenses (present or 'll …).**

1 If you .... that again, I .... (*say; scream*)
2 I .... surprised if she .... to sell that car. (*be; manage*)
3 If the boys .... to supper, I .... chicken breasts. (*come; cook*)
4 I .... some money if we .... out tonight. (*need; go*)
5 I .... you if we .... to Wales. (*miss; move*)
6 If you ...., I .... (*wash up; dry*)
7 Anna says she .... sorry if Helen .... to the party. (*be; not come*)
8 If you .... lonely, I hope you .... me – any time. (*get; phone*)
9 If you .... in the top drawer, you .... your passport. (*look; find*)
10 It .... funny if Norman .... the job. (*be; get*)

3 **Complete these sentences any way you like.**

1 I won't be surprised if ....
2 I'll be very happy if ....
3 I'll be sorry if ....

revise the basics: *If I had a million dollars, …*

We use *if* + past tense + *would* to talk about things that are **not real** or **not probable** now.

IF + PAST TENSE	WOULD + INFINITIVE (WITHOUT *TO*)
If I *had* a million dollars,	I would build myself a big house.
If you *were* the boss,	what would you do?
If she *didn't buy* so many clothes,	she'd have enough money for food.

After *I* and *we*, **should** is possible instead of *would*. (*Would* is more common.)

*If I had time, I **would/should** learn the saxophone.*

1 Put in the correct verb forms.

1 The kitchen .... better if we .... red curtains. (*look; have*)
2 Where .... if you .... a picture frame? (*you go; need*)
3 I .... this if I .... to. (*not do; not have*)
4 If I .... his address, I .... round and see him. (*know; go*)
5 What .... if you .... the lottery? (*you do; win*)
6 It .... quicker if you .... a computer. (*be; use*)
7 If you .... busy, I .... you how to play bridge. (*not be; show*)
8 If we .... some eggs, I .... you a cake. (*have; make*)
9 If you really .... me, you .... me diamonds. (*love; buy*)
10 If it .... so cold, I .... the garden. (*not be; tidy up*)
11 If I .... the keys, I .... you the cellar. (*have; show*)

After *if*, we often use **were** instead of *was*. In a formal style, *were* is considered more correct.

***If I were** rich, I would spend all my time travelling.*

2 Make sentences using *if … were*.

▶ He / a better dancer / her feet / not hurt.
   If he were a better dancer, her feet wouldn't hurt. ....

1 I / a rabbit / live in a hole
   ....

2 I / forty years younger / go dancing all night
   ....

3 I / Moroccan / speak Arabic
   ....

4 my nose / shorter / be quite pretty
   ....

5 it / not so cold / go for a walk
   ....

We often use the structure *If I were you …* to give **advice**.

***If I were you**, I'd get that car serviced.*   *I shouldn't worry **if I were you**.*

3 Write some sentences beginning *If I were you …* to a friend / your teacher / your mother / your father / your child / the President / the Pope …

....
....
....

In some answers, both contracted forms (for example *I'm, don't*) and full
forms (for example *I am, do not*) are possible. Normally both are correct.

revise the basics: *if I go* and *if I went*

The difference between, for example, *if I go ...* and *if I went ...* or *if I speak ...* and *if I spoke ...* is **not** a difference of **time**. They can **both** refer to the **present or future**.
The **past** tense (+ ***would***) usually suggests that the speaker thinks the situation is **less probable**, or **less definite**, or **impossible**, or **imaginary**. Compare:

*If I **become** President, I'll ...* (said by a candidate in an election)
*If I **became** President, I'd ...* (said by a schoolgirl)
*If I **win** this race, I'll ...* (said by the fastest runner)   *Is it all right if I **invite** John to supper?* (direct request)
*If I **won** this race, I'd ...* (said by the slowest runner) ***Would** it **be** all right if I **invited** John to supper?* (polite request)

1 **Choose the most sensible verb form.**

1 If I *live / lived* to be 70 ...
2 If I *live / lived* to be 150 ...
3 If I *am / were* better looking ...
4 If I *wake / woke* up early tomorrow ...
5 If Scotland *declares / declared* war on Switzerland ...
6 If the universe still *exists / existed* in five years' time ...
7 If everybody *gives / gave* ten per cent of their income to charity ...
8 If everybody *thinks / thought* like me ...
9 If there *is / was* nothing good on TV tonight ...
10 If my English *is / was* better next year ...
11 If the government *bans / banned* cars from city centres next year ...
12 If I *have / had* bad dreams tonight ...

2 **Choose the correct verb forms.**

1 If she *comes / came* late again, she'll lose her job.
2 I'll let you know if I *find / found* out what's happening.
3 If we *live / lived* in a town, life would be easier.
4 I'm sure he won't mind if we *arrive / arrived* early.
5 *We'll / We'd* phone you if we have time.
6 If I won the lottery, I *will / would* give you half the money.
7 It *will / would* be a pity if she married Fred.
8 If I'm free on Saturday, I *will / would* go to the mountains.
9 She *will / would* have a nervous breakdown if she goes on like this.
10 I know I'll feel better if I *stop / stopped* smoking.

3 **Make these requests less definite, and so more polite.**

▶ It will be nice if you help me a bit with the housework.
   It would be nice if you helped me a bit with the housework.

1 Do you mind if I go first?
   ....
2 If all of us come, will you have room in your car?
   ....
3 It will be good if you spend some time with the children.
   ....
4 Do you mind if I come round about seven o'clock?
   ....
5 Is it all right if I use your phone?
   ....

could = 'would be able to' *We could go cycling if ...*

We can use *could* to mean **'would be able to'**.

*If you arrived early, we **could** talk about the meeting.*   *If Joe came, he **could** help with the dog.*

Sometimes we use *could* twice: once as a **past tense** (to say that something is not real / not probable), and once for *would be able to*.

*If I **could** sell my car, I **could** buy a computer.*

1 Complete the sentences with *could* and expressions from the box.

ask her to help ✓   get up late   go and see him   go for a ride   go to the cinema more often
have breakfast in the garden   read the paper ✓   watch a film   write to Henry

▶ If Alice was here, ...*we could ask her to help.*...
▶ If I could find my glasses, ...*I could read the paper.*..
1 If John was at home, we ....
2 If the TV was working, we ....
3 If we had bikes, ...
4 If tomorrow was Saturday, I ....
5 If it was warmer, we ....
6 If I could find my address book, ...
7 If we lived in a town, ...

2 Andy is reading the job advertisements. Unfortunately he can't do much (see the box).
Look at the advertisements and write sentences with *if he ... he could ...*

Andy doesn't speak Japanese ✓   he doesn't have a passport   he can't drive ✓
he can't cook   he doesn't like children   he doesn't like animals   he can't swim

▶ .....*If he spoke Japanese, he could get a job*.......................... at the Grand Hotel.
1 If he could drive, ... at Calloway Ltd.
2 .... at Patterson Travel.
3 .... at Fred's Café.
4 .... at Crowndale School.
5 .... at the City Zoo.
6 .... at the Leisure Centre.

RECEPTIONIST

required immediately
at the Grand Hotel.
Must speak Japanese.
Phone 69423.

Calloway Ltd

needs energetic young
SALES ASSISTANT.
Must have driving licence.
Phone 33446.

Courier needed by
PATTERSON TRAVEL.
Must have passport.
Phone 44576.

ASSISTANT COOK

needed at Fred's Cafe.
Phone 65712.

Welfare officer
required at
Crowndale School.
Must like children.
Phone 88759.

The CITY ZOO requires
Assistant Keeper.
No experience necessary
but must like animals.

The Leisure Centre
needs Attendant,
starting immediately.
Must be able to swim.

In some answers, both contracted forms (for example *I'm, don't*) and full
forms (for example *I am, do not*) are possible. Normally both are correct.

IF ETC **257**

unreal past situations *If Jane hadn't helped me, …*

We can use *if* to talk about **unreal past** events and situations – about how things could have been **different**.
We use the **past perfect** and *would have* + past participle.

IF + PAST PERFECT	WOULD HAVE + PAST PARTICIPLE
If Mary had felt better,	*we would have gone swimming.* (But she didn't, so we didn't.)
If you had told me the truth,	*I would have respected you.* (But you didn't, so I didn't.)
If Jane hadn't helped me,	*I would have been in bad trouble.* (But she did, so I wasn't.)
If she hadn't gone climbing,	*she wouldn't have fallen and broken her arm.* (But she did.)

① **Write the sentences with the correct verb forms.**

▶ If I (*know*) you were coming, I (*invite*) some friends in.
   If I'd known you were coming, I'd have invited some friends in.

1 We (*get*) better tickets if we (*book*) earlier.
   ....

2 He (*go*) to university if his father (*not be*) ill.
   ....

3 If you (*say*) you weren't hungry, I (*not cook*) such a big meal.
   ....

4 The team (*win*) if Jones (*play*) better.
   ....

5 If they (*not cut*) off the electricity, I (*finish*) my work.
   ....

6 If Bell (*not invent*) the telephone, somebody else (*do*) it.
   ....

7 If you (*not spend*) so much time putting your make-up on, we (*not be*) late.
   ....

8 The burglars (*not get*) in if you (*remember*) to lock the door.
   ....

9 If he (*not be*) a film star, he (*not become*) President.
   ....

10 If she (*have*) more sense, she (*sell*) her car years ago.
   ....

11 If he (*not spend*) so much on his holiday, he (*have*) enough to pay for the house repairs.
   ....

12 You (*not catch*) cold if you (*take*) your coat.
   ....

13 You (*win*) if you (*run*) a bit faster.
   ....

14 It (*be*) better if you (*ask*) me for help.
   ....

15 'If Cleopatra's nose (*be*) shorter, the whole history of the world (*be*) different.' (Pascal)
   ....

Instead of *would have* … , we can use *could have* … (= 'would have been able to').

If he'd run a bit faster, he could have won.

2 **Write sentence chains with *if* to show how things could have been different.**

1 He worked hard ⟶ passed exams ⟶ went to university ⟶ studied languages ⟶ learnt
Spanish ⟶ went to Argentina ⟶ went climbing in the Andes ⟶ disappeared in a snowstorm

.....*If he hadn't worked so hard, he wouldn't have passed his exams.*.....
.....*If he hadn't passed his exams, he wouldn't have gone to university.*.....

If he hadn't gone to university, ...

....

....

....

....

....

2 He bought a bicycle ⟶ went for a ride in the country ⟶ fell off ⟶ woke up in hospital
⟶ met a beautiful nurse ⟶ wrote a bestselling novel about her ⟶ got rich ⟶ married the
beautiful nurse and had three charming children ⟶ lived happily ever after

If he hadn't bought a bicycle, ...

....

....

....

....

....

....

3 Mary's mother went out that evening ⟶ Mary cooked for herself ⟶ got interested in cooking
⟶ opened a very successful restaurant ⟶ had the Prime Minister as a customer ⟶ the PM
ordered mussels ⟶ the mussels poisoned the PM ⟶ the PM died ⟶ Mary went to prison for life

....

....

....

....

....

....

3 **Choose the correct forms to complete the cartoon caption.**

'Maybe things *had turned out* / *would have turned out*
better if I *would have put in* / *had put in* a whole week.'

In some answers, both contracted forms (for example *I'm*, *don't*) and full
forms (for example *I am*, *do not*) are possible. Normally both are correct.

IF ETC **259**

unless *Come tonight unless I phone.*

Unless means '**if not**', in the sense of '**except if**'.

Come tonight **unless** I phone. (= '... **if** I don't phone.' / '... **except if** I phone.')
I'll take the job **unless** the pay is too low.

Note that **after** *unless* we use a **present tense** to talk about the **future**.

1 **Change the words *in italics*.**

▶ Please don't call the doctor at weekends *if it's not important.* ...unless it's important...............

▶ *Unless you come with me*, I won't go to New York. ...If you don't come with me......

1 You can't go there *if you don't have a visa.* ....

2 *If you don't go now*, I'll call the police. ....

3 She always sees me on Wednesdays *unless she's travelling.* ....

4 I don't cook much *unless I've got visitors.* ....

5 We usually go sailing at the weekend *if Emma hasn't got a handball match.*

....

6 I'll go to bed early *if you don't want a game of cards.* ....

7 You can't see this film *unless you are 16 or over.* ....

8 I can't sell you a ticket *if you don't pay cash.* ....

9 I'm afraid we haven't got a table free *unless you have reserved.* ....

10 I'd like to talk to you, *if you're not too busy.* ....

2 **Join the beginnings and ends together and write the sentences using *unless* instead of *if not*.**

BEGINNINGS		ENDS	
0	I'll be back tomorrow	A	if he doesn't start working. ......
1	He'll get thrown out of school	B	if I don't phone to say I can't come. ......
2	You can't open the door	C	if you haven't heard it before. ......
3	I always watch TV in the evenings	D	if I don't go out. ......
4	I'll see you at ten	E	if it doesn't rain. ......
5	Let's have dinner out	F	if the children don't want it. ......
6	I'll tell you a good joke	G	if there isn't a change of government. ......
7	Things will go on getting worse	H	if there isn't a rail strike. ..0..
8	We're going to have a picnic	I	– if you're not too tired. ......
9	You can have the last sausage	J	if you don't know the code. ......

▶ I'll be back tomorrow unless there's a rail strike. ....

1 ....

2 ....

3 ....

4 ....

5 ....

6 ....

7 ....

8 ....

9 ....

if only and *I wish*: tenses *If only I knew…*

If only ...! and **wish** can be used with **would** and **past tenses**.
These structures express **regrets**, and wishes for **unlikely** or **impossible** things.
Past tenses are used to talk about the **present**.

*If only I **knew** more people!*   *I **wish** I **was** better looking.*

1 **Write sentences beginning *If only* or *I wish*.**

▶ The radio doesn't work. ..I wish the radio worked........ OR ..If only the radio worked!.......

1 He smokes. ....

2 I don't speak Russian. ....

3 I haven't got a car. ....

4 I'm not hard-working ....

5 I'm bad at sport. ....

6 I don't like dancing. ....

7 It rains all the time. ....

8 She works on Sundays. ....

9 I can't eat eggs. ....

We use **would** … after **wish / if only** to talk about things that we **would like people or things (not) to do.**
This often expresses dissatisfaction or annoyance: it can sound **critical.**

*I wish this damned car **would start**.*   *If only it **would stop** raining!*

2 **Write sentences with *If only … would* or *I wish … would ….***

▶ Somebody won't stop talking. ..I wish he would stop talking...........
   OR ..If only he would stop talking!..........

1 It's not snowing. ....

2 The phone keeps ringing. ....

3 The baby won't stop crying. ....

4 The kettle won't boil. ....

5 The traffic lights won't go green. ....

6 Frank hasn't written. ....

7 Patrick hasn't found a job. ....

8 The exam results haven't arrived. ....

9 Spring hasn't come. ....

We use a **past perfect** tense to express **regrets about the past.**

*I wish you **hadn't said** that.*   *If only she **hadn't told** the police, everything would be all right.*

3 **Complete the regrets with verbs from the box. Use the past perfect.**

be   choose   get   go   have   look after   save

1 I wish I .... my teeth properly.   5 I wish I .... a different career.

2 I wish I .... nicer to people.   6 I wish I .... married.

3 I wish I .... money.   7 I wish I .... children.

4 I wish I .... to university.

in case   *I'm taking my umbrella in case it rains.*

We use *in case* mostly to talk about **precautions** – things we do to be **ready for what might happen**. After *in case* we use a **present tense** to talk about the **future**.

*I wrote down her address **in case** I forgot it.*
*I've bought a chicken **in case** your mother **stays** to lunch.*

We can use *should* after *in case* – this gives the idea of 'by chance'.

*I've bought a chicken **in case** your mother **should** stay to lunch.*

Should is common in sentences about the **past**.

*I **wrote** down her address in case I **should** forget it.*

1 **A woman is packing to go on holiday in Austria. Make sentences:**

> SHE'S PACKING: a German phrase book ✓   a pack of cards   a tennis racket
> a thick sweater   a swimsuit   a swimsuit   aspirins   binoculars   her address book
> some books   walking boots

> IN CASE: she decides to send postcards   she has time to read
> she meets people who play bridge   she wants to go walking
> the hotel has a heated pool   the hotel staff don't speak English ✓
> the sun gives her a headache   the weather is cold   there is a tennis court
> she wants to go bird-watching

▸   *She's packing a German phrase book in case the hotel staff don't speak English.*
....
....
....
....
....
....
....
....

In case is **not** normally used like *if*. Compare:

*I'll buy a bottle of wine (now) **in case** Roger comes (later).*
*I'll buy a bottle of wine (later) **if** Roger comes. (and if he doesn't come I won't)*

2 *If* **or** *in case*?
1 I'm taking my umbrella with me ....it rains.
2 I'll open the umbrella............................it rains.
3 People phone the fire brigade ....their houses catch fire.
4 People insure their houses............................they catch fire.
5 We have a burglar alarm ....somebody tries to break in.
6 The burglar alarm will go off............................somebody tries to break in.
7 I'll let you know............................I need help.
8 I'll take my mobile phone............................I need to phone you.

it's time and *I'd rather*: tenses *It's time you had a haircut.*

After *it's time*, we can use an **infinitive** with *to*. After *would rather* (= 'would prefer'), we use an **infinitive** without *to*.
It's time to go out.   I'd rather stay in.

We can also use a **subject and verb** after these expressions. The verb is **past** (but with a present or future meaning).
It's time you had a haircut.   I'd rather they came tomorrow, not today.

1 Change the structure.

▶ It's time to stop. (*you*) ....It's time you stopped...

▶ It's time we went to bed. (*to*) .....It's time to go to bed..................................

1 It's time to clean the car. (*I*) ....

2 It's time you cooked supper. (*to*) ....

3 It's time to get a new fridge. (*we*) ....

4 It's time we had a party. (*to*) ....

5 It's time to go home. (*your mother*) ....

6 It's time to invite the Harrises. (*we*) ....

7 It's time to plan our holiday. (*we*) ....

8 It's time to see the dentist. (*you*) ....

9 It's time to stop work. (*I*) ....

10 It's time to get a job. (*that boy*) ....

2 Rewrite the *second* sentence in each conversation, starting with *I'd rather we/you* etc.

▶ 'You'd better phone Judy.' 'No, you phone her.' .....I'd rather you phoned her................

1 'Let's talk things over.' 'No, let's talk tomorrow.'
....

2 'Shall I come at nine?' 'Ten would be better.'
....

3 'I'll phone Sue.' 'No, don't.'
....

4 'Can she work with you?' 'Why doesn't she work with Maggie?'
....

5 'I'll cook tomorrow.' 'Tonight would be better.'
....

6 'Ask that policeman.' 'You ask him.'
....

7 'Mark wants to go out.' 'I'd prefer him to stay in.'
....

8 'Can they use our sheets?' 'It would be more convenient if they brought their own.'
....

9 'The government wants to cut taxes.' 'It would be better if they did something
about the homeless.'
....

10 'Let's get a new car.' 'No, let's spend the money on a trip round the world.'
....

In some answers, both contracted forms (for example *I'm, don't*) and full
forms (for example *I am, do not*) are possible. Normally both are correct.

IF ETC **263**

if etc: more practice

1 *If … would.* **Answer the questions. Use a dictionary if necessary.**

1 **If you heard a strange noise in your house in the night, would you:**
A go and look?   B phone the police?   C hide under the bedclothes?
If I heard a strange noise in my house in the night, I would ....
....

2 **If you found a lot of money in the street, would you:**
A keep it?   B try to find the person who had lost it?   C take it to the police?
....
....

3 **If you saw a child stealing from a shop, would you:**
A tell the child to stop?   B tell a shop assistant?   C do nothing?
....
....

4 **If a shop assistant gave you too much change, would you:**
A tell him/her?   B take the money and say nothing?
....
....

5 **If you found a dead mouse in your kitchen, would you:**
A throw it out?   B ask somebody to throw it out?   C run?
....
....

6 **If you found a suitcase on the pavement outside a bank, would you:**
A take it into the bank?   B take it to the police?   C take it home?   D leave it?
....
....

7 **If you found a friend's diary, would you:**
A read it?   B give it to him/her without reading it?
....
....

2 *If … would.* **What would you do if you had a free year and plenty of money?**
Write three or more sentences.
....
....
....
....

3 *If only, I wish.* **Write your own continuations for these sentences.**
If only I could ....
I wish I spoke ....
I wish I knew ....
If only I was ....
I wish I wasn't ....
I wish I had never ....

4 *If … would.* **Look at the pictures. What sentences do you think they illustrate?**

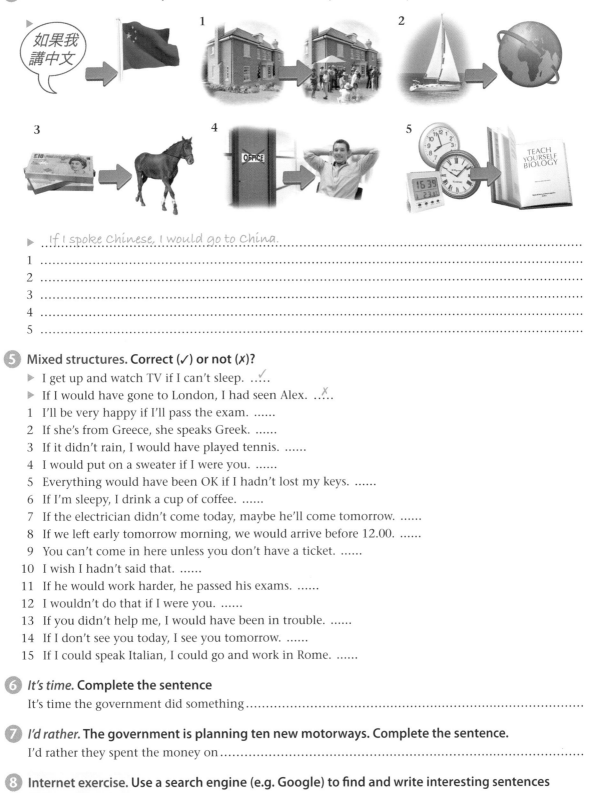

▶ ....If I spoke Chinese, I would go to China...
1 ....
2 ....
3 ....
4 ....
5 ....

5 **Mixed structures. Correct (✓) or not (✗)?**

▶ I get up and watch TV if I can't sleep. ...✓...
▶ If I would have gone to London, I had seen Alex. ...✗...
1 I'll be very happy if I'll pass the exam. ......
2 If she's from Greece, she speaks Greek. ......
3 If it didn't rain, I would have played tennis. ......
4 I would put on a sweater if I were you. ......
5 Everything would have been OK if I hadn't lost my keys. ......
6 If I'm sleepy, I drink a cup of coffee. ......
7 If the electrician didn't come today, maybe he'll come tomorrow. ......
8 If we left early tomorrow morning, we would arrive before 12.00. ......
9 You can't come in here unless you don't have a ticket. ......
10 I wish I hadn't said that. ......
11 If he would work harder, he passed his exams. ......
12 I wouldn't do that if I were you. ......
13 If you didn't help me, I would have been in trouble. ......
14 If I don't see you today, I see you tomorrow. ......
15 If I could speak Italian, I could go and work in Rome. ......

6 *It's time.* **Complete the sentence**

It's time the government did something ....

7 *I'd rather.* **The government is planning ten new motorways. Complete the sentence.**

I'd rather they spent the money on ....

8 **Internet exercise. Use a search engine (e.g. Google) to find and write interesting sentences beginning as follows.**

"If only we had" ....
"I wish everybody would" ....
"If I were more" ....

if etc: revision test

1 **Make sentences beginning with *if*.**

▶ I live in London, so I go to the theatre very often.
If I didn't live in London, I wouldn't go to the theatre very often.

1 We can't play bridge because Daniel isn't here.

2 Alice never listens to me, so I don't talk to her.

3 I don't understand physics because I don't know enough maths.

4 My father doesn't do exercise, so he's overweight.

5 I don't like cooking, so I don't make you wonderful meals.

2 **Right or wrong? Correct the mistakes or write 'Correct'.**

▶ I get up and go for a walk if I can't sleep. ....*Correct.*....

▶ We'll go and see Harry if ~~we'll pass~~ through London. ....*we pass*....

1 If we weren't all too tired, we would have played poker. ....

2 If she would smile more, people will like her. ....

3 Things would have been all right if the police hadn't stopped us. ....

4 If we took the 14.00 train, we would get to Oxford before six o'clock. ....

5 If I were you, I'd be more careful. ....

6 You can't get a job unless you don't have a work permit. ....

7 If I would have got up earlier, I hadn't missed the bus. ....

8 If Ann doesn't phone soon, there's something wrong. ....

9 If I'm sleepy, I go for a short walk. ....

10 I go home if I were you. ....

11 If she's from Turkey, she speaks Turkish. ....

12 If that child would stop shouting, everybody will be much happier. ....

13 I'd rather we had the meeting tomorrow, not today. ....

14 In case Peter phones, tell him I've gone out. ....

15 It's time we cleaned the windows. ....

3 **Read the story and write a sentence chain.**

CHOCOLATE IS GOOD FOR YOU

Anna felt very hungry, so she went out to buy chocolate. On the way back, she ran across the road in front of a cyclist; he fell off his bike and hit his head. He finished up in hospital, and Anna went to visit him. She decided he was very nice, so she went to visit him again, and met a really handsome doctor. She married the doctor and they lived happily ever after.

If Anna hadn't felt hungry, she wouldn't have gone out to buy chocolate.
If she hadn't gone out to buy chocolate, ...

In some answers, both contracted forms (for example *I'm, don't*) and full forms (for example *I am, do not*) are possible. Normally both are correct.

SECTION 19 relatives

GRAMMAR SUMMARY

who	(whom)	which	that	what	whose

We use **relative pronouns** to **join sentences** to **nouns**.
   The girl was only 15.   **She got the gold medal.**   *The girl who got the gold medal* was only 15.

We use *who* for **people** and *which* for **things**. We can also use *that* for **people and things**.
   *There's **the man who/that** built our garage.*   *They sent **a letter which/that** I didn't get.*

Whose is a possessive relative pronoun.
   *I want to talk to the man **whose** car is parked outside our house.*

Relative pronouns **replace** *he/she/it* etc. We don't use both.
   (**NOT** ~~The girl who she got the gold medal~~ …)

Where and *when* can be used as relatives referring to place and time.
   *I'll never forget **the day when** I first met you.* (= '… the day on which …')
   *Do you know **a shop where** I can find sandals?* (= '… a shop at which …')

We often leave out **object pronouns**, but not subject pronouns.
   *Here are those photos (**which/that**) you lent me.*
   *The photos **which/that** show the kids are lovely.* (**NOT** ~~The photos show the kids~~ …)

Prepositions can often go **in two places**.
   *The deal **about which** we were **talking** wasn't possible.* (formal)
   *The deal **that** we were **talking about** wasn't possible.* (informal)

We can use *what* to mean **'the thing(s) which'**.
   *You never get exactly **what** you want.*

Some **relative clauses identify** the noun that they go with; some do not. The grammar is a little different for the two kinds.
   *The woman **my brother is going to marry** is really nice.* (identifying)
   *Sandra Peters, **whom my brother is going to marry**, is really nice.* (non-identifying)

'Women have their faults
Men have only two:
Everything they say,
Everything they do.'
(*Traditional*)

'Everything I like is either illegal,
immoral or fattening.'
(*Traditional*)

'Nothing that is worth learning
can be taught.' (*Oscar Wilde*)

'No man can lose what he never had.'
(*Izaak Walton*)

'A politician is a statesman
who approaches every question
with an open mouth.' (*Adlai Stevenson*)

'It's really very simple, Miss Everhart. Now you just
move the cursor across the screen to the area of
the world you wish to destroy.'

revise the basics: *who(m)*, *which* and *that*

We can use **sentences** to describe **nouns**.
To join sentences to nouns, we use **relative pronouns**: *who* (for people) and *which* (for things).

*I've got **a friend. He collects stamps.*** ⟶ *I've got **a friend who collects stamps**.*
*There's **a problem. It worries me.*** ⟶ *There's **a problem which worries me**.*
*Holly's lost **the watch. I bought it for her.*** ⟶ *Holly's lost **the watch which I bought for her**.*

We use *who* or *which* instead of *he, him, she, it* etc. **Don't** use **both**.

*The man **who** lives opposite has been ill.* (**NOT** ~~The man who he lives opposite …~~)
*This is the report **which** you wanted.* (**NOT** … ~~which you wanted it.~~)

1 Join the sentences in the places marked *. Change *he, it* etc to *who* or *which*.

▶ I know a shop*. It sells good coffee. *I know a shop which sells good coffee.*

▶ Most of the people* work in London. They live in our village.
Most of the people who live in our village work in London.

1 The tomatoes* were mostly bad. You bought them.
....

2 The flowers* are doing well. I planted them.
....

3 A lot of the people* want a change of government. I know them.
....

4 Three of the prisoners* are still on the run. They escaped last night.
....

5 There's some cheese in the fridge*. It needs to be eaten.
....

6 I want some plates*. They can go in the microwave.
....

7 They haven't got the shirt* in your size. You wanted it.
....

8 The boy* has asked my sister out. He lives next door.
....

We often use *that* instead of *which*, and instead of *who* in an informal style.

*There's a problem **that** you don't understand.*   *I know some people **that** could help you.* (informal)

2 Rewrite sentences 1–5 from Exercise 1 using *that*.

1 ....
2 ....
3 ....
4 ....
5 ....

3 Write a true sentence beginning *Most of the people that I know* …

....

We normally use *that*, not *which*, after *all*, *everything*, *nothing*, *the only* … and **superlatives**.
We do **not** use *what* in these cases (see page 271).

*I've told you **everything that** I know.* (**NOT** … ~~everything what I know.~~)
***The only thing that** matters to me is your happiness.*

Whom can be used as an **object** for people. It is rather formal; in an informal style we often prefer *who*.

What is the name of that nurse **whom** *we met last week?* (formal)
What's the name of that nurse **who/that** *we met last week?* (informal)

Whom is always used **after prepositions**.

the woman **with whom** *I travelled* (**NOT** ~~the woman with who I travelled~~)

4 **Make these sentences more formal.**

1 He's one of those people that everybody likes.

....

2 There were three boys at my school that I'll never forget.

....

3 The woman that I didn't recognise was my old dentist.

....

4 The man who the police arrested said that he'd never met the woman.

....

5 We had a biology teacher who we couldn't stand.

....

After words for **time** and **place**, we can **use** *when* and *where* as relatives.

I'll never forget **the day when** *I first met you.* (= '… the day **on which** …')
Do you know **a shop where** *I can find sandals?* (= '… a shop **at which** …')

5 **Write your own completions for these sentences.**

1 I'll always remember the day when ....

2 I know a place where ....

6 GRAMMAR AND VOCABULARY. **Do you know the English words for countries and languages?**
Complete the sentences; use a dictionary to help you.

1 People who live in .... speak Greek.

2 The language that people speak in Hungary is called ....

3 The language .... most people speak in China is called ....

4 People who live in .... speak Italian.

5 .... live in .... Turkish.

6 The language .... Algeria is called Arabic.

7 The language .... some people .... Scots Gaelic.

8 The people .... Holland ....

9 The language .... some .... Irish.

10 The people .... Portugal ....

11 .... some .... Welsh.

12 .... Japan ....

7 **Write five more sentences like the ones in Exercise 6.**

....
....
....
....
....

In some answers, both contracted forms (for example *I'm, don't*) and full
forms (for example *I am, do not*) are possible. Normally both are correct.

revise the basics: leaving out relative pronouns

We can **leave out** object pronouns *who(m)*, *which* and *that*, but **not** usually **subject** pronouns.

Where's that letter that I saw this morning? → *Where's that letter I saw this morning?*

BUT NOT *Where's that letter that was on the table?* → ~~*Where's that letter was on the table?*~~

1 **Is the relative pronoun the subject or object in these clauses?**

▶ That's the woman *who* lives next door. ..S.

▶ Our doctor is a person *whom* I really respect. ..O.

1 He had a simple idea *which* changed the world. ......

2 I've lost that nice ring *which* Bill gave me. ......

3 It's a book *that* everybody talks about and nobody reads. ......

4 Once there were three rabbits *that* lived near a river. ......

5 That's the man *who* I wanted to see. ......

6 An orphan is a child *who* hasn't got any parents. ......

7 He keeps telling you things *which* you already know. ......

8 They never thanked me for the money *that* I sent them. ......

2 **In which three of sentences 1–6 can the relative pronouns be left out? Cross them out.**

▶ The strawberries ~~which~~ I bought weren't very good.

1 The job **that** he got wasn't very interesting.

2 A woman **who(m)** my sister knows has just bought the house next door.

3 The doctor **who** treated me didn't know what he was doing.

4 I'm sorry for people **who** haven't got a sense of humour.

5 Have you got anything **that** will clean this carpet?

6 Have you got a typewriter **that** I can use?

3 **Join the sentences in the places marked * without using *who(m)*, *which* or *that*.**

▶ You asked me to get you a paper. Here's the paper*.
   Here's the paper you asked me to get you.
   ....

1 You recommended a film. We went to see the film*, but we didn't think much of it.
   ....

2 My sister bought a new car last month. The car* has broken down four times already.
   ....

3 You didn't recognise an actor on television last night. The actor* was Jake McLean.
   ....

4 Jane had some friends at school. Only a very few of the friends* went on to university.
   ....

5 My father had an operation for his heart problem. The operation* was only a partial success.
   ....

6 Mark wrote an essay while we were on holiday. The essay* has won a prize in the school competition.
   ....
   ....

7 My daughter brings friends home. Some of the friends* are pretty strange.
   ....

→ For relative clauses ending in prepositions (e.g. *That's the girl I told you **about***), see page 273.

what = 'the thing(s) that' *Take what you like.*

We can use **what** to mean **'the thing(s) which/that'**, **'the stuff that'** or **'anything that'**.

What she said made me angry.   I gave him *what* he needed.
*Help yourself. Take *what* you like.*

We use **what** with a **singular** verb.

What I learnt at school **was** mostly useless.

1 **Rewrite the words *in italics*, using *what*.**

▶ *The things that she did* that morning *weren't* helpful. ...What she did......wasn't...........

1 *The things that he said* made everybody angry. ....

2 The date – that's *the thing that I forgot* to tell them! ....

3 I'll do *anything that I like*. ....

4 *The things that it said* in the paper *were* worrying. ....

5 Schoolchildren should read *anything that interests them*. ....

6 *The thing that matters* most is their happiness. ....

7 *The thing that I like best* is walking in the mountains. ....

8 I didn't understand *the things that she meant*. ....

9 Thanks for the handbag. It was *just the thing that I wanted!* ....

10 *The things that happened were* quite unexpected. ....

2 **Complete the definitions using *what* and the words in the box.**

> advertising   cheese ✓   grass   gravity   happiness   honey
> imagination   money   petrol   philosophy   power

▶ ...Cheese is what............. people make   6 .... economists
    from milk.   know about.

1 .... bees make.   7 .... poets need.

2 .... cows eat.   8 .... makes people

3 .... everybody wants.   buy things they don't want.

4 .... philosophers study. 9 .... makes cars go.

5 .... politicians want.   10 .... makes things fall.

We use **that**, not *what*, after **anything**, **something**, **nothing**, **everything**, **all** and **the only thing**.
*I'll give you **anything that** you need. (**NOT** ... ~~anything what you need.~~)*
*Music is **the only thing** that interests her.   They had **nothing that** was useful.*
All that I could do was listen to her.*

3 **Put in *that* or *what*.**

1 I don't believe anything .... she says.   6 .... you need is a rest.

2 .... he did shocked me.   7 I learnt nothing .... was important.

3 The only thing .... I forgot was soap.   8 Come and look at .... I've done.

4 I don't have time to read everything   9 I can eat .... I like.
   .... I want to.   10 He said something .... was

5 They told us .... we needed to know.   very upsetting.

→ For emphasising uses of *what*, see page 149.

In some answers, both contracted forms (for example *I'm, don't*) and full
forms (for example *I am, do not*) are possible. Normally both are correct.

RELATIVES **271**

whose *a girl whose beauty ...*

We can join sentences by putting *whose* in place of *his*, *her* or *its*. This structure is rather formal.

*I saw a girl. **Her** beauty took my breath away.* → *I saw a girl **whose** beauty took my breath away.*
*He went to a meeting. He didn't understand **its** purpose.* → *He went to a meeting **whose** purpose he didn't understand.*

Whose replaces *his/her/its*. We **don't** use **both** together.

NOT ... *whose her beauty took my breath away.*

Whose goes **together with a noun**. It cannot be used with *the*.

NOT *a man whose I had never heard*   NOT *a girl whose the beauty took my breath away*

1 **Complete the sentences with *whose*. The words in the box will help.**

books	children	food	houses ✓	patients	plants	students	tourists	
are happy	are read	die	fall down ✓	get lost	grow	learn	is enjoyed	

▶ A good builder is one ....*whose houses don't fall down.*..

1 A good parent is one ....

2 A good gardener ....

3 A good doctor ....

4 A good writer ....

5 A good teacher ....

6 A good tourist guide ....

7 A good cook ....

2 **In the Alpine village of Fernalm, everybody is related to everybody else. Combine the pieces of information in the correct order to make three sentences using *whose* (but with no other changes), so as to make everything clear.**

1 **Anton,**
   sister Anneliese also helps out in the sports shop
   brother Fritz helps him run the sports shop
   lives with Marika
   ....*Anton, whose brother Fritz*..
   ....
   ....

2 **Anneliese has**
   girlfriend Heidrun is an instructor at the ski school
   a younger brother Max
   wife Paula works in the restaurant run by Anton's other brother Toni
   ....
   ....
   ....

3 **The person who is**
   daughter Liesl runs the pizzeria
   wife Monika was national ice-dancing champion in her younger days
   but now works part-time for the baker down the road, Karsten
   in charge of the ski school is Anton's Uncle Erich
   ....
   ....
   ....

prepositions in relative clauses *the girl I was talking about*

In **relative clauses** (**after** *who*, *whom*, *which*, *that*), **verb + preposition** combinations usually **stay together**. This means that **prepositions** can be **separated** from their relative pronoun **objects**.

	OBJECT		VERB + PREPOSITION
something	*(that)*	*you can*	**write with**
the girl	*(whom)*	*I was*	**talking about**
the music	*(which)*	*we*	**listened to**

Prepositions can also go **before their objects**, but this is usually very **formal**.

something **with which** *you can write*   *the girl* **about whom** *I was talking*

1 **Complete the sentences with expressions from the box.**

a cup   a picture   a tap   a toy   a vase   a window

1 .... is something that a child plays with.   4 .... is something you can look through.
2 .... is something water comes out of.   5 .... is something that you drink out of.
3 .... is something that you can look at.   6 .... is something you put flowers in.

2 **Put the words in order. Which description goes with which picture?**

▶ bite you with things that *things that you bite with* E .... A
1 in something you sleep that ....
2 on you that something put things ....
3 valuables in you that put something ....
4 teeth with you that thing a your clean ....
5 on a thing hang that clothes you ....
6 with liquid dishes you wash that ....
7 can a fire start with you that something ....

3 **Make up similar descriptions for these things.**

a key ....
a purse ....
a chair ....
soap ....
furniture polish ....
olive oil ....
a knife ....
a razor ....
a notebook ....
money ....

4 **Make these expressions less formal.**

▶ the people with whom we went on holiday *the people (that) we went on holiday with*
1 a man with whom I sometimes play chess ....
2 somebody for whom I have great respect ....
3 the girl to whom I was writing ....
4 the problem about which I was worried ....
5 a car for which I paid too much ....

In some answers, both contracted forms (for example *I'm*, *don't*) and full forms (for example *I am*, *do not*) are possible. Normally both are correct.

RELATIVES **273**

reduced relative clauses *luggage left unattended*

We sometimes **leave out** *who/which/that* + *is/are/was/were* before **participles** (*-ing* and *-ed* forms).

*Do you know that man **standing** near the door?* (= '… who is standing …')
*The man **accused** of the killing said that he was at the cinema at the time.* (= 'The man **who was accused** …')
*Letters **posted** before twelve noon will usually be delivered by the next day.*

1 **Change the words** *in italics* **as shown in the examples.**

▶ *Paper that is made from rice* is sometimes used for stationery.
  ....Paper made from rice..

1 Who's that good-looking man *who is talking* to Alison?
....

2 *Luggage that is left unattended* will be taken away by police.
....

3 *The driver who was sent* to collect me at the airport went to the wrong terminal.
....

4 *The nurse who is looking after my aunt* is very kind to her.
....

5 *All the rubbish that is floating in the sea* is a real danger to health.
....

6 *Ham which is made in the traditional way* costs more, but tastes better.
....

7 *Women tourists who are wearing trousers* are not allowed in the temple.
....

8 James thought that *the man who was talking to his girlfriend* was her brother.
....

9 *The man who was bitten by my neighbour's dog* was her husband's boss.
....

2 **Join the sentences without using** *who/which/that.*

▶ There was a man. The man was seen running from the burning building.
  ....There was a man seen running from the burning building.....................

1 I keep dreaming about a woman. The woman is standing with her back to me.
....

2 James says he heard a shot. The shot was fired in the street.
....

3 Are those your trousers? The trousers are hanging over the balcony.
....

4 They live in a beautiful old house. The house was built 300 years ago.
....

5 The Navajo create beautiful jewellery. The jewellery is made of silver and turquoise.
....

6 Passengers are asked to keep behind the yellow line. The passengers are standing on Platform 2.
....

7 Pauline has a very strange old painting of a woman. The woman is holding a small dog.
....

non-identifying relative clauses *Kelly, who does my hair, ...*

Some relative clauses **identify** – they say **who or what** we are talking about.
Others **do not identify**, because it is already clear **who** or **what** we are talking about.

1 **DO IT YOURSELF** **Which relative clauses identify? Circle A or B.**
▶ (A) The woman **who/that does my hair** has just had a baby.
   B Kelly, **who does my hair**, has just had a baby.
1 A She married a man **(that/who/whom) she met on a bus.**
   B She married a nice architect from Belfast, **whom she met on a bus.**
2 A Have you got a book **that's really easy to read?**
   B I lent him *The Old Man and the Sea*, **which is really easy to read.**
3 A What did you think of the wine **(that) we had last night?**
   B I poured him a glass of wine, **which he drank at once.**

2 **DO IT YOURSELF** **Look at Exercise 1 again and answer the questions.**
1 Without the relative clauses, which make more sense – the **A** or **B** sentences? ....
2 Non-identifying clauses (in the **B** sentences) have commas (,,). Can you see why? ....
3 In which kind of clause can we use *that* instead of *who(m)* or *which* – **A** or **B**? ....
4 In which kind of clause can we leave out a relative pronoun when it is the object? ....
5 Do you think non-identifying clauses are more formal or more informal? ....

3 **Change *who/whom/which* to *that*, or leave it out, if possible.**
▶ This is Peter Taylor, who works with my sister. ..No change...................
▶ People ~~who~~ don't answer letters annoy me. ..that............................
1 What happened to the oranges which I bought yesterday? ....
2 This room, which isn't used any more, belonged to our eldest son. ....
3 My Uncle Sebastian, who travels a lot, has just gone off to Thailand. ....
4 We live in a village called Netherwold, which has 150 inhabitants. ....
5 I like a film which has a beginning, a middle and an end – in that order. ....
6 I've had a card from Sally, who used to live next door. ....
7 Do you remember those awful people who we met in Corfu? ....
8 We had good advice from James, whom we consulted about investments. ....

Note the use of *which* to refer to a **whole clause**. Compare:
*He took out **the teeth which/that** were causing the trouble.* (*which/that* = 'the teeth')
He took out two teeth, which *was a real pity.* (*which* = the clause 'He took out two teeth')

Note that *what* cannot be used in this way.

*He got the job, **which** surprised us all.* (**NOT** ... ~~what surprised us all.~~)

4 **Put in *which* or *what*.**
1 She cycles to work every day, ...
   keeps her healthy.
2 I very much liked .... you said at
   the meeting.
3 They gave me .... I asked for.
4 The lights suddenly went out, ...
   frightened Granny terribly.
5 This is .... I need.
6 Everybody arrived late, ... didn't
   surprise me in the least.
7 The door was locked, ... was a nuisance.
8 He wouldn't tell me .... I wanted to know.
9 She let me borrow one of her dresses,
   .... was very kind of her.
10 We're going to have to repair the roof,
   .... will cost a fortune.

In some answers, both contracted forms (for example *I'm, don't*) and full
forms (for example *I am, do not*) are possible. Normally both are correct.

RELATIVES **275**

reading sentences with relative clauses

Relative clauses can make sentences more **difficult to read**.

*A 36-year-old teacher **who was arrested in Cardiff after trying to set fire to a school** is said to have seriously injured two policemen.*

*The financial problems **which some of the company's branches have been facing over the last eighteen months** are mainly caused by increased foreign competition.*

1 DO IT YOURSELF **Why do the relative clauses make the above sentences harder to read? Circle the letter of the best explanation.**

A They separate the subject from the object.

B They separate the subject from the verb.

C They separate the verb from the object.

When **object relative pronouns are left out**, this can make reading even more difficult.

***Some people we met** when we were at a conference in Scotland last year have just written to invite us to stay with them.* (= 'Some people **that** we met ...')

Extra difficulty can be caused when relative clauses end in **prepositions**.

*The woman **my friend Barbara was out shopping with** was her stepmother.*
(= 'The woman **that** my friend Barbara was out shopping with ...')

2 Make these sentences easier to read by adding *that.*

▶ The earrings he gave her for Christmas must have cost at least £500.
   The earrings that he gave her ... .

1 The parcel he got that morning was addressed to someone else.
   ....

2 The sofa we bought last year is falling to pieces already.
   ....

3 Some papers I found lying in the street were secret government documents.
   ....

4 A picture my father bought for £5 has turned out to be worth £10,000.
   ....

5 The people he had hoped to introduce Lee to were not there.
   ....

6 The flat the terrorists hid the guns in was owned by an MP.
   ....

7 The song she could not remember the name of was *Rambling Boy*.
   ....

8 A boy I was at school with has just written a best-selling novel.
   ....

Relative clauses can put together **nouns and verbs that do not belong together**.

*The hair of the young woman sitting next to me on **the park bench was purple**.* (It was not the park bench that was purple.)

*The picture that I put in **Helen's room needs cleaning**.* (It's not the room that needs cleaning.)

3 Read the sentences and answer the questions.

1 The rosebush Sue gave to my little sister is growing beautifully.
Who or what is growing? ....

2 The two tall men we saw with Duncan and Jack were their nephews.
Who were the uncles? ....

3 The man my mother was working for before she met my father was very intelligent, but also very disorganised.
Who was disorganised? ....

4 A woman who lives near my sister has just won the national lottery.
Has my sister won the lottery? ....

5 The newspaper which first made contact with the kidnappers telephoned the police immediately.
Who telephoned? ....

6 Police called to a house in Brent, Derbyshire, after neighbours reported cries for help found 18-year-old Justin Evans stuck in a small window after being locked out of his home.
Who found him? ....

4 Find the beginnings of the sentences in the box.

> A A very ordinary-looking woman I got talking to at
> B A man I met by chance on a business trip to ✓
> C Some Polish people I was introduced to by
> D The dress my sister wore to
> E The little flat that I rented just after I moved out of
> F The house I lived in with

▶ ..B. Spain taught me things about myself I had never suspected.
1 ...... my wedding was bought in a little shop in Bath.
2 ...... my parents' home was the nicest place I've ever lived in.
3 ...... my first wife had holes in the roof.
4 ...... the airport in Memphis was going to Italy to collect a tiger for a zoo.
5 ...... my little cousin Pam had crazy plans for an expedition to the North Pole.

5 Can you write beginnings for these endings?

1 .... my brother was bright green.
2 .... the big armchair is Emma's boyfriend.
3 .... me doesn't work.

Reduced relative clauses (see page 274) can make sentences particularly hard to read.

*Most of **the people arrested** had been in trouble before.* (=' ... **the people who were arrested** ...')
*Three quarters of **those questioned** wanted more money.* (=' ... **those who were questioned** ...')
***Three children found** sleeping in Abbey Park late last night were taken to a foster home by social workers.*
(=' ... **children who were found** ...')
*A lot of **the buildings designed** by architects are unsuitable for young children.*

6 Put in *who were* three times to make the sentence easier to read.

Most of the of the people hoping to see the President remained calm, but a minority of those moved on by police became violent, and organisers claim that several of the people arrested suffered injuries.

Most of the people ....
....
....

relatives: more practice

1 **Reduced relative clauses. Change the sentences as in the examples.**

▶ Who is the woman who is standing at the bus stop?
Who is the woman standing at the bus stop?

▶ The forms that were sent to the embassy last week never arrived.
The forms sent to the embassy last week never arrived.

1 A road that was opened last Friday has had to be closed again for repairs.

....

2 The number of new cars that were sold in this country fell by 25% in January.

....

3 The men who are working on our house have been there for nearly three weeks.

....

4 Clothes that are made of artificial fibres often feel uncomfortable in hot weather.

....

5 Not many of the people who were invited turned up.

....

6 The money that is lying on the table is your change.

....

2 **Mixed pronouns. Choose the right pronouns.**

WHAT I LIKE
1 Rooms *who / that* smile at you when you walk into them.
2 People *who / which* like me.
3 Animals *what / that* belong to themselves and no one else.
4 People *which / who* have grown up, but *which /who* are still children.
5 Works of art *who / that* talk to us across the centuries.
6 People *who / what* say what I think better than I can.

WHAT I HATE
7 Strangers *who / which* address me by my first name.
8 People *what / who* think they know more than I do – especially when they're right.
9 Cold-callers *that / which* phone me trying to sell me things.
10 Places *who / that* play music that I didn't ask for.
11 Household gadgets *that / what* I can't understand.
12 Big car parks *whose / which* exits I can't find.

3 **Mixed pronouns. Write your list of what you like and what you hate, using**
who/which/that/whose.

WHAT YOU LIKE

....

....

....

WHAT YOU HATE

....

....

....

4 **Prepositions with relatives. Look at the table, and then write some descriptions ending in prepositions.**

NAME	PLAYS CHESS WITH	IS MARRIED TO	WORKS WITH
Bill	John	Alice	Anne
Ron	Anne	Sue	Mary
Peter	Alice	Anne	Sue
Sally	Mary	John	Alice

▸ *John is the man that Bill plays chess with.* ....
▸ *Sue is the woman Ron is married to.* ....

....
....
....
....
....

5 **Reading problems. Make these sentences easier to read by putting in *that*.**

▸ The woman/Pete's in love with doesn't know he exists.
   The woman that Pete's in love with ...

1 A man my brother met when he was travelling in Italy with his wife turned out to be a famous film director.   ....

2 Where does the wood that table's made of come from?
   ....

3 Because he forgot to write to the one person he really should have invited, his father was furious.
   ....

4 When he met the soldier he wanted to buy the guns from the police were watching him.
   ....

6 **Relatives in definitions. Choose the best way to start each definition.**

▸ ⟨*A critic*⟩ / *A banker* is somebody who knows the way but can't drive the car.

1 *A critic* / *A banker* is somebody who lends you an umbrella when the sun is shining, and takes it back when it starts raining.

2 *A boring person* / *A doctor* is somebody whose conversation is about himself instead of about you.

3 *A professional footballer* / *A boss* is a person who is in the office early when you're late and late when you're early.

4 *A dangerous driver* / *An actor* is a person who drives faster than you.

5 *A doctor* / *A teacher* is a person who translates your medical problems into Latin.

6 *A boss* / *A professional footballer* is a person who plays when he works and works when he plays.

7 *A teacher* / *A boss* is a person who used to think that she liked children.

8 *A teacher* / *An actor* is a person whose aim is to be everything except himself.

7 **Internet exercise. Use a search engine (e.g. Google) to find more definitions of the people in Exercise 6. Write some of them.**

1 A teacher is a person who ....
2 ....
3 ....

relatives: revision test

1 **Put in *which*, *what* or *that*.**

1   He spoke very fast, ... made it hard to understand him.
2   Thanks, but that's not .... I wanted.
3   I'll tell you something .... will surprise you.
4   I did .... I could.
5   I did everything .... I could.
6   She kept falling over, ... made everybody laugh.
7   He's a university professor, ... is hard to believe.
8   You can have anything .... you want.
9   Her sense of humour – that's .... attracts people to her.
10 He said nothing .... made sense.

2 **Right or wrong? Correct the mistakes or write 'Correct'.**

▶   Your birthday is the day ~~where~~ you were born.   *when*..............
▶   I've got an uncle who lives in Australia.   ..*Correct.*..........
1   I've found the papers I lost.   ....
2   Take anything what you like.   ....
3   He said something that I couldn't understand it.   ....
4   Have you got something that I can write with?   ....
5   I work for a man went to school with my father.   ....
6   I want to find the person whose the car is parked in front of my house.   ....
7   Money is what John likes most.   ....
8   The people with whom we travelled came from Chicago.   ....
9   Do you know the woman talking to Andrew?   ....
10 I'd like a car who doesn't break down.   ....
11 The man, who phoned just now, had the wrong number.   ....
12 Mr Smithers, that does our accounts, has been ill for a week.   ....
13 Peter was early, what surprised us all.   ....
14 We had a guide whose knowledge of English was extremely poor.   ....
15 People which have no sense of humour are very boring.   ....

3 **(a) Put in nothing at all (–), or**
    (b) if that is not possible, put in *that*, or
    (c) if that is not possible, put in *who(m)* or *which*.

1   This is Ann Hargreaves, ... runs the bookshop.
2   Have you heard about the problems .... Joe's having at work?
3   Never buy yourself anything .... eats.
4   I don't like people .... can't laugh at themselves.
5   We took the M4 motorway, ... goes straight to Bristol.
6   I'll never forget the first film .... I saw.
7   Harry James, ... writes detective stories, lives in our street.
8   I think this is the best holiday .... we've ever had.
9   I'm looking for something .... will clean leather.
10 We planted some birch trees, ... grow tall very quickly.

In some answers, both contracted forms (for example *I'm*, *don't*) and full forms (for example *I am*, *do not*) are possible. Normally both are correct.

SECTION 20 indirect speech

GRAMMAR SUMMARY

When we tell people **what somebody said or thought**, we often use **indirect speech**.
Tenses, here-and-now words (like *this, here, today*) and **pronouns** (like *I, you*) may **change**
in indirect speech after past reporting verbs. This is because the time, place and speaker
may be different.

> *'I'm going to stay **here** for the rest of **this** week.'* ⟶
> ***Susan said** that **she was** going to stay **there** for the rest of **that** week.*

Past perfect tenses and some modal verbs (e.g. ***should, must***) don't change in indirect speech.

> *'I **had seen** her somewhere before.'* ⟶ *I said I **had seen** her somewhere before.*
> *'You **must** fill in these three forms.'* ⟶ *They told me I **must** fill in three forms.*

We often **leave out *that***, especially after common verbs like ***say*** and ***think***.

> *Susan **said** she really liked it there.*

Indirect questions have a **different structure** from direct questions.

> *'Where**'s your luggage?**'* ⟶ *He asked me where **my luggage was**.*
> *'**Do you know** Karen?'* ⟶ *She asked me **if I knew** Karen.*

We can use **object + infinitive** after some verbs, like ***ask*** and ***tell***.

> *I **asked him to talk** more quietly.   We **told Oliver not to lock** the garage.*

And we can use **infinitives** after most **question words**.

> *Tell us **what to do**.   I don't know **how to switch on** this computer.*

He said he would love me for ever
  With a love that would never grow cool.
He said he would always be faithful.
  I believed every word. What a fool!
But now that he's no longer with me
  I'm glad to be free of his lies.
And if I am sorry, I'm sorry for him,
  For he'll be with himself till he dies.

  (*Leni McShaw, British poet, born 1936*)

There are so many kinds of awful men –
One can't avoid them all. She often said
She'd never make the same mistake again.
She always made a new mistake instead.

  (*Wendy Cope, British poet, born 1945*)

revise the basics: why things change

1 Look at the text, and write down all the words and expressions that are different in Tom's and Peter's sentences.

TOM (on Saturday evening): 'I don't like this party. I want to go home now.'

PETER (on Sunday morning):'Tom said that he didn't like the party, and he wanted to go home right away.'

....

....

2 **DO IT YOURSELF** Which do you think is the best explanation for the differences? Circle A, B or C.

A After verbs like *said*, you change tenses and pronouns in English.

B The time, place and speakers are different.

C If the main verb is past, the other verbs have to be past too.

3 Read the dialogue. Imagine that Theo talks to a friend the next day and tells him about the conversation, using indirect speech structures (*I said/told her that … ; so she asked if …*). Circle at least ten words in the conversation that would have to be changed or left out in Theo's report.

THEO: You're looking good today.

SUZY: Oh, thanks, Theo. You are sweet.

THEO: OK. If you sit down I'll get you a drink.

SUZY: There's nowhere to sit.

THEO: Yes, there is. Over there in the corner.

SUZY: I don't want to sit there. It's too dark. I'll sit here.

THEO: You can't. These seats are taken.

SUZY: No, they aren't.

THEO: Really, Suzy. Why do you always have to argue? They're taken.

SUZY: Excuse me. Are these seats taken?

JOE: Well, this one is, but the other one's free.

SUZY: OK. I'll sit here, then. Thanks.

JOE: You're welcome. What's your name?

THEO: Hey, what about me?

SUZY: Suzy. What's yours?

JOE: I'm Joe Parsons. Can I get you a drink?

SUZY: That's very kind. Can I have a bitter lemon?

THEO: I'm getting her a drink.

JOE: No, you're not, mate. I am.

THEO: I don't believe this. Suzy, what are you playing at?

SUZY: Really, Theo, I don't know what's wrong with you today. I'll see you around, OK?

revise the basics: 'here' and 'now' words

Some words may be changed in indirect speech because **the original speaker's 'here' and 'now' are not the same** as the reporter's.

1 **DO IT YOURSELF** The following sentence was said in England in November 2008:
'I've been in this part of the world since March this year.'

When does the first or second *this* have to be changed?

IF THE SENTENCE IS REPORTED	FIRST *THIS* CHANGED?	SECOND *THIS* CHANGED?
1 in England a week later	yes / no	yes / no
2 in England a year later	yes / no	yes / no
3 in Holland a week later	yes / no	yes / no
4 in Holland a year later	yes / no	yes / no

2 **Match the direct and indirect speech expressions.**

DIRECT SPEECH: *'here and now'* words				
0 here	5 today	A that day	F the next day ......
1 now	6 tonight	B that night	G there ..*0*..
2 this	7 last week	C that	H the week before ......
3 tomorrow	8 next week	D the day before	I then ......
4 yesterday		E the next week	

There is often more than one way of reporting 'here' and 'now' words.

'I don't like **this** house.' —→ *She said she didn't like **that** house / **the** house / **their** house / **the** house **she was visiting** …*

3 **Imagine these sentences were reported in another place a month later.**
Put in words and expressions from the box.

right away   that day   that evening   that morning   the   the day after ✓   the day before
the same night   the week before   there

▶ 'I'll see you tomorrow.' She said she'd see me ...*the day after*.......
1 'My brother's arriving here today.' She said her brother was arriving ....
2 'I'll phone you this evening.' He said he'd phone ....
3 'Do you like it here?' She asked if I liked it ....
4 'My uncle died last week.' He told me his uncle had died ....
5 'This meat tastes funny.' She said .... meat tasted funny.
6 'I'm leaving now.' He told us he was leaving ....
7 'I overslept this morning.' She told him she'd overslept ....
8 'The train leaves at 11.00 tonight.' I was told the train left at 11.00 ....
9 'Pete phoned me yesterday.' He said Pete had phoned him ....

In some answers, both contracted forms (for example *I'm*, *don't*) and full forms (for example *I am*, *do not*) are possible. Normally both are correct.

revise the basics: tenses

After reporting expressions like *he said*, *I asked*, *she thought*, **tenses** are usually **different** from those in the original words (because the reporter's time is different from the original speaker's time). Verbs become **more past**.

ORIGINAL WORDS (DIRECT SPEECH)	REPORTED WORDS (INDIRECT SPEECH)
You look nice.	*I told her she looked nice.*
	(**NOT** ~~I told her she looks nice.~~)
I can't swim.	*He pretended he couldn't swim.*
I'm learning French.	*She said she was learning French.*
Has he forgotten?	*I wondered if he had forgotten.*
John phoned.	*She told me that John had phoned.*
Will you marry me?	*I asked him if he would marry me.*

1 **DO IT YOURSELF** **Complete the table.**

DIRECT SPEECH	INDIRECT SPEECH
simple present	....
....	past progressive
present perfect	....
simple past	....
....	*would ...*

2 **Complete the reported sentences with the correct tenses.**

1 'I'm tired.' She said she .... tired.
2 'You play very well.' He told me I .... very well.
3 'Can you help us?' They asked if I .... help them.
4 'We're leaving.' They told us they ....
5 'She hasn't brushed her hair.' I noticed that she .... her hair.
6 'John's had an accident.' Pam rang to say that John .... an accident.
7 'I left school at fifteen.' Her letter said that she .... school at fifteen.
8 'She won't say anything.' I knew she .... anything.
9 'Nobody will know.' I thought nobody ....
10 'This letter has been opened.' I could see that the letter ....

Note the difference between *say* and *tell*.
Tell must have a **personal object**: we **tell somebody something**.

*They **told me** I was wrong.* (**NOT** ~~They told I was wrong.~~)   *Karen **told us** a joke.*

Say doesn't need a personal object: we **say something (to somebody)**.

*They **said** I was wrong.* (**NOT** ~~They said me I was wrong.~~)   *We **said** nothing to anybody.*

3 **Circle the correct answer.**

1 I *said / told* John I wanted to go home.
2 Lucy *said / told* that she would buy the tickets.
3 I didn't *say / tell* anyone that I was leaving.
4 Why did you *say / tell* you were ill?
5 My father *said / told* he needed help.
6 Andy *said / told* the doctor he couldn't walk.
7 Everybody *said / told* I looked happy.
8 Nobody *said / told* me that there was a strike.

4 **Put in the right tenses of the verbs in the boxes.**

| be | fancy ✓ | have | never meet | want |

(speech bubble: I've never met anybody like you before.)

(speech bubble: Do you want a lift home?)

I had a really funny evening yesterday, Mary. I got talking to this boy in the pub, very nice-looking he was, and I could see he ▶ ..*fancied*.... me. He said he ¹ .... anybody like me before, and he felt I ² .... a very unusual kind of beauty. Oh, yes? I said. Then he asked me if I ³ .... a lift home, so I said no, I ⁴ .... hungry, so we went out for a curry.

(speech bubble: What do you do for a living?)

(speech bubble: I'm doing some undercover work for the CIA.)

| call | can | can | do | do | move | think | want |

I asked him what he ⁵ .... for a living, and he said he ⁶ .... some undercover work for the CIA just now. He said he ⁷ .... not give me his address because he ⁸ .... around all the time. So I asked him why he ⁹ .... I ¹⁰ .... his address. Then he asked if he ¹¹ .... have my phone number. He said he ¹² .... me today to fix for me to go to America with him.

(speech bubble: I'm moving around all the time.)

(speech bubble: I'll call you tomorrow.)

| be | be | fall | go | have | leave | lie | not matter |
| think | want |

(speech bubble: Why do you want to take me to America?)

(speech bubble: I think I'm falling in love with you.)

So I asked him why he ¹³ .... to take me to America, and he said he ¹⁴ .... he ¹⁵ .... in love with me. I knew he ¹⁶ ...., but it was kind of fun. Anyway, I told him I ¹⁷ .... got a boyfriend already, but he said that ¹⁸ .... We ¹⁹ .... meant for each other, he said, and nobody ²⁰ .... to stand in our way, because our lives ²¹ .... written in the stars. Then he borrowed £20 from me to pay the bill because he said he ²² .... his wallet at home, and he went off to the toilet, and I never saw him again.

(speech bubble: We're meant for each other, and nobody is going to stand in our way.)

Tenses don't change after present or future reporting verbs, because there is no important change of time.

*He **says** he **doesn't** want to play any more. ('I **don't** want … ')*
*I'**ll tell** her your idea **is** great.*

Tenses do not usually change after **present perfect** reporting verbs, either.

*The government **has announced** that taxes **will be** raised.*

We often drop **that** after common reporting verbs.

*He **said (that)** he was falling in love with me.   I **knew (that)** he was lying.*

In some answers, both contracted forms (for example *I'm, don't*) and full forms (for example *I am, do not*) are possible. Normally both are correct.

INDIRECT SPEECH **285**

present situations *He proved that the earth is/was round.*

Situations that have not changed: if the original speaker was talking about a **present or future situation that is still present or future** when the words are reported, the tenses are sometimes **not changed** after a past reporting verb.

DIRECT SPEECH	INDIRECT SPEECH
The earth *is* round.	He proved that the earth *was/is* round.
'How old *are* you?' 'What?'	I asked how old you *were/are.*
Where *does* she *work*?	I've often wondered where she *worked/works.*
It *will be* windy tomorrow.	The forecast said it *would/will* be windy tomorrow.

1 Imagine these sentences were reported soon after they were said: change them to indirect speech in two different ways.

▶ I'm utterly fed up! (*I said*)
...*I said I was utterly fed up. I said I'm utterly fed up.*...

1 What day is it? (*I asked*) ....

2 What's the dark-haired child's name? (*I asked*) ....

3 It's raining. (*I told you*) ....

4 You'll get your money. (*I said*) ....

5 There will be a strike. (*This article I was reading said*) ....

6 The repairs will cost £5,000. (*Al told me*) ....

7 Is Jane coming to see us? (*I asked*) ....

8 You're going to the Glasgow office. (*Pat told me that*) ....

9 You won't pass your exam. (*I bet George £5 yesterday that he*) ....

10 They're getting married next week. (*Sue rang this morning, and she said*) ....

We do not keep the original speaker's tenses if we do **not agree** with what he/she said, or if we want to show that the ideas do not come from us.

*They were certain that the gods **lived** in the sky.*
*Did you hear that? She said she **was** fourteen!*
*He announced that profits **were** higher than forecast.*
*I didn't know she **was** ill.*

'Ed Roxey! I didn't know you were dead!'

Drawing by Joseph Farris; © 1994
The New Yorker magazine, Inc.

revise the basics: indirect questions

Indirect questions normally have the **subject before the verb**.

*He wanted to know when **I could start**.* (**NOT USUALLY** ... *when could I start*.)
*I asked where **the trainer and the team were staying**.*

Do is **not used** in indirect questions, and question marks (???) are not used.

*I wondered how **they felt**.* (**NOT** ... *how did they feel?*)

The same structure is used to report the answers to questions.

*I **knew how they felt**.*
*Nobody told me **why I had to sign the paper**.*

1 Turn these into indirect questions, beginning *I asked*.

▶ Where are my gloves? *I asked where my gloves were.* ....

1 What's Peter's address? ....

2 When's the new manager coming? ....

3 How does she know my name? ....

4 Why are all the windows open? ....

5 How many books does he want? ....

6 Where do they keep the money? ....

7 What time is the meeting? ....

8 When does the last train leave? ....

9 How does the photocopier work? ....

10 How often does Ann go shopping? ....

Yes/no* questions** are reported with ***if or ***whether***.

*The driver asked **if/whether** I wanted to go to the town centre.*

We prefer ***whether*** before ***or*** in a formal style.

*I enquired **whether** she was coming by road **or** by air.*

2 Turn these into indirect questions, beginning *I wondered*.

▶ Are the children all right? *I wondered if the children were all right.* ....

1 Do they like me? ....

2 Will I be ready in time? ....

3 Is there any food in the house? ....

4 Is service included or not? ....

5 Can I pay by cheque? ....

6 Does my hair look funny? ....

7 Has the postman been? ....

8 Do they speak English? ....

9 Am I doing the right thing? ....

10 Is the meeting on Tuesday or Wednesday? ....

We sometimes make indirect questions in the same way as direct questions in **informal speech** (but not in formal writing).

*He wanted to know **when could I start**.*

In some answers, both contracted forms (for example *I'm*, *don't*) and full forms (for example *I am*, *do not*) are possible. Normally both are correct.

INDIRECT SPEECH **287**

revise the basics: infinitives *He promised to write.*

We use **infinitives** to report sentences about future actions – for example **promises**, **agreements**, **orders**, **offers**, **advice**, **suggestions**, **requests**.

'I'll definitely write.' ⟶ *He promised **to write**.*
'OK, I'll wait until 6 o'clock.' ⟶ *She agreed **to wait** until 6 o'clock.*
'Do be careful, Andrew.' ⟶ *I told Andrew **to be careful**.*
'Shall I babysit tonight?' ⟶ *Ann has offered **to babysit** tonight.*
'You'd better think again.' ⟶ *The manager advised me **to think again**.*
'Please don't be late.' ⟶ *She asked us **not to be late**.*

1 **Change the sentences as shown.**

▶ I won't tell anybody. (*He promised*) .....He promised not to tell anybody.......
1 I'll cook supper. (*She offered*) ....
2 Leave early. (*He advised me*) ....
3 Please don't close the door. (*She asked me*) ....
4 I'll stop smoking. (*She promised*) ....
5 Why don't I do the shopping? (*He offered*) ....
6 You ought to tell the police. (*She advised me*) ....
7 Wait outside. (*I told her*) ....
8 OK, I'll pay half. (*He agreed*) ....
9 Don't park outside the house. (*She told me*) ....
10 We'll pay for the tickets. (*We offered*) ....

The structure **question word + infinitive** is common.

*He asked her **how to make** a white sauce.*   *Don't tell me **what to do**.*

2 **Complete the sentences with question words and the infinitives of the verbs in the box.**
(There is one verb too many.) Different answers may be possible.

break	come back	cook	give	park
play	start ✓	tell	wear	

▶ We'll let you know ....when to start............... work.
1 I don't know .... mah-jong.
2 Can you show me .... the car?
3 We don't know .... Oliver for
  his birthday.
4 I'm not sure .... John.
5 Do you know .... spaghetti carbonara?
6 I can't decide .... to Peter's wedding.
7 I'm leaving on Thursday, but I still haven't decided
  ....

'I told him to choose his weapons
and be here at six.'

Infinitives are **not used** after *suggest* or *say*.

*He **suggested trying** somewhere else.* (**NOT** *He suggested to try* …)
*The policeman **said I mustn't** park there.* (**NOT** … *said me not to park* …)

We can use *whether* but not *if* **before infinitives**.

*I don't know **whether to go** home.* (**NOT** … *if to go home.*)

indirect speech: special cases *He said I'd better go.*

Past tenses are changed to **past perfect** tenses after past reporting verbs, but only if this is necessary in order to make the time relations clear. Compare:

DIRECT SPEECH	INDIRECT SPEECH
I *saw* Penny a couple of days ago.	In his letter, he said he*'d seen* Penny a couple of days before.
Dinosaurs **were** around for 250 million years.	This guy on TV said that dinosaurs **were** around for 250 million years. (**NOT** … ~~had been around~~ …)

1 **Change these to indirect speech.**

1 I saw him once before in London. (*I knew*)

....

2 Shakespeare didn't speak French. (*The professor said*)

....

3 He died two years ago. (*When I got there, I found out*)

....

4 Three thousand years ago there were tigers in England. (*It said on this TV programme*)

....

5 Somebody threw a bomb at the Prime Minister. (*It said on this morning's news*)

....

6 The ancient Romans suffered from lead poisoning. (*I read in a magazine*)

....

Usually **unchanged** after past reporting verbs: **past perfect**, *had better*, *would*, *could*, *should*, *ought*, *might*, *must*.

DIRECT SPEECH	INDIRECT SPEECH
I *hadn't seen* him before. You*'d better* go.	She said she *hadn't seen* him before. He said I*'d better* go.

2 **Change these to indirect speech.**

1 Would you like a drink? (*She asked me*)

....

....

2 I couldn't help it. (*I said*)

....

....

3 We should be home about six. (*They thought*)

....

....

4 It might rain. (*The forecast said*)

....

....

5 She must be joking. (*Everybody said*)

....

....

6 I hadn't seen the notice. (*I explained*)

....

....

'I thought you'd like to know that the day after you died you won a $22.5 million lottery.'

In some answers, both contracted forms (for example *I'm*, *don't*) and full forms (for example *I am*, *do not*) are possible. Normally both are correct.

INDIRECT SPEECH **289**

indirect speech: more practice

① Tenses. Here are some things that people thought in the past. Report them, using indirect speech.

▶ 'I've found a new way to get to India.' (*Columbus*)
   .Columbus thought (that) he had found a new way to get to India............................

1 'The sun goes round the earth.' (*Ptolemy*)

....

2 'Brutus loves me.' (*Julius Caesar*)

....

3 'That boy will never be a scientist.' (*One of Einstein's teachers*)

....

4 'I can conquer Russia.' (*Napoleon and Hitler*)

....

5 'People are born again and again.' (*The ancient Egyptians*)

....

6 'The world has existed since October 23, 4004 B.C.' (*Bishop Ussher*)

....

7 'Modern ships cannot sink.' (*C J Smith, the future captain of the Titanic*)

....

8 'The land belongs to everyone.' (*Many native Americans*)

....

9 'The Beatles are more popular than Jesus.' (*John Lennon*)

....

10 'Capitalism will disappear.' (*Karl Marx*)

....

② Grammar in a text. Choose the right forms to complete the text.

I didn't feel at all well yesterday, so I looked in my book (*The Complete Home Doctor*, 2nd Edition) to see what I ¹ *have / had / did*. The book said it ² *is / was / would be* either mononucleosis or typhoid, but it wasn't clear which, so I went to the doctor. I wanted to see Dr Gibbons – he's always very understanding – but the receptionist said he ³ *isn't / wasn't / wouldn't* free, so I had to see Dr Parker, one of those new young doctors. I went in and told him what I ⁴ *have / had / did*. (I always tell the doctor what I ⁵ *have / had / did* got, it saves a lot of time.) But he just started asking a lot of stupid questions. He wanted to know how old ⁶ *I am / I was / was I*, if I ⁷ *smoke / smoked / was smoking*, how much ⁸ *I drink / I drank / did I drink*, if I ⁹ *take / took* exercise, if I ¹⁰ *live / lived* alone, if I ¹¹ *have / had* ever had mental problems, etc etc. So I told him that I ¹² *am / was / would be* perfectly all right, except that I either ¹³ *have / had / was having* mononucleosis or typhoid, and I ¹⁴ *do want / want / wanted* to know which. I explained that it ¹⁵ *is / was / will be* urgent, because typhoid ¹⁶ *is / is being / would be* very infectious. And he said I ¹⁷ *have / had / am having* a bad case of hypochondria, and I ¹⁸ *should take / should have taken / should be taking* two aspirins and come back in a week if I still felt ill. And he said ¹⁹ *I better throw / I'd better throw / I'd better have thrown* away the book. Throw away *The Complete Home Doctor*? It's been in my family for generations. I don't know what they do in medical school, but they don't learn ²⁰ *how talk / how talking / how to talk* to patients, and they certainly don't learn much about medicine. I'm surprised that I'm still alive.

3 GRAMMAR AND VOCABULARY: everyday jobs. What do you know how to do?
Write sentences beginning *I (don't) know how to …* Use a dictionary if necessary.

▶ (*boil an egg*) *I know how to boil an egg.* ....

1 (*mend a fuse*) ....

2 (*sew on a button*) ....

3 (*knit a sweater*) ....

4 (*clean a carpet*) ....

5 (*hang a picture on a wall*) ....

6 (*replace a tap washer*) ....

7 (*change a wheel on a car*) ....

8 (*make a cake*) ....

9 (*mend a puncture in a bike tyre*) ....

10 (*cook roast goose*) ....

4 *How to …* Write three other things that you know how to do, and three that you
don't know how to do.

....

....

....

....

....

....

5 Tenses. Choose the correct words to complete the cartoon caption.

'Don't ask me – I thought they *are / were / would be* yours.'

6 Internet exercise. Use the internet to find out some things that the ancient Greeks,
Chinese, Romans, Egyptians (or other people) believed. Write five or more things.

....

....

....

....

....

indirect speech: revision test

1 Mixed structures. Change these sentences to indirect speech (reported some time later).

▶ He's ill. (*She thought*) .....*She thought he was ill.*...........

1 I'll be back tomorrow. (*He said*)

....

2 Would you like a drink? (*She asked him*)

....

3 Where's the bus station? (*She asked me*)

....

4 Have you finished? (*I asked him*)

....

5 Three kilos should be enough. (*The book said*)

....

6 When is the car going to be ready? (*I asked*)

....

7 These figures can't be right. (*I knew*)

....

8 Her cat understands everything she says. (*She thought*)

....

9 Did Mary phone back? (*I wondered*)

....

10 Did dinosaurs lay eggs? (*I wondered*)

....

11 I don't like this music. (*She said*)

....

12 Do you want tea or coffee? (*He asked her*)

....

13 I'll clean the flat. (*She offered*)

....

14 What does the boss want? (*I asked*)

....

15 You should see the doctor. (*He advised me*)

....

2 Here are some famous predictions. Report them using indirect speech.

▶ 'There will be no war with Germany.' (*The Daily Express*, 1939)
   .....*The Daily Express told its readers that there would be no war with Germany.*..........

1 'The telephone will never have any commercial value.' (*J P Morgan*)

....

2 'TV will never become popular.' (*Mary Somerville*)

....

3 'We will never reach the moon.' (*An American astronomer in 1932*)

....

4 'We don't think the Beatles will be a commercial success.' (*Jay Livingstone of Capitol Records, 1964*)

....

5 'A black man will never be President of the United States.' (*Joseph George Caldwell, 2006*)

....

In some answers, both contracted forms (for example *I'm, don't*) and full
forms (for example *I am, do not*) are possible. Normally both are correct.

SECTION 21 prepositions

GRAMMAR SUMMARY

above	across	against	along	at	behind	between	by	down	during
for	from	in	in front of	into	near	off	on	opposite	out of	over
past	round	through	to	under	until/till	up

- Some prepositions are difficult because they have more than one meaning. (A preposition in one language often has several different translations into another language.) This is really a matter of vocabulary, not grammar, but grammar books often deal with the meanings of prepositions, and we include information about some problem points in this Section.

- We also list common fixed expressions consisting of **verb + preposition**, **noun + preposition** and **adjective + preposition**, and other common expressions that **begin with prepositions**. (To find out what preposition to use after other nouns, verbs and adjectives, see the *Oxford Advanced Learner's Dictionary*, the *Oxford Collocations Dictionary*, or any other good dictionary.)

- The grammar of prepositions is mostly covered in other Sections:
  For ***-ing* forms after prepositions**, see page 119.
  For the **position of prepositions**, see pages 107 (questions), 98 (passives) and 273 (relative clauses).

Note: for phrasal verbs (verb + adverb particle), see pages 150-151.

'Before you sentence me, I'd like to remind the court that I was just passing through the building looking for a bathroom.'

'Excuse me, but I think you're in my seat.'

revise the basics: time

1 **DO IT YOURSELF** Look at the examples in the box and complete the rule for the use of *at*, *in* and *on* to talk about time.

> in 2011   in June   in the morning   at 4.15   at lunchtime   on Sunday
> on Monday afternoon   at Christmas   at the weekend

Rule

..*at*........ + clock time or particular time

.... + part of a day

.... + part of a particular day

.... + particular day

.... + weekend, public holiday

.... + longer period

.... to say how long something takes

> MIKE WAS BORN AT 5.30
> IN THE MORNING
> ON A SATURDAY
> IN MARCH
> IN 1986.
> AND YOU?

2 **DO IT YOURSELF** Look at the examples in the box and complete the rule.

> I'll see you next Monday.   I'm not free this Thursday.   I train every day.
> Tell me what time it starts.   The exam's on my birthday.
> Let's meet one weekend.   She phoned this evening.

Rule

Before expressions of time beginning *this*, *next*, *every*, *one* and *what*, we usually ....

3 Put in *at*, *in*, *on* or – (= no preposition).

1 We're not going away .... Easter.

2 I spoke to Harry .... Tuesday.

3 Carole was born .... 1994.

4 We usually go to the gym .... the evening.

5 Are you free .... Friday evening?

6 The countryside is beautiful .... May.

7 I'll try to see you .... next Wednesday.

8 I don't know .... what time it starts.

9 Everybody will be here .... supper time.

10 There's no match .... this Sunday.

11 I'll always remember .... that afternoon.

12 Can I come and see you .... Sunday afternoon?

13 You'll be sorry for this .... one day.

14 I go to a maths class .... every Tuesday evening.

15 She learnt English .... six months.

16 When will I get married? .... this year, ... next year, some time, never?

17 .... what day are you seeing Frank?

18 I'm never very clear-headed .... the morning.

19 Are you going to have a party .... your birthday?

20 Let's go to the mountains .... the weekend.

revise the basics: place and movement

1 **DO IT YOURSELF** **Look at the examples and complete the rule correctly.**

> I met her **at** a concert.   Let's go **to** a concert.   He's **in** London.   I sent it **to** London yesterday.

Rule: *At* and *in* are used for *distance / position / movement*.
   To is used for *distance / position / movement*.

We often use *at* to talk about where something **happens** – for example, a meeting place or a point on a journey.
*We usually meet **at the pub**.*   *I had to change trains **at York**.*
*Turn right **at the petrol station**.*   *They kept me waiting **at the embassy**.*

And we often use *at* with words for **things that people do**, or the **places where they do them**.

at a match   *at* breakfast, lunch etc   *at* a restaurant   *at* work   *at* the office
at the theatre   *at* the cinema   *at* the station   *at* a party   *at* (the) college/university

At and *in* are often **both possible**. We prefer *in* when we are thinking more about the **place itself**,
and not just the activity. Compare:

*We **had dinner at** the Golden Dragon. It was very hot **in the big dining room**.*

At is not used with the names of very big places. Compare:

*We changed planes **at Kennedy**.*   *We changed planes **in New York**. (**NOT** … ~~at New York.~~)*
*She arrived **at school** late. (**NOT** … ~~arrived to~~ …)*   *She arrived **in London** on Tuesday.*

2 **Put in *in* or *at*.**

1 I'll see you ………. the party.
2 We spent two days ………. Bangkok.
3 There's no heating ………. my room.
4 We had problems ………. the office.
5 I'll pick you up ………. the station.

6 Get off the bus ………. Eden Square.
7 Joe's film crazy: he almost lives ………. the cinema.
8 You change trains ………. Cardiff.
9 Let's meet ………. my place at six.
10 I never talk ………. breakfast.

We use *in* with **3-dimensional spaces** like boxes, rooms, towns or countries.
We use *on* with **2-dimensional surfaces** like floors, tables, walls or ceilings.
We say that people are **in clothes**, and that clothes and jewellery are **on people**.

3 **Put in *in* or *on*.**

1 There's a spider ………. the bath.
2 Put this paper ………. the office door.
3 What's that bird ………. the roof?
4 Your lunch is ………. the table.
5 She had a ring ………. her first finger.

6 Who's the man ………. the funny hat?
7 There's a black mark ………. the ceiling.
8 Our football is stuck up ………. a tree.
9 Do you want your rice ………. a bowl or
   ………. a plate?

4 **Prepositions of movement: cross out the words that are wrong.**

▶ across *the road / ~~the tunnel~~*
1 through *the gate / the stairs*
2 down *the church / the hill*
3 under *the bridge / the crowd*
4 into *the supermarket / the table*
5 across *the river / the garage*
6 up *the mountain / the piano*

7 out of *the bank / the stairs*
8 along *the corner / the river*
9 off *the car park / the table*
10 over *the shop / the wall*
11 past *the floor / the station*
12 round *the corner / the road*

In some answers, both contracted forms (for example *I'm, don't*) and full
forms (for example *I am, do not*) are possible. Normally both are correct.

some preposition choices

by and *until*

1 **DO IT YOURSELF** Look at the examples in the box, and choose the best explanations of how to use *by* and *until*.

> 'Can you repair my watch if I leave it **until** Saturday?' 'No, but we can do it **by** next Tuesday.'
> You can have the car **until** this evening. But you must bring it back **by** six o'clock at the latest.

▶ to say that something **may or may not happen**, we use *BY* / *UNTIL* / (NEITHER) .
1 to say that **a situation will continue up to** a certain moment, we use *BY* / *UNTIL* / NEITHER .
2 to say that **something will happen around** a certain time, we use *BY* / *UNTIL* / NEITHER .
3 to say that **something will happen at or before** a certain moment, we use *BY* / *UNTIL* / NEITHER .

In an informal style we often use **till** instead of *until*. Before a **subject and verb**, we can use **by the time**.
*He'll be gone **by the time we get** home.*

2 Complete the sentences with *by (the time)* or *till/until*.
1 'Can I stay .... the weekend?'
2 'Yes, but you'll have to leave .... Monday midday at the latest.'
3 This form must be returned .... April 17.
4 We'll just have to wait .... he's ready to see us.
5 The visitors will have gone .... you get back.
6 Do you think you can finish the painting .... Easter?

'And returned by one o'clock. I go to lunch then.'

opposite and *in front of*

OPPO ◀ SITE   ◀ IN ◀ FRONT ◀ OF

3 **DO IT YOURSELF** Look at the picture. Which is *opposite* the house – the bus stop or the car? Which is *in front of* the house?

.... is opposite the house.
.... is in front of the house.

4 Put in *opposite* or *in front of*.
1 There's a supermarket .... my house.
2 .... me in the queue there was a very strange-looking woman.
3 I can't see the TV if you stand .... it.
4 The lifts are directly .... the reception desk.
5 Somebody's parked .... my garage door, and I can't get my car out.
6 She sat down .... me and started talking to me.

between and *among*

5 DO IT YOURSELF **Look at the examples in the box and complete the rules.**

> She was standing **between** Alice and Mary.
> Our house is **between** the woods, the river and the village.
> His house is hidden **among** the trees.
> We were in a little valley **between** high mountains.

We say .... a group, crowd or mass of things that are not seen separately.
We say .... two or more clearly separate people or things.
We say .... things on two sides.

6 **Look at the diagrams. Is X *between* or *among* the other things?**

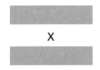

1 X is .... the other things.   2 X is .... the other things.

3 X is .... the other things.   4 X is .... the other things.

7 **Put in *between* or *among*.**
1 I saw something .... the wheels of the car.
2 She was standing .... a crowd of children.
3 We'll come and see you some time .... Christmas and Easter.
4 I found the letter hidden away .... some old photographs.
5 This is just one problem .... many.
6 Switzerland lies .... France, Germany, Austria and Italy.

for and *during*

8 DO IT YOURSELF **Look at the examples in the box. Which word tells you *how long* and which word tells you *when*?**

> My father was in hospital for six weeks during the summer. (**NOT** ... ~~during six weeks~~ ...)
> It rained during the night for two or three hours.

During tells you ....   *For* tells you ....

9 **Put in *for* or *during*.**
1 Drinks will be served .... the interval.
2 I'll come and see you .... a few minutes .... the afternoon.
3 They met .... the war.
4 He said nothing .... a long time.
5 I woke up several times .... the night.
6 She studied in America .... two years.

verbs with prepositions *Look at her.*

With some verbs, we put a preposition (*for, to, at* etc) before an object.

***Look at** her!* (**NOT** ~~Look her!~~)   *Please **listen to** me.* (**NOT** ~~Please listen me.~~)

We **don't** use a **preposition** if there is **no object**.

Look! (**NOT** ~~Look at!~~)   *Please **listen**.* (**NOT** ~~Please listen to.~~)

1 **Choose the correct preposition or no preposition (–).**

1 Let's go. We can't wait *for* / *at* / *on* / *–* Margaret any longer.
2 I'm going to take singing lessons. Don't laugh *at* / *for* / *to* / *–* .
3 'She's quite wrong.' 'I don't agree *to* / *at* / *with* / *–* .'
4 Sorry, I can't wait *for* / *at* / *on* / *–* any longer.
5 'Shall we go away next weekend?' 'I'll think *about* / *on* / *of* / *–* it.'

Not all verbs are followed by prepositions.

*She **married** a builder.* (**NOT** ~~She married with a builder.~~)

2 **Check your knowledge. Put a preposition into one sentence and – into the others.**

1 We're approaching .... the town centre.
2 I don't know what to do. Let's ask .... Harry.
3 I'm going to write .... my MP about this.
4 When we entered .... the room, it was too dark to see anything.
5 Shall I phone .... the tax office, or is it better to email .... them?
6 This soup lacks .... salt.
7 Can we discuss .... arrangements for the weekend?

3 **Check your knowledge. *Of, on, from* or –?**

1 She insisted *on paying* / *to pay*.
2 He went into hospital on Tuesday, and they operated *him* / *on him* yesterday.
3 Are you accusing me *lying* / *of lying* / *to lie* ?
4 I can't live *on* / *from* / *of* the money I earn in this job.
5 We may go to Wales at the weekend. It depends *on* / *from* / *of* the weather.
6 I think Alice is suffering *of* / *from* / *–* depression.
7 Can you take care *of* / *from* / *–* the children tomorrow?
8 Her parents prevented her *of marrying* / *from marrying* / *to marry* her internet boyfriend.

4 **Check your knowledge. Put in *at, in, to, into* or –.**

1 I don't believe .... ghosts.
2 She specialises .... psychiatry.
3 They divided us .... two groups.
4 The bus crashed .... a tree.
5 He'll never succeed .... business.
6 Do you want to take part .... an online game?
7 Can you translate this .... Dutch?
8 We arrived .... the airport at 10.40.
9 That baby smiles .... everybody.
10 I ran .... Peter in the bank yesterday.
11 Can you explain .... me how this works?

Here are some examples of other common **verb + preposition** combinations. Learn the ones you don't know.

fight with: *That child's always **fighting with** her brother.*
belong to/in: *This coat **belongs to** Maggie.   Cups **belong in** that cupboard.*
spend money/time on: *He **spends** all his money **on** clothes.   I **spend** a lot of time **on** language study.*
apply to somebody for something: *You have to **apply to** the consulate **for** a visa.*
happen to: *What's **happened to** your leg?*
consist of: *The human body **consists** mostly **of** water.*
blame somebody for something: *They **blamed** me **for** the accident, but it wasn't my fault.*
forgive somebody for something: *He never **forgives** anybody **for** anything.*
speak to/with: *I'd like to **speak to/with** the manager.*
thank you for: ***Thank you for** all your help.*

Some verbs can be used in more than one prepositional structure.
You **arrive at** a place, or **in** a very big place (**NOT** ~~to~~).

*The train **arrives at** Waverley Station at 18.15.   When did you **arrive in** London?*

You **get into** / **out of** a car; you **get on/off** a bus, train, plane, large boat or ship.

*She **got into** the car without saying goodbye.   You **get off** the bus at Queen's Square.*

You **pay** a person or a bill; you **pay for** something that you buy.

*'Have **you paid** Andy?' 'Yes, I **paid his bill** last week.'   Can you **pay for** the meal?*

5 Complete the sentences with *arrive, get* or *pay* and the correct prepositions.

▶ You haven't ..*paid for*.............. your drink.
1 What time does the plane .... Birmingham Airport?
2 You can't .... the bus without a ticket.
3 I haven't got enough money to .... the electricity bill.
4 You can .... the front of the car, because you've got long legs.
5 Do we .... the waiter, or do we pay at the cash desk?
6 When I first .... Paris I didn't speak a word of French.
7 The police told everybody to .... the car.
8 I'll .... the tickets if you .... dinner afterwards.
9 We had to .... the plane because there was a bomb.
10 When I .... the docks, I was just too late to .... the boat.

Shout/throw at are aggressive; *shout/throw to* are not.

*Don't **shout at** me like that.   I **shouted to** Mary to hurry up.*
*Why are you **throwing** stones **at** my car?   **Throw** the ball **to** me!*

Here are examples of some other verbs that can be used in more than one structure.

*I **asked** my brother.   I **asked for** help.*
*I often **dream about** you. (while asleep)   I often **dream of travelling** round the world. (in imagination)*
*What are you **thinking about**?   What do you **think of** the government? (= 'What's your opinion?')*
*Have you **heard** (the news) **about** John?   That girl has never **heard of** Shakespeare.*
*I'm **looking for** a good hotel. (= 'trying to find')   Can you **look after** the children? (= 'take care of')*
*She **reminded** me **about** the meeting. (I had forgotten)   You **remind** me **of** (= 'look or act like') my father.*
*The police **searched** everybody. They were **searching for** drugs.*

In some answers, both contracted forms (for example *I'm, don't*) and full forms (for example *I am, do not*) are possible. Normally both are correct.

PREPOSITIONS **299**

nouns with prepositions *lack of sleep*

Some **nouns** are followed by **particular prepositions**.

*I felt stupid because of **lack of** sleep.*   ***Congratulations on** your promotion.*

1 **Check your knowledge. Put in *of* six times and *for* four times.**

1 Can you show me an example .... your work?

2 Nobody really knows the reason .... the crisis.

3 Do you think there's enough respect .... older people these days?

4 The cost .... moving house is becoming enormous.

5 We voted for the Liberals in the hope .... a change.

6 The police are trying to establish the cause .... the accident.

7 There's not much demand .... our products at the moment.

8 Please give full details .... your career.

9 Enthusiasm is no substitute .... experience.

10 We'll need to see proof .... your age.

2 **One of sentences 1–7 has the wrong preposition. Correct the mistake or write 'Correct'.**

▶ She made no contribution to the discussion. ....*Correct.*......

▶ The rebels launched an attack ~~to~~ the police barracks. ...*on*...........

1 I don't know the answer to his question. ....

2 The explosion caused serious damage to the town centre. ....

3 I never got an invitation to his wedding. ....

4 There's no solution to this problem. ....

5 If there are any more increases to the prices, we'll be in trouble. ....

6 Have you got the key to the garage door? ....

7 We couldn't find the way to her house. ....

Here are some examples of other common **noun + preposition** combinations. Learn the ones you don't know.

*You need a good **knowledge of** Arabic for this job.*
*What's your **opinion of** the Prime Minister?*
*I don't like the **idea of** working in my father's business. (**NOT** …the idea to work …)*
*She hates the **thought of** getting old. (**NOT** … the thought to get old.)*
*The **price of** food is ridiculous. They'll put a **tax on** bread next.*
*I'm having **trouble/difficulty with** my visa application.*
*What's the **matter with** the electricity?*
*Some people say **belief in** yourself is important for **success in** life.*
*Do you think that an ear for music has a **connection/relationship with** language-learning ability?*
*Do you think there's a **connection/relationship between** an ear for music and language-learning ability?*

adjectives with prepositions *full of water*

Some **adjectives** are used with **particular prepositions**.

I'm **full of** energy today. (**NOT** … ~~full with energy~~ …)

Some **past participles** are used like adjectives. After these, we can use either **by** or another preposition (often **at** or **with**).

She's **astonished by/at** her own success.   They're **impressed by/with** her work.

1 Check your knowledge. Put in *at* five times and a different preposition once.

1 good .... sport
2 bad .... languages
3 surprised .... the result
4 bored .... studying
5 shocked .... her rudeness
6 clever .... maths

2 Put in *to* seven times and a different preposition once.

1 kind .... animals
2 married .... a designer
3 polite/rude .... people
4 accustomed .... hard work
5 similar .... the others
6 interested .... history
7 used .... hot weather
8 nice .... her colleagues

3 Put in *of* five times, *with* five times, and different prepositions twice.

1 That's typical .... him.
2 I'm responsible .... marketing.
3 We're pleased .... the results.
4 I'm tired .... travelling.
5 What's wrong .... you?
6 She's dressed .... her sister's clothes.
7 They're all angry .... me.
8 What are you afraid ....?
9 The train was crowded .... soldiers.
10 He's not satisfied .... my work.
11 I'm proud .... what I've done.
12 Are you aware .... the situation?

4 Put in *about* three times, *for* three times, and different prepositions twice.

1 excited .... going to America
2 prepared .... trouble
3 keen .... sport
4 worried .... the future
5 famous .... its old castle
6 ready .... anything
7 optimistic .... the exam
8 guilty .... murder

Here are some examples of other common **adjective + preposition** combinations.
Learn the ones you don't know.

> I feel **sorry for** his wife.   I'm **sorry for/about** the confusion.
> He's **dependent on** his parents.   She's **independent of** her parents.
> I'm **ashamed of** my behaviour.   She's very **fond of** you.   He's **capable of** extreme violence.
> She's **jealous of** her sister.
> It's **nice/kind/good/thoughtful/sweet of** you to help me.
> I'm not **sure/certain of/about** the exact time.
> We're not **happy with/about** the arrangements.
> He was **disappointed with/about** his exam results.
> I won't be **fit for** the match on Saturday.   We're very **angry about** what she said.
> Sally's **frightened of** the dark.   I'm **fed up with/of** all this useless discussion.
> She's very **different to/from** me.

expressions beginning with prepositions *at a party*

Some fixed expressions **begin** with a **particular preposition.**
*I met my girlfriend **at a party**.* (NOT … ~~in/on a party~~.)   *Is this car **for sale**?*
*We went there **by car**.*   *Please give me your report **in writing**.*

1 **Check your knowledge. Put in *in* eight times and a different preposition twice.**

1 .... my opinion	6 .... a raincoat
2 .... the picture	7 .... a hat
3 .... the rain	8 .... ink/pencil
4 .... a loud voice	9 .... cash
5 .... page 22	10 .... holiday

2 **Put in *on* eight times, *at* four times and a different preposition twice.**

1 .... the phone	8 .... cheque / credit card
2 .... the back	9 .... the internet
3 .... the side of the road	10 .... the screen
4 .... the radio	11 .... the left/right
5 .... TV	12 .... business
6 .... the middle of the road	13 .... a journey/trip
7 .... the front	14 .... the cinema/theatre

Note the differences between these expressions.
in time = 'not late', 'with time to spare'   ***on time*** = 'at exactly the right time'

*We got there **in time** to have a drink before the concert.*
*Trains never arrive **on time** in this country.*

in the way = 'in an inconvenient place'   ***on the way*** = 'during the journey'

*Can you move your bike out of the passage? It's **in the way**.*
*We stopped for a coffee **on the way**.*

at the end = 'after everything else'   ***in the end*** = 'after a long time or a lot of trouble'

At the end *of the performance the audience stood up and cheered.*
*It took him ages, but **in the end** he got the job he wanted.*

Here are some more fixed expressions beginning with prepositions. Learn the ones you don't know.

*a book **by** Dickens, a painting **by** Rembrandt, an opera **by** Mozart etc*
***In general**, I agree with you.*
*My address book is never **up to date**.*
*You can't use this ticket – it's **out of date**.*
*We can't spend all day driving – look at it **from** the children's **point of view**.*
*That house has been **on the market** for months.*
*I didn't step on your foot **on purpose** – I did it **by mistake/accident**.*
*My friend Henry became an actor purely **by chance**.*

prepositions: more practice

1 **Choose the correct prepositions.**

1 'Where's the police station?' 'Just *in front of / opposite* the public library.'
2 'Can I borrow your raincoat?' '*By / Until* when?'
3 She went on screaming *by / until* somebody came.
4 Andy was a teacher *for / during* a long time.
5 *By / Until* the time the police arrived, the bank robbers were miles away.
6 I couldn't see Maggie *between / among* the visitors.
7 I got to know John *for / during* my military service.
8 I had to do military service *for / during* two years.
9 Most accidents are caused by people driving too close to the car *in front of / opposite* them.
10 She stood there *between / among* piles of suitcases looking for a taxi.
11 Some time *in / during* the holiday we'd better go and see Sarah.
12 The ball hit him directly *between / among* the eyes.
13 The lift got stuck *between / among* two floors of the hotel.
14 The man sitting *in front of / opposite* me had a very friendly face.
15 There won't be any trees left *by / until* the year 2100.
16 You can go *in front of / opposite* me - I'm waiting for someone.
17 You don't see these animals *for / during* the day.
18 You ought to use this meat *by / until* tomorrow.

2 **Put in suitable prepositions from the box. You can use a preposition more than once. Different answers are possible.**

| in front of   opposite   by   on   in   at   over   between |

FRED: Where are we going to put the piano?
LIZ: ▶ ...*In front of*...... the window.
FRED: That means moving the big armchair.
LIZ: Yes, it can go over here ¹.................. the sofa.
FRED: So where are we going to put the bookcase?
LIZ: ².................. the piano.
FRED: ³.................. your mother's picture?
LIZ: Well, of course not. We'll put Mother's picture ⁴.................. that wall, ⁵.................. the TV.
FRED: So we can look at it if there's a really bad programme.
LIZ: That's not funny.
FRED: Sorry. So the coffee table will have to go ⁶.................. the piano and the sofa. Then where are we going to put Jim's computer?
LIZ: Well, that can go ⁷.................. the other table ⁸.................. the bookcase and the small armchair.
FRED: There isn't room. We'll have to put the small armchair somewhere else.
LIZ: Yes, I see what you mean.
FRED: How about on top of the piano?
LIZ: That's not funny.

prepositions: revision test

1 **All these sentences are wrong. Correct the mistakes.**

▶ I arrived ~~to~~ the station at six. ...at...............

1 I'm not very good in maths. ....

2 Our bus crashed against a parked car, but nobody was hurt. ....

3 My brother is looking after a new job. ....

4 Can we discuss about the holiday dates? ....

5 Have you ever read any novels of Tolstoy? ....

6 Do you know the man dressed with the blue raincoat? ....

7 There's an interesting article in page 12. ....

8 You forgot to pay the tickets. ....

9 You can be anything you want to. It depends of you. ....

10 Why are you talking with that strange voice? ....

11 We're not very interested by politics. ....

12 I didn't know the time, so I asked to a policeman. ....

13 We'll have to translate this in Japanese. ....

14 Her grandmother was very unkind with her. ....

15 Charlie is married with an economist. ....

16 The police allowed nobody to enter into the building. ....

17 Joe reminds me his father very strongly. ....

18 Congratulations for the prize. ....

19 Can you show me an example for your work? ....

20 I'm not responsible of the mistake. ....

21 He's forgotten again. That's typical for him. ....

22 What's the reason of the demonstration? ....

23 They've divided our department in two sections. ....

24 I often go walking under the rain. ....

25 At my opinion, you're right. ....

2 **Put in the correct prepositions.**

1 I've spent the day .... York.

2 Your key's .... the reception desk.

3 We usually meet .... the gym.

4 Why don't you take Joe .... the cinema?

5 Stop shouting .... me.

6 Throw the keys down .... me and I'll let myself in.

7 Belgium is .... Holland, Germany and France.

8 There's a bus stop on the other side of the road, just .... our house.

9 Children, please stop throwing snowballs .... Mrs Anderson.

10 Can you shout .... Paul and tell him he's wanted on the phone?

In some answers, both contracted forms (for example *I'm*, *don't*) and full forms (for example *I am*, *do not*) are possible. Normally both are correct.

SECTION 22 spoken grammar

GRAMMAR SUMMARY

The grammar of **informal spoken** English is **different** from the grammar of written English in some ways.

- Sentences are usually **less complicated**, with fewer kinds of conjunctions.
- Information is often **separated** more, and given piece by piece.
  That woman across the road, her brother, well, I was talking to him, and he said …
- We often **leave words out** if the meaning is clear.
  Seen Peter?   He said he'd pay, but I think he probably hasn't.
- We make several kinds of short sentence with **subject + auxiliary verb**.
  *The meeting's tomorrow, **isn't it?***
  *'Did you phone John?' 'No, **I didn't.'***
  *'The holiday was great.' '**Was it?** I'm so pleased.'*
  *'I'm playing tomorrow afternoon.' '**So am I.'***

Lonely? **Looking for friendship?**
Our discreet dating service can

Got a problem in the kitchen?
We can help.

Need short-term finance?
Contact **Brown Bros** today.

The market leaders for loans on attractive terms

Want to study in the City of London?

HARPER COLLEGE
offers a wide range of

Ready to take a break?
Sunrise Hotels

spoken sentence structure *It's difficult, the exam.*

The grammar of **informal spoken English** is **different** from the grammar of **written English** in some ways.
Sentences are usually **less complicated**, with fewer and simpler conjunctions.

FORMAL WRITING: *While the hotel was of quite a high standard, the food was disappointing.*
INFORMAL SPEECH: *The hotel was quite good, **but** the food was disappointing.*

Information is often **separated** out more, and given **piece by piece** – not always in the order
SUBJECT–VERB–OBJECT.

The woman across the road, her brother, well, I was talking to him, and he said …
Last Wednesday it was, I was just going to work, …
That lecture, I thought I was going to go to sleep.
They work very hard, most of the students.

1 **Change these spoken sentences into a more formal 'written' style. (Different answers are possible.)**

▶ That car of his, is he going to sell it?
  Is he going to sell his car?
  ....

▶ London, I think it was, where they met.
  I think they met in London.
  ....

1 It's pretty difficult, the final exam.
  ....

2 Copy paper, look, can I order six boxes, top quality?
  ....

3 She's not doing very well, Sheila, in her new job.
  ....

4 Who's going to win? Labour? Conservative? Well, nobody knows.
  ....

5 Sunday morning, I was fast asleep, the phone rang, it was Ellie.
  ....

6 Trust them? This government? Not me!
  ....

7 France, this year, we can't afford to go.
  ....

8 They're all the same, TV programmes these days.
  ....

9 George, his daughter, she's not going to university, not this year.
  ....

10 Without Henry, that job, we could never have finished it.
  ....

In **speech** we can emphasise one part of a sentence by saying it **louder** and on a **higher** pitch.

MARY sent a birthday card to the mayor. (NOT Mary's sister)
Mary sent A BIRTHDAY CARD to the mayor. (NOT a bomb)
Mary sent a birthday card to THE MAYOR. (NOT to the chief of police)

In writing, special structures have to be used to show emphasis (see pages 148-149).

***It was Mary who** sent a birthday card to the mayor.*

dropping sentence-beginnings *Must dash.*

In informal speech we often **drop unstressed beginnings** of sentences.
This happens mainly with **articles, possessives, personal pronouns, auxiliary verbs** and *be*, **demonstratives** and introductory *there is*.

Car's running badly. (= '**The** car's …')   *Shoelace is undone.* (= '**My** shoelace …')
Forgotten his umbrella again. (= '**He's** forgotten …')
You talking to me? (= '**Are** you talking …?')   *She ready?* (= '**Is** she ready?')
Must dash. (= '**I** must dash.')   *Won't work.* (= '**It** won't work.')
Be four pounds fifty. (= '**That**'ll be …')   *No reason to panic.* (= '**There's** no reason …')

1 **Put back the words that have been dropped and write the complete sentences.**

1 Wife's on holiday. ....
2 Couldn't understand a word. ....
3 Seen Joe? ....
4 Careful what you say. ....
5 Nobody at home. ....
6 Don't think so. ....
7 Train's late again. ....
8 Know what I mean? ....
9 Got a pen? ....
10 Lost my glasses. ....

2 **Make these sentences more informal by dropping words from the beginning.**

1 I've changed my job. ....
2 She doesn't know what she's doing. ....
3 That'll cost you £10. ....
4 Be careful of the flowers. ....
5 There's no time to waste. ....
6 The bus is coming. ....
7 Do you speak English? ....
8 I haven't been there. ....
9 He thinks he's clever. ....
10 Have you got a match? ....

We only drop pronouns **before stressed words**.

Like your tie.   *Haven't* seen him.   *Can't* swim.
BUT NOT ~~Have seen him., Can swim.~~ (Affirmative auxiliaries are usually unstressed.)

'You folks order the extra large?'

In some answers, both contracted forms (for example *I'm*, *don't*) and full
forms (for example *I am*, *do not*) are possible. Normally both are correct.

SPOKEN GRAMMAR **307**

dropping words after auxiliaries *'Get up!' 'I am!'*

In informal speech, we often use just an **auxiliary verb instead of repeating a longer expression.**

'Get up!' 'I am.' (= 'I am getting up.')
*He said he'd write to me, but he **hasn't.*** (= '… he hasn't written to me.')
'Talk louder.' 'I would if I could, but I can't.'

If there is **no auxiliary** to repeat, we use *do.*

*She said she would phone, and she **did.***

1 **Make these sentences more natural by cutting out unnecessary expressions after auxiliaries.**

▶ I can't see you today, but I can ~~see you~~ tomorrow.
1 She thinks I don't love her, but I do love her.
2 I've bought one of those tops, and Sue has bought one too.
3 'You wouldn't have won if I hadn't helped you.' 'Yes, I would have won.'
4 'That car needs cleaning.' 'It certainly does need cleaning.'
5 'You'd better phone Bill.' 'I have phoned Bill.'
6 'The photocopier isn't working.' 'Yes, it is working.'
7 She can't swim, but I can swim.
8 Phil doesn't want to go, and Celia doesn't want to go either.

2 **Read the text, and then write the expressions that have been dropped.**

"I've never understood how John puts up with her."
"No, I haven't ▶ either. He's a saint. He –"
"She's so rude. She just doesn't care how much she upsets people."
"She certainly doesn't [1]. I remember –"
"And having to work with her every day, it was getting on my nerves."
"Yes, I know it was [2]. I thought you –"
"I mean, I couldn't go on like that."
"Of course you couldn't [3], dear. You –"
"And then, she kept promising to take Sally to the zoo, and she never did [4]. Now if you make promises to children, you have to keep them, don't you [5]?"
"Yes, of course you do [6]. Children –"
"So in the end, I just told her what I thought of her."
"Well done. I'm glad you did [7]. Somebody had to [8]. If you hadn't [9], I would have [10]. I –"
"And another thing, …"

▶ ...*understood how John puts up with her*..
1 ....
2 ....
3 ....
4 ....
5 ....
6 ....
7 ....
8 ....
9 ....
10 ....

→ For *to* used in place of a complete infinitive (e.g. *I don't want to*), see page 122.

revise the basics: question tags *It's cold, isn't it?*

Question tags often **follow sentences** in speech and informal writing.
They are used to **check** whether something is true, or to **ask for agreement**.

*You haven't seen Joe, **have you**?*   *This tea isn't very nice, **is it**?*

Negative tags are usually **contracted** – we say for example ***isn't it*?** (NOT USUALLY *is it not?*)
(See page 321 for details of contractions). The contracted tag for *am I not?* is ***aren't I*?**

*Nice day, **isn't it**?*   *I'm late, **aren't I**?*

Question tags are usually negative (−) after affirmative (+) sentences, and not negative **after** negative
sentences. We do **not** normally put tags **after questions**.

*It is cold, **isn't it**?*   *It isn't warm, **is it**?*   (BUT NOT ~~Is it cold, isn't it?~~)

1 **Right (✓) or wrong (✗)?**

▶ You're Scottish, aren't you? ..✓..

▶ Are you ready, are you? ..✗..

1 She can't speak Chinese, can she? ......

2 It's been raining, hasn't it? ......

3 Have they paid, have they? ......

4 The film wasn't much good, wasn't it? ......

5 It'll be dark soon, won't it? ......

6 You've made a mistake, haven't you? ......

7 I'm in time for breakfast, aren't I? ......

8 Was the weather OK, was it? ......

If the main sentence has an **auxiliary verb** or **be**, this is used in the tag. If not, **do** is used.

*She **can** swim, **can't** she?*   *You **wouldn't** like a puppy, **would** you?*
*He **gave** you a cheque, **didn't** he?*

There can be used as a subject in tags.

***There's** a problem, **isn't there**?*

2 **These are sentences from real conversations. Put in the question tags.**

1 I'm cooking tonight, ...?

2 We're going to Mum's, then, ...?

3 Your brothers are not being kind to you today, ...?

4 I'm not quite myself, ...?

5 They weren't ready, ...?

6 She's not a baby now, ...?

7 That's the law, ...?

8 He's a lovely little boy, ...?

9 That fireman can see them, ... , Dave?

10 It must be a year now, ...?

11 It'll be all right, ...?

12 They look like big candles, ...?

13 They won't have bulbs, ...?

14 There's a light out there, ...?

15 Cathy's still got curly hair, ...?

16 She doesn't look well, ...?

17 They've been really horrible, ...?

18 I was first really, ...?

'Look, I'm sorry , mate – I'm only
doing my ****** job, aren't I?'

Instead of question tags, people also say *Right?, Yes?* or *No?*

*This is your coat, **right**?*   *We're seeing Hazel tonight, **no**?*

In some answers, both contracted forms (for example *I'm, don't*) and full
forms (for example *I am, do not*) are possible. Normally both are correct.

SPOKEN GRAMMAR **309**

more about question tags *Nobody phoned, did they?*

We use *they* to refer to *nobody/no one*, *somebody/someone*, *everybody/everyone* and *anybody/anyone*.

Nobody phoned, did *they*?   *Someone's* left the lights on, haven't *they*?

We use **non-negative** tags after words with a negative sense like *never*, *no*, *nobody*, *hardly*, *scarcely*, *little*.

She *never* smiles, *does she*? (NOT … *doesn't she?*)   It's *hardly* rained all summer, *has it*?

We use *it* in question tags to refer to *nothing*.

Nothing can happen, can *it*?

1 Put in suitable tags.

1 Everybody's here, aren't ....?
2 You're never happy, ...?
3 There's no milk, ...?
4 Nothing matters, ...?
5 Nobody likes her, do ....?

6 She hardly spoke, ...?
7 Somebody's forgotten their coat, ...?
8 There's scarcely enough time, ...?
9 You never wrote, ...?

Informal questions/requests often use **negative sentence + question tag.**

You *haven't* seen Liz around, *have you*?   You *can't* lend me £5, *can you*?

2 Change the structure.

▶ Do you know where Harry is?   *You don't know where Harry is, do you?*
1 Have you picked up my keys?   ....
2 Could you help me for a minute?   ....
3 Is that your brother?   ....
4 Can you give me a lift?   ....

After **imperatives**, we can use *won't you?* to invite people to do things, and *will/would/can/can't/could you?* (informal) to **tell** or **ask** people to do things.

Do sit down, won't you?   *Give me a hand, will you?*   *Shut up, can't you?*

After a **negative imperative** we use *will you?* After *Let's* we use *shall we?*

Don't forget, will you?   *Let's have a party, shall we?*

3 Complete the sentences with tags from the box.

| could you?   shall we?   will you?   won't you?   would you? |

1 Do have some more tea, ...
2 Don't drive too fast, ...
3 Let's start again, ...

4 You couldn't tell me the time, ...
5 Pass me the newspaper, ...

If a tag is a **real question**, it has a **rising intonation**: the music of the voice goes ᵘᵖ.
If the tag only **asks for agreement**, it has a **falling intonation**: the voice goes ᵈᵒʷⁿ.

The meeting's at four o'clock, isn't it?   *Nice day, isn't it?*

4 Real question or not? Draw arrows (⬈ or ⬊).

1 Sweet child, isn't she?

2 That's Fred, isn't it?

3 This is boring, isn't it?

4 We finish at twelve, don't we?

revise the basics: short answers and reply questions

In conversation, we often give **short answers** using **pronoun + auxiliary verb**.

'Can he swim?' 'Yes, *he can*.'   'Has the rain stopped?' 'No, *it hasn't*.'
'Don't forget to phone.' '*I won't*.'   'She likes cakes.' '*She* certainly *does*.'

1 **Write short affirmative (➕) or negative (➖) answers for these sentences.**

1 'Are you ready?' ➖ ....
2 'Do you speak English?' ➕ ....
3 'It's too hot.' ➕ ....
4 'Don't be late.' ➖ ....
5 'Send me a postcard.' ➕ ....
6 'Have you seen Les?' ➕ ....
7 'Can you understand him?' ➖ ....
8 'He plays well.' ➕ ....
9 'She sounded tired.' ➕ ....
10 'Say hello to Linda for me.' ➕ ....

Reply questions using **auxiliary verb + pronoun** (like question tags) can express **attention**, **interest** or **surprise**.

'It was a terrible party.' '*Was it?*' 'Yes, … '
'We had a lovely holiday.' '*Did you?*' 'Yes, we went … '
'I've got a headache.' '*Have you*, dear? I'll get you an aspirin.'
'John likes that girl next door.' 'Oh, *does he?*'
'I don't understand.' 'Oh, *don't you*? I'm sorry.'

Negative reply questions answering affirmative sentences can express **emphatic agreement**.

'It was a lovely concert.' 'Yes, *wasn't it*! I did enjoy it.'
'She's lost a lot of weight.' 'Yes, *hasn't she?*'

2 **Read the text and then rewrite a few lines of it as a conversation, using reply questions.**

It was a lovely wedding. Though I didn't think much of Maggie's dress. That colour doesn't suit her at all. Anyway. I don't really go for church weddings. The service went on for ages. And I was sitting right at the back, so I couldn't hear the vicar. The music was nice, though. They played that hymn about sheep. Lovely. I must say I didn't enjoy the reception much. The food wasn't very good. And the bride's father made such a stupid speech. And I got one of my headaches. Champagne always gives me a headache. And I was sitting next to that Mrs Foster from down the road. I can't stand that woman. She's always criticising. Anyway, I must go. Nice to talk to you. It really was a lovely wedding.

'It was a lovely wedding.' 'Was it?' 'Yes. Though … '
....
....
....
....
....
....
....
....
....
....

In some answers, both contracted forms (for example *I'm*, *don't*) and full forms (for example *I am*, *do not*) are possible. Normally both are correct.

revise the basics: *so am I* etc

So am I means '**I am too**'; *so does he* means 'he does too'; and so on.
Neither/Nor am I means '**I'm not either**', and so on.

She's from Scotland, and **so am I.**   I was tired, and **so were the others.**
'I've lost their address.' '**So have I.**'   I like dancing, and **so does he.**
I can't swim, and **neither can Bill.**   'She didn't understand.' '**Nor did I.**'

1 **Complete the sentences with *so am I* etc or *neither/nor am I* etc.**

1 He's tall, and .... his sister.
2 'I haven't paid.' '..................................... I.'
3 Penguins can't fly, and .... ostriches.
4 'I love this music.' '..................................... I.'
5 'I lost my passport.' '..................................... Nicola.'
6 I don't like her, and .... my friends.
7 The food was bad, and .... the wine.
8 Sue won't be there, and .... her mother.
9 'Pete looks ill.' '..................................... you.'
10 'I wasn't surprised.' '..................................... I.'

2 **Look at the pictures, and make sentences about pairs of things using *so is* etc or *neither/nor is* etc.**

The cat has got four legs, and so has the dog.   The pram is not alive, and neither is the car.
....
....
....
....
....
....
....
....

We can use short sentences (**subject + auxiliary verb**) to say that **A is not the same as B**.

*'I'm not ready.' '**I am.**'   Ann doesn't like the new neighbours, but **I do**.*
*'I want to go home.' '**I don't.**'   The room was OK, but **the food wasn't**.*

3 Complete the sentences using expressions from the box, to say that things are not the same.

| gas cookers   her second   little Lucy   mine   Robert   the other one ✓ |
| the sofa   the windows |

▶ 'This driver speaks English.' *'The other one doesn't.'*
1 'My room doesn't cost a lot.' '...'
2 Most of the children can sing, but ....
3 Her first marriage didn't work out very well, but ....
4 'Electric cookers take a long time to heat up.' '...'
5 'Mike has found a job.' 'Yes, but ....'
6 The door was locked, but ....
7 'The armchair isn't very comfortable.' '...'

4 Here are some facts about some people. Are you the same as them, or different?
Write your answers, using *So am I, Neither/Nor do I, I have, I can't* etc.

▶ A lot of people have got brown eyes. ...*So have I.*... or ...*I haven't*....
▶ Some people don't like fish. ...*I do*.......... or ...*Nor do I*.....
1 Most people are interested in sport. ....
2 Quite a lot of people have climbed a mountain. ....
3 A lot of people can sing. ....
4 Some people like old books. ....
5 A lot of people speak Chinese. ....
6 Some people aren't very sociable. ....
7 Most people haven't got a dog. ....
8 Some people can't drink milk. ....
9 Some people don't like travelling. ....
10 A lot of people don't understand computers. ....

We can also use *too* or *not either* to say that **A is/does the same as B**.

*'I'm hungry.' 'I am **too**.'   Lucy hasn't written, and Carol hasn't **either**.*

In informal conversation we often say *Me too* instead of *So do I, I do too* etc.

*'I've got a headache.' '**Me too**.'* (NOT *~~I also.~~*)

5 Write a few sentences comparing yourself with somebody you know.
Use the structures that you have just practised.

....
....
....
....
....
....
....
....
....
....

In some answers, both contracted forms (for example *I'm, don't*) and full
forms (for example *I am, do not*) are possible. Normally both are correct.

structures with *so* and *not* *I (don't) think so. I hope so/not.*

We often use *so* in answers, instead of a *that*-clause. This is common after **be afraid**, **hope**, **suppose**, **think**.

'*Did you lose?*' '**I'm afraid so.**' (= 'I'm afraid that we did.')
'*Do you think we'll have good weather?*' '*Yes, **I hope so.**' (NOT *Yes, I hope.*)
'*Are you ready?*' '**I suppose so.**' (unwilling agreement)
'*Is Alex here?*' '**I think so.**' (NOT *I think it.* OR *I think.*)

1 Here are some exchanges taken from recorded conversations. See if you can guess which of the following expressions was used in each exchange: *I'm afraid so, I hope so, I suppose so* or *I think so.*

1 'Is it working?' 'Yes, ...'
2 'Dead, aren't they?' '......................................'
3 'Do we want it?' 'Not sure. ....'
4 'Is that when she said it?' '......................................'
5 'It should be warmer in April.' '......................................'
6 'Did he know who you were?' 'Oh, yes, ...'
7 'When is it? Tomorrow?' 'Yes, ...'
8 'You're mean, aren't you?' '......................................'
9 'It should be quite easy, though.' '......................................'
10 'I could borrow one of your dresses, couldn't I?' '......................................'
11 'Complete disaster, isn't it?' '......................................'
12 'This really is the last job for today, right?' 'Well, ...'

Negatives are: *I'm afraid not*, *I hope not*, *I suppose not* and (usually) *I don't think so.*

'*Have we finished?*' '**I'm afraid not.**'   '*Is this our hotel?*' '**I hope not.**'
'*John won't want to come with us.*' '**I suppose not.**'
'*Is there a later train?*' '**I don't think so.**'

2 Complete the negative answers.

1 'Did you find out?' '......................................' (*afraid*)
2 'Will you be home late?' 'No, ...' (*think*)
3 'We're not going to have lunch too early, are we?' '......................................' (*hope*)
4 'It's not a good idea, is it?' 'No. ....' (*suppose*)
5 'Do they serve tea here?' '......................................' (*afraid*)
6 'I think she's got a new boyfriend?' '......................................' (*hope*)
7 'We won't be in time for the train.' '......................................' (*suppose*)
8 'Is this where she lives?' '......................................' (*think*)
9 'Can you come round tonight?' '......................................' (*afraid*)
10 'This isn't going to work, is it?' '......................................' (*suppose*)
11 'Is it going to rain again?' '......................................' (*hope*)
12 'Does Alice know what's going on?' '......................................' (*think*)

spoken grammar: more practice

1 **Dropping sentence-beginnings. Cut out unnecessary expressions after auxiliaries.**

▶ I haven't checked the car, but Andy has ~~checked the car~~.

1 'Ann isn't coming in tomorrow.' 'Yes, she is coming in tomorrow.'
2 I don't speak Spanish, and Maggie doesn't speak Spanish either.
3 I'm going to buy a bike, and Phil is going to buy a bike too.
4 'You would have overslept if I hadn't woken you up.' 'No, I wouldn't have overslept.'
5 He thinks we don't know what he's doing, but we do know what he's doing.
6 'You'd better tell the police.' 'I have told the police.'
7 None of them can cook, but I can cook.
8 'We need some new plates.' 'We certainly do need some new plates.'

2 **Dropping sentence beginnings. Put back the words that have been dropped.**

▶ Want the newspaper? *Do you want the newspaper?* ....

1 Got any money on you? ....
2 Heard from Peter? ....
3 Careful how you drive. ....
4 Know what I think? ....
5 Anybody at home? ....
6 Couldn't find his house. ....
7 Don't suppose so. ....
8 Door's locked. ....
9 Carpet's very dirty. ....
10 Forgotten her phone number. ....

3 *So am I* **etc. Look at the table and write sentences about the people.**

	SPEAKS ARABIC	CAN SING	LIKES ANIMALS	HAS BEEN TO PERU	PLAYS TENNIS	IS SHY
ROBERT	✓	✗	✓	✓	✗	✓
SARAH	✓	✓	✗	✗	✗	✓
MIKE	✗	✗	✗	✓	✗	✗
ANN	✓	✓	✓	✓	✓	✓
JULIE	✗	✓	✗	✗	✓	✗
PETER	✓	✓	✗	✗	✓	✓

▶ *Ann speaks Arabic, and so does Peter.* ....
▶ *Robert can't sing, and neither can Mike.* ....
▶ *Ann likes animals, but Sarah doesn't.* ....
▶ *Julie isn't shy, but Peter is.* ....

....
....
....
....
....
....
....
....
....
....
....

spoken grammar: revision test

1 Right or wrong? Correct the mistakes or write 'Correct'.

▶ Are you English, ~~are you~~? ...Are you English?........

▶ It's cold, isn't it? ...Correct.........................

1 She's funny, that girl. ....

2 'Open the window.' 'I would if I could, but I can't.' ....

3 There weren't enough chairs, were there? ....

4 'I didn't like the party much.' 'Didn't you?' ....

5 'Can you swim?' 'Yes, I do.' ....

6 'My father plays a lot of tennis.' 'So mine does.' ....

7 The President didn't answer my letter, and neither did the Foreign Minister.

....

8 I haven't seen many films this year, but my sister has seen. ....

9 Lost your key? ....

10 Nobody understood, did they? ....

11 You don't know what time it is, do you? ....

12 'Is it going to rain?' 'I don't hope so.' ....

13 Don't be late, will you? ....

14 Let's stop now, shall we? ....

15 'I'm tired.' 'I also.' ....

2 Put in the missing words (one word or two).

1 I'm late, ... I?

2 She never smiles, ... she?

3 'I haven't seen John recently.' '.............. you?'

4 'My father plays golf every weekend.' 'So .... mine.'

5 'That's Sandra over there.' 'No, ...'

6 'You could have got here earlier.' 'No, I ....'

7 Hold this for a minute, ...?

8 'I didn't enjoy the concert.' '.............. ....? I'm sorry.'

9 'We're not going to be on time.' 'I suppose ....'

10 Let's go home now, ...

11 I haven't done much work today.' 'Nor ....'

12 We can't come tomorrow, but .... on Sunday.

13 'I'm hungry.' '.............. too.'

14 Celia wasn't around today, and Max wasn't ....'

15 'I've got a headache.' '.............. ....? Let me get you an aspirin.'

In some answers, both contracted forms (for example *I'm*, *don't*) and full forms (for example *I am*, *do not*) are possible. Normally both are correct.

appendix 1 common irregular verbs

(These are the most common irregular verbs. For a complete list, see a good dictionary.)

INFINITIVE	SIMPLE PAST	PAST PARTICIPLE	INFINITIVE	SIMPLE PAST	PAST PARTICIPLE
be	was/were	been	lay	laid	laid
beat	beat	beaten	lead	led	led
become	became	become	learn	learnt/learned	learnt/learned
begin	began	begun	leave	left	left
bend	bent	bent	lend	lent	lent
bet	bet	bet	let	let	let
bite	bit	bitten	lie	lay	lain
bleed	bled	bled	lose	lost	lost
blow	blew	blown	make	made	made
break	broke	broken	mean	meant	meant
bring	brought	brought	meet	met	met
build	built	built	pay	paid	paid
burn	burnt	burnt	put	put	put
buy	bought	bought	read /ri:d/	read /red/	read /red/
catch	caught	caught	ride	rode	ridden
choose	chose	chosen	ring	rang	rung
come	came	come	rise	rose	risen
cost	cost	cost	run	ran	run
cut	cut	cut	say	said	said
deal	dealt	dealt	see	saw	seen
dig	dug	dug	sell	sold	sold
do	did	done	send	sent	sent
draw	drew	drawn	shake	shook	shaken
dream	dreamt/dreamed	dreamt/dreamed	shine	shone	shone
drink	drank	drunk	shoot	shot	shot
drive	drove	driven	show	showed	shown
eat	ate	eaten	shut	shut	shut
fall	fell	fallen	sing	sang	sung
feed	fed	fed	sink	sank	sunk
feel	felt	felt	sit	sat	sat
fight	fought	fought	sleep	slept	slept
find	found	found	smell	smelt	smelt
fly	flew	flown	speak	spoke	spoken
forget	forgot	forgotten	spell	spelt	spelt
forgive	forgave	forgiven	spend	spent	spent
freeze	froze	frozen	stand	stood	stood
get	got	got	steal	stole	stolen
give	gave	given	swim	swam	swum
go	went	gone/been	take	took	taken
grow	grew	grown	teach	taught	taught
hang	hung	hung	tear	tore	torn
have	had	had	tell	told	told
hear	heard	heard	think	thought	thought
hide	hid	hidden	throw	threw	thrown
hit	hit	hit	understand	understood	understood
hold	held	held	wake	woke	woken
hurt	hurt	hurt	wear	wore	worn
keep	kept	kept	win	won	won
know	knew	known	write	wrote	written

appendix 2 active and passive verb forms

	ACTIVE		PASSIVE: TENSE OF *BE* + PAST PARTICIPLE	
INFINITIVE	*(to) watch*	*(to) write*	*(to) be watched*	*(to) be written*
-ING FORM	*watching*	*writing*	*being watched*	*being written*
SIMPLE PRESENT	*I watch*	*I write*	*I am watched*	*It is written*
PRESENT PROGRESSIVE	*I am watching*	*I am writing*	*I am being watched*	*It is being written*
SIMPLE PAST	*I watched*	*I wrote*	*I was watched*	*It was written*
PAST PROGRESSIVE	*I was watching*	*I was writing*	*I was being watched*	*It was being written*
PRESENT PERFECT	*I have watched*	*I have written*	*I have been watched*	*It has been written*
PAST PERFECT	*I had watched*	*I had written*	*I had been watched*	*It had been written*
WILL FUTURE	*I will watch*	*I will write*	*I will be watched*	*It will be written*
GOING TO FUTURE	*I am going to watch*	*I am going to write*	*I am going to be watched*	*It is going to be written*
MODAL VERBS	*I can watch*	*I can write*	*I can be watched*	*It can be written*
	I must watch	*I must write*	*I must be watched*	*It must be written*
	I should watch	*I should write*	*I should be watched*	*It should be written*
	etc	etc	etc	etc

→ For the use of the different tenses, see Sections 2–5.
→ For the use of passives, see Section 7.
→ For the spelling of *-ing* forms, see page 16.
→ For the spelling of third-person present forms (*writes, watches, sits, goes* etc), see page 16.

appendix 3 capital letters (A, B, C etc)

We use CAPITAL LETTERS to begin the names of **people, places, organisations, nationalities, languages, days, months** and **holidays.**

Charles Dickens   Shanghai   Universal Export   French   Arabic   Friday   May   Easter

Titles like *Mr, Mrs, Miss, Doctor/Dr, Professor/Prof, General* begin with capital letters.
We also use capital letters to begin the most important words in the titles of **books, films** etc.

A Tale of Two Cities   Gone with the Wind

And we use a capital letter for the **first word in a sentence,** and for the pronoun *I.*

When I was younger I wanted to be a musician.

appendix 4 punctuation

This section summarises the most important rules of punctuation.

the basic sentence
We don't separate the basic parts of a sentence (**subject** and **verb**, **verb** and **object**, etc).
>   *The Export Department should not have lost **so much money**.*
>   (**NOT** ~~*The Export Department, should not have lost* **so much money.**~~
>   **OR** ~~*The Export Department should not have lost,* **so much money.**~~)

before the basic sentence
If we put **long adverbial expressions** (saying *when*, *where* etc) before the basic sentence, we often use a comma (,). Compare:
>   *Last year the Export Department should not have lost so much money.*
>   *Between January 2010 and March 2011, the Export Department should not have lost so much money.*

after the basic sentence
We don't usually use commas when **adverbial expressions** come **after** the basic sentence.
>   *The Export Department should not have lost so much money **between January 2010 and March 2011**.*

inside the basic sentence
When adverbial expressions come **between** or inside parts of the basic sentence, we usually put commas before and after them.
>   *The Export Department, **between January 2010 and March 2011**, lost an absolute fortune.*

noun phrases
We don't usually separate a noun from the adjectives or other expressions that go with it.
>   *the very strange men* (**NOT** ~~*the very strange, men*~~)
>   *the very strange men in the London office* (**NOT** ~~*the very strange men, in the London office*~~)
>   *the very strange men in the London office who run the Export Department*
>   (**NOT** ~~*the very strange men in the London office, who run the Export Department*~~)

However, we do use **commas** to separate **non-identifying expressions** (see page 275) after nouns.
>   *Mr Sackbottle and Mr Pertwee, who run the Export Department, …*

sentences with conjunctions
We often put **commas** in sentences with conjunctions, especially in longer sentences. (See page 240.) Compare:
>   *Things will be different **when** the head of the Export Department retires.*
>   *Things will be very different after next December, **when** the head of the Export Department retires.*

We **usually** use a **comma** if we **start** with the conjunction.
>   ***When** the head of the Export Department retires, things will be different.*

indirect speech
We **don't put commas** after verbs of saying, thinking etc in **indirect speech**.
>   *Annie **says that** the Export Department is in deep trouble.* (**NOT** ~~*Annie says, that …*~~)
>   *I don't **know how much** they're going to lose this year.* (**NOT** ~~*I don't know, how much …*~~)

We **don't put question marks** (?) in **indirect questions**.
>   *I **asked why** the police were here.* (**NOT** ~~*I asked why the police were here?*~~)

a useful rule: no comma before *that*
We **don't put commas** before *that* (conjunction or relative pronoun).
>   *I **know that** the police have questioned **the men that** run the Export Department.*

between separate sentences

Between separate sentences (with no conjunction), we use a full stop (.) or a semi-colon (;), but **not a comma**. Compare:

The police have been here, **and** *they have arrested the head of the Export Department.* (comma and conjunction)
The police have been here. They have arrested the head of the Export Department.
OR *The police have been here; they have arrested the head of the Export Department.*
BUT NOT ~~The police have been here, they have arrested the head of the Export Department.~~

lists

We use commas to separate the different things in a list (but not before *and*).

The police are questioning his wife, his sister, his girlfriend, his secretary and his secretary's boyfriend.

abbreviations (short forms of words)

We use full stops after some abbreviations, like *e.g.* (meaning 'for example'). *Mr* and *Mrs* have full stops in American English, but not usually in British English.

The police have also arrested some of his other associates, **e.g.** *the head of the Marketing Department,* **Mrs** *Oliver.*

quotation marks ('…' or "…")

Quotation marks are used to show direct speech (somebody's actual words).

Mrs Oliver says, 'I can explain everything.' (**NOT** <*I can explain everything*> **OR** *– I can explain everything.*)

figures

We use commas after thousands and millions, and full stops in decimal fractions.

losses of € 5,500,000 (= 'five million, five hundred thousand euros')
losses of € 5.5m (= 'five and a half million euros')

apostrophes (')

For apostrophes in contractions (e.g. *isn't*), see Appendix 5. For apostrophes in possessives (e.g. *John's*), see page 207.

appendix 5 contractions

Contractions like **she**'s, **isn**'t represent the pronunciation of **informal speech**.
They are common and correct in **informal writing**, but are unusual in formal writing.

AFFIRMATIVE (⊞) CONTRACTIONS: PRONOUN + 'M, 'RE, 'S, 'VE, 'D, 'LL	NEGATIVE (⊟) CONTRACTIONS: AUXILIARY VERB / BE + N'T	
I am ⟶ I'm	are not ⟶ aren't	shall not ⟶ shan't
we are ⟶ we're	is not ⟶ isn't	would not ⟶ wouldn't
she is ⟶ she's	have not ⟶ haven't	should not ⟶ shouldn't
he has ⟶ he's	has not ⟶ hasn't	cannot ⟶ can't
I have ⟶ I've	had not ⟶ hadn't	could not ⟶ couldn't
you had ⟶ you'd	do not ⟶ don't	might not ⟶ mightn't
you would ⟶ you'd	does not ⟶ doesn't	must not ⟶ mustn't
they will ⟶ they'll	did not ⟶ didn't	need not ⟶ needn't
	will not ⟶ won't	ought not ⟶ oughtn't

With *be*, two negative forms are common: *you're not / you aren't, she's not / she isn't* etc.
With other verbs, forms with *n't* are more common.

Am not is contracted to *aren't* only in questions.
I'm late, aren't I? (**BUT** *I'm not late*, **NOT** ~~I aren't late.~~)

The contraction *'s* (= *is* or *has*) can be written after pronouns, nouns, question words, *there* and *here*.
It's late.   Your father's gone home.   How's everything?
There's the phone.   Here's your money.
The contractions *'re, 've, 'd* and *'ll* are normally only written after pronouns.

Don't confuse *it's* (= *it is/has*) with **its** (possessive – see page 190).
*The cat isn't hungry. It's only eaten half of **its** food.*

Don't confuse *who's* (= *who is/has*) with **whose** (possessive – see page 190).
*Who's the woman in the green coat?   **Whose** car is that?*

In very informal speech, *going to, want to* and *got to* are often pronounced like *gonna, wanna* and *gotta*.
They are sometimes written like this, especially in American English.

① Change the words *in italics* to contractions.

▶ *I am* ...I'm... tired.

1 My *car has* .... broken down.
2 *She is* .... French.
3 *She has* .... forgotten.
4 *They have* .... finished.
5 I thought *you had* .... left.
6 *We will* .... tell you tomorrow.
7 I wish *he would* .... stop.
8 *How is* .... your mother?
9 *Nobody is* .... perfect.

10 *Do you not* .... like this?
11 You *need not* .... worry.
12 I *cannot* .... swim.
13 The door *will not* .... close.
14 It *does not* .... matter.
15 I *have not* .... forgotten.
16 *I am not* .... sorry.
17 Why *are you not* .... in bed?
18 I'm right, *am I not* ....?

Affirmative contractions are **not usually stressed**. When an affirmative auxiliary verb is stressed
(for example at the end of a sentence) we don't use a contraction. Compare:

*'You're late.' 'Yes, **we are**.'* (**NOT** ~~'Yes, we're.'~~)   *'**He's** forgotten.' 'I think **he has**.'* (**NOT** ~~I think he's.~~)

Negative contractions can be stressed, and are possible in any position.
'It **isn't** true.' 'No, it **isn't**.'

2 **Rewrite the words _in italics_ only if contractions are possible.**

▶ Can you tell me where _she is_ staying? ..she's..........

▶ 'Remember to take your medicine.' 'Yes, _I will_.' ....—..........

1 Do you know where _she is_? ....

2 'Have you paid?' 'No, I _have not_.' ....

3 'It _is not_ true.' ....

4 'On the contrary, _it is_ true.' ....

5 'Would you like another cup?' 'Yes, _I would_.' ....

6 I _do not_ believe they are fresh. ....

7 Telephone if you _cannot_ come. ....

8 'Can you help me?' 'No, I _cannot_ just at the moment.' ....

3 **Complete the poem with the contracted forms of the expressions in the box.**

cannot	he has	he would	I will	that is	there is	we have	you have

Mother, 1 .... a strange man
Waiting at the door
With a familiar sort of face
You feel 2 .... seen before.

Says his name is Jesus
Can we spare a couple of bob*
Says 3 .... been made redundant
And now 4 .... find a job.

Yes I think he is a foreigner
Egyptian or a Jew
Oh aye, and that reminds me
5 .... like some water too.
Well shall I give him what he wants
Or send him on his way?
6 .... give him 5p
Say 7 .... all 8 .... got today.

(From _Roger McGough: Three Rusty Nails_)

*a couple of bob (shillings): a little money

appendix 6 word order

This section summarises the most important rules of word order that you can find in other parts of the book.

sentences
The basic word order of English sentences is SUBJECT – VERB – OBJECT.
> *I like jazz.* (NOT ~~I jazz like.~~)

questions
In questions we usually put an auxiliary verb before the subject.
> ***Did you*** *see my email?* (NOT ~~Saw you my email …?~~)   ***Must you*** *go?*

For more details, see pages 103–107.
This does not usually happen with **indirect questions.**
> *I asked her **what she wanted.*** (NOT ~~I asked her what did she want.~~)

For more details, see page 287.

adjectives
Adjectives usually go before, not after, nouns.
> *an **interesting book*** (NOT ~~a book interesting~~)

Adjectives can go after *be*, *seem* and similar verbs.
> *I think he **is unhappy**.*

For more details, see pages 215–219.

adverbs
Different adverbs can go in different places in a sentence.
> ***Yesterday*** *I stopped work early.   I've **just** seen Peter.   She's talking very **strangely**.*

They do **not** usually go **between the verb and the object**.
> *I **bought some shoes yesterday**.* (NOT ~~I bought yesterday some shoes.~~)
> *You speak **English very well**.* (NOT ~~You speak very well English.~~)

For more details, see pages 220–222.

prepositions
Prepositions often go **at the ends of questions**, especially in spoken English.
> *Who do you work **for**?   Where did you get that **from**?*

For more details, see page 107.
Prepositions can also go **at the ends of passive clauses** and (especially in spoken English) **at the ends of relative clauses**.
> *That child needs **to be spoken to**.*
> *The team **that I play for** has won its last six matches.*

For more details, see pages 98 and 273.

exclamations
In exclamations, the adjective, adverb or object comes at the beginning of the sentence, just after *how* or *what*.
> ***How cold*** *it is!* (NOT ~~How it is cold!~~)   ***What a stupid mistake*** *I made!*

For more details, see page 145.

phrasal verbs
The objects of **phrasal verbs** (but not prepositional verbs) can often **go between the two parts of the verb**.
> *Shall I **switch the TV off**?* (OR *Shall I **switch off the TV**?*)

Pronoun objects always go between the two parts of a phrasal verb.
> *I **switched it off**.* (NOT ~~I switched off it.~~)

For more details, see pages 150–151.

ago

Ago follows an expression of **time**.

>*She went to bed **two hours ago**.* (NOT … *ago two hours*)

enough

Enough usually goes **before nouns** but **after adjectives and adverbs.**

>*We haven't got **enough milk**.* (NOT … *milk enough*)

>*Is your coffee **hot enough**?* (NOT … *enough hot?*)   *I didn't study **hard enough**.*

so do I etc

Note the word order in ***so do I***, ***so am I*** etc (see page 312).

>*My sister sings in a choir, and **so do I**.* (NOT … *so I do.*)

appendix 7 numbers

A hundred, *a thousand* etc are less formal than *one* hundred etc. Compare:

*I'll let you have it for **a hundred** pounds.*
*We are prepared to sell the item for a sum of **one hundred** pounds.*

We use *one* hundred etc when we wish to sound **precise**.

*It costs exactly **one hundred** dollars.*

We use *one hundred* etc, not *a hundred* etc, just before another number or inside a larger number.

1,300: **one** thousand, three hundred (**NOT** ~~a thousand, three hundred~~)
£1.70: **one** pound seventy   six thousand, **one** hundred and eleven (**NOT** ~~six thousand, a hundred~~ ...)

1 Write the figures in words.

1 We drove about 100 miles. ....
2 He wants £1,450 for the car. ....
3 'What's the population of your village?' 'Oh, 1,000, I suppose.' ....
4 3,144 ....
5 $1.85 ....
6 (*on a cheque*): Pay G S Hallam £1,000 only ....

Dozen, *hundred*, *thousand* and *million* have **no -s** after a number, *few* or *several*.

*three **dozen** bottles* (**NOT** ~~three dozens (of) bottles~~)
*a few **hundred** times   six **thousand** miles   several **million** pounds*

In other cases we use *dozens (of)*, *hundreds (of)* etc.

*We've got **dozens** of bottles.   He's done it **hundreds** of times.   She made **millions** in the property market.*

2 Put in *dozen(s) (of)*, *hundred(s) (of)*, *thousand(s) (of)* or *million(s) (of)*.

1 He had to sign his name five .... times. (*hundred*)
2 We export 40 .... tons a year. (*million*)
3 I just need to borrow a few .... pounds. (*hundred*)
4 I've told you .... times. (*million*)
5 .... refugees are flooding into the country. (*thousand*)
6 Could I have two .... eggs? (*dozen*)

3 Do you know how to spell ordinal numbers? Write these in words.

1st *first* ....   2nd ....   3rd ....
4th ....   5th ....   6th ....
7th ....   8th ....   9th ....
10th ....   12th ....   16th ....
20th ....   21st ....   30th ....
100th ....   1000th ....

We use **ordinal numbers** to say the names of **kings**, **queens** and **popes**.

Henry VIII → *Henry the **Eighth***   *Elizabeth II* → *Elizabeth the **Second***   *Pius the **Twelfth***

'I'm afraid you've got the wrong
number. This is Louis XV.'

WRITING DATES: *30 March 2008; 10 June 1980*

SAYING DATES: *the thirtieth of March / March the thirtieth, two thousand and eight*
the tenth of June / June the tenth, nineteen eighty

4 **Change these from written to spoken or from spoken to written form.**

1 the tenth of April, two thousand and six

....

2 September the seventeenth, nineteen eleven

....

3 the sixteenth of June, nineteen seventy-nine

....

4 16 May 1970

....

5 12 March 2003

....

6 14 January 1996

....

Telephone and credit card numbers and similar numbers are usually said **one number at a time.**

*3174522: three one seven four five two two (**OR** ... double two)*
*20645: two oh (**OR** zero) six four five*

5 **Write the following all in words:**

1 your telephone number

....

2 your date of birth

....

3 the approximate population of your home village/town and your country

....

appendix 8 word problems

This section tells you about some words that are difficult to use correctly. We explain some other word problems in other sections of the book: see the Index.

after We **don't** usually say *and after*, X happened. We prefer *afterwards* or *after that*.
  *I did the washing, and **afterwards / after that** I went shopping. (NOT ... ~~and after, I went~~ ...)*

ago *Ago* goes **after** a time expression. Compare *ago* with *for* and *since* (see page 56).
  *I started this job **six months ago**. I've been working here **for six months, since October**.*

ago and *before* *Ago* means 'before now'. To say 'before a particular past time', we use *before*.
  *A man came to my office a few days **ago**. When I saw him, I knew that we had met years **before**.*
  (NOT … ~~we had met years ago.~~)

born We say that somebody *is/was born* (passive).
  *I **was born** in Glasgow.   Children who **are born in the summer start school younger than others**.*

both We often **drop** *the* and/or *of* after *both*.
  ***Both (the)** chairs are broken. **Both (of)** my brothers are out of work.*

do and *make* Common expressions with *do* and *make*:
  ***do** work, a job, shopping, washing, ironing, business; **do** something, nothing, anything, everything*
  ***make** a suggestion, a decision, a phone call, a noise, a journey, a mistake, money, a bed, a fire, love*

do + *...ing* Common expressions:
  ***do** the shopping; **do** some (a lot of / a bit of) walking, swimming, reading, climbing, sailing, skiing*

else We use *else* to mean *other* after *something*, *anything*, *somebody*, *nobody* etc.
  *Would you like **anything else**?   I understand her, but **nobody else does.***

ever is used mostly in **questions**, or with **present perfect + superlative**.
  *Do you **ever** get depressed?   Have you **ever** been to Brazil?*
  *This is the worst meal I've **ever** eaten.   This the most interesting job I've **ever** had.*

explain is **not** used with **two objects** (see page 143).
  Can you explain the rules to me? (NOT ~~Can you explain me the rules?~~)

half We often **drop** *of* after *half*.
  *He spends **half (of)** the night playing computer games.*

hear and *listen to* We can **hear** something **without trying**. When we **listen to** something, we **want** to hear it.
  *I **heard** a strange noise upstairs.   You're not **listening to** me. (NOT ... ~~listening me.~~)*
We often use *can* with *hear*.
  *I **could hear** the children playing in the garden.*

home We **leave out** *to* before *home*.
  *Are you going **home** now? (BUT There's nobody **at home**.)*

hope We often use *so* and *not* after *hope*.
  *'Are you free on Saturday?' 'I **hope so**.'   'Is there a meeting tomorrow?' 'I **hope not**.'*

if and *when* We use *if* for things that **may happen**, and *when* for things that **will happen**.
  ***If** I make a lot of money ...   **If** John phones ...   **When** I die ...   **When** it stops raining ...*

just has several meanings: 1) *right now* 2) *a short time ago* (with present perfect, see page 51)
3) *exactly* 4) *really* 5) *only*
  1) *I can't talk now – I'm **just** going out.*   2) *Her plane has **just** landed.*
  3) *It's **just** eight o'clock.*   4) *I **just** hate the way he talks to people.*
  5) *'Can I help you, sir?' 'No, I'm **just** looking round, thanks.'*

let and *make* If I **let** you do something, I say that you **can** do it. If I **make** you do it, I say that you **must**. After *let* and *make*, we use **object + infinitive without *to***.

>*My parents **let** me leave school. But they **made** me get a job.*

quite often comes **before an article**.

>*It was **quite a** good film.*

rather often comes **before an article**.

>*We've had **rather a** difficult year.*

see, look and *watch* We can **see** something **without trying**. When we **look at** something, we **want** to see it.

>*I **saw** Joanna at the station yesterday.   **Look at** that sunset! (NOT ~~Look that sunset!~~)*

We often use **can** with **see**.

>*If you look out of the window you **can see** John working in the garden.*

We **watch** things that **move**, **change** or **happen**.

>*I hardly ever **watch** TV.   Did you **watch** the match last night?*
>*Can you **watch** the children for a few minutes?*

still, yet and *already* We use **still** to say that something **is continuing**; *yet* to ask if it **has happened** (or to say it **hasn't**); *already* to say it **has happened earlier** than we expected.

>*Pete's **still** in the bathroom.   'Has Carl phoned **yet**?' 'No, not **yet**.'*
>*I've **already** done three hours' work, and it's only nine o'clock.*

than, as and *that* Use **than** after **comparatives** (see page 229); *as* in the structure *as ... as* (see page 231); *that* after *say*, *think* etc and as a **relative pronoun** (see page 268).

>*He's **older than** me.   My hands are **as cold as** ice.   I think **that** you're wrong.*
>*Where's the bread **that** I bought?*

think We often use **so** after **think**. **Don't** use an **infinitive** after *think*.

>*'Are we ready?' 'I **think so**.'   'Is Peter in?' 'I don't **think so**.'*
>*I'm **thinking of changing** my job. (NOT ~~I'm thinking to change~~ ...)*

very and *too* **Too** means '**more than we want**'; *very* doesn't.

>*'This curry's **very** hot.' 'Yes, a bit **too** hot for me.' 'Oh, it's OK for me.'*

wait We often use **wait for** with **object + infinitive** (with *to*).

>*I'm **waiting for my sister to phone**.*

whom In a very **formal** style, we use **whom** as an **object** in questions and relative clauses.

>***Whom** did they arrest?   For **whom** did she work?   The man **whom** they elected did a very bad job.*

In an **informal** style, *who* is more normal in questions, and *that* (OR nothing) in relatives.

>***Who** did they arrest?   **Who** did she work for?   The man they elected did a very bad job.*

why and *because* **Why** asks for a reason. *Because* **gives** a reason.

>*'**Why** are you laughing?' '**Because** John has just said something very funny.'*

answer key

page 2

1 1 were 2 is 3 are; was 4 will be 5 was
6 were; was 7 will be 8 am 9 was
10 was; were 11 are / will be 12 are

2 1 Will you be here tomorrow?
2 Was Anne's father a teacher?
3 We are not ready.
4 When was your birthday?
5 Those chocolates were not very good.
6 Mary will not be at home next week.
7 Was the train late this morning?
8 I am not ready for the exam.
9 Are my gloves in the car?
10 My brother and I were not happy at school.
11 Is there a telephone in the kitchen?
12 There will not be a lesson tomorrow.

3 1 We don't have a car.
2 Do they have any children?
3 Does James have a cold?
4 My mother doesn't have a cat.
5 Does Cindy have any brothers or sisters?
6 I don't have enough work.
7 Does John have a girlfriend?
8 Why do you have two bicycles?
9 This house doesn't have a garden.
10 Do you and Alan have an evening free next
week?

page 3

4 1 Has she got a brother?
2 She hasn't got a car.
3 She's got three dogs.
4 She hasn't got a lot of money.
5 Has she got long hair?
6 She hasn't got any sisters.
7 Has she got a nice flat?
8 She's got a good job.
9 She's got problems with her family.
10 She hasn't got much free time.

5 1 We're all here.
2 They're tired.
3 I'm ready.
4 My name's Mike.
5 You're very kind.
6 Nina's got a headache.
7 I don't have a car.

8 They're not / They aren't ready.
9 I'm not well.
10 You're not / You aren't very polite.
11 What's your name?
12 What's the dog got in its mouth?
13 Where's the station?
14 I didn't have a good time at school.
15 The house doesn't have central heating.
16 There's not / There isn't much cheese in the
fridge.

6 1 ✗ 2 ✗ 3 ✓ 4 ✗ 5 ✗ 6 ✓ 7 ✗ 8 ✗
9 ✗ 10 ✓

7 1 Are 2 has 3 is 4 am 5 have 6 is
7 Are 8 are 9 are 10 has

page 4

1 1 There is 2 There were 3 there was
4 there will be 5 There is 6 Are there
7 There have been 8 There aren't
9 There has been 10 there isn't / there won't be
11 there are 12 Was there
13 There is (going) to be 14 there aren't
15 have there been 16 there is
17 There won't be 18 There have (never) been
19 Is there (going) to be 20 has there been

page 5

1 1 K 2 I 3 C 4 J 5 H 6 E 7 D 8 F
9 B 10 A

2 1 There's 2 There's 3 It's 4 It's
5 There's; It's 6 There's 7 It's 8 There's
9 It's 10 There's

page 6

1 1 got 2 Has 3 got 4 have 5 Did (you)
have 6 haven't 7 have (you) got OR Do (you)
have 8 haven't got OR don't have 9 Have
(you) got OR Do (you) have 10 haven't got OR
don't have

In these answers, we usually give **either** contracted forms (for example *I'm, don't*)
or full forms (for example *I am, do not*). Normally both are correct.

ANSWER KEY **329**

2 *(possible answers)*
1 If you're bald, you haven't got any hair.
2 If you're penniless, you haven't got any money.
3 If you're childless, you haven't got any children.
4 If you're unemployed, you haven't got a job.
5 If you're toothless, you haven't got any teeth.
6 If you're lonely, you haven't got any friends.
7 If you're starving, you haven't got any food.
8 If you're an orphan, you haven't got any parents.
9 If you're unmarried, you haven't got a wife or husband.
(Other answers are possible.)

page 7

3
1 Have you got; I've got; I've got; I haven't got
2 have you got?
3 've got; it's got
4 I've got
5 have you got; I've got
6 Have I got; you've got
7 's got; he's got; he's got
8 Have you got; he's got
9 've got; 's got
10 have you got

4
1 We don't have a TV.
2 Have you got a dog?
3 Bill hasn't got a job any more.
4 My mother doesn't have time for a holiday.
5 Luke hasn't got any friends.
6 I don't have a very good temper.
7 Why do you have that funny hat on?
8 Have we got a meeting this evening?
9 Does anybody have a map of the town?
10 Do you have time to look at something?

page 8

3
1 have exams   2 has a service   3 have terrible headaches   4 have (those) bad dreams
5 have meetings   6 have a medical check-up
7 have long holidays   8 have difficulty

page 9

1
1 (You can) have a shower.
2 (You can) have a swim.
3 (You can) have dinner.
4 (You can) have a game of cards.
5 (You can) have a game of tennis.
6 (You can) have a drink.
7 (You can) have a rest.
8 (You can) have coffee.
9 (You can) have a shave.

2
1 She's going to have a baby.
2 They're going to have a fight.
3 He's going to have an operation.
4 She's going to have a nervous breakdown.
5 He's going to have an accident.

page 10

4
1 Rule B is correct.

page 11

5 *(possible answers)*
The woman in advertisement 2 is natural. She is 37. She is intelligent and fun-loving. She is tall. She has got brown hair, blue eyes and a good sense of humour.
The woman in advertisement 3 is attractive. She is black. She is slim. She is 5ft 6 in. She has got a nice smile.
The man in advertisement 4 is successful. He is attractive. He is tanned. He has got a nice home and a yacht.
(Other answers are possible.)

6
I've always got a moment.
Have you got a problem?
I've got a small problem.
I've got a question.
Have you got a dog?
I've got three.
I've got a garden.
I've got no flowers.
I've got no idea what you're talking about.
I've got a gun.
I've got work to do.

7
1 There is a large living room.
2 There is a small study.
3 There is a downstairs cloakroom.
4 There are two bathrooms.
5 There are four bedrooms.
6 There is gas central heating.
7 There is a double garage.
8 There is a large garden.

page 12

1
1 There's   2 There's   3 There's   4 It's
5 There's   6 There's; It's   7 There's
8 It's   9 It's   10 It's

2 1 There seems to be a problem.
2 There is too much salt in the soup.
3 There is likely to be snow tomorrow.
4 I don't want there to be any trouble.
5 Were there any letters for me?
6 There is something wrong with the car.
7 There was a woman singing on the bus.
8 There is no need to shout.
9 There must be somebody at home.
10 Will there be an exam next week?

3 1 Yes. 2 Yes. 3 No. 4 Yes. 5 No.
6 Yes. 7 No. 8 Yes. 9 Yes. 10 Yes.
11 Yes. 12 No 13 No. 14 Yes. 15 Yes.

4 1 ✗ 2 ✓ 3 ✗ 4 ✗ 5 ✓ 6 ✓
7 ✗ 8 ✗ 9 ✓ 10 ✓

page 14

1 1 PP 2 SP 3 PP 4 SP 5 SP 6 PP 7 PP

2 1 He often reads poems, but now he is reading an autobiography.
2 She often reads comics, but now she is reading a grammar.
3 He often reads short stories, but now he is reading a cookery book.
4 I often read biographies, but now I am reading a newspaper.
5 They often read newspapers, but now they are reading a notice.
6 He often reads magazines, but now he is reading poems.

page 15

3 1 read; make   2 'm making   3 do you speak
4 're doing   5 plays   6 's playing
7 's she playing   8 Does she play   9 plays
10 's playing   11 's cooking   12 shop; cooks
13 doesn't work   14 isn't working

4 1 think   2 are you looking   3 Do you know
4 don't understand   5 are you driving
6 do you mean   7 hate   8 Are you talking
9 don't remember   10 is raining

6 am standing

page 16

1 1 A 2 A 3 C 4 B 5 B

2 boxes, brushes, buys, completes, cries, defends,
excites, expects, fries, guesses, looks, prays,
reaches, rushes, spends, wants, watches

3

	Just add -ing	Double the last letter and add -ing	Change the end to y and add -ing	Drop the end and add -ing
most verbs	✓			
verbs ending in -e				✓
verbs ending in -ie			✓	
short verbs ending in one vowel and one consonant		✓		

4 1 breaking, cleaning, coming, dying, dreaming,
enjoying, feeling, getting, going, hitting,
jumping, living, making, playing, putting,
robbing, shopping, shouting, sitting, slimming,
standing, turning, washing, writing

5 answering, preferring, opening, galloping,
upsetting, visiting

page 17

1 *(possible answers)*
1 Milk is getting more expensive
2 Newspapers are getting more expensive.
3 Haircuts are getting cheaper.
(Other answers are possible.)

page 18

1 The police station.

2 *(possible answer)*
When you come out of the station you turn left.
Then you take the first right and keep straight on
till you come to a T-junction. You turn right, and
then take the first left.
(Other answers are possible.)

page 19

4 *(possible answer)*
You put water in a saucepan. Then you put it on
the cooker. When the water boils you put the egg
in. You wait for four and a half minutes and then
you take it out.
(Other answers are possible.)

In these answers, we usually give **either** contracted forms (for example *I'm, don't*)
or full forms (for example *I am, do not*). Normally both are correct.

ANSWER KEY **331**

6 1 A woman is sitting in a railway carriage when she notices that the man opposite her is holding an orange in his hand and looking out of the window.

2 Suddenly the man opens the window, throws out the orange and closes the window again.

3 'Excuse me,' the woman asks, 'but why did you do that?'

4 'Because we are going through the mountains. Oranges keep the elephants away.'

5 'But there are no elephants in these mountains,' says the woman.

6 'You see,' says the man. 'It works.'

page 20

1 1 believe/know
2 Do (you) like/prefer/hate
3 needs/wants
4 need/want
5 believe/know; know/like/remember/understand
6 forget/know
7 hates/loves/likes/understands; hate/love/like/understand
8 prefer
9 remember/forget
10 does ('explicate') mean
11 seem
12 know/understand; wants/needs
13 Do (you) know/remember
14 know/remember
15 need/want

2 1 belongs   2 suppose   3 owns   4 matter
5 contains   6 depends   7 realise   8 mind
9 suppose   10 agree

page 21

4 1 are seeing   2 think   3 is (that woman) looking   4 do (not) have / have (not) got
5 looks   6 see   7 are (you) thinking
8 feel / am feeling   9 is having   10 feel

page 22

1 1 I watch   2 Correct.   3 I don't know
4 is getting   5 goes; asks; says   6 Correct.
7 Correct.   8 Correct.   9 I don't understand
10 Correct.

2 writes, works, replies, answering, tries, forgetting, making, wishes, beginning, looking, completing, getting, teaches, enjoys, hoping

3 1 is going down   2 is increasing   3 are getting
4 is getting   5 is continuing   6 are continuing
7 is becoming less common.

page 23

4 1 doesn't matter.   2 don't remember
3 don't remember/recognise   4 don't believe
5 don't mind   6 don't agree.

5 1 I don't understand.   2 I hope so.   3 It doesn't matter.   4 It depends.   5 I don't remember.
6 I think so.   7 I don't agree.   8 I don't mind.

7 is (your English) getting on; is getting

page 24

1 answers, answering; begins, beginning; breaks, breaking; buys, buying; catches, catching; completes, completing; cooks, cooking; eats, eating; enjoys, enjoying; fetches, fetching; fixes, fixing; forgets, forgetting; frys, frying; gallops, galloping; happens, happening; hopes, hoping; makes, making; misses, missing; offers, offering; opens, opening; parks, parking; pays, paying; pushes, pushing; says, saying; shops, shopping; sits, sitting; sleeps, sleeping; starts, starting; teaches, teaching; tries, trying; waits, waiting; washes, washing

2 1 don't eat   2 is coming   3 goes   4 play
5 's sitting   6 happens   7 drinks
8 She's wearing   9 are you looking
10 'm staying   11 usually stay   12 runs
13 are you doing   14 gets   15 fly

3 1 think   2 know; mean   3 looks like
4 feel; are making   5 is melting; take; break
6 am thinking   7 believe; is changing
8 don't see   9 are you looking   10 understand
11 is getting   12 are going up
13 doesn't matter   14 depends   15 are seeing

page 26

1 1 She is going to have a baby.
2 He is going to get on a/the bus.
3 She is going to open/read a letter.
4 She is going to drink (a cup of) coffee.
5 he is going to open a bottle.
6 The cat / It is going to catch a mouse.
7 The children / The boys / They are going to fight.

2 1 going to try; going to spend
2 going to do; going to spend; going to start
3 going to do; going to be; going to work; going to stay
4 going to decorate; going to spend; going to start

page 27

1
1. She's playing tennis on Sunday morning.
2. Matthew is coming to see her on Sunday afternoon.
3. She's having lunch with James at 12.30 on Wednesday.
4. She's flying to Amsterdam on Thursday.
5. She's meeting Mrs Parsons in the Oxford office.
6. She's going to the meeting with Mrs Parsons by train.
7. She's going to a funeral on Wednesday morning.
8. She's meeting the accountants at 4 p.m. on Monday.
9. She's going to the theatre on Friday evening.
10. She's spending Saturday at the races.

page 28

1
1. Tomorrow will be mainly dry, but there will be some rain in the north. There will be strong winds from the south-west later in the day. It will be quite warm in the south, but Scotland will be cold, and in the north of Scotland the rain will turn to snow during the afternoon.

3
1. I think / don't think it will snow tomorrow.
2. I think / don't think I will get a letter from America tomorrow.
3. I think / don't think I will be rich in ten years.
4. I think / don't think I will be famous in ten years.
5. I think / don't think people will speak English everywhere in the year 2100.

page 29

1
1. 'll wash 2 'll go 3 won't tell 4 won't eat.
5. 'll answer 6 'll tell 7 'll write 8 won't come
9. 'll call 10 'll send

2
1. Will you deliver the furniture on Friday?
2. Will you send the bill to the office?
3. Will you stop shouting?
4. Will you lock all the doors?
5. Will you put the meat in the oven?

3
1. Would you switch the lights on?
2. Would you open a window?
3. Would you buy some bread?
4. Would you phone for a taxi?
5. Would you wake me up at 8.00?

page 30

1
1. Jack is arriving at 4.00.
2. I'm flying to Glasgow tomorrow.
3. We're spending next week in Ireland.

2
1. will 2 will 3 is going to 4 will
5. 's going to

3
1. I'll 2 I'll 3 I'm going to 4 I'll 5 I'll

page 31

1
1. does 2 are going 3 will stop 4 are
5. have 6 doesn't 7 will come
8. am playing 9 does 10 will post

2
1. How do I start the car?
2. Where do I put my coat?
3. Who do I write to?
4. Where do I go for the interview?
5. When do I apply?
6. How do I make spaghetti bolognese?
7. When do I start?
8. Who do I ask?
9. How much do I give the driver?
10. Where do I sign?

page 32

1
1. At 8.30 he'll be driving to work.
2. At 9.05 he'll be teaching maths.
3. At 10.15 he'll be correcting papers.
4. At 10.30 he'll be having coffee.
5. At 11.15 he'll be teaching French.
6. At 2.15 he'll be training the football team.
7. At 4.00 he'll be having a shower.
8. At 6.00 he'll be cooking supper.
9. At 7.30 he'll be watching TV.

2
1. What time will you be getting up?
2. What will you be wearing?
3. How will you be travelling to work?
4. How soon will you be leaving?
5. Will you be taking the car?
6. Will you be having lunch out?
7. What time will you be coming back?
8. Where will you be sleeping?
9. How will you be paying?
10. When will you be going back home?

page 33

1 *(Examples of possible answers)*
After arriving at the airport, the President is to inspect a guard of honour.
At 9.00 the President is to have a working breakfast with President Jensen.
From 11.00 to 13.00 the President is to make a tour of Star City and meet the mayor and civic leaders.
At 13.00 the President is to have lunch with Foreign Minister Svendsen and his guests.
From 14.00 to 16.00 the President is to visit inner city schools and open a new eye hospital.

In these answers, we usually give **either** contracted forms (for example *I'm, don't*) **or** full forms (for example *I am, do not*). Normally both are correct.

At 16.00 the President is to meet business leaders. From 20.00 to 23.00 the President is to attend a State Dinner as the guest of President and Mrs Jensen.

2 *(possible answers)*
1 You're to do your piano practice.
2 You're not to give chocolate to the cat.
3 You're to go to bed by ten o'clock.
4 You're not to leave dirty socks on the floor.
5 You're not to leave empty crisp packets lying around.
6 You're not to make hour-long phone calls.
7 You're to make your own bed.
8 You're not to open the door to strangers.
9 You're to polish your shoes.
(Other answers are possible)

page 34

1 1 would be married. 2 was to regret
3 was going to ring 4 was leaving
5 would spend 6 was to change
7 was going to say 8 would be terrible
9 was catching 10 was going to happen.

2 1 were going to do 2 was going 3 was going to be 4 was joining 5 was to report
6 was to get 7 was going to do something
8 would come back 9 was starting 10 was to
11 would become well known 12 would marry
13 would sometimes envy 14 was going to stay

page 35

1 1 will have left home 2 will have finished
3 will have saved 4 will have driven
5 will have won

3 1 She will have written 100 pages.
2 She will have written (about) 300 pages.
3 She will have written 3,650 pages.
4 She will have written (about) 36,500 pages.
5 She will have finished her first book in a month.
6 She will have written 12 books.
7 She will have been writing for ten years.
8 She will have made $12,000,000.

page 36

1 *(possible answers)*
1 I promise I'll write.
2 I promise I won't smoke.
3 I promise I'll go to church.
4 I promise I won't stay out late / stay late at parties.
5 I promise I won't drink.
6 I promise I'll study hard.
7 I promise I'll go to lectures.
8 I promise I won't fight.

9 I promise I'll do exercises / go to the gym / keep fit.
10 I promise I'll get up early.
11 I promise I'll wash my clothes.
12 I promise I'll think of you.
(Other answers are possible.)

2 1 She is going to switch off the radio.
2 She is going to turn up the radio.
3 She is going to turn down the radio,
4 She is going to switch on the TV.
5 She is going to switch off the TV.
6 She is going to turn on the tap.
7 She is going to turn off the tap.
8 She is going to plug in the iron.
9 She is going to unplug the iron.
10 She is going to plug in the hair-dryer.
11 She is going to unplug the hair-dryer.

page 37

3 1 ✓ 2 ✓ 3 ✗ 4 ✗ 5 ✓ 6 ✓ 7 ✗

4 1 It's going to rain 2 it will snow
3 is going to have 4 will have 5 I'm playing
6 He'll win 7 She'll tell 8 won't start
9 will have 10 She's getting married

5 1 will be walking 2 will have finished
3 are to go 4 will have been studying
5 were going to get 6 will be visiting
7 was going to rain 8 would not pay
9 Will you be going out 10 will have arrived

page 38

1 1 is going to have 2 Correct. 3 I'll pay
4 Correct. 5 I'm going 6 I'll find
7 it'll rain / it's going to rain 8 You'll fall
9 Correct. 10 Correct.

2 1 I 2 C 3 G 4 K 5 F 6 J 7 H
8 B 9 E 10 A

3 1 will be thinking 2 will have been working
3 are to tidy 4 will have saved 5 was going to 6 is to open 7 wouldn't enjoy 8 would go 9 will you be getting 10 will have finished

page 40

1

to make regular simple past forms	Add -ed	Just add -d	Double the last letter and add -ed	Change the -y to -i and add -ed
most verbs	✓			
verbs ending in -e		✓		
verbs ending in vowel + -y (-ay, -oy)	✓			
verbs ending in consonant + -y				✓
short verbs ending in one vowel and one consonant			✓	

2 annoyed, arrived, carried, changed, cooked, cried, fitted, hated, hurried, jumped, lived, passed, prayed, rained, robbed, shaved, shopped, shouted, slimmed, slipped, started, stayed, studied, turned, walked, watched

3 visited, regretted, developed, galloped, opened, answered, referred

4 became, began, broke, brought, caught, came, drank, ate, fell, felt, forgot, got, gave, heard, held, kept, knew, learnt, left, let, made, paid, put, read, said, shut, sat, spoke, stood, took, told, thought, wrote.

page 41

1 1 were all talking 2 lived 3 was coming; was shopping 4 met; was travelling 5 was talking; walked; stole 6 came; stopped 7 looked; saw; were flying 8 woke; was pouring 9 broke; was playing

2 *(possible answers)*
1 Fred was frying fish in Folkestone.
2 Harry was having a haircut in Hamburg.
3 Barbara was buying books in Birmingham.
4 Steve was stealing socks in a supermarket.
5 Ruth was riding racehorses in Rome.
6 Pete was playing poker in Paris.
(Other answers are possible.)

page 42

1 1 was shopping 2 stopped 3 said
4 were talking 5 broke 6 was working
7 sat down 8 took 9 was carrying

2 1 was standing 2 went 3 took
4 was dancing 5 played 6 was getting
7 worked 8 got 9 went 10 was going

page 43

1 1 How many days did you intend to stay?
2 Could you give me a hand?
3 We could ask Peter to help us.
4 I thought it would be a good idea to invite Simon.
5 I wondered if you needed any help.
6 We hoped you would stay for dinner.
7 Were you planning to be here next week?
8 Did you want to pay now?
9 Would you tell Annie to come to my office?
10 It might be a good idea to apologise.

2 1 were wondering; had 2 Were
3 was wondering; could 4 were thinking; was
5 was hoping; didn't

page 44

1 1 Mrs Allen told the police that she was feeding pigeons, but actually she was robbing a bank.
2 Bill told the police that he was playing chess, but actually he was burgling a house.
3 Pete told the police that he was singing, but actually he was shoplifting.
4 Mrs Oliver told the police that she was painting, but actually she was poisoning her husband.
5 Miss Fry told the police that she was studying French, but actually she was forging banknotes.
6 Jim told the police that he was fishing, but actually he was selling stolen property.
7 Mr Lucas told the police that he was praying, but actually he was holding up a security van.

page 45

2 1 got; was repairing 2 looked 3 played
4 came 5 smoked 6 understood
7 was flying 8 protected; went
9 found; was sitting 10 wrote
11 didn't like; were playing; walked

3 1 were hoping; could 2 wondered; felt
3 thought; would 4 were 5 Would
6 might; drove 7 were wondering 8 Were

4 1 were throwing 2 were dancing
3 were/was not dancing 4 was grinning
5 was holding 6 came 7 ordered 8 asked

page 46

1 agreed, answered, arrived, became, began, believed, carried, developed, dropped, enjoyed, fitted, galloped, hoped, left, opened, planned, preferred, regretted, replied, robbed, seemed, slept, slimmed, slipped, started, stayed, stopped, studied, visited, wrote.

2 D.

In these answers, we usually give **either** contracted forms (for example *I'm, don't*) **or** full forms (for example *I am, do not*). Normally both are correct.

ANSWER KEY **335**

3 1 was having   2 was sailing   3 knew
   4 Correct.   5 Correct.   6 learnt   7 had
   8 Correct.   9 saw   10 Correct.   11 Correct.
   12 Correct.   13 smoked   14 lived
   15 stopped; was carrying

4 1 thought / was thinking; was   2 wondered /
   was wondering; could   3 Were   4 Did
   5 wondered / was wondering; had

page 48

1 begun, broken, brought, bought, come, drunk,
   eaten, fallen, forgotten, given, heard, held, kept,
   known, learnt, left, let, made, paid, put, read, said,
   shut, sat, stood, taken, told, thought, written

2 *(possible answers)*
   1 The Foreign Minister is dead.
   2 Lucy has (got) a baby.
   3 Your coat is torn.
   4 My leg is broken.
   5 He can't find his address book. / His address
     book is lost.
   6 Is there tea?
   7 The washing up is done.
   8 She's working for the BBC.
   9 We don't know where he is.
   10 The noise isn't going on. / There isn't any noise.
   11 I don't/can't remember your name.
   12 She knows/speaks French.
   (Other answers are possible.)

page 49

1 1 PROBABLY NOT   2 YES   3 YES   4 YES
   5 DON'T KNOW   6 YES   7 NO   8 NO / PROBABLY NOT
   9 DON'T KNOW   10 NO

2 1 've told   2 've forgotten   3 've made
   4 've bought   5 left   6 has lost
   7 never reached   8 got   9 studied   10 built

page 50

1 1 two days ago, last month, then, yesterday,
     when?, in 2007, before I was born, just after I
     got up, when I was nine

2 1 ✗   2 ✓   3 ✗   4 ✗   5 ✗   6 ✗   7 ✗   8 ✓
   9 ✓   10 ✗

3 1 Have you seen Carol today?
   2 Has Simon come back from Spain yet?
   3 Has the baby had anything to eat?
   4 I haven't played tennis this year.
   5 Has Alex spoken to you lately?
   6 Rob has never written to me.
   7 Have you ever lost your passport?
   8 My mother has never travelled by air.

   9 Have you ever written a love letter?
   10 I have never seen an iceberg.

4 1 haven't seen   2 've never seen   3 've done
   4 left   5 did you get   6 haven't finished
   7 've often wondered   8 caught   9 read
   10 Have you seen

page 51

1 1 've already told   2 I've already read
   3 've already bought   4 has already found
   5 I've already sold

2 1 Have you had breakfast yet?
   2 Cheryl hasn't found a flat yet.
   3 Have you finished the painting yet?
   4 Has John phoned yet?
   5 Carole hasn't come back from holiday yet.
   6 The newspaper hasn't come yet.

page 52

1 1 B   2 A   3 B   4 A   5 B   6 A   7 B
   8 B   9 A   10 A

2 1 were   2 have not read   3 Have you visited
   4 lived   5 did not discover; knew   6 has lost
   7 gave   8 have you been
   9 have never enjoyed   10 Did you hear

page 53

3 1 have drunk eight   2 have written six
   3 have read five   4 has driven 40,000
   5 have lived (in) eight   6 has eaten twenty

4 1 have played   2 has had   3 ran
   4 have you made   5 came   6 wrote
   7 has written   8 cooked; have cooked
   9 have made   10 have lost

page 54

1 1 has eaten   2 has gone   3 have won
   4 has stolen   5 has come   6 has died

2 1 has married   2 has died   3 has delayed
   4 has left   5 has closed   6 have set fire
   7 has disappeared   8 has given
   9 has discovered   10 have arrested

page 55

1 1 has left; didn't like   2 have bought; found
   3 have sold; got   4 has found; did (he) find
   5 has gone; went; sent   6 has had; fell
   7 have heard; sent   8 have told; did (she) say
   9 have died; lost   10 have not arrived; took

2 1 Did he get good marks? 2 When did she go?
  3 When did he tell you? 4 Where did he stay?
  5 Why did he sell it? 6 How much did it cost?
  7 Where did he meet her? 8 Why did you stop?

page 56

1 1 has been raining 2 have been learning
  3 has been playing 4 have(n't) been living
  5 has been walking 6 have been working
  7 has been crying 8 has been playing
  9 Have (you) been waiting
  10 have been waiting

2 1 for 2 since 3 since 4 for 5 since
  6 since 7 for 8 for 9 since 10 since
  11 for 12 since

page 57

3 1 My father has been repairing his car for five
    days.
  2 We have been travelling for five hours.
  3 We have been waiting for the train since 7.30.
  4 Mr Andrews has been making violins for
    30 years.
  5 Prices have been going up fast since last year.
  6 I have been writing my great novel since January.
  7 The water has been rising for eight hours.
  8 The people next door have been playing loud
    music for five hours.
  9 I have been trying to explain things to her for
    an hour.
  10 The dog has been barking since six o'clock.

4 1 H 2 G 3 F 4 A 5 C 6 J 7 B 8 D
  9 I

page 58

1 1 been raining 2 broken 3 told
  4 been driving 5 read 6 been waiting
  7 been sitting 8 written 9 been learning
  10 learnt

2 1 been living 2 lived 3 worked
  4 been working 5 farmed 6 been farming
  7 been running 8 run 9 spent
  10 been spending

page 59

3 1 How long have you known Mike?
  2 How long have you been a student?
  3 How long has your brother been a doctor?
  4 How long has Andrew had that dog?
  5 How long have David and Elizabeth been
    together?
  6 How long has Mary had her job?

  7 How long have your parents been married?
  8 How long have you known about Carl's
    problem?

4 1 has been snowing 2 have had
  3 has been working 4 has been
  5 have you known 6 have been repairing
  7 have not been enjoying
  8 has been helping 9 have had 10 has been

page 61

1 1 had never seen; went
  2 understood; had got
  3 arrived; had already started
  4 didn't play; had hurt
  5 had looked; found
  6 didn't recognise; had grown
  7 told; had been
  8 was; had snowed
  9 hadn't made; refused
  10 had done; sat down; read

2 1 got; had washed 2 met; had worked
  3 had seen; was 4 had not checked; broke down
  5 had lent 6 did not know; had hidden
  7 did not travel 8 found; had forgotten
  9 came; had been 10 had already started;
  arrived

page 62

1 1 After he had tried on six pairs of shoes, he
    decided he liked the first ones best.
  2 When Mary had done all the shopping, she
    took a short walk round the park.
  3 After I had washed and dried the last plate, Paul
    came in and offered to help.
  4 He went to the café in the square for a cup of
    coffee after he had said goodbye to the visitors.
  5 I started on the dark chocolate when I had
    eaten all the milk chocolate.
  6 When Peter had done his karate training, he
    phoned his mother.
  7 Mike had a long hot shower after he had been
    for a run.
  8 Sandra went to bed after she had phoned the
    office to say she was ill.

2 1 had not been 2 arrived 3 decided
  4 spent 5 had had 6 saw 7 had shared
  8 had lost 9 had not seen 10 called
  11 looked 12 turned 13 realised 14 had
  15 saw 16 went 17 explained 18 had got
  19 was not 20 felt 21 had not passed
  22 had said 23 had arrived 24 had
  25 thought 26 had 27 got 28 began
  29 had happened

In these answers, we usually give **either** contracted forms (for example *I'm, don't*)
or full forms (for example *I am, do not*). Normally both are correct.

page 63

1 1 had been repairing   2 had been working
3 had been lying   4 had been driving

2 1 Kate, because she had been gardening.
2 Stephanie, because she had been playing tennis.
3 Robert, because he had been practising karate.
4 Rebecca, because she had been horse-riding.
5 Philip, because he had been painting (the ceiling in his room).
6 Roger, because he had been swimming.

page 64

1 1 have seen   2 have sung   3 had made
4 had had   5 had (ever) seen   6 have drunk
7 had been   8 have eaten   9 have said
10 have bought

2 1 It was the first time he had worn a uniform.
2 It was the first time he had had to make his own bed.
3 It was the first time he had cleaned his own boots.
4 It was the first time he had fired a gun.
5 It was the first time he had walked more than a mile.

page 65

1 Peter has just offered me a new job. He said I was just the person he needed.
Ana Gomez, of Peru, has set a new record for the marathon. She covered the 42 km in just over 2 hours and 11 minutes.
Novelist Maria Santiago has married actor Tony Delaney. They met while working on the screenplay for the film *Sun in the Morning*.
Police have found missing schoolgirl Karen Allen. She was at a friend's house in Birmingham.
The World Cup team have arrived home. Five thousand fans were at the airport.
Two prisoners have escaped from Caernarvon high security prison. They stole dustmen's uniforms and walked out through the main gate.
Three climbers have died in the Alps. They fell just before reaching the summit of Mont Blanc (4,807m).

2 1 He has been playing ice hockey.
2 He has been playing chess.
3 He has been playing darts.
4 He has been playing polo.
5 She has been playing poker.

page 66

4 1 have known   2 have been   3 ago
4 came   5 has been doing   6 have opened
7 have just asked   8 hasn't decided
9 has never lived   10 bought   11 talked

5 1 came   2 didn't like   3 told   4 've been lying
5 've never been   6 's been raining   7 didn't come   8 ('ve) paid   9 got   10 have left
11 has moved   12 died   13 's been   14 was
15 's gone   16 've been   17 for
18 's always been   19 has left   20 wasn't
21 haven't trusted   22 broke   23 said
24 was   25 hasn't been   26 have taken

page 67

6 1 F 2 F 3 T 4 F 5 T

7 1 he had lost his glasses.
2 he had lost his/the ticket.
3 he had lost his money.
4 he had lost the address.
5 he had lost his/the key.
6 he had lost his appetite.
7 he had lost his memory.

8 1 Rule 3.

9 has gone (Present-tense sentence: He is dead.)
have you done?

page 68

1 1 I spent three days in hospital last month.
2 … She has had bad luck all her life.
3 I wanted to be a doctor until I was fifteen.
4 He has been unemployed ever since he left school.
5 How long have you lived / been living in this town?
6 I didn't learn much in my last job.
7 I didn't work very hard when I was at university.
8 Joe lived in Durban for a year before he got married.
9 He was ill before Christmas, but he has been fine since then.
10 I have had trouble sleeping all this week.
11 I had trouble sleeping all last week.
12 I have learnt a lot in this job.
13 My boyfriend and I have known each other for ages.
14 When I saw her, I knew that we had met before.
15 I felt very tired this morning, but I'm OK now.

2 1 After I had written to my boyfriend, I watched television for an hour or so.
2 After everybody had had a chance to say what they thought, we took a vote.
3 After I had posted the letter, I felt much better about everything.
4 After she had stopped trying to lose weight, she looked much healthier.
5 After he had bought presents for everyone in his family, he bought something for himself as well.

page 69

3 1 started   2 spoken   3 hoping
4 have known   5 have come   6 wrote
7 had lost   8 I've been studying
9 had been   10 drunk   11 did you leave
12 for years   13 I had a headache
14 I'd finished   15 had forgotten

4 1 Yes.   2 No.   3 No.   4 No.   5 Yes.   6 No.
7 Yes, she is.   8 Yes.   9 No.   10 Yes.   11 No.
12 Yes.

5 1 haven't heard   2 had received   3 have had
4 have been trying   5 for   6 saw
7 had just come back   8 had been/gone
9 lost   10 were fishing

page 70

1 1 has crashed; hit; had put
2 turned; went; had forgotten
3 have been doing; have cleaned
4 was lying; rang
5 started; had not been/gone
6 have been playing
7 got; was watching
8 have not seen
9 have you been learning
10 has changed; came
11 have you seen; have seen
12 have never seen
13 got
14 have often wondered; met
15 Have you read
16 have just discovered
17 Did you hear
18 has been
19 was talking; started; broke
20 had done
21 has been standing
22 has stood
23 got; have spent/ have been spending
24 was; played
25 had finished; sat
26 met; had been working
27 have never learnt
28 Have you finished

29 lived; was
30 has had

page 72

1 1 The infinitive without *to*.   2 *ought*   3 no -*s*
4 no *do*

2 1 play   2 to be   3 to do   4 go   5 leave
6 to get   7 make   8 pass   9 to phone
10 to move

3 1 Can I stay here?   2 Must you go?
3 May we sit down?   4 Can she drive?
5 Could she do it?   6 Would you like to?
7 Should he pay now?   8 Must I change here?

page 73

4 1 be able to   2 have to   3 to have to
4 been able to   5 to be able to   6 been able to
7 to have to   8 had to   9 been allowed to
10 be able to

6 1 Can   2 must   3 might   4 ought
5 couldn't   6 must   7 Can   8 may   9 can't
10 must

7 be able to

page 74

1 1 should   2 must   3 should   4 must
5 must   6 should   7 must   8 must
9 should   10 should

3 1 Should I move to London?
2 How long should I wait?
3 What should I do at the weekend?
4 Where should I park?
5 When should I pay the tax bill?
6 Should I take a taxi?

page 75

1 1 must   2 has to   3 must   4 must
5 have to   6 have got to   7 have to
8 must   9 must   10 have got to

2 1 must take more exercise.
2 must phone him.
3 has (got) to pay income tax.
4 have (got) to hold a general election
5 must give my love
6 has (got) to work
7 must do some shopping.
8 must get a haircut.
9 have got to pay.
10 must try to get

1 1 must not   2 do not have to   3 must not
4 must not   5 do not have to   6 must not
7 don't have to   8 don't have to   9 mustn't
10 don't have to   11 mustn't   12 don't have to
13 mustn't   14 don't have to   15 mustn't

2 1 In rugby you mustn't pass the ball forwards.
2 In tennis you needn't hit the ball before it bounces.
3 In chess you needn't move fast.
4 In boxing you mustn't hit your opponent below the belt.
5 In a 100m race you mustn't start before the gun.
6 In hockey you mustn't lift the stick above your shoulder.
7 In golf you needn't run from one hole to the next.
8 In soccer you mustn't touch the ball with your hands.
9 In bridge you mustn't look at other people's cards.

1 1 A 'd better not drink   2 F 'd better not sit
3 C 'd better phone   4 E 'd better go
5 D 'd better stop   6 K 'd better remember
7 J 'd better see   8 I 'd better give
9 H 'd better do   10 G 'd better invite

2 1 'd better   2 should   3 'd better   4 should
5 'd better   6 should   7 'd better   8 should
9 'd better   10 'd better

1 1 are supposed to cure headaches.
2 are supposed to go to church
3 supposed to phone
4 was supposed to have
5 supposed to do
6 were supposed to come
7 supposed to go
8 are supposed to be
9 are supposed to pay for
10 supposed to smoke

3 1 It's supposed to be a house.
2 It's supposed to be an aeroplane.
3 It's supposed to be a horse.
4 It's supposed to be a fire engine.
5 It's supposed to be a tiger.
6 It's supposed to be the sun.

1 1 He must want something.
2 She must be French.
3 He must read a lot.
4 That must be interesting.
5 He must have very big feet.
6 You must know Paul Baker.
7 She must have a problem.
8 You must be crazy.
9 They must be rich.
10 He must have another woman.

2 1 He can't be American.
2 He can't be a teacher.
3 She can't have many friends.
4 We can't need petrol.
5 He can't be hungry.
6 The film can't be very good.
7 You can't be serious!
8 You can't want another pair.
9 She can't have six children.
10 You can't like that rubbish.

1 1 It may not snow.
2 may get a dog.
3 Joe may not be well.
4 Ruth may need money.
5 The baby may be sleepy.
6 I may not move house.
7 She may be unhappy.
8 He may not like you.
9 She may not be ready.
10 I may not pay.

2 1 may/might not   2 may/might not
3 may/might not   4 can't   5 can't
6 may/might not   7 can't   8 may/might not
9 may/might not   10 can't

1 1 May I leave early?
2 Could I use your phone?
3 May I stop work now?
4 Could I pay you tomorrow?
5 Could I speak to Jane?
6 Can I have a beer?
7 May I hang up your coat?
8 Can I do your shopping?

2 1 Students may not use this lift.
2 You may have these tickets.
3 Nobody can ride my horse.
4 You can't come into my room.
5 Employees may not make personal phone calls.

3 1 Can you translate this letter for me?
    2 Could you feed the dogs?
    3 Can you tell me when it's time to go?
    4 Could you watch my luggage for a minute?
    5 Can you switch on the TV?

page 82

1 1 Where shall I put the coats?
    2 When shall I pay you?
    3 Shall I lock the door?
    4 What time shall I come tomorrow?
    5 Shall I go now?
    6 Shall I clean the windows?
    7 How many potatoes shall I buy?
    8 When shall I come for the next lesson?
    9 What shall I buy for lunch?
   10 Shall I get your coat?

2 1 Shall we go to France or Scotland?
    2 Shall we go to the seaside or the mountains?
    3 When shall we go?
    4 How long shall we go for?
    5 Shall we fly, or go by train, or drive?
    6 Shall we stay in one place or travel around?
    7 Shall we stay in a hotel or camp?
    8 What shall we do with the dogs?
    9 Shall we take Granny?
   10 Shall we go with the Jacksons?

page 83

1 1 can 2 can 3 will be able to 4 will be
able to 5 can 6 will be able to 7 can't; can
8 will be able to 9 won't be able to
10 will be able to 11 will be able to
12 will be able to; won't be able to

2 1 could 2 managed to 3 managed to
4 couldn't 5 managed to 6 could; could
7 managed to 8 managed to 9 could
10 managed to 11 couldn't 12 managed to

page 84

1 1 Anna used to have lots of boyfriends. Now she's
married.
    2 John used to study mathematics. Now he
studies physics.
    3 Mary used to climb mountains. Now she cycles.
    4 Joe used to be a builder. Now he's a driver.
    5 Gary used to work in Germany. Now he works
in England.
    6 Claire used to live in Scotland. Now she lives in
Ireland.
    7 I used to like meat. Now I prefer fish.
    8 We used to go to the cinema. Now we watch TV.

2 1 People used to travel by horse.
    2 People used to cook on wood fires.
    3 People didn't use to live so long.
    4 People used to fight with spears.
    5 People used to hunt with bows ands arrows.
    6 People used to believe in ghosts and devils.
    7 People didn't use to be able to vote.
    8 People used to think the earth was flat.
    9 People used to have bigger families.
   10 Children used to work.

page 85

1 1 will keep 2 will play 3 will talk
4 will listen 5 will land 6 will ring; will be
7 will tell 8 will drive

2 1 would swim 2 would skate 3 would take
4 would go 5 would find 6 would make
7 would go 8 would come 9 would exchange

3 1 A 2 C 3 B 4 H 5 E 6 F 7 D

page 86

1 1 should have locked 2 shouldn't have eaten
3 should have been 4 shouldn't have spent
5 should have put 6 shouldn't have gone
7 should have brought 8 shouldn't have played
9 should have arrived 10 should have brought

page 87

1 1 She may have broken her leg.
    2 I may have lost my keys.
    3 Alice may have gone back home.
    4 My great-grandfather may have been a soldier.
    5 I may have found a new job.
    6 This house may have been a school once.
    7 I may have made a mistake.
    8 We may have taken the wrong road.
    9 I may have caught a cold.
   10 Life may have begun on another planet.

2 1 She must have gone home.
    2 I must have left it on the bus.
    3 She must have forgotten.
    4 John must have taken it.
    5 Peter can't have been shopping.
    6 It must have rained in the night.
    7 She can't have got the job.
    8 Jenny must have posted them.
    9 I must have said the wrong thing.
   10 You can't have watered them.

3 1 must have been 2 had to get 3 had to learn
4 must have been 5 must have done
6 had to get up 7 had to go 8 had to call
9 had to show 10 must have heard it

In these answers, we usually give **either** contracted forms (for example *I'm, don't*)
or full forms (for example *I am, do not*). Normally both are correct.

ANSWER KEY **341**

1 1 could have married   2 could have lent
3 could have studied   4 could have won
5 could have been   6 could have hit
7 could have been   8 could have gone
9 could have phoned   10 could have got

2 1 He needn't have taken a Spanish dictionary.
2 He needn't have taken sunglasses.
3 He needn't have taken running shoes.
4 He needn't have taken a swimsuit.
5 He needn't have taken climbing equipment.
6 He needn't have taken a tennis racket.
7 He needn't have taken playing cards.
8 He needn't have taken books.
9 He needn't have taken his driving licence.
10 He needn't have taken an alarm clock.

3 *(possible answers)*
1 It can't be true.   2 It can't be true.
3 It may be true.   4 It can't be true.
5 It must be true.   6 It may be true.
7 It can't be true.   8 It can't be true.
9 It may be true.   10 It must be true.
(Other answers are possible)

4 1 Can you give me a receipt?
2 Can you bring me the menu?
3 Can you give me an estimate?
4 Can you give me your price list?
5 Can you bring me the bill?
6 Can I pay by credit card?
7 Can you explain this paragraph in the contract?
8 Can you send me your catalogue?

5 1 She must like chocolate.
2 She must speak Italian or English.
3 She must have long blonde/fair hair
4 She must/may have a lot / plenty of money.
5 She must play golf.
6 She must be interested in (Russian) history.
7 She must have a dog.
8 She must/may have children.
9 She may/must be a doctor.
10 may/must be a spy.

6 1 used to live   2 used to stand
3 used to look after   4 used to play.
5 used to take   6 used to look at
7 used to go   8 used to buy
9 used to keep   10 used to have

8 1 can't have gone   2 could have killed
3 may have gone   4 must have been
5 could have gone   6 should have been
7 should have taken   8 must have had
9 can't have got   10 may have been

9 1 A   2 C   3 C   4 B   5 B   6 B   7 A   8 C
9 B   10 B

1 1 I can't   2 to be able to   3 should work
4 tell   5 had to work   6 will be able to
7 do not have to do   8 can't be
9 ought to phone   10 managed to catch

2 1 C   2 A   3 C   4 B   5 A   6 B   7 B   8 A
9 A   10 B   11 B   12 C   13 B   14 B   15 C

3 1 should have phoned
2 shouldn't/needn't have put
3 could/should have asked
4 could have killed
5 should/may have finished
6 can't have forgotten
7 needn't have bought
8 may/must have gone
9 may not / can't have addressed
10 had to walk.

1

	PASSIVE
PRESENT PROGRESSIVE	is being made
FUTURE	will be made
SIMPLE PAST	was made
PAST PROGRESSIVE	was being made
PRESENT PERFECT	has been made
PAST PERFECT	had been made

2 1 is spoken   2 was built   3 will be opened
4 is being interviewed   5 was being watched.
6 has been invited   7 had been stolen.
8 are asked   9 was destroyed
10 will be examined

3 1 is being repaired   2 was being followed.
3 were being examined.   4 is being painted.
5 is being interviewed   6 is being done.
7 were being translated.   8 is being checked

4 1 has not been told.   2 had been lost.
3 had been agreed.   4 has been cancelled.
5 had been arrested.   6 has been hurt
7 has been found   8 had been eaten.

5 The expressions can be crossed out in sentences 2, 3, 5 and 6.

page 96

1
1 He wants to be remembered.
2 She wants to be respected.
3 They want to be elected.
4 She wants to be listened to.
5 He wants to be looked at.
6 She doesn't want to be forgotten.
7 He doesn't want to be talked about.
8 She doesn't want to be paid.

2
1 She can't be criticised.
2 This mustn't be folded.
3 This should be kept cool.
4 Ann ought to be told.
5 He may be invited.
6 This can't be sent through the post.
7 This should be opened immediately.
8 This mustn't be opened before Christmas.

page 97

1
1 We were brought papers to sign.
2 Henry was given a clock when he retired.
3 The children were read stories.
4 I'm owed £5,000.
5 I've been offered a new job.
6 We are taught French by Mrs Lee.
7 I've been lent a car for the week.
8 We were promised a full explanation.
9 I was told a lot of lies by the secretary.
10 I am often sent presents by my children.

2
1 All the passengers were given meal tickets.
2 Meal tickets were given to all the passengers.
3 The plans for the new building have been shown to Ellen.
4 Ellen has been shown the plans for the new building.
5 All the office workers have been promised a week's holiday.
6 A week's holiday has been promised to all the office workers.
7 A bill for the repairs was sent to Laura.
8 Laura was sent a bill for the repairs.
9 All the facts were not told to the police.
10 The police were not told all the facts.

page 98

1
1 read/talked to 2 talked/spoken about
3 spoken/talked to. 4 slept in. 5 sat in/on.
6 paid for. 7 heard of 8 played with. /
talked to. 9 looked at. / spoken to. / talked to.
10 shouted at.

2 *(possible answers)*
Who was electricity discovered by?
Who was the film *The Birds* directed by?
Who was the novel *Anna Karenina* written by?
Who was *Hamlet* written by?
Who was *Happy Birthday to You* composed by?
Who was penicillin discovered by?
Who was radio invented by?
Who was television invented by?
Who was the Eiffel Tower built by?
Who was the Taj Mahal built by?
Who was the Mona Lisa painted by?
Who was the planet Neptune discovered by?
Who was Antarctica discovered by?
Who was the film *Casablanca* directed by?

page 99

1
1 Polly's mother made this sweater.
This sweater was made by Polly's mother.
2 Carla paid the electricity bill last week.
The electricity bill was paid by Carla last week.
3 The first television was built by J. L. Baird in 1924.
J. L. Baird built the first television in 1924.

2 1 B 2 B 3 A 4 B 5 A

page 100

1 1 ✗ 2 ✓ 3 ✓ 4 ✗ 5 ✗ 6 ✗ 7 ✗ 8 ✓
9 ✗ 10 ✗

2 *(possible answers)*
The houseboats have been turned into floating restaurants.
The Super Cinema has been turned into a casino.
A new car park has been built.
New schools have been built.
The old fire station has been turned into a supermarket.
The opera house has been modernised.
A ring road has been built.
The station has been rebuilt.
Some streets have been widened.
A statue of you has been put up in the park.
The town centre has been turned into a pedestrian area.
Your house has been turned into a museum.
(Other answers are possible.)

3
1 be broken; be dropped 2 be heard
3 be handled 4 be trusted 5 be read
6 be eaten (or) drunk 7 be understood
8 be eaten 9 be found 10 be blown up

In these answers, we usually give **either** contracted forms (for example *I'm, don't*) or full forms (for example *I am, do not*). Normally both are correct.

ANSWER KEY **343**

5 1 had been told   2 had been given   3 was shown   4 was given   5 was given   6 had never been taught   7 was sent   8 was offered   9 was promised   10 wasn't being paid

6 1 was taken   2 was told   3 had been expected   4 will be carried out   5 will be fulfilled.   6 was brought   7 will be sacrificed   8 was brought   9 was attended   10 was given   11 was dressed   12 was played   13 was governed   14 will be sacrificed   15 was taken   16 were removed   17 was made   18 to be sacrificed.

1 1 French is taught in most schools in Britain.
2 I have a shower every morning.
3 The town hall is just being / has just been rebuilt.
4 I could see that the room hadn't been cleaned for months.
5 Our bread is freshly baked every day.
6 Our car was stolen last year.
7 Your car will be ready soon; it's being repaired now.
8 I've been given some beautiful flowers by my boyfriend.
9 These computers are made in Korea.
10 The work will be finished tomorrow.

2 1 be (listened) to   2 is (still) being   3 had   4 been   5 be   6 was   7 will (definitely) be   8 is spoken/taught/used   9 Have   10 be seen

3 1 A   2 B   3 B   4 A   5 B

1 1 Is she   2 does he think   3 see   4 can I sit   5 does the bus leave   6 Can you   7 does 'vast' mean   8 did you go   9 is she   10 must I do

2 1 Will Jane and her mother be staying in Ireland?
2 Do John and Susan want to play golf on Saturday?
3 Have the Sunday newspapers arrived?
4 Has the secretary from the accounts office telephoned?
5 What did the big man with the grey beard say?
6 When did Mrs Potter's two boys play football?
7 Why were the people who were sitting at the back of the bus singing?
8 Where has Sally planted all those flowers that she bought?

3 1 What size   2 What colour
3 What sort/kind/type of   4 What make/type of
5 What sort/kind/type of   6 What size/colour
7 What make of   8 What make of / size
9 What sort/kind/type of   10 What time

4 1 'What's the new teacher like?'
2 'How's your mother?'
3 'How's work going?'
4 'How's business?'
5 'What's Anne's boyfriend like?'
6 'How's school?'
7 'What's Manchester like?'
8 'How are things at home?'
9 'What's your village like?'
10 'What are the neighbours like?'

1 1 played   2 caused   3 came   4 helps
5 do you mean   6 told   7 happened   8 costs
9 suit   10 does the letter say

2 1 (a) What did Alice break?   (b) Who broke her arm?
2 (a) What did Paul find?   (b) Who found a necklace?
3 (a) What did the bomb destroy?   (b) What destroyed a school?
4 (a) Who lost the map?   (b) What did Fred lose?
5 (a) What does Julie teach?   (b) Who teaches Japanese?
6 (a) Who prefers classical music?   (b) What kind/sort/type of music does his wife prefer?
7 (a) How many people does room 6 hold?   (b) Which room holds 600 people?
8 (a) Whose baby keeps us awake at night?   (b) Who does her baby keep awake at night?
9 (a) Who can't wear red?   (b) What colour can't Sheila wear?
10 (a) Who caught the first train?   (b) Which train did Peter catch?

1 1 'What are you thinking about?'
2 'Who did you buy it from?'
3 'Who did she send it to?'
4 'What will you carry it in?'
5 'What can I eat it with?'
6 'What did she hit him with?'
7 'Who does your father work for?'
8 'Who did you make it for?'
9 'What's the book about?'
10 'Who were you talking to?'

2
1 'What are you waiting for?'
2 'What are you worried about?'
3 'What are you talking about?'
4 'Who do you want to speak to?'
5 'Who do you work for?'
6 'What are you looking at?'
7 'What are you looking for?'
8 'What are you interested in?'
9 'Who are you writing to?'
10 'What are you thinking about?'

3
1 'Who from?'   2 'Who for?'   3 'Where to?'
4 'Who with?'   5 'Who to?'   6 'What about?'
7 'Who with?'   8 'What for?'   9 'What with?'
10 'What with?'

page 108

1
1 Shakespeare wasn't French.
2 Austrians don't speak Japanese.
3 Roses aren't green.
4 Cats can't fly.
5 George Washington didn't live in Russia.
6 Fridges don't run on petrol.
7 The sun doesn't go round the earth.
8 Telescopes don't make things smaller.
9 There aren't seventeen players in a rugby team.
10 Bananas don't grow in Scotland.

2
1 I don't like your new glasses.
2 I understood nothing.
3 Nothing happened.
4 Sally doesn't like dancing.
5 Nobody wants to sing.
6 There's nowhere to sit down.
7 My mother never drives fast.
8 I hardly go out.
9 We'll never get there.
10 We won't get there.

page 109

3
1 no   2 not   3 no   4 not   5 no   6 not
7 not   8 Not   9 no   10 NO

4
1 mustn't   2 don't understand
3 didn't go anywhere / went nowhere   4 not
5 I never eat   6 wait   7 I hardly watch
8 didn't phone   9 not well
10 didn't see anything / saw nothing

5   1 F   2 B   3 E   4 D   5 C

page 110

1
1 Can't you swim?
2 Don't you speak Spanish?
3 Weren't the shops open?
4 Hasn't Ann arrived?
5 Didn't she know him?
6 Why aren't you working?
7 Hasn't the postman come?
8 Isn't your mother at home?
9 Aren't you ready yet?
10 Don't they understand?

2
1 Don't you believe me?
2 Didn't she pass the exam?
3 Haven't you paid for your ticket?
4 Didn't you lock the door?
5 Can't you understand English?
6 Don't you like my cooking?
7 Didn't you get the letter I sent?
8 Didn't you enjoy the film?
9 Aren't you and John going to get married?
10 Don't you want any more potatoes?

page 111

3
1 Don't you speak Arabic?
2 Isn't that Bill over there?
3 Didn't you study at Oxford?
4 Isn't this your coat?
5 Isn't her mother a doctor?
6 Wasn't Joe at the party?
7 Aren't you hot in that sweater?
8 Didn't you get a letter from Harry?
9 Didn't they lose money last year?
10 Isn't she Irish?

4
1 Aren't they stupid!
2 Doesn't she look tired!
3 Isn't that child dirty!
4 Isn't it hot!
5 Doesn't John work hard!
6 Wasn't that film terrible!
7 Isn't he funny!
8 Isn't it a pity!
9 Doesn't she complain!
10 Don't those flowers smell nice!

5   1 No   2 No   3 Yes   4 Yes   5 Yes   6 No
7 No   8 Yes   9 Yes   10 No

page 112

1
1 voted against him?'   2 did Jane buy?'
3 belongs to your uncle?'   4 does Roger own?'
5 does Carl like?'   6 like hunting?'
7 dog dug up your roses last night?'
8 of books does Mary write?'
9 matches did you lose?'
10 vegetables make you ill?'

In these answers, we usually give **either** contracted forms (for example *I'm, don't*)
or full forms (for example *I am, do not*). Normally both are correct.

2 1 Correct.   2 What are you thinking about?
3 I hardly ever go   4 What colour eyes
5 Correct. 6 Correct.   7 No, I'm not. / Yes, I am.
8 Correct.   9 What … like   10 not
11 Correct.   12 I hardly went out   13 Correct.
14 Correct.   15 is your brother's football match
starting   16 What made   17 Correct.
18 can never   19 Correct.   20 Correct.

3 1 What do you cut metal with? A hacksaw.
2 What do you cut bread with? A breadknife.
3 What do you make holes with? A drill.
4 What do you shave with? A razor.
5 What do you cut grass with? A lawnmower.
6 What do you cut wood with? A saw/axe.
7 What do you cut hair with? A pair of scissors.

page 113

4 *(possible answers)*
1 Where do the three families live?
2 What sort of house do they live in?
3 How many children have Alice and George got?
4 Who has a baby daughter?
5 What do Joe and Sue do?
6 What does Alice take care of?
7 Where does Joe work?
8 What does he design?
9 What does Pam do?
10 How many children go to school in the village?
11 How do the oldest children go to school?
12 Where is their school?

1 Who does the cooking?
2 Who does most of the housework?
3 Who does the repairs?
4 Who takes care of the garden?
5 What is their biggest worry?
6 What needs replacing?
(Other answers are possible.)

page 114

1 1 Why did Alex go home?
2 What did Judy write?
3 What happened?
4 Who took the keys?
5 What was Mike making?
6 How did Carol pass her exam?
7 What time did Jenny arrive?
8 What fell off the roof?
9 Who shouted 'Help!?
10 What does the dog want?

2 1 Will all the family be there next week?
2 Correct.   3 Correct.   4 What is John talking
about?   5 Correct.   6 Aren't you   7 Alice
hardly ever phones me.   8 Correct.   9 What are
all the children doing?   10 What colour hair

11 Correct.   12 What is their new house like?
13 Correct.   14 Correct.   15 not enough
16 Correct.   17 Correct.   18 No, I'm not.
19 Correct.   20 What time did you get home?

3 1 … close the window for?   2 Why are all
the people …?   3 What were you …?
4 What time does …?   5 … have lunch with?
6 Where are you …?   7 … work for?
8 Where from?   9 What about?
10 … the table with?

page 116

1 1 You should eat enough.
2 I won't have lunch.
3 I might go sailing this summer.
4 She expects to get married in June.
5 I agreed not to tell her father.
6 We must make careful plans.
7 He seems to be ill.
8 I wish I could change my job.
9 I hope to come and see you next week.
10 You needn't apologise.
11 I decided not to go back.
12 I promise to pay you on Saturday.
13 I didn't manage to find the ticket office.
14 I had better not go.
15 She refused to see him again.
16 I've learnt to play chess.

2 1 to know   2 to be ill   3 Correct.   4 Correct.
5 Correct.   6 mustn't expect   7 Correct.
8 to get   9 had better think   10 Correct.
11 Why not go   12 Correct.   13 to study
14 not to go

page 117

1 *(possible answers)*
1 You go to a bookshop to buy books.
2 You go to a bank to get money out.
3 You go to a cinema to see a film.
4 You go to a theatre to see a play.
5 You go to a swimming pool to swim.
6 You go to a gym to (take) exercise / work out.
7 You go to a driving school to learn to drive.
8 You go to a station to get a train.
9 You go to an airport to get a plane.
10 You go to a travel agent to book a holiday.
11 You go to a church to pray.
12 You go to a football stadium to watch a match.
13 You go to a post office to buy stamps.
14 You go to a restaurant to have a meal.
15 You go to a supermarket to buy food.
(Other answers are possible.)

3 1 You use scales to weigh things.
2 You use a saucepan to boil things.
3 You use a frying pan to fry things.
4 You use a bowl to mix things.
5 You use a knife to cut things.
6 You use an oven to bake things.

page 118

1 + INFINITIVE: decide, expect, hope, learn, manage, need, offer, promise, seem, would like
+ *-ING* FORM: finish, give up, keep (on), mind, practise, spend (time)

2 1 to hear   2 to spell   3 to write   4 driving
5 to be   6 smoking   7 talking   8 studying
9 to find   10 to see   11 passing   12 watching
13 to help   14 talking   15 to stay   16 to talk

3 1 B   2 Both.   3 A   4 Both.   5 B   6 A
7 Both.   8 Both.   9 Both.   10 A

page 119

1 1 I'm thinking of going to Australia.
2 I'm interested in working with children.
3 I'm tired of listening to her.
4 She's good at painting.
5 I'm bad at listening.
6 Thank you for helping me.
7 I stayed in bed instead of going to work.
8 You can't live without eating.
9 We talked about having a party.
10 He passed the exam in spite of doing no work.

page 120

1 1 to be working   2 be repaired   3 to go
4 to have seen   5 be having   6 to listen
7 to be chosen   8 not to be   9 have told
10 to be interrupted

2 1 She seems to /could / may / must be drinking.
2 She seems to /could / may / must be driving.
3 She seems to /could / may / must be playing tennis.
4 She seems to /could / may / must be washing.
5 She seems to /could / may / must be (tele)phoning.
6 She seems to /could / may / must be brushing her hair.
7 She seems to /could / may / must be reading.

page 121

1 1 I'm glad to have met you.
2 I was sorry to have disturbed him.
3 I expect to have passed all my exams by June.
4 You seem to have made a mistake.

5 I'm happy to have had a chance to talk to you.
6 I was disappointed to have missed the party.
7 She seems to have got lost.
8 She was pleased to have found the house.

2 1 I would like to have seen his face when he realised what had happened.
2 He meant to have finished all his work by three o'clock.
3 We were to have spent a week skiing.
4 It was to have been the happiest week of my life.
5 She meant to have said goodbye to everybody before she left.
6 I would like to have lived in the seventeenth century.
7 He was to have played in the Cup Final.

page 122

1 1 'Well, I'm starting to.'
2 'If you'd like to.'
3 'I'll try to, but I can't promise.'
4 'Sorry, I forgot to.'
5 'No, but I used to.'
6 'He seems to.'
7 'I don't really want to – it's too cold.' or 'I'd like to, but I'm working late.'
8 'Yes, she expects to.'
9 'We'd love to.'
10 'I intend to. They make far too much noise.'
11 'I'd like to, but I'm working late.' or 'I don't really want to – it's too cold.'
12 'We don't need to – there's always plenty of room.'
13 but we can't afford to.

page 123

1 1 Drinking   2 paying   3 hearing   4 lying
5 skiing; climbing   6 Learning   7 saying
8 Forgetting   9 Watching   10 Answering; typing

3 1 Do you mind me giving you some advice?
2 I don't appreciate you shouting at me.
3 I couldn't understand Toby wanting to pay for everybody.
4 What's the use of them asking all these questions?
5 The delay was caused by Peter needing to see a doctor.
6 I was astonished at you expecting us to give you a room.
7 The holiday was ruined by Ann having to go home early.
8 She can't stand me telling her what to do.

In these answers, we usually give **either** contracted forms (for example *I'm, don't*) **or** full forms (for example *I am, do not*). Normally both are correct.

ANSWER KEY **347**

page 124

1
1. She didn't dare to say anything.
2. Columbus failed to reach India.
3. I happened to see Annie when I was out shopping.
4. They're planning to build two new hospitals here next year.
5. I'm preparing to leave the country.
6. He pretended to be rich.
7. My uncle refused to lend me any money.
8. I wish to see the manager.

2
1. cooking   2. going to sleep   3. being
4. working   5. seeing   6. passing   7. waking
8. losing   9. spending   10. listening to
11. asking   12. studying   13. planning
14. making

page 125

1
1. You can go fishing.   2. You can go swimming.
3. You can go sailing.   4. You can go skiing.
5. You can go skating.   6. You can go riding.

page 126

1
Things people did: *-ing* form.
Things people are/were supposed to do: infinitive.
1. going   2. to write   3. changing   4. to pay
5. to announce

2
Change: infinitive.
Continuation: *-ing* form.
1. running   2. to talk   3. to study   4. playing

3
Activity stops: *-ing* form.
Reason for stopping: infinitive.
1. seeing   2. to think   3. talking   4. to have

4
after *would*
1. A   2. A, B   3. B   4. A, B

page 127

5
When there is no object: *-ing* form.
When there is an object: infinitive.
1. to talk   2. parking   3. eating and drinking
4. to stay; to work

6
Action going on: object + *-ing* form.
Completed action: object + infinitive without *to*.
1. digging   2. running   3. take   4. explode.
5. climbing   6. playing

7
1. meeting   2. to post   3. not visiting
4. to talk   5. learning   6. to make   7. visiting
8. watching / to watch   9. to spend

10. to come.   11. waiting   12. break
13. running   14. to get   15. working   16. to tell

page 128

1   *(possible answers)*
1. Her boss wants her to work harder.
2. Her daughter wants her to buy her a car.
3. Her husband wants her to cook supper.
4. Her mother wants her to leave her husband.
5. Her son wants her to buy him some new clothes.
6. The butcher wants her to pay his bill.
7. The dog wants her to take him for a walk.
8. The government wants her to pay taxes.
9. The priest wants her to go to church.
(Other answers are possible.)

2
1. They didn't allow us to look at the house.
2. I asked Jake to be more careful.
3. She encouraged me to try the exam.
4. I expect him to come tomorrow.
5. I left him to solve the problem.
6. Did you mean me to pay?
7. The captain ordered the men to attack.
8. I reminded Sue to buy coffee.
9. She taught me to cook.
10. I would prefer you not to tell anybody.

page 129

3
1. Her parents made her do the washing up.
2. Her parents made her clean up her room.
3. Her parents let her read what she liked.
4. Her parents made her iron her own clothes.
5. Her parents made her do her homework.
6. Her parents let her drink beer.
7. Her parents made her go to church.
8. Her parents let her have parties.
9. Her parents let her choose her own school.

6   you to serve

page 130

1   fine, lazy, unusual, well

2
1. We were glad to get home.
2. Are you ready to go?
3. We were lucky to get tickets.
4. Lucy was surprised to get a letter from Pete.
5. I was shocked to hear about your accident.
6. I'll be happy to help you.
7. Are you willing to work at weekends?
8. You were right to ask for my advice.
9. I was wrong to believe what you said.
10. I'm sorry to be late.

3 1 Camels are capable of going without water for a long time.
2 I'm bad at remembering names.
3 I'm bored with going to business meetings.
4 We're excited about seeing our Greek friends next weekend.
5 Anna is annoyed at having to do all the housework.
6 I'm fond of sitting in the garden doing nothing.
7 I'm fed up with seeing the same faces every day.
8 My brother is tired of working in a bank.
9 Josh was guilty of breaking the speed limit.

page 131

1 1 to go   2 in reading   3 of arriving
4 of leaving   5 to reserve   6 to spend
7 of losing   8 to get   9 to meet

2 1 to think before I speak.   2 of flying
3 in keeping her temper.   4 of dying
5 to get angry.   6 to start a business.
7 to get up.   8 of giving

page 132

1 1 potatoes to peel.   2 complaint to make.
3 message to pass on   4 letter to write.
5 clothes to wash.   6 information to give

2 1 nothing to do   2 somewhere to sit.
3 anywhere to stay   4 somebody/someone to help   5 something to finish.   6 anything to eat
7 nothing to buy.   8 something to read.
9 nothing to understand.   10 somewhere to sleep.

page 133

1 1 There's no need for the meeting to start before eight.
2 It's time for the postman to come.
3 It's unusual for him to be late.
4 I'm anxious for the children to go to a good school.
5 It's a bad idea for John to go to Australia.
6 It would be a mistake for Tanya to change her job just now.
7 Is it possible for Paul to come to the meeting?
8 It's important for the car to have regular services.
9 It's normal for him to stay up late on Saturdays.
10 I'd be happy for you to take a holiday.

2 *(Our opinions. Other answers are possible.)*
1 It's unnecessary for teachers to be able to dance.
2 It's very important for teachers to be good listeners.
3 It's not very important fort teachers to be able to draw.
4 It's very important for teachers to speak clearly.

5 It's important for teachers to like people.
6 It's unnecessary for teachers to be good-looking.
7 It's important for teachers to be patient.
8 It's important for teachers to have lots of energy.
9 It's not important for teachers to have a good sense of humour.

page 134

1 *(possible answers)*
English is easy to learn.
Chinese is hard to read.
Small children are interesting to listen to.
Silver is difficult to clean.
Boiled eggs are nice to eat.
Lobster is difficult to cook.
Maths is impossible to understand.
Modern music is boring to listen to.
(Other answers are possible.)

page 135

1 1 after swimming   2 Since passing her exam
3 before visiting her   4 after breaking her leg
5 Before crashing his car   6 since getting her new job

3 1 By switching on the ignition.
2 By playing loud music.   3 By robbing a bank.
4 By oiling it.   5 By looking in a dictionary.
6 By taking an aspirin.   7 By using an extinguisher.

4 *(possible answers)*
A paperclip is for holding papers together.
Soap is for washing.
A saucepan is for cooking.
A knife is for cutting things.
Money is for buying things.
A hairbrush is for brushing hair.
A pen is for writing.
A bag is for carrying things.
(Other answers are possible.)

page 136

1 1 A   2 C   3 B

2 1 to walking   2 to receiving   3 to coming
4 getting up   5 to paying   6 to seeing
7 to dealing   8 to sleeping   9 to having
10 to going away

page 137

1 1 to be lying   2 have gone   3 to be asked
4 to take   5 to have met
6 to have misunderstood   7 be repaired
8 to have finished   9 have told
10 to have seen

*In these answers, we usually give **either** contracted forms (for example I'm, don't) or full forms (for example I am, do not). Normally both are correct.*

2 *(possible answers)*

I got the money by selling things.
I've been much happier since leaving home.
I like to sit and read the paper after getting home in the evening.
He passed his exam in spite of not doing any work.
I apologise for disturbing you.
I like walking as well as playing football.
I sometimes dream of having time to read all my books.
I'm fed up with answering that child's questions.
I'm not capable of understanding this – it's too difficult.
I'm tired of cooking.
She succeeded in convincing the police that she was not a burglar.
She talks about/of changing her job, but I don't think she will.
This key is for unlocking the windows.
Always look in the mirror before driving off.
Thank you for telling me the truth.
You can't live without eating.
We're thinking of moving to Canada.
Why don't you come out with us instead of cooking?
(Other answers are possible.)

page 138

4
1 Their house is hard to find.
2 Grammar is sometimes difficult to understand.
3 That mountain is impossible to climb.
4 This shirt is nice to wear.
5 The word 'sixth' is hard to pronounce.
6 This furniture is easy to clean.
7 My uncle is impossible to dislike.
8 Those apples are not good to eat.
9 Good restaurants are not easy to find.
10 The front door is difficult to open.

5
1 Correct. 2 to see 3 meeting 4 Correct.
5 in getting 6 Correct. 7 of getting
8 to tell 9 falling 10 Correct. 11 Correct.
12 of cooking 13 to pay 14 working
15 Correct. 16 to write 17 of going
18 Correct. 19 Correct. 20 Correct.

page 139

7
To see his woods fill up with snow.
To stop without a farmhouse near
To ask if there is some mistake.
But I have promises to keep
And miles to go before I sleep,
And miles to go before I sleep.

8
to go; have; having
to do

page 140

1
1 with cooking 2 going 3 to stop 4 to sell
5 of travelling 6 going 7 to help Andy
8 to see 9 in climbing 10 of flying
11 you to lose 12 want to 13 to see
14 of studying 15 easy to find 16 to seeing
17 eating 18 going 19 to help
20 of drawing

2
1 C 2 A 3 B 4 A 5 B 6 C 7 B 8 C
9 B 10 A 11 B 12 C 13 B 14 B 15 A
16 C 17 B 18 A 19 B 20 A

page 142

1
1 Always check 2 Don't believe 3 Never cook
4 Don't wait 5 Always unplug 6 Count
7 Never put off 8 Never say 9 Don't be

2
1 Let's not go swimming. 2 Let's play tennis.
3 Let's go for a walk. 4 Let's not play cards.
5 Let's play chess. 6 Let's go to Paris.
7 Let's not go dancing. 8 Let's go skiing.
9 Let's do the washing up.
10 Let's have dinner.

page 143

1
1 Could you send the bill to me?
2 I've bought you a present.
3 Leave some potatoes for me.
4 I lent £5 to Henry yesterday.
5 Show your picture to Granny.
6 Read me the letter, will you?
7 She teaches French to adults.
8 I took Mrs Samuels the report.
9 Would you get a beer for me?
10 We owe the bank £20,000.
11 I offered free tickets to the class.
12 I wrote the doctor a letter.
13 Sing a song to the children.
14 Can you bring me the newspaper?
15 Pay €200 to Mrs Jones, please.

page 144

1
1 It would be nice to have/get some more electric sockets put in.
2 We have/get our knives sharpened once a year.
3 We're going to have/get the roof repaired next summer.
4 I must have/get my jacket cleaned. And I'd better have/get my raincoat reproofed.
5 'Do we need to have/get the car serviced?' 'Well, we'd better have/get the oil changed.'
6 When she had/got her jewellery valued, she found it wasn't actually worth much.

7 You need to have/get your tennis racket re-strung.
8 Shall we have/get the kitchen redecorated, or shall we do it ourselves?
9 I need to have/get some business cards printed.
10 The water isn't running away. We must have/get the drains unblocked.

2 1 He hasn't had it reproofed.
2 He hasn't had them cleaned.
3 He hasn't had it serviced.
4 He hasn't had them sharpened.
5 He hasn't had it repaired.
6 He hasn't had them redecorated.
7 He hasn't had them cleaned.

page 145

1 1 What beautiful flowers!   2 What a nuisance!
3 How terrible!   4 How boring!   5 What a stupid hat!   6 What a star!

2

| 1A | 2C | 3B |

3 1 How well he cooks!
2 How wrong we were!
3 What a lot of nonsense he talks!
4 What funny clothes she wears!
5 How badly she plays!
6 What a fool I was!

4 1 Doesn't he cook well!
2 Weren't we wrong!
3 Doesn't he talk a lot of nonsense!
4 Doesn't she wear funny clothes!
5 Doesn't she play badly!
6 Wasn't I a fool!

page 146

1 1 I do agree with you.
2 I do apologise for disturbing you.
3 I do hate cooking.
4 Peter did enjoy the party.
5 Alice does talk a lot.
6 Do be home early tonight.
7 Do give John my love.
8 I do like your hairstyle.

2 1 I'll be ready in a minute, but I do have to make a phone call.
2 'You don't love me.' 'I do love you.'
3 I may not be educated, but I do know something about life.
4 She doesn't really like sport, but she does play a bit of tennis sometimes.
5 Although she didn't say much, she did give me her phone number.

6 I'm not sure she'll be there, but if you do see her (do) give her my love.
7 My wife does the housework, but I do iron my own trousers.
8 I made her go to the doctor's, and she did have a broken finger.
9 It's a small house, but it does have a nice big kitchen.
10 There's nobody at home. They did say eight o'clock, didn't they?

page 147

1 1 It's easy to speak languages in your head.
2 It annoys me to hear her talk like that.
3 It takes four hours to get from here to York.
4 It's silly to get upset about small things.
5 It's nice to get up in the morning, but it's nicer to stay in bed.
6 It makes me tired to watch him.
7 It upsets me to hear her complaining.
8 It's hard to say no to people.

2 1 It is necessary that everybody should say what they think.
2 It's a good thing that she's got some money saved.
3 It doesn't bother me that he's got long hair.
4 It worried her that John never talked to her.
5 It is essential that she should be told immediately.
6 It was strange that he didn't remember my name.
7 It's a pity that he can't come.
8 It's important that the children should get to bed early.
9 It's not true that wolves attack people.
10 It shocked me that she kept stealing from shops.

page 148

1 1 It was Sarah that/who hid Dad's shoes this morning.
It was Dad's shoes that Sarah hid this morning.
It was this morning that Sarah hid Dad's shoes.
2 It was Maria that/who married Harry last week.
It was Harry that Maria married last week.
It was last week that Maria married Harry.
3 It was Carl that/who broke the kitchen window today.
It was the kitchen window that Carl broke today.
It was today that Carl broke the kitchen window.
4 It was Mark that/who met Cathy in Germany in 2002.
It was Cathy that Mark met in Germany in 2002.
It was in Germany that Mark met Cathy in 2002.
It was in 2002 that Mark met Cathy in Germany.

In these answers, we usually give **either** contracted forms (for example *I'm, don't*) **or** full forms (for example *I am, do not*). Normally both are correct.

2
1 It's not Greek that he speaks, it's Dutch.
2 It's not you that I love, it's Peter.
3 It's not Carol that's/who's the boss, it's Sandra.
4 It's not the music that I hate, it's the words.
5 It wasn't my glasses that I lost, it was my keys.
6 It's not Ryan that's/who's getting married, it's Clive.
7 It wasn't Judy that I saw, it was Jill.
8 It's not maths that he's studying, it's physics.
9 It's not Max that's/who's crazy, it's you.
10 It's not a nail that you need, it's a screw.

page 149

3
1 What shocked me was her rudeness.
2 What I need is a drink.
3 What I like is her sense of humour.
4 What I hate is his jealousy.
5 What keep me fit is cycling.
6 What makes the job interesting is the travelling.
7 What I want is five minutes' rest.
8 What I found was something very strange.
9 What stopped us was the weather.
10 What I don't understand is why she stays with him.

page 150

1
1 awake, (explode), disintegrate, return, rise, leave, continue, postpone, return, consider, arrive

2
1 away   2 on paper   3 not working
4 quieter   5 further   6 to various people
7 further   8 higher   9 working   10 louder

3
1 up   2 over   3 back   4 off   5 up
6 up   7 pick   8 bring   9 take
10 Look   11 switch; switch   12 cut

page 151

4
1 Could you turn the radio off?
Could you turn it off?
2 I'll throw these old plates away.
I'll throw them away.
3 Do take your coat off.
Do take it off.
4 Please write my address down.
Please write it down.
5 Get Mary to fill this form in.
Get Mary to fill it in.
6 I'll switch all the lights off.
I'll switch them off.
7 We'd better put the next meeting off.
We'd better put it off.
8 We'll have to give the money back.
We'll have to give it back.
9 I'll think your suggestion over.
I'll think it over.

10 I couldn't put the book down, it was so interesting.
I couldn't put it down, it was so interesting.

page 152

1
1 Scottish people don't speak Japanese, but they do speak English.
2 In England it doesn't snow a lot, but it does rain a lot.
3 Banks don't sell beer, but they do lend money.
4 Napoleon didn't fight against China, but he did fight against Britain.
5 Cats don't eat potatoes, but they do eat mice.
6 Blue cheese doesn't smell good, but it does taste good.
7 Antibiotics don't kill viruses, but they do kill bacteria.
8 Ostriches don't fly, but they do run fast.

3
arrive: turn up
calculate: work out
clean: wash up
consider: think over
continue: go on
demolish: pull down
destroy: break up
distribute: give out
heat: warm up
pause: break off
postpone: put off
remove: take off

page 153

4
1 Warm it up.   2 Send them back.
3 Write them down.   4 Look it up.
5 Tidy it up.   6 Switch it off.   7 Cool it down.
8 Throw them away.

5
1 Always think   2 Correct.   3 the weather is
4 Correct.   5 hard he works   6 Correct.
7 What a   8 It's strange   9 Correct.
10 Correct.

6
1 It's not the violin that he plays, it's the guitar.
2 It wasn't a sweater that I bought, it was jeans.
3 It's not Andy who's/that's the captain, it's Pete.
4 It's not German that I speak, it's Dutch.
5 It wasn't a cup that I broke, it was a glass.

page 154

1
1 did   2 It   3 up   4 wash   5 off.   6 a
7 get/have   8 How   9 that   10 do

2
1 A, B   2 A   3 A, B   4 B   5 B   6 A   7 B
8 A   9 A, B   10 A, B

3 1 Let's not / Don't let's go out this evening.
 2 This coat's dirty; I must have it cleaned.
 3 The eggs were all bad, so I threw them away.
 4 Can I put off our meeting until next week?
 5 What I need now is a drink.
 6 It's not important to have a perfect pronunciation.
 7 Can you tell me your name?
 8 What a beautiful garden!
 9 Always lock the door at night.
 10 I always have my hair cut at the same place.

page 156

1 1 an 2 a 3 an 4 a 5 a 6 an 7 a
 8 a 9 a 10 an 11 an 12 a 13 a 14 an
 15 a 16 a 17 an 18 a

2 1 One 2 a 3 an 4 one 5 a 6 one
 7 a 8 a 9 one

page 157

1 1 is a musician. 2 is a hairdresser.
 3 is a scientist. 4 is a lorry driver.
 5 is a doctor. 6 is a builder. 7 is a mechanic.
 8 is a photographer. 9 is a gardener.

2 1 He's got a big moustache.
 2 He's got a long neck.
 3 He's got a long beard.
 4 She's got a big smile.
 5 He's got a long nose.
 6 He's got a small moustache.
 7 She's got a big mouth.
 8 He's got a loud voice.
 9 He's got a small mouth.

page 158

1 1 A telescope 2 A lens 3 A barometer
 4 A compass 5 A microscope 6 A mirror
 7 A speedometer 8 A thermometer
 9 A screen 10 A torch

page 159

1 1 the 2 the 3 a 4 a 5 The; the
 6 the; the 7 the; the 8 a; the 9 the
 10 The

2 1 the 2 the 3 an 4 the 5 a 6 the
 7 the 8 A 9 a 10 the 11 the 12 the

3 (possible answers)
 1 No. The light over the door. 2 Yes. 3 Yes.
 4 Yes. 5 No. The place where I put my bike.
 6 Yes. 7 No. The house across the street.

8 Yes. 9 Yes. 10 Yes. 11 Yes.
12 No. The restaurant I went to last night.
(Other answers are possible.)

page 160

1 1 – 2 – 3 – 4 – 5 – 6 the 7 the
 8 the 9 the 10 –

page 161

1 1 the wheel 2 the novel 3 the computer.
 4 The violin 5 the ballpoint pen 6 the dog;
 the wolf 7 the whale 8 The X-ray machine
 9 the train 10 the camera

2 1 the violin 2 the piano 3 the guitar
 4 the harp 5 the cello 6 the saxophone
 7 the organ 8 the trumpet

page 162

1 1 China 2 United Kingdom 3 Republic of
 Ireland 4 Oxford Street 5 Norway
 6 Mediterranean 7 USA 8 Himalayas
 9 Ritz 10 Mont Blanc

2 1 – 2 – 3 – 4 – 5 the 6 the 7 the
 8 – 9 the 10 the 11 – 12 the 13 –
 14 – 15 the 16 the 17 – 18 the
 19 – 20 the

page 163

1 1 on foot; by bus 2 at work; to bed
 3 to school 4 on holiday; at home
 5 at university; at home / in bed 6 to church
 7 by underground; by bus 8 by bicycle
 9 in prison

2 1 – 2 a 3 the 4 – 5 a 6 an 7 the
 8 a 9 a 10 –

page 164

1 1 Life 2 Correct. 3 the cinema
 4 the mountains 5 go to school
 6 the Dragon Restaurant
 7 I climbed Mont Blanc 8 elected
 President 9 Correct. 10 Correct.

2 1 a; a 2 a; an 3 –; a; a 4 A; the 5 –; –; –
 6 An; a 7 –; – 8 –; a 9 –; –; –; – 10 –
 11 a; the 12 a; the; the 13 –; a 14 a; the
 15 a; an; the

In these answers, we usually give **either** contracted forms (for example *I'm, don't*) **or** full forms (for example *I am, do not*). Normally both are correct.

ANSWER KEY **353**

page 165

4 1 the trumpet.   2 the cello.   3 the guitar.
4 the violin.   5 the piano.   6 Ann Moore
7 Galileo Galilei   8 Mary Anderson
9 Grace Hopper   10 Alexander Graham Bell

5 –; a   –; –; –; –; –; –

page 166

1 1 an   2 an   3 a   4 a   5 an   6 a   7 a
8 a   9 a   10 a

2 1 one   2 a   3 one   4 one   5 a   6 one
7 a   8 one   9 a   10 one

3 1 a   2 the   3 –; –   4 the   5 the   6 a
7 the   8 the;   9 –; –   10 an   11 a
12 a   13 the; the   14 the   15 –   16 the
17 an   18 the   19 –   20 a

4 1 the   2 –   3 the   4 –   5 –   6 –   7 the
8 –   9 –   10 the   11 the   12 the   13 –
14 the   15 the   16 the   17 the   18 the
19 the   20 –

page 168

2 THIS/THESE: happening now, just about to start,
here, near
THAT/THOSE: finished, said before, over there,
distant, unwanted

3 1 this   2 that   3 these   4 that   5 those
6 this   7 this   8 those   9 that   10 That
11 that   12 that   13 this; that.   14 this.
15 these

4 this

page 169

1 1 any; some   2 anybody   3 some   4 some
5 any   6 some   7 anything   8 somebody
9 anything   10 some   11 any   12 any
13 somebody   14 any

2 1 refuses   2 doubt   3 hardly   4 never
5 seldom   6 without

3 1 any   2 something   3 anything
4 anything   5 something   6 any   7 some;
some   8 anything   9 any   10 anything

page 170

1 1 D   2 E   3 C   5 B   6 H   7 L   8 K   9 J

10 I   11 G

2 1 mustard.
2 some mushrooms; mushrooms.
3 carrots.
4 He didn't buy any vinegar, because he doesn't
like vinegar.
5 He bought some rice, because he likes rice.
6 He didn't buy any pepper, because he doesn't
like pepper.
7 He bought some cornflakes, because he likes
cornflakes.
8 He didn't buy any oil, because he doesn't like oil.

page 171

1 1 She doesn't speak any German.
2 He hasn't written any letters to her.
3 We get no rain here.
4 There's no post on Sundays.
5 She's got no brothers or sisters.

2 1 None.   2 no   3 none   4 None   5 no; none

3 1 no   2 Nobody   3 No   4 none   5 No
6 None   7 no   8 nobody   9 None
10 no; no; no

4 1 Sorry, no milk.   2 Any phone calls for me?
3 No more money.   4 Any problems today?

page 172

1 1 any boy   2 Any colour   3 any supermarket.
4 any question   5 any problems   6 Any day
7 any bank.   8 any bus

2 1 F Anywhere   2 A anything.   3 B anybody.
4 C anywhere   5 E anything.

3 1 Any   2 No   3 anything   4 nothing
5 can't hear   6 any   7 nobody   8 anybody

page 173

2 1 so much   2 as many   3 too much
4 as many   5 too many   6 as many

page 174

1 *Enough* normally comes after an adjective or
adverb.
Enough normally comes before a noun.

2 1 enough champagne   2 big enough
3 enough money; enough time   4 enough
friends   5 old enough   6 hard enough
7 clever enough; enough confidence

3 Before an adjective without a noun, or an adverb, we use *too*.
Before a noun (with or without an adjective), we use *too much/many*.

4 *(possible answers)*
1 There were too many people for one car.
2 No, he's speaking too quickly.
3 She was too busy.
4 It's too expensive.
5 There's too much traffic
6 I wrote too slowly.
7 There's too much noise in this room.
(Other answers are possible.)

page 175

5 1 too many people   2 not enough people
3 not enough water   4 too much water
5 too much work   6 too many cats
7 not enough food   8 too much food

6 1 well enough to decide
2 too tired to think about
3 well enough to listen
4 strong enough to move
5 too bored to concentrate
6 too quietly for me to hear
7 clean enough for people to swim
8 too dark for us to see
9 too fast for the police to catch
10 clean enough to wear

page 176

1 1 little   2 little   3 few   4 few.   5 little
6 little   7 few   8 Few

2 1 little   2 a little   3 Few   4 a few   5 a few
6 a little; a little   7 little   8 few

3 1 We haven't got many / We've only got a few friends.
2 There isn't / There's not much / There's only a little that I can do for you.
3 Not many / Only a few people wanted to help her.
4 They didn't have much / They only had a little money, but they were pretty happy.
5 Not many / Only a few children are as difficult as Robert.
6 I don't dislike many / I only dislike a few people.
7 My father doesn't do much / My father only does a little exercise.
8 I don't need much / I only need a little sleep.
9 Vermeer didn't paint many / Vermeer only painted a few pictures.
10 I don't speak much / I only speak a little Japanese.

page 177

1 1 the least; the fewest   2 fewer; less   3 fewer; less   4 less; less   5 the least   6 the fewest   7 fewer   8 the least   9 the fewest   10 less

2 *(possible answers)*
1 less optimistic   2 the least selfish
3 less fluently   4 less prosperous
5 less quickly   6 the least boring
7 less religious   8 the least important
9 less interesting   10 The least intelligent
(Other answers are possible.)

page 178

1 1 The marketing people all like Oliver.
2 All our children speak French.
3 All the tourists went back home.
4 These cars all cost too much.
5 Meetings all take too long.
6 All my friends thought I was crazy.
7 My old friends all live a long way away.
8 All the classes started late.

2 1 The museums all close on Tuesdays.
2 The interviews will all start next week.
3 We all stopped for a rest.
4 Your clothes are all ready.
5 We all went to Paris for Easter.
6 Sorry, the buses have all left.
7 These children can all speak English.
8 The apples have all gone bad.

3 1 They are all in Asia except Melbourne.
2 They are all in China except Delhi.
3 They are all in Europe except Japan.
4 They are all in England except Edinburgh.
5 They are all in German-speaking countries except Athens.
6 They are all in South America except Mexico City.
7 They are all in the United States except Toronto.
8 They are all seaports except Madrid.

page 179

1 1 Not every bird can fly.
2 I've read every newspaper.
3 Please listen to every word.
4 Every road was under water.
5 Every language is difficult in one way or another.
6 Every London train is cancelled today.
7 The police have interviewed every employee.
8 Every plate is dirty.
9 Not every change is good.
10 Every computer is down today.

2 1 All   2 everybody   3 All   4 all; everybody
5 everybody   6 all

3 1 All   2 everything   3 everything   4 All
5 everything   6 everything   7 everything
8 everything.   9 All

page 180

1 1 has   2 Correct.   3 each
4 Every/Each child is different. / All children
are different.   5 Correct.   6 each

2 1 Each   2 every   3 each   4 each   5 each
6 Every   7 each

3 1 Every one   2 every   3 every one.
4 Every one; every one   5 every   6 every one.
7 every   8 Every one

page 181

1 1 Both   2 Either   3 either   4 both
5 Both; neither   6 Both; neither   7 Either
8 either; both   9 either   10 either; Both
11 both   12 both

2 1 both hands.   2 both hands and both feet
3 either foot.   4 either hand.   5 either hand.
6 both hands.   7 both eyes   8 either eye.
9 either hand   10 both feet

page 182

1 1 which   2 What   3 Which/What   4 Which
5 What   6 Which   7 What   8 What   9 Which
10 Which

2 1 Which   2 Which   3 which   4 What
5 Which   6 Who   7 What   8 which   9 Who
10 Which

page 183

1 1 others   2 other   3 others   4 others.
5 other   6 other   7 others   8 others.
9 other   10 Other

2 1 more clothes   2 more friends
3 another child   4 another hour
5 another mile   6 more sleep   7 another job
8 more possibilities   9 more money
10 more time / another time   11 more freedom
12 more holidays   13 another problem
14 another question   15 more tickets

3 1 another few days   2 another hundred pounds
3 another twenty miles   4 another few mistakes
5 another million dollars

page 184

1 1 of   2 of   3 –   4 –   5 –   6 of   7 of   8 –
9 of   10 of   11 –   12 –   13 –   14 –

2 1 Most people   2 Most of the people
3 most of the people   4 Most people
5 most people   6 Most of the people
7 most people.   8 Most of the people
9 Most of the people   10 Most people

page 185

1 1 any petrol   2 some money   3 anyone
4 any   5 pretty toes   6 a little   7 few
8 the least   9 other   10 bear   11 have all left
12 are all   13 each   14 Both   15 What

2 1 any petrol station / garage; any supermarket /
pet shop; any post office; any sports shop; any
bookshop
2 any English teacher; any lawyer/solicitor; any
accountant; any photographer; any farmer

3 1 Nobody   2 None of   3 nobody
4 a lot of / plenty of   5 (much) too slowly
6 enough chairs   7 warm enough   8 'Yes, a lot.'
9 with no difficulty / without any difficulty
10 Correct.   11 everybody   12 the least bad
13 either   14 more meat   15 everything

page 186

4 *(possible answers)*
1 Nobody in the family speaks French.
2 None of them.
3 Nobody speaks seventy-six languages.
4 There's no food in the house.
5 Sorry, I've got no coffee.
6 There's nobody at home.
7 There's nothing good on.
8 I had no money.
9 I had nothing to say.
(Other answers are possible.)

5 a) Few people learn foreign languages perfectly
as adults. The majority of us make many
mistakes when we are speaking another
language. The best policy is to aim for a
reasonable level of accuracy, but not to be too
perfectionist. Many common mistakes have
little effect on communication.

b) Not many people learn foreign languages
perfectly when they're grown up. Most of us
make a lot of mistakes when we're speaking
another language. It's best to try to get most
things right, but not to be too perfectionist.
A lot of common mistakes don't have much
effect on communication.

page 187

7   1 anywhere; anybody; any   2 less   3 any
        4 anything

page 188

1   1 none of   2 anybody   3 enough rain
        4 Most of   5 beautiful   6 no   7 another two
        8 anything   9 a lot of / lots of   10 least
        11 warm enough   12 any   13 Every one of
        14 each/every   15 were all   16 Everybody
        17 either/each   18 a little   19 have all gone
        20 too

2   1 that man   2 any time   3 Correct.
        4 will all be   5 bird   6 Correct.   7 Which
        8 a lot of   9 everything   10 Correct.
        11 Correct.   12 We understood little / We didn't
        understand much   13 That was   14 Correct.
        15 Correct.   16 more coffee   17 enough rooms
        18 Correct.   19 without any salt / with no salt
        20 Correct.

page 190

1

I	me	my	mine
you	you	your	your
he	him	his	his
she	her	her	hers
it	it	its	–
we	us	our	ours
you	you	your	yours
they	them	their	theirs

2   1 theirs   2 It's 30 miles   3 I've forgotten
        4 their   5 them   6 yours   7 his mother
        8 It's Tuesday   9 this is mine   10 your
        11 It's December   12 I like it

3   1 him; me.   2 my; yours   3 her   4 his
        5 mine; mine; hers.   6 her   7 they; us
        8 it   9 them   10 its

4   1 its   2 Whose; It's   3 who's   4 It's; its

page 191

1   1 these silly cats of ours
        2 that unemployed brother of hers
        3 another good friend of mine
        4 a brilliant idea of mine
        5 these stupid plans of his
        6 those old books of yours
        7 some distant relations of his

        8 a beautiful cousin of hers
        9 this wonderful news of yours
       10 that lazy son of ours

2   1 my sweater   2 her foot   3 its tail
        4 their coats   5 my raincoat   6 your mouth
        7 my head   8 His lips   9 your shoes
        10 your eyes

page 192

1   1 me   2 he; him   3 Me   4 me.   5 me; him.
        6 he; her.   7 him   8 me   9 me   10 her

2   1 Anne's got the same car as I have.
        2 They're been here longer than we have.
        3 I'm much taller than he is.
        4 'He is going to Mexico.' 'I am too.' / 'So am I.'
        5 'Who said that?' 'She did.'
        6 We're not as old as them.
        7 He had a bigger meal than me.
        8 I'm not as quick as her.
        9 'We're from York.' 'Me too.'
        10 'Who wants a drink?' 'Me.'

page 193

3   1 She   2 it   3 It's   4 She/It   5 it   6 Who
        7 It   8 it   9 who   10 it

page 194

1   1 herself   2 herself; her.   3 itself   4 ourselves
        5 him   6 yourself   7 himself   8 you   9 me
        10 himself

2   1 ourselves.   2 herself   3 himself
        4 themselves   5 myself.   6 itself   7 himself.
        8 yourselves   9 herself.   10 yourself.

page 195

3   1 each other   2 themselves   3 each other
        4 yourselves   5 each other   6 each other
        7 ourselves   8 themselves.   9 themselves.
        10 each other.

4   1 ourselves.   2 him   3 each other   4 myself.
        5 her   6 me/us   7 myself   8 each other
        9 itself   10 themselves   11 yourself.
        12 you; them

5   1 behave yourselves   2 shave   3 make
        yourself   4 Help yourself.   5 Enjoy yourselves.
        6 hurry.   7 feel   8 by myself.   9 washes.
        10 dress

In these answers, we usually give **either** contracted forms (for example *I'm, don't*) **or** full forms (for example *I am, do not*). Normally both are correct.

1 1 You can't get into the US without a passport.
2 You can't fly directly from Birmingham to Canberra.
3 You can't be a physicist if you're bad at maths.
4 You can't grow oranges in a cold climate.
5 You can't get a driving licence at age 15.
6 You can't eat soup with a fork.
7 You can't see animals in the forest if you get up late.
8 You can't learn languages in your sleep.
9 You can't see the Director without an appointment.
10 You can't make an omelette without breaking eggs.

2 1 One cannot get into the US without a passport.
2 One cannot fly directly from Birmingham to Canberra.
3 One cannot be a physicist if one is bad at maths.
4 One cannot grow oranges in a cold climate.
5 One cannot get a driving licence at age 15.
6 One cannot eat soup with a fork.
7 One cannot see animals in the forest if one gets up late.
8 One cannot learn languages in one's sleep.
9 One cannot see the Director without an appointment.
10 One cannot make an omelette without breaking eggs.

3 1 They 2 they 3 they 4 They 5 You
6 you 7 your 8 you 9 you 10 they
11 you 12 them.

4 1 they 2 their 3 their 4 they; them.
5 them. 6 her 7 theirs 8 they 9 them
10 her

1 1 It's 2 their 3 him 4 ourselves
5 Who's; It's 6 Hurry 7 its 8 whose 9 me.
10 enjoy yourselves

2 1 Correct. 2 Correct. 3 each other
4 Correct. 5 his/her/their own room
6 Correct. 7 Correct. 8 Me too./So am I.
9 yourself 10 your/a raincoat

6 1 throw 2 balance 3 put 4 tie 5 dive
6 use 7 give 8 wrap 9 throw 10 build

8 you; herself
It's; We; you; ours

1

~~me~~ I	me	my	mine	myself
you	~~your~~ you	your	yours	yourself
he	him	his	his	himself
she	her	~~hers~~ her	hers	herself
it	it	~~it's~~ its	–	itself
we	us	our	ours	ourselves
you	you	your	yours	yourselves
they	them	their	~~their~~ theirs	~~theirselves~~ themselves

2 1 yours; hers 2 Whose; ours 3 your; Its
4 his; her 5 their 6 our; theirs 7 my; mine
8 each other 9 feel 10 herself 11 he is
12 your 13 my 14 myself 15 him

3 1 Correct. 2 Who's 3 than her / than she is
4 Correct. 5 ourselves 6 a friend (of mine) / my friend 7 Correct. 8 Correct. 9 Hurry.
10 Correct. 11 Correct. 12 shave this morning
13 Correct. 14 except me 15 Correct.

1 COUNTABLE: book, cup, flower, mountain, piano, river, song, table, wall
UNCOUNTABLE: dust, flour, happiness, knowledge, love, milk, meat, music, oil, rain, snow

2 1 a glass 2 glass. 3 wood. 4 a wood.
5 pity. 6 a pity. 7 Time 8 times 9 beers
10 Beer 11 experience. 12 an experience
13 a chicken 14 chicken

3 some baggage, some bread, a bus, a dishwasher, some furniture, a holiday, a house, some luck, some knowledge, a magazine, a problem, some research, a table, some travel, some work

1 1 luggage, a suitcase bread, a loaf furniture, a table information, a fact money, a dollar publicity, an advertisement traffic, cars travel, a journey work, a job

2 an item/piece of news   a flash of lightning
a stroke of luck   a clap of thunder
a blade of grass   a bar of soap OR chocolate
a loaf of bread   a game of chess

3 A word of advice …
… baggage has …

page 204

1 1 Add -*s*.   2 Change *y* to *i* and add -*es*.
3 Add -*s*.   4 *s*, *z*, *sh*, *ch*, *x*   5 echo, hero, potato,
tomato

2 addresses, boxes, brushes, computers, desks,
faces, guys, lists, losses, messes, patches, patios,
peaches, plays, poppies, replies, toys, trees,
witches, worries

page 205

1 1 crisis – crises, means   2 aircraft, sheep
3 dozen, thousand   4 shelf – shelves,
wolf – wolves   5 mouse – mice, tooth – teeth
6 mathematics, news   7 police, scissors

page 206

1 1a school has   1b school have
2a club have   2b club has
3a staff do   3b staff does
4a class is   4b class are
5a orchestra are   5b orchestra is

2 1 have   2 is   3 is   4 have; are   5 is   6 are
7 are   8 is   9 are   10 are   11 has   12 were
13 Is   14 have

page 207

1 *(possible answers)*
1 your sister's clothes   2 Jonathan's health
3 Emily and Claire's address   4 those women's
clothes   5 my teachers' ideas   6 Katie's legs
7 our dog's nose   8 Simon and Jill's car
9 most people's ideas   10 doctors' education
11 Katie's fear of heights   12 Jonathan's father
13 your sister's address   14 most people's
education   15 Emily and Claire's father
(Other answers are possible.)

2 1 Correct.   2 Are you Al's daughter?
3 Correct.   4 Here's Barry's address.   5 Correct.
6 Correct.   7 Correct.   8 Correct.   9 Alice's
10 Carol's

page 208

1 Angela's leg; the highest branches of the trees;
the lock of my suitcase; your dog's mouth; the
bank's branch in Paris; the floor of your office; the
mouth of the river; my family's name; the town's
atmosphere / the atmosphere of the town; our
company's best sales manager; the police force's
main problem; next week's timetable; last night's
party; today's news

2 1 Helen's story, the story of the French Revolution
2 the bed of the stream, the patient's bed
3 the policy of full employment, the company's
policy
4 my favourite author's style, the style of the
1930s
5 the place of language education, women's
place
6 the ideas of modern physics, my son's ideas
7 the club's rules, the rules of football
8 the committee's view, the view of the lake
9 the cat's head, the head of the queue
10 the arm of the chair, John's arm

page 209

1 1 H   2 C   3 I   4 B   5 A   6 D   7 F   8 J
9 E   10 G

2 1 a music shop   2 a Birmingham man
3 a picture frame   4 mint tea
5 the station clock   6 a space rocket
7 a biscuit factory   8 soap powder
9 garden furniture   10 a road sign
11 a toothbrush   12 wildlife programmes
13 a wine bottle   14 a school play
15 an evening paper

3 *(possible answers)*
antique shop, bicycle race, bus station, cowboy
film, grape juice, kitchen door, newspaper
publisher, road map
(Some other answers are possible.)

page 210

1 1 a chocolate cake   3 a kitchen cupboard
4 a matchbox   5 toothpaste   7 the kitchen
door   8 a wine bottle   9 a train timetable
11 garden chairs

page 211

1 1 small metal one   2 white cotton one.
3 Unsweetened orange.   4 ones that I've read.
5 new ones.   6 long sunny one.   7 Chinese.
8 solid practical ones.   9 sharp one.   10 cold.

In these answers, we usually give **either** contracted forms (for example *I'm, don't*)
or full forms (for example *I am, do not*). Normally both are correct.

ANSWER KEY **359**

2 1 One 2 one. 3 Mine 4 some 5 one
6 any 7 hers. 8 some.

page 212

1 criteria, fish, thieves, fungi, phenomena, series, analyses, tomatoes, geese

2 billiards S cattle P clothes P
congratulations P economics S exam N
glass N gymnastics S hand N idea N
meal N measles S paper N physics S
research S scissors P thanks P trousers P

3 1 have 2 have 3 is 4 is 5 agree
6 are; want 7 has 8 think 9 is 10 want

4 1 one 2 bus timetable 3 the school's
4 Mark 5 book about Napoleon
6 postman's van 7 a friend of John's
8 the arm of the chair 9 wine bottle
10 Maggie's.

5 the meaning of the word
the results of your tests

page 213

6 1 sunset 2 sunflowers 3 suncream; sunburn
4 sunstroke 5 sunspots 6 sunglasses.
7 suntan. 8 sundial 9 sunrise

7 1 their grandparents' 2 children's
3 the other children's 4 Josie and Cara's
5 girls' 6 a man's 7 the shopkeeper's
8 local people's

page 214

1 some advice, an artist, some bread, a company,
a curtain, some furniture, some information, a job,
a joke, a journey, some money, some publicity,
some traffic, a train, some travel

2 boys, buses, cities, crossroads, deer, echoes,
loaves, gases, halves, kilos, monkeys, phenomena,
pianos, series, watches

3 1 a flower shop 2 raspberry juice 3 a shoe
brush 4 a car radio 5 a morning paper
6 water bottles 7 rat poison 8 university
exams 9 a marmalade factory 10 a bathroom
cupboard

4 1 furniture 2 Athletics is 3 Correct.
4 Correct. 5 want 6 is having 7 Mine are
8 fruit juice 9 the rules of basketball
10 Correct. 11 Correct. 12 Correct. 13 the
baby's bottle 14 I've got green. 15 table
tennis 16 Are you Maria's sister? 17 Correct.

18 some information / a piece of information
19 Correct. 20 These old jeans are … new
ones. OR This old pair of jeans is … a new one.

page 216

1 1 calm 2 unhappily. 3 beautifully.
4 terrible. 5 calmly 6 slow 7 beautiful
8 terribly 9 slowly. 10 unhappy.

2 1 amazingly 2 sure 3 real 4 amazing
5 slightly 6 badly 7 wonderful; awful
8 cleverly 9 completely 10 unbelievably

page 217

1 1 surprised 2 surprising 3 tiring. 4 tired.
5 disappointing. 6 disappointed. 7 excited
8 exciting 9 shocked 10 shocking.
11 confusing. 12 confused. 13 annoyed
14 annoying

2 The visitors.

3 1 A botanist is interested in plants.
2 A cook is interested in food.
3 A doctor is interested in medicine.
4 An explorer is interested in unknown places.
5 A fashion designer is interested in clothes.
6 A geographer is interested in places.
7 A historian is interested in the past.
8 A linguist is interested in languages.
9 A mathematician is interested in numbers.
10 A zoologist is interested in animals.

page 218

1 1 the blind 2 the young. 3 the poor
4 the young; the old 5 the rich. 6 the living
7 The poor; the rich 8 the dead; the living.

2 1 Dutch 2 Irish 3 French 4 Welsh
5 English

page 219

1 1 modern industrial buildings 2 red silk
evening dress 3 narrow colourless eyes
4 black nylon swimming trunks 5 flat gold
frame 6 blue woollen tie 7 short leather
jacket 8 French ski boots

2 1 beautiful little Belgian city 2 excellent cold
dinner 3 lovely old furniture 4 strange new
ideas 5 depressing grey concrete university

3 1 hot breezy 2 untidy red 3 young and
bearded 4 cold and rough 5 old and
ugly. 6 quiet tense 7 yellow and grey
8 red and blue

page 221

4
1. Her mum always cooks a meal in the evenings.
2. We usually book that April holiday in January.
3. They probably think that we have got bread.
4. You should always look where you're going.
5. She is probably going to stay overnight.
6. Chocolate cakes are definitely the best.
7. I will probably be able to get it cheaper.
8. I have never had an illness in my life.
9. We never saw sweets in those days.
10. I definitely remember buying some.
11. Do you usually read upside down?
12. I can usually manage to get there.
13. She has never done that before.
14. Something is definitely burning.
15. She has always been nervous.
16. I never feel cold in your house.
17. They were always against me.
18. We are definitely going to win.
19. February is usually the worst.
20. It is sometimes very difficult.
21. I always buy them in boxes.
22. I have often tried to find it.
23. They are always fighting.
24. She often saw this ghost.
25. You are probably right.

page 222

1
1. He even sings in his sleep.
2. I am only doing this because I love you.
3. She even gets up at six on Sundays.
4. He even wears a suit on holiday.
5. She only ate a piece of dry toast.
6. I can only play very easy music.
7. He can't even write his own name.
8. They even make you pay for a carrier bag.
9. I'm sorry. I was only trying to help.
10. You can even ski there in summer. / You can ski there even in summer.

2
1. I don't think she plays tennis very well.
2. He always moves very slowly in the morning.
3. She was crying quietly in her room.
4. We talked about it briefly at lunchtime.
5. I'm going to break the eggs carefully into the bowl.
6. Ann works at the village shop on Saturdays.
7. I paid the bill at once.
8. She speaks Japanese fluently.
9. I can't explain my feelings clearly.
10. The team played brilliantly yesterday.
11. I think we'd better open the parcel now.
12. I always worked very hard at school.
13. She practises the piano here every evening.
14. He read every word slowly.
15. Put the butter in the fridge at once.

page 223

1
1. late 2. daily 3. early 4. well. 5. weekly
6. loud. 7. hard/late 8. daily 9. late.; late.
10. loud 11. hard 12. well 13. monthly
14. early

2
1. deadly 2. likely 3. lovely 4. silly 5. lonely
6. lively 7. cowardly 8. ugly

3 *(possible answers)*
1. friendly, lively, lovely, silly, ugly
2. daily, weekly, monthly, early, late
3. early, loud, lively, lovely, silly
4. loud.
5. daily, monthly, weekly, yearly.
6. hard, lovely, silly
7. hard, cowardly, lively, lonely, lovely, silly, ugly
8. likely
9. early, late, lovely
10. well, cowardly, lively, lonely, silly, ugly
11. early, late
12. hard
13. deadly
14. daily, hard, lonely
15. hard, lonely, lovely
(Some other answers may be possible.)

page 224

1
1. cheaply. 2. gently 3. soft 4. clearly.
5. happy 6. completely 7. stupid; extremely
8. bad. 9. carefully. 10. badly

2
1. coldly 2. wonderful 3. Correct. 4. Correct.
5. deaf man/woman/person 6. Japanese very well 7. in a very friendly way / gives me a very friendly smile 8. Correct. 9. old blue
10. bored 11. is usually 12. beautifully in the church last night 13. interested 14. Correct.
15. Correct.

3
1. even on Sundays. 2. even brush their teeth
3. She even likes rats. 4. Even the cat thinks
5. Only the clock 6. only for a few minutes.
7. Even the guides got lost. 8. only watch tennis

page 225

4
1. impatient 2. bad-tempered 3. practical
4. mean 5. shy 6. sociable 7. reserved
8. lazy 9. optimistic 10. quick-thinking

6
Wrong rules: C and E.

7
1. loud 2. hard 3. lonely 4. daily 5. friendly
6. ugly

In these answers, we usually give **either** contracted forms (for example *I'm, don't*) or full forms (for example *I am, do not*). Normally both are correct.

1
1 That girl always spends hours in the bathroom.
2 I have never been to Jamaica.
3 We got home very late last night.
4 Somebody was definitely trying to open the door.
5 He even puts tomato ketchup on cornflakes.
6 Life is sometimes hard.
7 I know some French, and I speak Russian very badly.
8 We have never been invited to Jamie's parties.
9 Alice probably needs somebody to help her.
10 The water was usually too cold for swimming.

2
1 Correct. 2 is always 3 in a friendly way/voice 4 interested 5 Correct. 6 even took
7 beautiful 8 completely 9 Correct.
10 carefully 11 intelligent 12 big old
13 Correct. 14 very well yesterday
15 new black

1
1 add -r, -st. 2 add -er, -est. 3 change y to i and add -er, -est. 4 put *more* and *most* in front.
5 put *more* and *most* in front.

2 4 is the correct completion.

3
1 more boring, most boring
2 cheaper, cheapest
3 finer, finest
4 funnier, funniest
5 greener, greenest
6 more handsome, most handsome
(*also possible*: handsomer, handsomest)
7 harder, hardest
8 more interesting, most interesting
9 lazier, laziest
10 more nervous, most nervous
11 sadder, saddest
12 sillier, silliest
13 slimmer, slimmest
14 wetter, wettest

4
1 better 2 best. 3 farthest/furthest
4 worse 5 worst. 6 elder, eldest 7 elder
8 further 9 most; least 10 less 11 farther/further

5 (*Examples of possible answers*)
Hotel Y is more comfortable than Hotel X.
Hotel Y is the most comfortable of the three hotels.
Hotel Z is more efficient than the other two hotels.

Hotel Z is much more efficient than Hotel X.
Hotel Y is the friendliest of the three hotels.
Hotel X is the most convenient.
Hotel Y is the farthest/furthest from the city centre.

1
1 faster 2 more beautifully/clearly 3 (the) hardest. 4 earlier 5 the most beautifully/clearly. 6 more peacefully 7 the latest
8 the most fluently

3 A more slowly B faster

1 (*examples of possible answers*)
Jake didn't go to the same university as Susie.
Susie went to the same school as Jake.
Susie isn't / Susies's not so/as tall as Jake.
Susie doesn't weigh so/as much as Jake.
Jake has/does the same job as Susie.
Jake isn't / Jake's not so/as old as Susie.
Susie earns twice as much as Jake.
Jake doesn't work for the same firm as Susie.
Susie's holiday isn't so/as long as Jake's.
Jake lives in the same street as Susie.
Susie hasn't got so/as many children as Jake.
Jake speaks the same languages as Susie.
Jake's French is as good as Susie's, but he doesn't speak German so/as well as her.
Jake doesn't read so/as much as Susie.

2
1 as black as night 2 as flat as a pancake
3 as green as grass 4 as hard as iron
5 as old as the hills 6 as pretty as a picture
7 as quiet as a mouse / the grave
8 as red as a beetroot 9 as thin as a rake
10 as white as a sheet

1
1 faster and faster 2 taller and taller
3 hotter and hotter 4 more and more difficult / harder and harder 5 fatter and fatter
6 more and more tired 7 more and more expensive

2
1 is getting harder and harder / more and more difficult
2 is getting better and better
3 are getting younger and younger
4 is getting worse and worse
5 is getting harder and harder / more and more difficult
6 is getting more and more boring
7 are getting more and more expensive
8 are getting longer and longer

page 233

3 *(possible answers)*
1 The more; the less   2 The longer; the more
3 The warmer; the more   4 The more; the less
5 The more; the angrier   6 The faster; the louder
7 The more; the more   8 The older; the darker
(Other answers are possible)

4 *(examples of possible answers)*
The Amazon is much longer than the Thames.
The Atlantic is very much bigger than the Mediterranean.
A parrot is far more intelligent than a cat.
My mother is a little taller than my father.
Living in the country is a bit more boring than living in the city.
A horse is a lot bigger than a dog.
My teacher speaks English even better than my boss.
A computer is no more beautiful than a pen.
The Taj Mahal isn't any nearer to my home than the White House.

page 234

1 1 of   2 in   3 of   4 in   5 in   6 in   7 of
8 of   9 in   10 of

2 1 Who is the youngest of your three sisters?
2 Which is the cheapest of these three jackets?
3 For a time, my grandfather was the most famous footballer in the country.
4 Cassie and Louise are the fastest swimmers in the team.
5 When I was a child, I was the tallest boy in my class.
6 For me, the early morning is the best time of the day.
7 Andy is very quiet, but he is the most interesting person in the group.

page 235

1 1 as   2 like   3 as   4 as   5 like   6 like
7 as   8 like   9 like   10 As

2 1 so   2 so   3 such   4 such   5 such   6 so
7 so   8 such   9 such   10 so

page 236

1 worse, worst   cleaner, cleanest   dirtier, dirtiest
more famous, most famous
farther, farthest OR further, furthest   fitter, fittest
greener, greenest
happier, happiest   lazier, laziest   more modern, most modern
nicer, nicest   redder, reddest   shorter, shortest
slimmer, slimmest

sweeter, sweetest   taller, tallest
thinner, thinnest
more tiring, most tiring   whiter, whitest

2 1 as cold as ice   2 in the world   3 later
4 Correct.   5 The more I learn, the more I forget.
6 Correct.   7 warmer and warmer   8 The more money he has   9 Correct.   10 as you
11 Correct.   12 is nicest   13 as a tourist guide
14 Correct.   15 than

3 1 Is this box stronger than that one? Is it the strongest you've got?
2 Alistair is taller than anyone else in the team. He's the tallest in the team.
3 The state of Alaska is bigger than any of the other states. It's the biggest in the US.
4 This wine is more expensive than that one. It's the most expensive in the world.
5 Max's party was better than Rob's party. It was the best I've ever been to.
6 This job is worse than my last one. It's the worst I've ever had.

page 237

4 1 The more ice cream he eats, the fatter he gets. And the fatter he gets, the more ice cream he eats.
2 The more he reads, the more he forgets. And the more he forgets, the more he reads.
3 The more she ignores him, the more he loves her. And the more he loves her, the more she ignores him.
4 The more shoes she buys, the more shoes she wants. And the more shoes she wants, the more shoes she buys.
5 The more money we spend, the more friends we have. And the more friends we have, the more money we spend.
6 The more I sleep, the more tired I am. And the more tired I am, the more I sleep.

5 1 tallest   2 longest   3 largest   4 longest
5 fastest   6 fastest   7 largest   8 longest
9 highest   10 smallest

page 238

1 more boring, most boring   brighter, brightest
cheaper, cheapest
cleaner, cleanest   more distant, most distant
more exciting, most exciting
farther, farthest OR further, furthest   fitter, fittest
funnier, funniest
more honest, most honest   lazier, laziest
nicer, nicest
plainer, plainest   safer, safest   shorter, shortest
slimmer, slimmest
thinner, thinnest   better, best   wetter, wettest

In these answers, we usually give **either** contracted forms (for example *I'm, don't*) **or** full forms (for example *I am, do not*). Normally both are correct.

2　1　eldest　2　than　3　the same as　4　further
　　　5　the worst　6　an easier　7　best　8　as
　　　9　the most　10　The more; the more

3　1　stranger than　2　in the world　3　Correct.
　　　4　cheaper and cheaper　5　as usual
　　　6　The more tired he gets　7　Correct.　8　further
　　　9　Correct.　10　Correct.　11　as cold as ice
　　　12　more and more bored　13　in the world
　　　14　the most famous　15　Correct.

page 240

1　The following words could come before '…she
　　went home', and are conjunctions:
　　although, and, as, because, before, if, or, since, so,
　　that, unless, until, when, whether

2　1　After I've finished work, I'll come round to
　　　　your place.
　　　2　When the weather gets better, let's have a
　　　　weekend in the country.
　　　3　Before you go back to Canada, you ought to
　　　　see Paula.
　　　4　Not possible.
　　　5　Although I didn't understand everything,
　　　　I enjoyed the lecture.
　　　6　Not possible.

3　1　after　2　–　3　–　4　or　5　that　6　so　7　–
　　　8　unless

page 241

1　1　have; will write　2　Will you stay; takes
　　　3　arrive; will phone　4　get　5　will see; am
　　　6　will open; stops　7　bring　8　will wait; have
　　　9　finish; will have　10　will be; get

2　1　your brother is in England.
　　　2　my father goes into hospital
　　　3　the new car's ready
　　　4　he goes back to work.

page 242

1　1　as long as　2　until　3　so that　4　while
　　　5　as if　6　until　7　as if　8　provided that
　　　9　so that　10　Whereas

2　1　so that　2　as long as　3　so that
　　　4　as long as　5　as long as　6　so that

3　1　While she's very clever, she's got no common
　　　　sense at all.
　　　2　While I know how you feel, I think you're
　　　　making a mistake.
　　　3　While the job's well paid, it's deadly boring.
　　　4　While I'm interested in economics, I wouldn't
　　　　want to work in a bank.

　　　5　While the hotel was nice, it was a long way from
　　　　the beach.

page 243

4　1　He looks as if he's lost something.
　　　2　She looks as if she's been painting.
　　　3　He looks as if he's got a cold.
　　　4　She looks as if she's had bad news.
　　　5　He looks as if he's seen a ghost.
　　　6　It looks as if it's going to rain.
　　　7　He looks as if he's had good news.

5　1　Because of my unhappiness …
　　　2　In spite of her hunger …
　　　3　… because of the heat.
　　　4　… because of the rain.
　　　5　… in spite of the cold.
　　　6　… because of my work.
　　　7　In spite of his interest in the lesson, …
　　　8　… because of my tiredness.
　　　9　In spite of my thirst …

page 244

1　1　It's funny　2　Were you surprised　3　You knew
　　　4　Did you know　5　I believe　6　He suggested
　　　7　I'm glad　8　Tell me　9　I heard　10　I expect

2　1　provided that　2　so　3　Now　4　such … that
　　　5　so that　6　provided　7　Now that
　　　8　provided　9　so　10　Now

page 245

1　1　He speaks neither English nor French.
　　　2　It was either Tuesday or Wednesday. …
　　　3　I neither like nor dislike her.
　　　4　You're neither right nor wrong.
　　　5　I both admire and distrust him.
　　　6　He either lied to us or made a mistake. …
　　　7　Both Paul and Sally are on holiday.
　　　8　Neither the secretary nor the accountant had
　　　　the file.
　　　9　The play was both funny and shocking.
　　　10　He collects both paintings and jewellery.

page 246

1　1　When I've finished my exams I'm going to sleep
　　　　for a week.
　　　2　I'll go shopping as soon as it's stopped raining.
　　　3　After I've done the washing up I'm going to
　　　　have a bath.
　　　4　I'll phone Sally when I've found her number.
　　　5　Let's wait here until Peter's arrived.
　　　6　When I've finished the report I'll ask you to read it.

2 1 After he'd tried on six pairs of shoes, he decided he liked the first ones best.
2 When Mary had done all the shopping, she took a short walk round the park.
3 As soon as I had washed and dried the last plate, Paul came in and offered to help.
4 He went to the café in the square for a cup of coffee after he had said goodbye to the visitors.
5 I ate all the dark chocolate when I had eaten all the milk chocolate.
6 Peter didn't start his karate training until he had phoned his mother.

page 247

1 1 has been; got up   2 have been; lost
3 took up; has had   4 has been; got
5 went; haven't heard   6 has been; had
7 haven't seen; came   8 met; has been
9 We've lost; left   10 have you been; I last saw

3 (possible answers)
1 He looks much younger since he shaved off his beard.
2 It's nearly three years since he had a job.
3 It's only a week since I met her, but it seems like years.
4 It's too long since we last had a proper talk.
5 She's a lot happier since she stopped going out with Pete.
6 Things are better since we got our own flat.
(Other answers are possible.)

page 248

1 1 before   2 while   3 After   4 when
5 since   6 before   7 while/when   8 since
9 while/when   10 while/when

2 1 after eating.   2 while driving.   3 since failing
4 before/after talking   5 while exercising
6 Since coming   7 after returning
8 when/while/before travelling

3 1 The parcel will arrive within 24 hours if sent by express delivery.
2 Warm slowly until completely melted.
3 Guarantee: your money back if not satisfied.
4 When examined, he was found to have a fractured skull.
5 Stir the sugar until dissolved.

page 249

1 1 Having left school at twelve, he had no qualifications.
2 Fried in butter and sprinkled with lemon juice, it tastes delicious.
3 Walking over to her desk, she picked up a paper.

4 The water came into the houses, flooding the downstairs rooms.
5 Knowing his tastes, I took him a large box of expensive chocolates.
6 Putting on his coat, he went out.
7 A lorry broke down in Bond Street, causing a massive traffic jam.
8 Not wanting to frighten her, I phoned before I went round.
9 Sent first class, it should arrive tomorrow.
10 At 3 a.m. Simon came in, waking everybody in the house.

2 1 feeling   2 looking at   3 pulling   4 finding
5 giving up   6 Invested   7 taking care of
8 Turning away   9 Fixing

page 250

1 1 A,B   2 A   3 A,B   4 A,B   5 B   6 A,B
7 B   8 B   9 A   10 A   11 B   12 B   13 B
14 A,B   15 A

2 1 When George had eaten all the chocolate biscuits, he started eating the lemon ones.
2 After I had turned off the lights in the office, I locked the door and left.
3 When you've finished with the newspaper, I'll read it.
4 Zach had a long hot shower after he had done his exercises.
5 As soon as I've told Jackie the good news I'll go to bed.
6 I'll stay by his bed until he's gone to sleep.
7 As soon as the opera had started, Mike went to sleep.
8 After I had locked the door, I realised the children were still outside.
9 When Deborah has left school, she'd going straight into an office job.
10 They watched me until I had gone out of the door.

page 251

3 1 although she was   2 since we had
3 Although it was expensive, he bought it.
4 before it starts   5 nor play   6 after eating
7 Because you were so nice to me, here are
8 had told her   9 I'll take you   10 in spite of

4 1 until   2 while   3 so that   4 provided
5 because of   6 if   7 although   8 as long as
9 After   10 so that   11 either   12 or
13 Although   14 in spite of   15 provided
16 After

In these answers, we usually give **either** contracted forms (for example *I'm, don't*) or full forms (for example *I am, do not*). Normally both are correct.

ANSWER KEY **365**

page 252

1
1. We stopped playing because of the rain.
2. Although we drove as fast as we could, we got there late.
3. They went on climbing in spite of the snow.
4. Because we hadn't got much money, we went on a camping holiday.
5. He got the job in spite of his poor qualifications.
6. When I had finished the shopping, I took the car in for a service.
7. She has neither come to see me nor answered my emails.
8. Going over to his desk, he picked up a small black book.
9. While the film was interesting, it was much too long.
10. Everybody felt sleepy because it was hot.

2
1. as long as 2. until 3. so that 4. provided
5. While 6. if 7. – 8. although 9. going
10. went

3
1. it gets 2. Correct. 3. I've finished
4. Correct. 5. Correct.

page 254

1
1. say you're with me. 2. you don't know what's going on? 3. you won't need to do it again.
4. I never get anything done. 5. I'm sure I can't.
6. she was lying. 7. you park near the station.
8. you're not feeling up to it. 9. we can catch the early train. 10. you want to learn a musical instrument.

2
1. say; 'll scream 2. 'll be manages 3. come; 'll cook 4. 'll need; go 5. 'll miss; move
6. wash up; 'll dry. 7. 'll be doesn't come
8. get; 'll phone 9. look; 'll find 10. 'll be gets

page 255

1
1. would look; had 2. would you go; needed
3. wouldn't do; didn't have to 4. knew; would go
5. would you do; won 6. would be; used
7. were not; would show 8. had; would make
9. loved; would buy 10. was/were not; would tidy up 11. had; would show

2
1. If I were a rabbit, I would live in a hole.
2. If I were forty years younger, I would go dancing all night.
3. If I were Moroccan, I would speak Arabic.
4. If my nose were shorter, I would be quite pretty.
5. If it were not so cold, I would go for a walk.

page 256

1
1. live 2. lived 3. were 4. wake 5. declared
6. exists 7. gave 8. thought 9. is 10. is
11. banned 12. have

2
1. comes 2. find 3. lived 4. arrive 5. We'll
6. would 7. would 8. will 9. will 10. stop

3
1. Would you mind if I went first?
2. If all of us came, would you have room in your car?
3. It would be good if you spent some time with the children.
4. Would you mind if I came round about seven o'clock?
5. Would it be all right if I used your phone?

page 257

1
1. could go and see him. 2. could watch a film.
3. we could go for a ride. 4. could get up late.
5. could have breakfast in the garden. 6. I could write to Henry. 7. we could go to the cinema more often.

2
1. If he could drive, he could get a job at Calloway Ltd.
2. If he had a passport, he could get a job at Patterson Travel.
3. If he could cook, he could get a job at Fred's Café.
4. If he liked children, he could get a job at Crowndale School.
5. If he liked animals, he could get a job at the City Zoo.
6. If he could swim, he could get a job at the Leisure Centre.

page 258

1
1. We would have got better tickets if we had booked earlier.
2. He would have gone to university if his father had not been ill.
3. If you had said you weren't hungry, I wouldn't have cooked such a big meal.
4. The team would have won if Jones had played better.
5. If they hadn't cut off the electricity, I would have finished my work.
6. If Bell hadn't invented the telephone, somebody else would have done it.
7. If you hadn't spent so much time putting your make-up on, we wouldn't have been late.
8. The burglars wouldn't have got in if you had remembered to lock the door.
9. If he had not been a film star, he would not have become President.

10 If she had had more sense, she would have sold her car years ago.

11 If he hadn't spent so much on his holiday, he would have had enough to pay for the house repairs.

12 You wouldn't have caught cold if you had taken your coat.

13 You'd have won if you'd run a bit faster.

14 It would have been better if you'd asked me for help.

15 'If Cleopatra's nose had been shorter, the whole history of the world would have been different.'

page 259

2 1 If he hadn't gone to university, he wouldn't have studied languages. If he hadn't studied languages, he wouldn't have learnt Spanish. If he hadn't learnt Spanish, he wouldn't have gone to Argentina. If he hadn't gone to Argentina, he wouldn't have gone climbing in the Andes. If he hadn't gone climbing in the Andes, he wouldn't have disappeared in a snowstorm.

2 If he hadn't bought a bicycle, he wouldn't have gone for a ride in the country. If he hadn't gone for a ride in the country, he wouldn't have fallen off. If he hadn't fallen off, he wouldn't have woken up in hospital. If he hadn't woken up in hospital, he wouldn't have met a beautiful nurse. If he hadn't met a beautiful nurse, he wouldn't have written a best-selling novel about her. If he hadn't written a best-selling novel about her, he wouldn't have got rich. If he hadn't got rich, he wouldn't have married the beautiful nurse and had three charming children. If he hadn't married the beautiful nurse and had three charming children, he wouldn't have lived happily ever after.

3 If Mary's mother hadn't gone out that evening, Mary wouldn't have cooked for herself. If she hadn't cooked for herself, she wouldn't have got interested in cooking. If she hadn't got interested in cooking, she wouldn't have opened a very successful restaurant. If she hadn't opened a very successful restaurant, she wouldn't have had the Prime Minister as a customer. If she hadn't had the Prime Minister as a customer, he wouldn't have ordered mussels. If he hadn't ordered mussels, they wouldn't have poisoned him. If they hadn't poisoned the Prime Minister, he wouldn't have died. If the Prime Minister hadn't died, Mary wouldn't have gone to prison for life.

3 would have turned out; had put in

page 260

1 1 unless you have a visa 2 Unless you go now
3 if she's not travelling 4 if I haven't got visitors
5 unless Emma's got a handball match
6 unless you want a game of cards
7 if you're not / you aren't 16 or over
8 unless you pay cash 9 if you haven't reserved
10 unless you're too busy

2 1 A He'll get thrown out of school unless he starts working.
2 J You can't open the door unless you know the code.
3 D I always watch TV in the evenings unless I go out.
4 B/I I'll see you at ten unless I phone to say I can't come. / – unless you're too tired.
5 I/B Let's have dinner out – unless you're too tired. / unless I phone to say I can't come.
6 C I'll tell you a good joke unless you've heard it before.
7 G Things will go on getting worse unless there's a change of government.
8 E We're going to have a picnic unless it rains.
9 F You can have the last sausage unless the children want it.

page 261

1 1 If only / I wish he didn't smoke.
2 If only / I wish I spoke Russian.
3 If only / I wish I had a car.
4 If only / I wish I was/were hard-working.
5 If only / I wish I was/were good at sport. / I wasn't/weren't bad at sport.
6 If only / I wish I liked dancing.
7 If only / I wish it didn't rain all the time.
8 If only / I wish she didn't work on Sundays.
9 If only / I wish I could eat eggs.

2 1 If only / I wish it would snow.
2 If only / I wish the phone would stop ringing / wouldn't keep ringing.
3 If only / I wish the baby would stop crying.
4 If only / I wish the kettle would boil.
5 If only / I wish the traffic lights would go green.
6 If only / I wish Frank would write.
7 If only / I wish Patrick would find a job.
8 If only / I wish the exam results would arrive.
9 If only / I wish spring would come.

3 1 had looked after 2 had been 3 had saved
4 had gone 5 had chosen 6 had got
7 had had

In these answers, we usually give **either** contracted forms (for example *I'm, don't*) **or** full forms (for example *I am, do not*). Normally both are correct.

ANSWER KEY **367**

page 262

1
1 She's packing a pack of cards in case she meets people who play bridge.
2 She's packing a tennis racket in case there is a tennis court.
3 She's packing a thick sweater in case the weather is cold.
4 She's packing a swimsuit in case the hotel has a heated pool.
5 She's packing aspirins in case the sun gives her a headache.
6 She's packing binoculars in case she wants to go bird-watching.
7 She's packing her address book in case she decides to send postcards.
8 She's packing some books in case she has time to read.
9 She's packing walking boots in case she wants to go walking.

2
1 in case   2 if   3 if   4 in case   5 in case
6 if   7 if   8 in case

page 263

1
1 It's time I cleaned the car.
2 It's time to cook supper.
3 It's time we got a new fridge.
4 It's time to have a party.
5 It's time your mother went home.
6 It's time we invited the Harrises.
7 It's time we planned our holiday.
8 It's time you saw the dentist.
9 It's time I stopped work.
10 It's time that boy got a job.

2
1 I'd rather we talked tomorrow.
2 I'd rather you came at ten.
3 I'd rather you didn't.
4 I'd rather she worked with Maggie.
5 I'd rather you cooked tonight.
6 I'd rather you asked him.
7 I'd rather he stayed in.
8 I'd rather they brought their own.
9 I'd rather they did something about the homeless.
10 I'd rather we spent the money on a trip round the world.

page 265

4 *(examples of possible answers)*
1 If I had a big house, I would invite lots of people.
2 If I had a yacht, I would go round the world.
3 If I had plenty of money, I would buy a horse.
4 If I didn't have a job, I'd be happier.
5 If I had more time, I'd study biology.

5   1 ✗   2 ✓   3 ✗   4 ✓   5 ✓   6 ✓   7 ✓   8 ✓
9 ✗   10 ✓   11 ✗   12 ✓   13 ✗   14 ✗   15 ✓

page 266

1
1 If Daniel were/was here, we could play bridge.
2 If Alice listened to me, I would talk to her.
3 If I knew enough maths, I would understand physics.
4 If my father did exercise, he wouldn't be overweight.
5 If I liked cooking, I would make you wonderful meals.

2
1 If we hadn't been OR we would play
2 If she smiled more, people would like her. / If she smiles more, people will …   3 Correct.
4 Correct.   5 Correct.   6 unless you have OR if you don't have   7 If I had got up earlier, I wouldn't have missed the bus.   8 Correct.
9 Correct.   10 I would go   11 Correct.
12 If that child stopped … everybody would be … / If that child stops … everybody will be …
13 Correct.   14 If Peter phones   15 Correct.

3
… she wouldn't have run across the road in front of a cyclist. If she hadn't run across the road in front of a cyclist, he wouldn't have fallen off his bike and hit his head. If he hadn't fallen off his bike and hit his head, he wouldn't have finished up in hospital. If he hadn't finished up in hospital, Anna wouldn't have gone to visit him. If she hadn't gone to visit him, she wouldn't have decided that he was very nice. If she hadn't decided that he was very nice, she wouldn't have gone to visit him again. If she hadn't gone to visit him again, she wouldn't have met a really handsome doctor. If she hadn't met a really handsome doctor, she wouldn't have married him. If she hadn't married him, they wouldn't have lived happily ever after.

page 268

1
1 The tomatoes which you bought were mostly bad.
2 The flowers which I planted are doing well.
3 A lot of the people who I know want a change of government.
4 Three of the prisoners who escaped last night are still on the run.
5 There's some cheese in the fridge which needs to be eaten.
6 I want some plates which can go in the microwave.
7 They haven't got the shirt which you wanted in your size.
8 The boy who lives next door has asked my sister out.

2
1. The tomatoes that you bought were mostly bad.
2. The flowers that I planted are doing well.
3. A lot of the people that I know want a change of government.
4. Three of the prisoners that escaped last night are still on the run.
5. There's some cheese in the fridge that needs to be eaten.

page 269

4
1. He is one of those people whom everybody likes.
2. There were three boys at my school whom I will never forget.
3. The woman whom I did not recognise was my old dentist.
4. The man whom the police arrested said that he had never met the woman.
5. We had a biology teacher whom we could not stand.

6
1. People who live in Greece speak Greek.
2. The language that people speak in Hungary is called Hungarian
3. The language that/which most people speak in China is called Chinese/Mandarin.
4. People who/that live in Italy speak Italian.
5. People who/that live in Turkey speak Turkish.
6. The language that/which people speak in Algeria is called Arabic.
7. The language that/which some people speak in Scotland is called Scots Gaelic.
8. The people who/that live in Holland speak Dutch.
9. The language that/which some people speak in Ireland is called Irish.
10. The people who/that live in Portugal speak Portuguese.
11. The language that/which some people speak in Wales is called Welsh.
12. The language that/which people speak in Japan is called Japanese.

page 270

1 1 S 2 O 3 O 4 S 5 O 6 S 7 O 8 O

2
1. The job he got …
2. A woman my sister knows …
6. … a typewriter I can use.

3
1. We went to see the film you recommended, but we didn't think much of it.
2. The car my sister bought last month has broken down four times already.
3. The actor you didn't recognise on TV last night was Jake McLean.
4. Only a very few of the friends Jane had at school went on to university.

5. The operation my father had for his heart problem was only a partial success.
6. The essay Mark wrote while we were on holiday has won a prize in the school competition.
7. Some of the friends my daughter brings home are pretty strange.

page 271

1
1 What he said 2 what I forgot 3 what I like
4 What it said; was 5 what interests them
6 What matters most 7 What I like best
8 what she meant 9 just what I wanted
10 What happened was

2
1 Honey is what 2 Grass is what 3 Happiness is what 4 Philosophy is what 5 Power is what
6 Money is what 7 Imagination is what
8 Advertising is what 9 Petrol is what
10 Gravity is what

3
1 that 2 What 3 that 4 that 5 what
6 What 7 that 8 what 9 what 10 that

page 272

1
1 whose children are happy. 2 is one whose plants grow. 3 is one whose patients don't die.
4 is one whose books are read. 5 is one whose students learn. 6 is one whose tourists don't get lost. 7 is one whose food is enjoyed.

2
1. Anton, whose brother Fritz helps him run the sports shop, lives with Marika, whose sister Anneliese also helps out in the sports shop.
2. Anneliese has a younger brother Max, whose wife Paula works in the restaurant run by Anton's other brother Tony, whose girlfriend Heidrun is an instructor at the ski school.
3. The person who is in charge of the ski school is Anton's Uncle Friedrich, whose wife Monika was national ice-dancing champion in her younger days, but now works part-time for the baker down the road, Karsten, whose daughter Liesl runs the pizzeria.

page 273

1
1 A toy 2 A tap 3 A picture 4 A window
5 A cup 6 A vase

2
1. Something that you sleep in. G
2. Something that you put things on. C
3. Something that you put valuables in. D
4. A thing that you clean your teeth with. F
5. A thing that you hang clothes on. B
6. Liquid that you wash dishes with. H
7. Something that you can start a fire with. A

In these answers, we usually give **either** contracted forms (for example *I'm, don't*) **or** full forms (for example *I am, do not*). Normally both are correct.

4 1 A man (that) I sometimes play chess with.
2 Somebody (that) I have great respect for.
3 The girl (that) I was writing to.
4 The problem (that) I was worried about.
5 A car (that) I paid too much for.

page 274

1 1 talking to Alison 2 Luggage left unattended
3 The driver sent 4 The nurse looking after my
aunt 5 All the rubbish floating in the sea
6 Ham made in the traditional way 7 Women
tourists wearing trousers 8 the man talking
to his girlfriend 9 The man bitten by my
neighbour's dog

2 1 I keep dreaming about a woman standing with
her back to me.
2 James said he heard a shot fired in the street.
3 Are those your trousers hanging over the
balcony?
4 They live in a beautiful old house built 300
years ago.
5 The Navajo create beautiful jewellery made of
silver and turquoise.
6 Passengers standing on Platform 2 are asked to
keep behind the yellow line.
7 Pauline has a very strange old painting of a
woman holding a small dog.

page 275

1 1 A 2 A 3 A

2 1 The 'B' sentences.
2 Because they are not a necessary part of the
meaning of the noun that they follow.
3 A.
4 A.
5 More formal.

3 1 that (or leave it out) 2 No change. 3 No
change. 4 No change. 5 that 6 No change.
7 that (or leave it out) 8 No change.

4 1 which 2 what 3 what 4 which 5 what
6 which 7 which 8 what 9 which
10 which

page 276

1 B

2 1 The parcel that he got …
2 The sofa that we bought …
3 Some papers that I found …
4 A picture that my father bought …
5 The people that he had hoped to introduce
Lee to …
6 The flat that the terrorists hid the guns in …

7 The song that she could not remember the
name of …
8 A boy that I was at school with …

page 277

3 1 The rosebush. 2 Duncan and Jack.
3 The man the mother was working for. 4 No.
5 The newspaper. 6 Police.

4 1 D 2 E 3 F 4 A 5 C

6 Most of the people who were hoping to see the
President remained calm, but a minority of those
who were moved on by police became violent,
and organisers claim that several of the people
who were arrested suffered injuries.

page 278

1 1 A road opened last Friday has had to be closed
again for repairs.
2 The number of new cars sold in this country fell
by 25% in January.
3 The men working on our house have been
there for nearly three weeks.
4 Clothes made of artificial fibres often feel
uncomfortable in hot weather.
5 Not many of the people invited turned up.
6 The money lying on the table is your change.

2 1 that 2 who 3 that 4 who; who 5 that
6 who 7 who 8 who 9 that 10 that
11 that 12 whose

page 279

4 *(possible answers)*
Alice is the woman (that) Bill is married to / Sally
works with / Peter plays chess with.
Anne is the woman (that) Ron plays chess with /
Peter is married to / Bill works with.
Sue is the woman (that) Peter works with.
Mary is the woman (that) Ron works with / Sally
plays chess with.
Bill is the man (that) John plays chess with / Alice
is married to / Anne works with.
Ron is the man (that) Anne plays chess with / Sue
is married to / Mary works with.
Peter is the man (that) Alice plays chess with /
Anne is married to / Sue works with.
Sally is the woman (that) Mary plays chess with /
John is married to / Alice works with.

5 1 A man that my brother met …
2 … the wood that that table's made of …
3 … the one person that he really should have
invited.
4 … the soldier that he wanted to buy the guns
from …

6 1 A banker   2 A boring person   3 A boss
4 A dangerous driver   5 A doctor
6 A professional footballer   7 A teacher
8 An actor

page 280

1 1 which   2 what   3 that/which   4 what
5 that   6 which   7 which   8 that   9 what
10 that

2 1 Correct.   2 that   3 that I couldn't understand.
4 Correct.   5 a man who went   6 whose car
7 Correct.   8 Correct.   9 Correct.
10 which/that   11 The man who phoned just
now had …   12 who does   13 which surprised
14 Correct.   15 who have

3 1 who   2 –   3 that   4 that   5 which   6 –
7 who   8 –   9 that   10 which

page 282

1 1 I/he, don't/didn't, this/the, want/wanted, now/
right away

2 B

3 *Words and expressions that would have to be
changed or left out are in **bold type**:*

THEO: **You're** looking good **today**.
SUZY: **Oh, thanks**, Theo. **You are** sweet.
THEO: **OK. If you sit** down **I'll** get **you** a drink.
SUZY: **There's** nowhere to sit.
THEO: **Yes, there is. Over there** in the corner.
SUZY: I **don't** want to sit there. It's too dark. **I'll** sit
here.
THEO: **You can't. These** seats are taken.
SUZY: **No**, they **aren't**.
THEO: **Really**, Suzy. Why **do you** always **have** to
argue? **They're** taken.
SUZY: **Excuse me. Are these** seats taken?
JOE: **Well, this** one **is**, but the other one**'s** free.
SUZY: **OK. I'll** sit **here**, then. **Thanks**.
JOE: **You're** welcome. **What's your** name?
THEO: **Hey**, what about **me**?
SUZY: Suzy. **What's yours**?
JOE: **I'm** Joe Parsons. **Can I get you** a drink?
SUZY: **That's** very kind. **Can I** have a bitter lemon?
THEO: **I'm** getting **her** a drink.
JOE: **No, you're** not, **mate. I am**.
THEO: **I don't** believe **this**. Suzy, what **are you** playing
at?
SUZY: **Really**, Theo, **I don't know what's** wrong with
you today. I'll see **you** around, OK?

page 283

1 1 no; no   2 no; yes   3 yes; no   4 yes; yes

2 1 I   2 C   3 F   4 D   5 A   6 B   7 H   8 E

3 1 that day.   2 that evening.   3 there.   4 the
week before.   5 the   6 right away.   7 that
morning.   8 the same night.   9 the day before.

page 284

1

DIRECT SPEECH	INDIRECT SPEECH
simple present	simple past
present progressive	**past progressive**
present perfect	past perfect
simple past	past perfect
will …	***would …***

2 1 was   2 played   3 could   4 were leaving.
5 hadn't brushed   6 had had   7 had left
8 wouldn't say   9 would know.
10 had been opened.

3 1 told   2 said   3 tell   4 say   5 said   6 told
7 said   8 told

page 285

4 1 had never met   2 had   3 wanted   4 was
5 did   6 was doing   7 could   8 was moving /
moved   9 thought   10 wanted   11 could
12 would call   13 wanted   14 thought
15 was falling   16 was lying   17 had
18 didn't matter   19 were   20 was going
21 were   22 had left

page 286

1 1 I asked what day it was/is.
2 I asked what the dark-haired child's name was/is.
3 I told you it was / it's raining.
4 I said you'd / you'll get your money. (OR I said
he/she … his/her …)
5 This article I was reading said there would/will
be a strike.
6 Al told me the repairs would/will cost £5,000.
7 I asked if Jane was/is coming to see us.
8 Pat told me that I was / I'm going to the
Glasgow office.
9 I bet George £5 yesterday that he wouldn't /
won't pass his exam.
10 Sue rang this morning, and she said they were /
they're getting married next week.

In these answers, we usually give **either** contracted forms (for example *I'm, don't*)
or full forms (for example *I am, do not*). Normally both are correct.

ANSWER KEY **371**

page 287

1
1. I asked what Peter's address was.
2. I asked when the new manager was coming.
3. I asked how she knew my name.
4. I asked why all the windows were open.
5. I asked how many books he wanted.
6. I asked where they kept the money.
7. I asked what time the meeting was.
8. I asked when the last train left.
9. I asked how the photocopier worked.
10. I asked how often Ann went shopping.

2
1. I wondered if/whether they liked me.
2. I wondered if/whether I would be ready on time.
3. I wondered if/whether there was any food in the house.
4. I wondered if/whether service was included or not.
5. I wondered if/whether I could pay by cheque.
6. I wondered if/whether my hair looked funny.
7. I wondered if/whether the postman had been.
8. I wondered if/whether they spoke English.
9. I wondered if/whether I was doing the right thing.
10. I wondered if/whether the meeting was on Tuesday or Wednesday.

page 288

1
1. She offered to cook supper.
2. He advised me to leave early.
3. She asked me not to close the door.
4. She promised to stop smoking.
5. He offered to do the shopping.
6. She advised me to tell the police.
7. I told her to wait outside.
8. He agreed to pay half.
9. She told me not to park outside the house.
10. We offered to pay for the tickets.

2
1. I don't know how to play mah-jong.
2. Can you show me where to park the car?
3. We don't know what to give/cook Oliver for his birthday.
4. I'm not sure what to give John. OR …what/when/how to tell John.
5. Do you know how to cook spaghetti carbonara?
6. I can't decide what to wear to Peter's wedding.
7. I'm leaving on Thursday, but I still haven't decided when to come back.

page 289

1
1. I knew I'd seen him once before in London.
2. The professor said Shakespeare didn't speak French.
3. When I got there, I found out he had died two years before.

4. It said on this TV programme that three thousand years ago there were tigers in England.
5. It said on this morning's news that somebody had thrown a bomb at the Prime Minister.
6. I read in a magazine that the ancient Romans suffered from lead poisoning.

2
1. She asked me if I would like a drink.
2. I said (that) I couldn't help it.
3. They thought (that) they should be home about six.
4. The forecast said (that) it might rain.
5. Everybody said (that) she must be joking.
6. I explained that I hadn't seen the notice.

page 290

1
1. Ptolemy thought (that) the sun went round the earth.
2. Julius Caesar thought (that) Brutus loved him.
3. One of Einstein's teachers thought (that) he would never be a scientist.
4. Napoleon and Hitler thought (that) they could conquer Russia.
5. The ancient Egyptians thought (that) people were born again and again.
6. Bishop Ussher thought (that) the world had existed since October 23, 4004 B.C.
7. C J Smith thought (that) modern ships could not sink.
8. Many native Americans thought (that) the land belonged to everyone.
9. John Lennon thought (that) the Beatles were more popular than Jesus.
10. Karl Marx thought (that) capitalism would disappear.

2
1. had 2. was 3. wasn't 4. had 5. have
6. I was / I am 7. smoked / smoke
8. I drank / I drink 9. took / take 10. lived / live
11. had / have 12. was 13. had 14. wanted
15. was 16. is 17. had 18. should take
19. I'd better throw 20. how to talk

page 291

5 were

page 292

1
1. He said he would be back the next day.
2. She asked him if/whether he would like a drink.
3. She asked me where the bus station was.
4. I asked him if/whether he had finished.
5. The book said (that) three kilos should be enough.

6 I asked when the car was going to be ready.
7 I knew (that) those figures couldn't be right.
8 She thought (that) her cat understood everything she said.
9 I wondered if/whether Mary had phoned back.
10 I wondered if/whether dinosaurs laid eggs.
11 She said (that) she didn't like that music.
12 He asked her if/whether she wanted tea or coffee.
13 She offered to clean the flat.
14 I asked what the boss wanted.
15 He advised me to see the doctor.

2 1 J P Morgan said that the telephone would never have any commercial value.
2 Mary Somerville said that TV would never become popular.
3 An American astronomer said that we would never reach the moon.
4 Jay Livingstone / Capitol records didn't think that the Beatles would be a commercial success.
5 Joseph George Cordwell said that a black man would never be President of the United States.

page 294

1 *in* + part of a day
on + part of a particular day
on + particular day
at + weekend, public holiday
in + longer period
in to say how long something takes

2 … put/have no preposition.

3 1 at 2 on 3 in 4 in 5 on 6 in 7 –
8 – 9 at 10 – 11 – 12 on 13 – 14 –
15 in 16 –;– 17 – 18 in 19 on 20 at

page 295

1 *At* and *in* are used for position.
To is used for movement.

2 1 at 2 in 3 in 4 at 5 at 6 at 7 in
8 at 9 at 10 at

3 1 in 2 on 3 on 4 on 5 on 6 in 7 on
8 in 9 in; on

4 1 the gate 2 the hill 3 the bridge
4 the supermarket 5 the river 6 the mountain
7 the bank 8 the river 9 the table
10 the wall 11 the station 12 the corner

page 296

1 1 UNTIL 2 NEITHER 3 BY

2 1 till/until 2 by 3 by 4 till/until
5 by the time 6 by

3 The bus stop is opposite the house.
The car is in front of the house.

4 1 opposite 2 In front of 3 in front of
4 opposite 5 in front of 6 opposite

page 297

5 We say *among* a group, crowd or mass of things not seen separately.
We say *between* two or more clearly separate people or things.
We say *between* things on both sides.

6 1 between 2 between 3 between 4 among

7 1 between 2 among 3 between 4 among
5 among 6 between

8 *During* tells you **when**. *For* tells you **how long**.

9 1 during 2 for; during 3 during 4 for
5 during 6 for

page 298

1 1 for 2 – 3 – 4 – 5 about

2 1 – 2 – 3 to 4 – 5 –;– 6 – 7 –

3 1 on paying 2 on him 3 of lying 4 on
5 on 6 from 7 of 8 from marrying

4 1 in 2 in 3 into 4 into 5 in 6 in
7 into 8 at 9 at 10 into 11 to

page 299

5 1 arrive at 2 get on 3 pay 4 get into
5 pay 6 arrived in 7 get out of 8 pay for/get; pay for 9 get off 10 arrived at; get on

page 300

1 1 of 2 for 3 for 4 of 5 of 6 of 7 for
8 of 9 for 10 of

2 1 Correct. 2 Correct. 3 Correct. 4 Correct.
5 increases in 6 Correct. 7 Correct.

In these answers, we usually give **either** contracted forms (for example *I'm, don't*) **or** full forms (for example *I am, do not*). Normally both are correct.

ANSWER KEY **373**

1 1 at 2 at 3 at 4 with 5 at 6 at

2 1 to 2 to 3 to 4 to 5 to 6 in 7 to
8 to

3 1 of 2 for 3 with 4 of 5 with 6 in
7 with 8 of 9 with 10 with 11 of 12 of

4 1 about 2 for 3 on 4 about 5 for 6 for
7 about 8 of

1 1 in 2 in 3 in 4 in 5 on 6 in 7 in
8 in 9 in 10 on

2 1 on 2 at 3 at 4 on 5 on 6 in 7 at
8 by 9 on 10 on 11 on 12 on 13 on
14 at

1 1 opposite 2 Until 3 until 4 for 5 By
6 among 7 during 8 for 9 in front of
10 among 11 during 12 between
13 between 14 opposite 15 by
16 in front of 17 during 18 by

2 1 opposite/by 2 Opposite/By 3 In front of
4 on 5 over 6 between 7 on 8 between

1 1 good at 2 crashed into 3 looking for
4 discuss the holiday dates 5 by Tolstoy
6 dressed in 7 on page 12 8 pay for
9 depends on 10 in that strange voice
11 interested in 12 asked a policeman
13 into Japanese 14 unkind to 15 married to
16 enter the building 17 reminds me of
18 Congratulations on 19 example of
20 responsible for 21 typical of 22 reason for
23 into two sections 24 in the rain
25 In my opinion

2 1 in 2 at 3 at 4 to 5 at 6 to
7 between 8 opposite 9 at 10 to

1 *(possible answers)*
1 The final exam is pretty difficult.
2 Can I order six boxes of top quality copy paper?
3 Sheila is not doing very well in her new job.
4 Nobody knows who is going to win: Labour or
Conservative.

5 On Sunday morning Ellie phoned when I was
fast asleep.
6 I do not trust this government.
7 We cannot afford to go to France this year.
8 TV programmes are all the same these days.
9 George's daughter is not going to university
this year.
10 We could never have finished that job without
Henry.
(Other answers are possible.)

1 1 My wife's on holiday.
2 I couldn't understand a word.
3 Have you seen Joe?
4 Be careful what you say.
5 There's nobody at home.
6 I don't think so.
7 The train's late again.
8 Do you know what I mean?
9 Have you got a pen?
10 I've lost my glasses.

2 1 Changed my job.
2 Doesn't know what she's doing.
3 Cost you £10.
4 Careful of the flowers.
5 No time to waste.
6 Bus is coming.
7 Speak English?
8 Haven't been there.
9 Thinks he's clever.
10 Got a match?

1 1 … but I do. 2 … Sue has too.
3 … 'Yes, I would.' 4 … 'It certainly does.'
5 … 'I have.' 6 … Yes, it is.' 7 … but I can.
8 … and Celia doesn't either.

2 1 care how much she upsets people
2 getting on your nerves
3 go on like that
4 take Sally to the zoo
5 have to keep them
6 have to keep them
7 tell her what you thought of her
8 tell her what they thought of her
9 told her what you thought of her
10 told her what I thought of her

1 1 ✓ 2 ✓ 3 ✗ 4 ✗ 5 ✓ 6 ✓ 7 ✓ 8 ✗

2 1 aren't I 2 aren't we 3 are they 4 am I
5 were they 6 is she 7 isn't it 8 isn't he

9 can't he   10 mustn't it   11 won't it
12 don't they   13 will they   14 isn't there
15 hasn't she   16 does she   17 haven't they
18 wasn't I

page 310

1 1 they   2 are you   3 is there   4 does it
5 they   6 did she   7 haven't they   8 is there
9 did you

2 1 You haven't picked up my keys, have you?
2 You couldn't help me for a minute, could you?
3 That isn't your brother, is it?
4 You can't give me a lift, can you?

3 1 won't you?   2 will you?   3 shall we?
4 could you?   5 would you?

4 1 isn't she?
2 isn't it?
3 isn't it?
4 don't we?

page 311

1 1 'No, I'm not.'   2 'Yes, I do.'   3 'It (certainly) is.'
4 'I won't.'   5 'I will.'   6 'Yes, I have.'
7 'No, I can't.'   8 'He (certainly) does.'
9 'She (certainly) did.'   10 'I will.'

2 (some possible exchanges with reply questions)
'It was a lovely wedding.' 'Was it?'
'… I didn't think much of Maggie's dress.'
'Didn't you?'
'… I don't really go for church weddings.'
'Don't you?'
'… The service went on for ages.' 'Did it really?'
'… I couldn't hear the vicar.' 'Couldn't you, dear?'
'… They played that hymn about sheep.'
'Oh, did they?'
'… I didn't enjoy the reception much.' 'Didn't you?'
'… The food wasn't very good.' 'Wasn't it?'
'… And the bride's father made such a stupid
speech.' 'Did he really? What a pity.'
'… And I got one of my headaches.' 'Did you,
dear? I am sorry.'
'… Champagne always gives me a headache.'
'Oh, does it?'
'… I can't stand that woman.' 'Can't you?'
'… She's always criticising.' 'Is she really?'

page 312

1 1 so is   2 Neither/Nor have   3 neither/nor can
4 So do   5 So did   6 neither/nor do
7 so was   8 neither/nor will   9 So do
10 Neither/Nor was

3 1 Mine does.   2 Robert / Little Lucy can't.
3 her second did.   4 Gas cookers don't.
5 Robert hasn't.   6 the windows weren't.
7 The sofa is.

page 314

1 (These are the sentences that the people said, but
other answers are possible.)
1 I think so.   2 I'm afraid so.   3 I suppose so.
4 I think so.   5 I hope so.   6 I think so.
7 I think so.   8 I'm afraid so.   9 I hope so.
10 I suppose so.   11 I'm afraid so.   12 I hope so.

2 1 I'm afraid not.   2 I don't think so.
3 I hope not.   4 I suppose not.   5 I'm afraid not.
6 I hope not.   7 I suppose not.
8 I don't think so.   9 I'm afraid not.
10 I suppose not.   11 I hope not.
12 I don't think so.

page 315

1 1 … Yes, she is.   2 … Maggie doesn't either.
3 … and Phil is too.   4 … No, I wouldn't.
5 … but we do.   6 … I have.   7 … but I can.
8 … We certainly do.

2 1 Have you got any money on you?
2 Have you heard from Peter?
3 Be careful how you drive.
4 Do you know what I think?
5 Is (there) anybody at home?
6 I couldn't find his house.
7 I don't suppose so.
8 The door's locked.
9 The carpet's very dirty.
10 I've forgotten her phone number.

3 (examples of possible answers)
Robert speaks Arabic, and so does Sarah.
Mike doesn't play tennis, and neither does Robert.
Julie can sing, and so can Peter.
Peter hasn't been to Peru, and nor has Sarah.
Peter is shy, but Mike isn't.
Julie doesn't like animals, but Ann does.
Ann plays tennis, but Sarah doesn't.

page 316

1 1 Correct.   2 Correct.   3 Correct.   4 Correct.
5 'Yes, I can.' OR 'Do you swim.'   6 'So does mine.'
7 Correct.   8 my sister has.   9 Correct.
10 Correct.   11 Correct.   12 'I hope not.'
13 Correct.   14 Correct.   15 'So am I.' OR 'Me too.'

2 1 aren't   2 does   3 Haven't   4 does
5 it isn't.   6 couldn't.   7 will you

In these answers, we usually give **either** contracted forms (for example *I'm, don't*)
or full forms (for example *I am, do not*). Normally both are correct.

8 Didn't you   9 not.   10 shall we.   11 have I.
12 we can   13 Me   14 either   15 Have you

page 321

1 1 car's   2 She's   3 She's   4 They've   5 you'd
6 We'll   7 he'd   8 How's   9 Nobody's
10 Don't you   11 needn't   12 can't   13 won't
14 doesn't   15 haven't   16 I'm not   17 aren't
18 aren't I

page 322

2 1 –   2 haven't   3 isn't   4 it's   5 –   6 don't
7 can't   8 can't

3 1 there's   2 you've   3 he's   4 can't   5 he'd
6 I'll   7 that's   8 we've

page 325

1 1 a hundred
2 one thousand, four hundred and fifty pounds
3 a thousand
4 three thousand, one hundred and forty-four
5 one dollar (and) eighty-five (cents)
6 one thousand pounds

2 1 hundred   2 million   3 hundred   4 millions
of   5 Thousands of   6 dozen

3 second; third; fourth; fifth; sixth; seventh; eighth;
ninth; tenth; twelfth; sixteenth; twentieth; twenty-
first; thirtieth; hundredth; thousandth

page 326

4 1 10 April 2006
2 17 September 1911
3 16 June 1979
4 the sixteenth of May / May the sixteenth,
nineteen seventy
5 the twelfth of March / March the twelfth, two
thousand and three
6 the fourteenth of January / January the
fourteenth, nineteen ninety-six

index